Shantideva's Guide to Awakening

SHANTIDEVA'S
GUIDE TO AWAKENING

A Commentary on the Bodhicharyavatara

Geshe Yeshe Tobden

Foreword by His Holiness the Dalai Lama

Edited by Fiorella Rizzi

Translated from the Italian by
Manu Bazzano and Sarita Doveton

Wisdom

Wisdom Publications, Inc.
199 Elm Street
Somerville, MA 02144 USA
wisdompubs.org

Library of Congress Cataloging-in-Publication Data

Names: Tobden, Geshe Yeshe, 1926– author. | Rizzi, Fiorella editor. | Śāntideva, active 7th century, author. Bodhicaryāvatāra. English
Title: Shantideva's guide to awakening: a commentary Shantideva's Bodhicharyavatara.
Other titles: Commentario al testo di Shantideva Bodhisattvacharyavatara. English | Commentary Shantideva's Bodhicharyavatara
Description: Somerville, MA: Wisdom Publications, 2017. | Reprint of translation: The way of awakening. 2005. |
Identifiers: LCCN 2017003554 (print) | LCCN 2017014659 (ebook) | ISBN 9781614294559 (ebook) | ISBN 1614294550 (ebook) | ISBN 9781614294306 (pbk.: alk. paper) | ISBN 1614294305 (pbk.: alk. paper)
Subjects: LCSH: Śāntideva, active 7th century. Bodhicaryāvatāra. | Mahayana Buddhism—Doctrines.
Classification: LCC BQ3147 (ebook) | LCC BQ3147 .T6315 2017 (print) | DDC 294.3/85—dc23
LC record available at https://lccn.loc.gov/2017003554

ISBN 978-1-61429-430-6   ebook ISBN 978-1-61429-455-9

21 20 19 18 17
5   4   3   2   1

Cover and interior design by Gopa&Ted2, Inc. Cover line art by Andy Weber.
Set in AGaramond 10.75 pt. / 14 pt.

This book was originally published in Italian as *Commentario al testo di Shantideva, Bodhisattvacharyavatara: Una guida allo stile di vita del Bodhisattva* (Pomaia, Italy: Chiara Luce Edizione, 1997, 1999, 2001). Previously published in English as *The Way of Awakening*.

Printed in the United States of America

Please visit fscus.org.

PUBLISHER'S ACKNOWLEDGMENT

The publisher gratefully acknowledges the kind help of the Hershey Family Foundation in sponsoring the printing of this book, as well as Richard Gere and the Gere Foundation for sponsoring the translation.

TABLE OF CONTENTS

FOREWORD

The *Bodhicharyavatara* was composed by the renowned Indian scholar Shantideva, who was accepted by all Buddhist schools in Tibet as one of the most reliable and inspiring of teachers. The book focuses mainly on cultivating and enhancing the awakening mind of bodhichitta, and as such, it is a Mahayana text. At the same time, Shantideva's philosophical viewpoint as revealed particularly in the ninth chapter on wisdom follows the Madhyamaka tradition of Chandrakirti.

The major emphasis of the book is on nurturing a mind wishing to benefit other sentient beings. In my life I have read this book and listened to explanations of it many times. I have thought deeply about the meaning it contains and have even had the good fortune on many occasions to teach it myself. Consequently, I have some experience of the advice contained here, and can confidently say that it continues to be relevant and useful today. If we sincerely try to put the core of these teachings into practice, we need have no hesitation about whether they will be effective. Cultivating qualities like love, compasion, and generosity not only benefits us on a personal level, it benefits all sentient beings and even helps maintain harmony with the environment. This is why I encourage people to observe such practices; it's not merely so that the tradition may be preserved.

The present work contains a thorough, practical guide by Geshe Yeshe Tobden to the *Bodhicharyavatara*. He has that rare distinction not only of being qualified as a scholar but also of having gained long acquaintance through many years of meditation in the mountains. As a result his explanation of teachings such as these has the special flavor of heartfelt personal experience. I am delighted that this record of Geshe-la's explanation is being published and offer my prayers that readers may be inspired to take it to heart for the greater peace and happiness of all sentient beings.

Tenzin Gyatso, The Fourteenth Dalai Lama

Editor's Preface

Tsewang Rabten, destined to later become the master Geshe Yeshe Tobden, was born in 1926 to a family of wealthy farmers in Ngadra, a village one day's walk south of the city of Lhasa. As a child, he lived with his father, Kelsang Tsering; his mother, Yangzom Bhuti; and his sister, Yeshe Tsomo.

One day a great lama who was visiting the area to give an initiation saw him and predicted that his life would be in danger unless he took monastic vows. So his mother, with the help of a cousin who lived in Lhasa, entrusted the twelve-year-old boy to the Venerable Damchoe of Sera Monastery. There Geshe-la began his monastic studies.

His mother died when he was eighteen, and Geshe-la always spoke of her with undying affection, explaining that he had been overwhelmed by a tremendous feeling of gratitude for all the love and attention she had given him. At the same time he spoke with regret for having been unable to repay her kindness while she was still alive. A year later his younger sister also died, and immediately after that his father passed away as well. Geshe-la was the only one left, and he did not hesitate to sell all his family's possessions and offer the proceeds to his monastery. Later on, so as not to be a burden on the Venerable Damchoe, who had helped him like a mother but who had other monks to take care of as well, Geshe-la decided to go and live alone in a small house near the monastery.

In those years Geshe-la was extremely poor; the door to his house had no lock, and there was nothing inside that anyone would want. Anything that he received from others he would share with the most needy, never keeping anything for the next day. Those who knew him recount that his immediate, spontaneous reaction after accepting a gift was to offer it enthusiastically to those who might enjoy it or have need of it, keeping for himself only a few indispensable items, as long as they were simple and unpretentious.

During this time he studied vigorously, receiving numerous teachings from great masters, among whom he remembered with special devotion Geshe Lodoe Sangpo and his own root guru, Chusang Rinpoche. A few years ago Chusang Rinpoche's reincarnation was found in Tibet in the form of a young monk. The Dalai Lama recognized him at the age of twelve, and as a result, he later came to live in India.

With the Chinese invasion of 1959, Geshe-la was arrested and imprisoned near Lhasa but managed to escape after four months. He was caught, suffered two months of hardship in prison, and escaped again. On the road to India he was caught yet again by the Chinese, but he managed to escape to safety. He once recounted how he had kept a few *chulen* pills (pills made of flower essence, minerals, and various blessed substances) in his luggage, as well as a text with instructions on how to prepare new ones when needed. He was determined that if he did not succeed in crossing the border, he would hide in some remote corner in the mountains and survive on these pills.

At the end of 1963, after a year and a half of trials and adversities, having crossed occupied Tibet on foot, finally he reached the eastern border of India, but the frontier guards imprisoned him because they did not believe his story. By then Tibet's border was closed, the flux of refugees interrupted, and they believed no one could face such a journey alone and without any resources at his disposal. The Indians treated Geshe-la with suspicion, thinking he might be a spy working for the Chinese.

News of all this came to a frontier guard named Tashi, a Tibetan who had at one time been a monk. He went to meet Geshe-la, and to the astonishment of the others present, he recognized Geshe-la and confirmed his tale, vouching for him and thus securing his freedom. He welcomed Geshe-la into his home, and there Geshe-la learned that the main Tibetan monasteries had been rebuilt in India. He refused financial help from Tashi and set out on a journey to Buxa, a refugee settlement of Tibetan monks in West Bengal, where he resumed his studies. At the age of thirty-seven, having completed the entire course of studies at Sera Me Monastery, he obtained the highest honor—the title of Geshe Lharampa, a special recognition that in those days was given to only one or two monks a year who passed their exams.

Geshe-la taught at the monastery for several years and subsequently was sent by His Holiness the Dalai Lama for three years to the university in Varanasi as a teacher of Buddhist philosophy. Here he disclosed to his old friend Geshe Rabten, himself a teacher at the university, his true aspiration—to retire to the mountains and meditate. Sometime later Geshe Rabten told His Holiness about this, and the Dalai Lama indicated his wish to learn the reasons behind this desire from Geshe Tobden himself. With utmost simplicity, Geshe-la explained that he wished to meditate on renunciation, bodhichitta, and emptiness. His Holiness asked when he had first felt such an aspiration, and Geshe Tobden replied that he remembered having it since he was a small boy. His Holiness the Dalai Lama was impressed by his statement and released him from his post at the university. His Holiness also offered his support in case Geshe-la needed advice or help with any difficulties that might arise in his meditation practice.

At the age of forty-four Geshe-la was at last able to fulfill his dream and retreat to a tiny stone house above McLeod Ganj, which remained his residence from that time on. His house consisted of a single room with an altar, a bed, a hearth in the corner, and a small courtyard for cooking. He placed the few things he possessed inside and protected the entrance from wild animals. Tibetans who lived in the nearby valley gradually developed a profound devotion toward him and would address or speak about him using a title that means "saint."

In 1976 Geshe-la became seriously ill but refused what he called the "luxury" of hospitalization. However, he accepted accommodation offered by Lama Thubten Yeshe. It was then that some Italian students had their first opportunity to meet him and were greatly impressed. A while later Lama Yeshe asked the Dalai Lama if Geshe Yeshe Tobden could be a Dharma teacher in Italy, and His Holiness, with truly enlightened vision, decided that he should go to Pomaia. It was our great good fortune to have Geshe-la as the first resident lama at the Lama Tsong Khapa Institute in 1979 and 1980. His teachings guided and helped those early practitioners at the institute who were taking their first steps on the path of spiritual practice. Geshe-la's presence alone was an inspiration to those who had the privilege of meeting him. Every one of his disciples can recount episodes in which Geshe-la manifested, even with just a simple gesture or a small remark, enormous wisdom, profound compassion, and the power that arises from these qualities.

In 1981 the time came for Geshe-la to return to India, to his quiet mountain retreat. He did not hide his joy, but he promised to return in the future, and until 1997, he came back every two years, thus keeping the commitment he had made to his old students in Italy. He also accepted invitations from newer Western disciples, who asked him to come and teach in their own countries—Switzerland, France, the United States, and Canada.

With the echo of that original promise to return still vivid in their hearts, the students of the Lama Tsong Khapa Center of Villorba, near Treviso, Italy (a Dharma center founded in 1980 under the spiritual guidance of Lama Zopa Rinpoche), wrote to him at the end of 1981, inviting him to give a series of teachings at their center the following summer. This request was based on the profound connection the students at Villorba had always felt with Geshe-la, who had provided their first exposure to the Dharma as well as the inspiration to found a center for Buddhist studies in their town. When the center started, Geshe-la himself gave news of it to His Holiness the Dalai Lama. After requesting His Holiness's advice, Geshe-la accepted the invitation, saying, "I am coming with the hope that I can be of some help, and also because you have insisted, and in spite of the fact that I would rather not leave my meditation place. If the energy is right, I will remain, otherwise I will leave immediately."

The Commentary on Shantideva's Bodhicharyavatara

Planning for the trip took longer than expected, but Geshe-la finally arrived and between July and October 1983 offered a complete commentary to Shantideva's *Bodhicharyavatara,* a key text based on the fundamental practices of Mahayana Buddhism. The oral translation of the teachings from Tibetan into English was done by Acharya Ngawang Sherab, teacher at the University of Buddhist Studies at Varanasi, India, and now a geshe. The translation from English into Italian was done mainly by Dario

Tesoroni. The students at the center remember that time as spiritually rewarding, filled with enthusiasm, and buzzing with activity. Geshe Yeshe Tobden gave teachings on the ninth, or "wisdom," chapter every evening, drawing on the Tibetan commentary by Gyeltsab Je, one of Lama Tsongkhapa's two main disciples, and he taught on the remaining chapters on the weekends. All these teachings were recorded.

When the time came for Geshe-la to leave the center, his students wished to keep his incomparable gift alive and make it available to others, so they transcribed his words patiently from the many audio tapes. I wish to express here my gratitude to these people and to all those who have in various ways contributed to making this book possible, particularly the following people: Caterina and Bruno Bellotto, Carla and Piero Malfatto, Carla Granata, Margherita De Biasi, Luigina De Biasi, Mariangiola Fracasso, Annamaria De Pretis, Giovanna Pescetti, and Vincenzo Tallarico.

Naturally, the manuscript needed to be revised and corrected, and after some time Margherita Giordana offered to edit the chapter on wisdom and published a preliminary version in 1989. This was later revised for publication in the complete edition, which I was fortunate enough to have been given the opportunity to undertake. Annalisa Lirussi has helped me with word processing, as well as provided me with consistent help and valuable suggestions. Pietro Sirianni gave momentum to the entire project and designed the Italian edition.

The teachings upon which the present work is based were delivered over a long period of time and were attended by the students at the center as well as by several disciples visiting from elsewhere. With infinite kindness, Geshe-la offered the teachings that would be most beneficial to the audience he faced each time. Often, when he thought it profitable, he did not hesitate to review key subjects that he had already explained during previous talks. Having to present the content in book form, the general orientation has been to make the material as accessible as possible, avoiding repetition and, where appropriate, combining sections covering similar subjects that may have been discussed on multiple occasions. I wanted to keep the simple but effective style that is typical of direct oral teachings, refraining from literary formalities.

Bearing in mind that the teachings were based directly on Shantideva's text, it is advisable to combine the reading of this commentary with the reading of the root text. The result will be a clearer understanding of particular examples and statements. Several translations of the text in English are available. It is also crucial to remember Shantideva's historical and cultural context. He was a great Indian sage of the eighth century whose audience was composed of monks at Nalanda's monastic university, to which he belonged. To make the correlation to the root text easier, the chapter names correspond to the titles of Shantideva's chapters, and the number of the stanza being discussed is included in brackets. Verses that are omitted are either covered by the explanation immediately before or after or else not commented upon because their meaning is relatively self-evident.

The Venerable Geshe Yeshe Tobden was informed of and endorsed the above decisions. During several meetings, thanks to the translation by his close disciple Lobsang Dondhen (who also accompanied him on his travels), he clarified certain points for me and provided further explanations to others.

He urged me to use utmost accuracy, especially with regard to the ninth chapter, whose weight is equal to its complexity, and in September 1997, at the Lama Tsong Khapa Center of Villorba and the Cian Ciub Ciö Ling Center of Polava (Udine), he discussed stanzas that had remained uncommented upon. At the time, Norbu Lamsang did the direct translation from Tibetan into Italian, an invaluable service that he has been providing for several Buddhist centers in Italy, while Gelong Lobsang Tharchin provided notes and tapes, which I then edited for the new entries. The guidelines that enabled me to put together the synthesis of the ninth chapter (expressly requested by Geshe-la and produced in the appendix) are the result of explanations Geshe-la personally gave me in India in October 1998, translated into English by his Tibetan disciple, the composer, musician, and one-time monk Ngawang Khechog.

Not long afterward, Richard Gere met with Geshe Yeshe Tobden in McLeod Ganj at the suggestion of His Holiness the Dalai Lama, who had praised Geshe-la as a great meditator and scholar. During his visit to the mountain hermitage, Mr. Gere, having thanked Geshe-la for both personal and Dharma advice given during their meetings, expressed regret for not having had the opportunity to attend any of his courses, particularly those on emptiness. Geshe-la then told him of his complete commentary to the *Bodhicharyavatara* published in Italian, and Mr. Gere expressed the wish to be able to read it in English. He generously offered to sponsor this translation, thereby making the teachings available to many others. In 2000 the project received the approval of His Holiness the Dalai Lama, who provided me with the main guidelines on how to manage the translation, particularly the choice of the translator. We were lucky to have found Manu Bazzano and Sarita Doveton for this task, which they accomplished excellently. The staff at Wisdom Publications further edited the work for publication in English.

In spite of the diamond-like purity of every single word of the teachings transmitted by Venerable Geshe Yeshe Tobden, and in spite of my best attempts to relate them faultlessly, some errors may still remain. This is due mainly to the limits of my knowledge, for which I apologize. I hope, however, that I have provided some people with an opportunity to approach the invaluable treasure of wisdom of this perfect master, my holy guru, the kindest and most compassionate among all the buddhas of past, present, and future.

Postscript

On July 31, 1999, the eve of his departure to Italy from Dharamsala for another series of courses at Buddhist centers abroad, the Venerable Geshe Yeshe Tobden instead transmitted his final teaching—on impermanence—manifesting the death of his own body. From that moment, for twelve days and twelve nights, his mind remained in deep absorption, but his body showed no sign of decay and instead emitted a kind of fragrance and luminosity. According to His Holiness the Dalai Lama, this demonstrated the tremendous power of Geshe-la's meditative concentration. After the signs of the last phase of absorption of subtle awareness had manifested and the entire death process had come to an end, the cremation ceremony began in the presence of various monks and disciples. The fire burned for more than two hours without producing any smoke, and shortly before sunrise a half rainbow appeared, which was considered particularly auspicious for Geshe-la's swift reincarnation. There was then a fierce rain followed by a strong wind, and finally, in gaps between the clouds, one could see snowy mountain peaks (in August!).

The next day, before gathering the ashes, the remains of the fire—which had been devotedly guarded the whole time—were examined. In the center, toward the West, one could make out the footprints of a small child— another special sign, interpreted as further indication that Geshe-la will soon be back among us.

Fiorella Rizzi

Annotated Table of Contents

INTRODUCTION

THE THRESHOLD of Buddhist practice is going for refuge to the Three Jewels—the Buddha, Dharma, and Sangha. The Buddha shows us the true path, the Dharma is the path itself, and the Sangha provides help while we travel on it. We can think of the Buddha as a doctor, the Dharma as medicine, and the Sangha as nurses. When we have a physical illness, it is vital to take medicine under the guidance of a physician; likewise, it is important to cure mental disturbance through the medicine of the Dharma. In order to become acquainted with the Dharma, we need to listen to it; then we need to study it so that we know how to apply it to our own lives; and finally we need to practice it. Following this order is fundamental.

Suffering and Its Causes

Since no one wants to experience unhappiness, let alone see it protracted over time, we must find a way to avoid it. When we are hungry we do our best to relieve our hunger. In much the same way, we need to seek out relief from suffering. For some kinds of suffering we already have solutions, albeit temporary ones. For example, if we are hot we can use a fan, and if we are cold we can bundle up. For other situations, however, remedies are not so easily found.

We could seek material means as the antidote to pain. If all problems could be solved this way, however, then the wealthy would never experience any discomfort. We all know that this is not the case. Generally, what we call "life problems" are rooted in three types of suffering. The first is the *suffering of pain,* as in the pain caused by illness. This type of suffering is easy to comprehend. The second is the *suffering of change.* This is not usually considered to be suffering but is revealed to be such upon close examination. For example, if we walk, after a while we need to rest, and this is usually considered happiness. But if we rest for too long we will experience discomfort, and the "rest" will eventually turn to pain. Likewise, if we eat more than is needed, the solution to hunger turns into the suffering of having eaten too much. In these cases too we speak of suffering, for although we experience pleasure at first as a result of remedies, later on, if we continue to apply them, they turn into more suffering.

The third type of suffering is *all-pervading suffering,* marked by the fact that we have no control over our lives. We are born because of karma and mental defects, and we must die without a choice. Birth, old age, and death are part of it, and it is called "all-pervading" because it is common to all beings and is the foundation for the first two types of suffering.

We become interested in the Dharma because we do not want to experience suffering, only to discover soon thereafter that the subject is extensively discussed. We may think it is better not to hear about it, but analyzing suffering is essential for understanding how it manifests—this is a prerequisite to becoming free of it. When the Buddha started to give teachings, one of the first topics was the necessity of acknowledging suffering—not an easy task in the case of the suffering of change and all-pervading suffering, but nevertheless a task we must try to accomplish. Lama Tsongkhapa, the great fourteenth-century Tibetan yogi and founder of the Gelug school, said that if one does not discover the truth of suffering, one cannot generate renunciation; and if one lacks the understanding of the origin of suffering, one cannot cut the root of samsara, the root of cyclic existence.

Suffering experienced within the realm of samsara is usually divided into six types. The first is *dissatisfaction.* No matter how many material objects we might have, we always remain dissatisfied—very few people say that they are now wealthy enough and that they will no longer try to accumulate more money. The second is the *uncertainty* about friends and enemies. Someone can be a friend for a while and then turn into an enemy; a person who is a friend during the first half of our lives can become an enemy in the second half. The third type of suffering is the pain of having to *leave our body.* The fourth is the suffering of having to be *continuously reborn;* in our conditioned existence we are forced to be conceived again and again. The fifth is the *uncertainty of our social status,* of our condition, and of our power. The sixth is *loneliness.* This refers primarily to the fact that we are born and die alone.

Each realm of samsara is also characterized by specific types of suffering. Eight of them are typical of a human rebirth: the sufferings of birth, illness, old age, and death, the suffering of having to leave behind objects and situations that we cherish, the suffering of having to meet objects and situations that we abhor, the suffering of not being able to satisfy our desires, and the suffering of having a body.

If, having examined suffering, we just try to avoid it, we won't solve the problem in a satisfactory way. We must instead seek its causes in order to prevent its effects. For this purpose we need to analyze existent phenomena. These are divided into two categories: *produced phenomena* (impermanent) and *phenomena without a cause* (permanent). The former exist because there is a preceding cause, while the latter do not have any cause.

Among phenomena, those that have a cause have a bigger influence on us. Among them we can distinguish external phenomena and inner, mind-related phenomena. Even in relation to mental phenomena the law of the external world is valid, according to which if we interrupt the cause of a certain phenomenon, the phenomenon itself also ceases. For example, when we extinguish a cigarette, the smoke that comes out of it also disappears.

In our reality, we have pleasant and unpleasant experiences. If we desire the former and dislike the latter, we must collect or avoid their specific causes. External phenomena that create our conditions are easy to comprehend. Among mental phenomena, it is useful to differentiate between those that benefit us and those that harm us, such as anger, desire, and ignorance. Let's take a few examples.

If we are sitting quietly by ourselves and someone comes along and says something unpleasant, immediately our peaceful state of mind disappears and unhappiness sets in, caused by the anger we now feel. If we are experiencing a pleasant mental state but then encounter objects we find attractive, we instantly lose our happiness when the desire for those objects arises and grows within us. Or, if we think of ourselves as important but others don't pay any attention to us, we feel wounded because of our pride.

When we experience anger we must search for its true causes rather than becoming angry. And if someone insults us, we must think that the same person might have helped us immensely in the past, in both our present and previous lives. Why then, because of a brief incident, would we harbor aversion against him or her? If we reflect in such a way, we can change our attitudes and experience a special consideration for this person, thus keeping our minds serene.

When it comes to envy, we should investigate why we create it in the first place: a particular person has what we wish to possess. If we think, however, that it is right for others to have what we desire, envy will disappear and we will preserve our peace of mind.

When it comes to pride, we can reflect that we have so many shortcomings and so it's not appropriate to have such a high opinion of ourselves; then the inflated opinion will shrink.

Let us look now at the suffering of a rich person and a poor person. A poor person becomes happy when he has enough food and shelter, perfectly satisfied with the little he has, and his specific problems are generally solved. The problems of the poor relate mainly to survival. The rich, however, though not worried by a lack of material things, experience mental discomfort.

In samsara there are six kinds of existence: three of them, including the human realm, are favorable, and three, including the animal realm, are unfavorable. Animals are born as animals because of negative karma accumulated in previous lives, and suffering among humankind is also a result of negative karma.

In summary, the causes of all forms of suffering are the three main afflictions—anger, attachment, and ignorance—but there are antidotes to them. They are, respectively, compassion, non-attachment, and wisdom. By *wisdom* we don't mean ordinary, common wisdom, but the wisdom that recognizes the ultimate nature of all phenomena. If the three afflictions bring suffering, the three respective antidotes bring happiness, so if we want to eliminate suffering, we have to eradicate the afflications and cultivate the antidotes. No external means are of any help, only the Dharma.

Therefore, we have to become acquainted with it. The Dharma's function is to destroy the enemy within us, the mental attitude that from time immemorial has caused us enormous suffering. If we become acquainted

with the nature and the function of the Dharma, a genuine interest will
be born in us that will establish causes for happiness. The purposes of the
Dharma are vast, and among them we can choose those that are suitable
for us in this moment.

We must recognize the nature of anger and understand the reason it
creates suffering in our minds. Then we must investigate the reasons anger
arises, and when it manifests, make an effort to avoid and control it. It will
be hard at first, but if we keep thinking of the harm anger creates for us,
the moment will come when we will be able to eliminate it completely.

We experience attachment for many reasons, and one of them is our
bodies. If we examine the body carefully, we realize that it is made up of
many impurities, and our attachment will decrease.

You must not see such afflictions as negative only because Buddha says
so or because I say so. As soon as an affliction arises, check for yourself
whether it gives you happiness and well-being, or whether it creates problems for you. You never find someone who says, "I am so glad that I got
angry!" In fact, you find quite the opposite.

In our analysis we must proceed in the following way: karma is the cause
of all suffering; the causes of karma are anger and desire; the cause of anger
and desire is ignorance—not knowing things in the right way. Ignorance
clings to phenomena as if they existed independently, from their own side,
but this is a deluded view—like someone who, seeing a scarecrow in the
middle of a field, mistakes it for a person. Similarly, we think that phenomena exist as they appear to us, and because of this mistaken perception
of reality, anger and desire arise. Seeing a scarecrow from a distance and
believing it to be a person, we can experience anger or desire. However,
when we get close and see the scarecrow for what it is, the misconception
disappears. We have traded the wrong perception for the right one.

The great Indian pandit Dharmakirti said that because of ignorance, we
first conceive "I," and then, on this basis, generate desire and anger, which
respectively bring us attraction and repulsion for things. By *ignorance* we
mean a wrong view of phenomena. When we start perceiving reality correctly, this type of ignorance is erased and with it the other afflictions.
Erasing the afflictions allows us to refrain from creating the nonvirtuous
actions that are motivated by them, and thus, because we have not produced negative karma that leads to suffering, problems cease.

In order to destroy ignorance we need to generate the wisdom that knows emptiness. The view of emptiness counters ignorance's view that phenomena are self-existent with the understanding that phenomena only exist interdependently. With the wisdom that realizes emptiness, we see phenomena as they really are, and because of that, anger and desire don't arise in our minds any longer. In this way we avoid creating negative karma and therefore reach the final stage in which we don't have to experience suffering, since its cause is extinguished.

Creating the Causes for Happiness

In Buddhist teachings we differentiate between the Hinayana path and the Mahayana path. Followers of the Hinayana path, aware of samsara's suffering, emphasize the elimination of mental defects and obtain cessation of mental suffering for themselves. The Mahayana practitioner, however, holds dear the end of suffering for all beings, and followers of this path therefore try to obtain perfect enlightenment in order to be able to help others do the same.

When a Hinayana follower has eliminated all his afflictions, he obtains cessation of his personal suffering—what we also call *nirvana*, or personal peace—but he does not yet possess the omniscient mind of a buddha. We differentiate between overt afflictions and their imprints, which constitute the obstacles to omniscience. The Hinayana follower who has completely realized his path has eradicated the former but has not yet eradicated the latter; having obtained the cessation of suffering and having totally removed any problems for himself, he is completely satisfied. Someone who is also concerned about others, however, will not be satisfied with this kind of achievement, but desires instead the enlightened state. In order to obtain that state, we need to generate *bodhichitta*, or the mind of awakening.

In a poor family, the main concern of the head of that family is finding a means of survival and solving problems for those he is responsible for. Likewise, bodhisattvas, Mahayana followers, want to eliminate the problems of other beings as well as their own, and to this end they will strive to attain the state of a buddha, for only then will they be able to really help others. It is not enough, however, to have only the desire and the determination to attain such a state; we must also follow the path that leads to this state, the bodhisattva path, through the practice of the six *paramitas,* the transcendental perfections.

Every being thinks in a different way, has different problems, and needs specific help to solve them, and only a buddha is able to give appropriate help to everyone. It is for this reason that the bodhisattva tries to obtain perfect enlightenment, though at the same time he completely solves all his own problems, having extinguished the cause of suffering and developed all positive qualities in himself. If we need water, we need a container, the main object of desire being not the receptacle itself but the water. In the same way, a bodhisattva tries to obtain the state of a buddha first, for the sake of all beings. We must therefore perform beneficial actions and avoid harmful actions toward all beings as much as possible.

If we want to follow the Dharma, we must make the determination "If until now I have been angry with others, from now on I won't allow it, and I won't repeat any negative action I have committed in the past." This kind of determination to change one's mind must be developed before deciding to practice the Dharma.

His Holiness the Dalai Lama summarized the Buddha's teachings in two sentences: "If we can, we must benefit others. If we cannot, at least we must avoid hurting them." The more we succeed in being of benefit to others, the happier we will be, and the more we succeed in avoiding hurting others, the less suffering we will experience. When we start behaving in this way and practice the Dharma, people close to us will start loving us, and therefore we will experience happiness in this life as well as in future ones.

A Tibetan saying goes, "If we walk an arduous path, we must first prepare with our hands the place where we will put our feet, and then we have to dig a firm spot for our next step." If we wish for something positive tomorrow, we must do something positive today. In order to have a peaceful and stable old age, we need to have a good education, a good job, and we must try to save money. In order for a politician to gain votes and consensus, he will first need to work assiduously at it. He who does not take care of his own education and occupation right now will experience difficulties and problems later on. Likewise, if we want to earn a good future birth, it is necessary that we create its causes right now.

Hence we can conclude that whether we are happy or unhappy right now, it is because we have created the causes for either condition. In the end, we can point only to ourselves.

The Example of Ben Kungyel

There was once a famous geshe named Ben Kungyel who had been a farmer in the first half of his life. Dissatisfied with the fruit of his labor, he would rob travelers. One day a woman bumped into him and asked him whether he had seen the dreadful robber Ben Kungyel, and when he replied, "That's me!" the woman, overwhelmed by fear, dropped dead on the spot. At that moment Ben Kungyel understood his situation clearly; he saw the terror people felt at the simple utterance of his name and that he himself was the cause of so much suffering. Then and there he decided to change his ways and started practicing the Dharma and meditation. He would keep a pile of white and black pebbles, which he used to keep track of his every deed and every thought that arose in his mind. If it was a positive thought or deed, he would put aside a white pebble—if negative, a black one—and by evening he could weigh the entire day. He would do this every day. At first the black pebbles greatly outnumbered the white ones; by improving himself day by day, however, the black pebbles gradually decreased in number and the white ones increased. As time went by and he progressed in his practice, he was counting almost exclusively white pebbles and almost no black ones, and this was because he had managed to dissolve desire, anger, and the other afflictions, thus ceasing to create negative karma.

Likewise, when we feel compassion and love for others, there is no space for hatred and antagonism, because our mind is permeated by positive feelings. One of the main causes for the negative karma we create is aversion, the dislike we feel for others. Substituting this attitude with love and compassion, we eliminate the causes that produce it, and we don't even consider harming anyone.

Ben Kungyel used to say that when he was a robber he was full of desire—the loot was never enough; he was never satisfied with it. From the moment he became a practitioner, it was quite another matter—food couldn't find his mouth.

Changing Our Way of Thinking

Someone who is acquainted with the Dharma and practices it will be able to endure enormous difficulties far better than someone who does not practice. He knows they are the inevitable result of actions he himself has committed. If two people suffer the same complaint and one of them is practicing the Dharma, the Dharma practitioner will reflect that he finds himself in a conditioned existence where suffering is natural; he will endure physical discomfort more easily than the other one, although the pain they experience is exactly the same.

Those who do not have the support offered by the Dharma will work hard to earn money and then will have problems saving and spending it, and in spite of their efforts they will not achieve the happiness they desire. If we open our cupboards and drawers we will see that they are full of objects, and yet we are not happy. Our state of mind is very different from Milarepa's, who lived and meditated in caves and did not possess anything at all. In Tibet many monks who practiced the Dharma were so poor that they only managed to obtain water, yogurt, and toasted flour, which they would mix together into a meal, but because they practiced, they were completely satisfied with their lot. They could not light a fire for many months in their rooms, but their minds were warm and happy.

If we know the Dharma intimately and possess a right understanding of reality, our existence will progress very easily, and even if we have to give our life for others we will do it happily, without resistance.

In one of his past lives, when he was still a bodhisattva, the Buddha gave his body to a hungry tigress, and he did so with great joy, thinking that human life is short, and that doing some good for others is far more important. He weighed the value of his own life against the value of performing virtuous actions and understood that to perform these, even for one moment, is far more precious. In accordance with these Dharma realizations he offered his own body without hesitation.

Since we want to better ourselves, we need to know how to bring about this change. Right now we consider this life of ours to be more important than future lives, this month more important than future months, this present moment more important than future moments, and we consider ourselves to be the most important among all the beings in the universe.

We must reverse such a way of thinking and regard others as more important than ourselves, and the future as more important than the present. We must not, however, be in a hurry to change, because in so doing we could create even greater problems and difficulties; on the contrary, we have to bring about such change gradually.

When we listen to the teachings, we must avoid three errors, which are illustrated by the following metaphors. We must avoid being like an upside-down vessel, into which, no matter how much water is poured, not even one drop enters. This refers to the error of having a closed mind. Instead of this, we should pay attention to the teachings and try to receive them. We must also avoid being like a leaky vessel, into which the water that is poured seeps out. This refers to the error of forgetting the teachings in spite of having listened to them with an open mind. Instead of this, we should remember them and reflect on them. Then there is the error of being like a dirty vessel, which pollutes the clean water that is poured into it. This refers to having a motivation limited to personal gain, in spite of having listened to the teachings and in spite of remembering them. A mind befitting the teachings must be absolutely pure.

The Law of Cause and Effect

Dharma practice depends upon belief in karma—the law of cause and effect—and acting on it. It does not matter how profound our knowledge of the Dharma is: if we do not follow the law of cause and effect, we cannot claim to be true practitioners. A true practitioner is one who understands and acts upon this law, however limited his knowledge might be. If, due to right understanding, we get to the point where we avoid even the smallest negative action, then we have become truly intimate with the path.

Karma has four characteristics:

1. It is certain. If we create positive or negative causes, the results will surely be of the same kind.
2. It is expandable. Tiny seeds will give a great amount of fruit.
3. If we do not create a certain type of karma, we will not experience

its consequences. We certainly will not be able to experience karma created by another, and in the same way, others will not experience our karma.

4. Created karma never dissipates.

Understanding and following the four characteristics or laws of karma means observing karma generally. Particular karma refers to specific actions of body, speech, and mind. There are three negative actions created by the body:

- killing
- stealing
- sexual misconduct

There are four negative actions created by speech:

- lying
- divisive speech
- harsh words
- idle, senseless talk

There are three negative actions created by the mind:

- covetousness
- malice
- wrong views

All negative karmas can be included in these ten. The determination to not want to commit negative karma is the practice of morality. In order to achieve a favorable situation in the future, we must observe the ten virtuous karmas, which means abstaining from the ten nonvirtues.

Since we do not see the effects of various actions right now, we might be led to think that it is pointless to practice and observe these precepts. But let us look at an animal and the sufferings its state entails, and ask ourselves if we would be able to endure them if we found ourselves in its position. This will provide us with the answer to the question of the usefulness of practicing the ten precepts. In the future we must try to avoid these negative actions, without worrying too much about those we have committed in the past; we can purify them, if we so wish.

It is easy, now that we have the opportunity, to avoid creating karma that can lead us to unfortunate rebirths, whereas once we find ourselves in one of these rebirths, it will be extremely difficult to generate the causes for a future happy existence. We must bear this in mind and, even if practicing the Dharma is very demanding, make all possible efforts. If during our lifetime we ended up in prison for a while, this might not be so unpleasant, because even if the conditions were harsh, we could still continue to practice the Dharma. But if we were born poor, in an unbearably hot or cold climate, with no food or water, we would probably live like this not just for a month or a year, but for our entire lives.

There are states of so much suffering, even worse than those of animals, that we can neither imagine nor bear to hear about. If we are attacked and beaten, someone can come to our rescue, but this does not happen among animals—they are constantly afraid of being hurt, and the difference here is that we human beings for the most part refrain from committing negative actions. Many animals, even where I live, do not reveal themselves during the day for fear of being killed. They come out at night, driven by hunger. Theirs is a hopeless situation, to the point that they cannot do anything for themselves, not even cry. If we compare our situation to that of animals, we can understand how lucky we are. The bigger one eats the smaller—this is their law! What would we do if we were to be reborn in a similar condition? We cannot even bear the thought of it. If we constantly keep ourselves on the path of the Dharma, we guard ourselves from being reborn in inferior realms, where we will not only suffer immensely, but also accumulate nothing but negative karma. Let us try then to avoid creating the causes for such existence.

What we enjoy as a result of virtuous actions also depends on what motivates us to abstain from improper behavior, since the quality of results depends on the motivation and on the satisfaction we place in our activities.

The same goes for negative actions. If, because of a strong mental affliction, we kill an animal and derive great satisfaction from that, we will be reborn in the hell realm. If the intensity of the two factors is not so strong, we will be reborn as a hungry ghost, a *preta;* if it is slight, we will be reborn in the animal realm or even in the human realm, but our lifespan will be short. We will have to suffer such consequences because, having taken an animal's life, we caused suffering. On the other hand, if we resolve not to kill anymore, we will, as a result, enjoy a long life.

In the case of stealing, the strength of motivation and satisfaction also produces different results. If it is strong, we will be reborn in the hell realm; if it is not so intense, as a hungry ghost; if it is slight, as an animal, or as a human, forced to suffer theft, fire, and poverty, since we have caused others the suffering of being deprived of their possessions.

The consequence of committing adultery is that in the future we will not be able to enjoy a serene married life; our partner will have affairs, and there will be marital discord. A happy married life is the result of having refrained from sexual misconduct in previous lives.

The effect of telling lies is that no one believes what we say.

The consequence of divisive speech is not being loved. If someone harshly criticizes somebody else, we must not repeat his words; on the other hand, if positive things are being said about someone, it is good to do so.

Naturally, nobody likes to hear harsh words; and if we say harsh words, we'll be forced to hear them too.

Idle talk is a waste of our precious time—it would be more profitable to read or listen to meaningful things. Among Tibetans, the greatest waste of time is chatting; among Westerners, watching television.

Being covetous is pointless, because whoever has money can buy the desired goods and whoever doesn't have money gains absolutely nothing by watching shop windows and envying what others have.

If we sow the seeds of malice toward others, we will find ourselves reaping plenty of it ourselves.

Because our views are wrong, we must be careful when, reading a text, we do not grasp parts of it. We should refrain from assuming that they are wrong, for many subjects need time to be properly understood. If we conclude right away that they are not correct only because we do not understand them, this can easily turn into a wrong view. On the subject of rebirth, for example, even if the logic is not clear to us, we must not reject it indiscriminately, because in so doing we engender a wrong view; this must be avoided.

The ten paths of the virtuous actions can be practiced all the time: while eating, walking, working, and even sleeping, since if before falling asleep we determine to avoid any negative action, sleep itself will be a practice of accumulating virtue. If we follow the paths of the ten virtuous actions we will obtain human rebirths, and we will be able to accumulate more positive karma for the accomplishment of buddhahood.

It is not necessary to be a monk or a special being—anyone can practice the Dharma perfectly: in retreat, with the family, in the office, or anywhere else. Many yogis have said that if we practice, nirvana is between the walls of our home, but if we do not practice, we sow the causes for an unfortunate rebirth, even though we might be in solitary retreat.

Great Effort and Its Results

The Buddha we refer to is not a legendary character, but a historical one. To this day there are artifacts of his coming and evidence of his life. He was born in India, in Lumbini, which today is part of Nepal, into the royal family of Shakya. He obtained enlightenment at Bodhgaya and gave his first teachings in Sarnath, near Varanasi. We have had the opportunity to know these places directly, through documentation, or by other people's testimonials, and the teachings he gave in Sarnath and elsewhere are preserved to this day, gathered in the texts of the *Tripitaka*. Shakyamuni Buddha appeared approximately two thousand five hundred years ago in India, but he is not the only buddha who has manifested; many came before him. However, the time between the coming of one buddha and the next is millions of years. Even in the present eon, three other buddhas came into this world before Shakyamuni, and 996 of them will appear in the future. The next one will be Maitreya Buddha.

At first Buddha was an ordinary human being like us, full of shortcomings and faults. However, these can be completely eradicated and all virtues completely realized, and he proved this by succeeding in attaining enlightenment. Therefore, it is possible to understand logically that we can do the same. Buddha reached this state as a result of his perseverance and great effort, whereas we continue to wander in cyclic existence from beginningless time due to laziness and indolence.

We also know Milarepa's story—his master Marpa asked him to build towers, destroy them, and then to build them again. Marpa made him endure many other hardships as well, in order to help Milarepa purify his karma and mental defects. We also find ourselves having to endure various problems: some of us perhaps do not eat regularly, others sleep badly. We endure many kinds of discomfort for some gain, but if we work many hours at the office, for example, the result will be limited to this life. What we gain by listening to the Dharma and enduring the difficulties of practice, however, goes far beyond this. Simply hearing the name of a buddha or a bodhisattva is in itself a great purification, and we gain benefits simply by listening to the story of the Buddha, or by wishing to be like him—one who has purified all negativity and accumulated all virtues.

If we possess solid foundations in the Dharma, even the ordinary dimensions of our daily life will not present us with difficulties. It will bring no benefit, on the other hand, to put spirituality aside and dedicate ourselves exclusively to the material aspects of existence. If we compare a person whose whole life has been dedicated to these material concerns to someone who also took care of his own spiritual development and mental training, we'll notice not only that the latter has suffered less in this life but that he has something to take with him after death.

Those who dedicate their lives to spiritual practice, such as monks or nuns, may be poorer, but they are also much happier. Buddha said that his followers would never suffer hunger, not even in times when, in order to eat, humans will only be able to sow seeds in fields as tiny as a fingernail, or when rice will be swapped for equal quantities of jewels. Those who follow a spiritual path will have difficulties, but also realizations.

However, we should not cultivate the kind of haste that makes us desire to achieve great results the very next day after hearing the teachings. If we plant the seeds of a tree, we can't possibly expect it to bear fruit the following year. Even when sowing grain or wheat, we need to wait five or six months for the harvest. We have the opportunity to listen to the teachings and embark on our spiritual training, but in order to see the results we must be patient and wait.

When we leave this existence we will have to leave behind all our possessions and the riches we consider so important, as well as our friends, relatives, loved ones who are now close to us, and our parents who cherish us so much. But, if we have practiced it, the Dharma will not abandon us, and if we have not destroyed it with anger and wrong views, positive karma will accompany us.

If we realize renunciation, bodhichitta, and the right understanding of the mode of existence of phenomena, it will be impossible for the afflictions to annihilate our inner wealth. For this reason, the Dharma is the most important and the most precious thing, and it is therefore essential to practice it. In order to practice it, we must become acquainted with it, and we can do this through the text of the *Bodhicharyavatara*. Dharma practice must depend not on the help we might receive from others, but solely on ourselves. We must reflect, assimilate the explanations that will be given here with our own personal experience, and try to gain a clear understanding of what will be presented.

As long as we dwell within conditioned existence we will not be of any real help to other beings; in order to be able to help them we must therefore attain buddhahood and with such resolution start our journey on the bodhisattva path. However, in order to understand the *Bodhicharyavatara*, a Mahayana teaching, we must first prepare ourselves through the various stages of the Hinayana path that have been explained so far. In general, there are three levels of Dharma practice: the lesser, the middling, and the great. Once we are trained in the first two levels, we will then be ready for the teachings unique to the third level, the Mahayana teachings.

The *Bodhicharyavatara* teaches the practice of a bodhisattva. It was written by Shantideva for our benefit—he left it to us with the same love as a mother writing her will for her son before her death! We are truly fortunate to be able to listen to and grow acquainted with this text, and I myself consider it a privilege to give teachings on it.

❧ I ❧
THE BENEFITS OF THE
AWAKENING MIND

THE TITLE of the *Bodhicharyavatara* is in Sanskrit, the ancient language of India, because it was written in the eighth century by the Indian acharya Shantideva. Only later was it translated into Tibetan.

At the monastic university of Nalanda, to which Shantideva belonged, there were many great scholars who disparaged Shantideva's behavior; they felt his conduct brought them shame. Shantideva was a perfect Dharma practitioner, but since he was practicing quietly, the other monks thought he was not practicing at all; in fact, they thought that all he was doing was eating, sleeping, and defecating, and because of this he was nicknamed "the one who practices only three things." In order to get him expelled, they planned to play a trick on him. It was the tradition in the monastery that every monk would periodically give teachings. When it was Shantideva's turn, they prepared a very high teaching throne that had no steps to allow him to climb it. When Shantideva arrived, however, he lowered the throne with one hand and sat down.

After this demonstration of high powers, he asked the assembled monks what kind of teachings they wished to hear, and a pandit replied, "You who are famed for your big appetite, we would like to hear something we have never heard before." Thus, Shantideva began to teach the *Bodhicharyavatara*. The teachings were profound, revealing deep spiritual understanding, and everybody was astonished. When Shantideva reached the ninth chapter, he began to levitate from the throne and disappear; only the pandits who possessed special realizations were able to continue to listen to him and write down his words, and they begged him not to abandon them. This is the story of how the *Bodhicharyavatara* came to be.

In Tibet it was once decreed that every text translated from Sanskrit had to be categorized into one of the three baskets, or *pitakas:* the *Vinaya Pitaka,* which contained the teachings on discipline and morality; the *Sutra Pitaka,* which contained the teachings on concentration; or the *Abhidharma Pitaka,* which contained the teachings on wisdom. In order to differentiate between translated texts and to indicate the group to which it belonged, a text was introduced with a particular verse of deference. For texts belonging to the Vinaya Pitaka, the verse was addressed to the Buddha; for texts belonging to the Sutra Pitaka, it was addressed to all buddhas and bodhisattvas; and for texts belonging to the Abhidharma Pitaka, it was addressed to Manjushri. At the beginning of the text we are studying at present, there is a single verse of homage written by the Tibetan translator that states, "I pay my respects to all buddhas and bodhisattvas." This indicates that the text belongs to the Sutra Pitaka.

Expressing such tribute, and with it the determination to bring the task to completion in verse, was a literary tradition of India, aimed at ensuring the success of the undertaking and the elimination of obstacles. It is always a good idea when we begin any work to pray to the Three Jewels of refuge—the Buddha, Dharma, and Sangha—to remove obstacles, and allow us to complete the work in the best possible way. The tribute in the first stanza is followed by verses in which Shantideva commits himself to completing the work, since a wise person does not leave a promise unfulfilled. The author then proceeds to explain the reasons for writing the text: to bring awareness into the mind of the reader and enable the reader's understanding to arise more easily.

The text says, "I respectfully prostrate myself to the sugatas, who are endowed with the dharmakaya." [stanza 1]

The *sugatas,* or those who have obtained a blissful state, are the buddhas, who possess the *dharmakaya,* the mind that has perfectly purified itself of all afflictions and accumulated all virtues. They are also endowed with the realization of the two truths. The eradication of mental afflictions in the mind of a buddha has three characteristics: it is perfect, it is permanent, and it concerns the totality of afflictions in all their aspects.

A being abiding in *samadhi,* the mind stabilized through meditation, perceives the five aggregates of the desire realm as unattractive and eliminates deceptive appearances, recognizing them as projections fueled by attachment. Among afflictions we find two levels: manifest and potential. For example, you are probably not angry right now; there is no obvious hatred. The seeds of anger and hatred, however, are present. A being in samadhi has eliminated the first aspect of the mental afflictions but has not yet eliminated the second. He does not perceive ordinary objects as attractive, and as a result he is able to withdraw his mind from them, directing it instead toward a higher level, the world of form. The only way to eliminate the seed of desire, however, is by perceiving emptiness directly. Only then has this being erased the mental afflictions completely. If he does not reach such a state, his afflictions can still manifest after he comes out of samadhi.

There are two paths that act as methods to erase the mental afflictions. The first is the supermundane or transworldy path, by which we arrive at the direct perception of emptiness, and thus at the complete and perfect eradication of the afflictions. The second is the worldly path, by which, not perceiving emptiness directly, we eradicate only the manifest level of the afflictions. Non-Buddhists, such as *rishis,* also follow this path. Therefore the eradication of mental afflictions in the mind of a buddha is superior to that of an *arhat* on the Hinayana path, for the latter has eliminated the obstructions of afflictions, but not, because of the imprints of the afflictions, the obstructions to omniscience.

Our minds, like those of all beings, are empty, lacking intrinsic existence. Mind is by nature pure; in ordinary beings, however, it is temporarily obscured, whereas in the state of complete enlightenment it is not polluted, either naturally or temporarily. Because mind is intrinsically pure, it is possible to attain perfect enlightenment. Since obscuration is only temporary, the mind can be purified. Fire is by nature hot, while iron is burning hot only in given circumstances. In the same way, the minds of all beings are by nature pure, but temporarily obscured.

The prostration in the initial verse is directed not only toward the buddhas, but also toward all those who are worthy of praise—namely, the bodhisattvas, here called "noble sons" (or "noble offspring") because they will eventually become buddhas. There are three kinds of homage: physical, verbal, and mental. We pay homage to the higher beings in order to encourage ourselves to seek their qualities within our own minds.

The teachings we are discussing at present have been given by the Buddha, and in the beginning it is essential to inquire as to whether he is effectively guiding us on the right path. For this reason we need to analyze whether the Buddha possesses the necessary wisdom and ability to do this. Bodhisattvas who have obtained the *path of seeing* can see that the attributes of a buddha are so many that they cannot be numbered, and that is why we will try to get acquainted with them through the bodhisattvas' experience. It was not possible for us to meet the Buddha and listen to his teachings ourselves, but these bodhisattvas have the capacity to perceive him directly. We are fortunate to be able to learn something about him through these beings.

The attributes of a buddha can be divided into those belonging to the body, those belonging to the speech, and those belonging to the mind. Let us look at the *ten powers* of a buddha.

The first is that a buddha knows without any doubts the positive and negative effects of virtuous and nonvirtuous karma, he knows what is possible and what is not possible, and the truth of his statements is undeniable. The second is that he knows even the smallest consequence of a specific cause, as well as any relation between a cause and its effect. For example, there are various colors in the feathers of a peacock's tail, each with a particular cause, and a buddha knows all of them in the finest detail. Thanks to this power, there is no question he is not able to answer. The third power is that he knows the various attitudes and dispositions of each individual, and hence he understands each being's inclination, be it toward the Hinayana or the Mahayana path. This power allows a buddha to guide all beings according to their specific needs, requirements, and characteristics. Able to satisfy the demands of all, the buddhas were worshipped in the past and continue to be worshipped in the present. His Holiness the Dalai Lama has this very same power, and therefore he has been helpful to many people.

The fourth power of a buddha is that he knows the disposition of each individual, and gives teachings accordingly. The fifth is that he knows the ability of each individual, and offers teachings in a concise form to those with a higher capability, and in a detailed and expansive form to those with a lower capability. The sixth is that he knows all paths and their respective causes. For example, he understands the causes that bring a human or god rebirth, the causes for obtaining liberation, and so forth.

The seventh is that he knows all the *dharmas*, or phenomena, that must be abandoned, and the dharmas that must be sought after. The eighth is that he knows all former lives. The ninth is that he knows the transmigration of beings in the universe in detail. The tenth is that he knows the extinction of all forms of contamination.

A buddha has all these powers and knowledge. Therefore, his advice can only be right and useful to us. An expert physician is able to provide the best cure for his patients. In the same way, a buddha can be the best guide for a practitioner.

Now let us examine the *four fearlessnesses* typical of an enlightened being. The first is that he can categorically state that he is all-knowing, and there is no possibility that anyone could challenge him. If we take all the trees of the earth, burn them, and scatter their ashes in the ocean, and then bring some of these ashes to a buddha and ask him to identify to which tree a single particle belonged and in what area it was found, he will be able to answer in great detail.

Once there was a person who did not believe what Shakyamuni Buddha had told him regarding his previous lives. The Buddha sent him to a village, suggesting that he write the names of every resident on a different piece of paper. These were sealed and mixed together, and then presented to Buddha, who guessed all of them correctly.

The second fearlessness is that Buddha is able to say, without fear of being challenged, that afflictive emotions are a hindrance to liberation, and that their imprints are a hindrance to perfect enlightenment.

The third fearlessness is that he can fearlessly assert that different paths lead to different realizations.

The fourth fearlessness is that he can declare to have extinguished any kind of obstacle or fear within himself.

A buddha also possesses the *four perfect individual knowledges,* which are as follows. First, he knows every phenomenon in the universe. Second, he knows the characteristics of each phenomenon. Third, he knows the terms by which one refers to all the various phenomena in the world, in the various existing languages. He does not need any translation when he gives teachings. On this point, since we believe His Holiness the Dalai Lama to be a *nirmanakaya,* a manifestation of Buddha himself, the question could arise as to why he would need a translator. The answer to this is that His Holiness has not appeared in this world in the form of a buddha; if he had done so we would not be able to see him and benefit from him. His

Holiness has appeared instead as an ordinary being. Having manifested as such, he must act accordingly and give the appearance of not knowing the various languages. The fourth perfect individual knowledge is that a buddha has no hindrances to his knowledge of nature, or his knowledge of the type and classification of each phenomenon.

In addition to these characteristics, a buddha also possesses eighteen qualities known as the *eighteen unshared attributes of buddhas.*

The first is that if a mad elephant charges him, he is not afraid. The second is that if he finds himself in a dark forest that echoes with terrifying noises, he is not afraid. Third, he has the special quality of not being forgetful, and when given the opportunity to benefit a particular being, he will be mindful. Fourth, he can spontaneously and simultaneously help all beings perceive emptiness directly. Fifth, to a buddha, *samsara* and *nirvana* are equal, since both are without intrinsic, self-sustaining existence.

The sixth attribute is that a buddha constantly possesses the awareness of the appropriate times to benefit various beings. As one driving down a street filled with traffic is constantly aware and alert, a buddha is always mindful of the needs of all beings, so that he can give his help whenever possible.

Seventh, a buddha invariably wishes to help all beings, and to this aim he is always present in those places where he can be helpful. This is possible because, during his training as a bodhisattva, he generated bodhichitta for the welfare of all beings. With this motivation, he practiced the transcendental perfections over a long period of time, and because of this he achieved perfect enlightenment. Having realized all there is to realize, a buddha has no difficulty being present where needed.

A buddha will continue to help all beings until their final liberation, because his body, unlike ours, is not subject to decay. Whenever someone is ready to receive his help and his teachings, a buddha is ready to give them in the most appropriate form—as a layman, a monk, or even as an animal, according to the situation and the level of the being who is to benefit. He can even manifest himself as a blind man or as a beggar.

There are areas in the woods where hunting is permitted, and areas where it is forbidden. Animals who take shelter in protected areas are safe; few among them are aware of these areas, yet they do their best to take others to these safe places. These beings could indeed be buddhas or bodhisattvas.

As clouds are not endowed with a particular desire to produce rain, buddhas benefit all beings effortlessly, naturally, and spontaneously. As the moon reflects in all puddles of water without a will of its own, in the same way wherever a buddha is needed, he will spontaneously manifest.

When we pray, meditate, and invite the Buddha, he is present even if we are not able to see him. If we have paintings or statues or an altar in our home and make offerings to them with the wish that the Buddha visit us, this will happen even if we are not able to perceive him.

Asanga went into retreat in order to have a vision of Maitreya. He stayed there three years, constantly meditating, but failed. Discouraged, he came out and continued on his journey. Along the road he happened to meet an old man who was filing a big iron bar with cotton. Intrigued, Asanga asked the old man what he was doing, and the man replied that he was trying to shape the iron bar into a pin. Asanga thought that if the old man had such strong determination as to think it possible to create a pin from an iron bar, how much more perseverance should he have in meditation if he was to have the vision of Maitreya Buddha. He went back to his solitary place, where he resumed and abandoned his task several times. After twelve years, disappointed, he finally gave up. As he was leaving, he saw a female dog with a wounded, putrefied thigh infested with worms. Moved to great compassion, Asanga tried to think of a way to help the dog. He did not want to take the worms off and throw them away because they would die, nor did he want to leave them on the wound, because the dog was suffering. So Asanga decided to put the worms on a piece of his own flesh that he cut from his body. Fearful of harming them by grabbing them with his bare hands, he bent down to catch them with his mouth. Disgusted at the sight, he closed his eyes, and when he opened them again, he saw Maitreya standing there in place of the dog.

Upon seeing Maitreya, Asanga complained that he had appeared only after twelve long years. Maitreya explained that he had been beside Asanga since the beginning of his retreat, and, as proof, he showed his clothes marked with Asanga's spit from all that time. Maitreya told Asanga that he had been unable to perceive him because he was lacking compassion but that the strong compassion he had generated toward the dog as he left his retreat was the final condition for his sight to be cleared.

The eighth attribute is that a buddha goes to all places where there are beings to be benefited. The ninth is that he knows all methods to benefit all beings. The tenth is that he has the ability to maintain the state of samadhi. The eleventh is that he has the special quality of discriminating wisdom. The twelfth is that, since a buddha has eliminated all hindrances and he has obtained all realizations, it is not possible for him to lose them. The thirteenth is that his actions are such that his disciples feel reverence for him at the mere sight of him. Just by seeing the body of a buddha, we create merit.

The fourteenth attribute is that anything a buddha says is meaningful and constitutes a Dharma teaching. This is the case with His Holiness the Dalai Lama. The fifteenth quality is that the mind of a buddha is always full of love and compassion for all. The sixteenth is that he possesses the full ability to know the past. The seventeenth is that he possesses the full ability to know the present. And the eighteenth is that he possesses the full ability to know the future. A buddha can benefit all beings profoundly because he possesses these attributes.

If we wish and ask for guidance, it will be given according to our capabilities and dispositions. If we practice what has been taught, it is possible to achieve what we aspire to. Given that one of the qualities of a buddha is knowing at all times when a being can be benefited, it is not possible that someone who is ready will not receive the help that he or she needs in that very moment. Indeed, there is no need for that person to physically be present in a place where a buddha is, because a buddha is present wherever he is needed.

Since a buddha possesses all these qualities, there is never a situation in which he is not helpful to his disciples.

The text continues, "Here I shall explain how to engage in the conduct of the Buddha's sons, the meaning of which I have condensed in accordance with the scriptures."

The thought might arise that since Shantideva has written this text by extracting it from existing scriptures, his was a superfluous job. In fact, it is true that the subjects he discusses are found in a great number of scriptural volumes, but in the *Bodhicharyavatara,* whose content addresses the six transcendental perfections, or *paramitas,* they are presented in a simple and concise form. If, through the study of this text, we are able to familiarize ourselves with the paths and the fruit of the Mahayana and, by practicing it, attain enlightenment or nirvana, the purpose of its composition will be accomplished. There is nothing in this text that is not present already in the teachings of the Buddha; it has been written for those who are not able to access those teachings through the more extensive scriptures.

Shantideva states that, not having much hope to be able to benefit all beings, he writes specifically to acquaint his mind with the teachings he has heard, and he wishes that, in so doing, his own faith and that of others equal in fortune to himself may increase, and that his words may be meaningful to them. [3]

Shantideva was already familiar with these teachings and had therefore accumulated merit in relation to them. In writing the text, he paid attention to the details, thus accumulating even more merit. However, reading the text augments the merit and virtue of people who have the opportunity to do so, such as ourselves. Shantideva's aim is that new qualities might be born in those who have not come across these teachings before, and increase in those who have already received them.

In order to be able to listen to the Dharma and practice it, we need a human form, with all the freedom and material means that come with it. Such a condition is indeed rare. Upon close examination, we realize exactly how uncommon this type of rebirth is. However, we ourselves have gained it, and we must fully recognize our good fortune. Thanks to our precious human condition we can attain the state of a buddha, liberation, or any form of happiness in this life. In fact, virtually anything we wish, we can attain. If we do not take advantage of this opportunity, how will we obtain a similar rebirth in the future? Our lives are as rare and fleeting as sudden lightning on a dark night, and it is only because of the power of a buddha that at times a virtuous thought arises in our mind. [5]

We can easily verify this when we reflect on the fact that on earth there are billions of human beings. There are millions of beings in Italy, but only a few are here to listen to the teachings. This is therefore a very fortunate occurrence, which rarely takes place. Negative karma is prevalent and intense; positive karma is weak and incidental. The former is consequently more common than the latter. In the teachings on the gradual path, the *lamrim,* particular emphasis is placed on the fact that this precious human rebirth is indeed rare. Furthermore, because of its great significance, it is necessary to fully realize its value by making the best of it and by understanding that we can and must practice the Dharma. Reflecting upon the fact that in the future we may no longer have such an opportunity, we understand the urgency of practicing right now. If, for example, we feel inclined to practice in the latter part of our lives instead of now, we must remember impermanence, and, to avoid wasting this opportunity, commit ourselves to starting from this very moment.

Our negative karma is strong, and we have been accumulating it from beginningless time. As a result, we could not possibly defeat it by the strength of ordinary virtue. That being the case, bodhichitta alone is the extraordinary weapon able to defeat our negative karma. The buddhas have realized it, and since bodhichitta is the best weapon at our disposal, it is also something that we must develop in our own minds.

Bodhichitta, the altruistic aspiration for buddhahood, is of great benefit to countless sentient beings, and it can instantly or rapidly bring us to supreme enlightenment. In cyclic existence we suffer and experience many problems, but all of them can be solved with the help of bodhichitta. Bodhisattvas should never abandon or betray this mind of enlightenment; with the help of bodhichitta we can attain the state of a buddha, and thus become able to help all beings effectively.

There are two ways to accumulate merit: with or without bodhichitta. The latter is comparable to a banana tree that dries up once it has produced fruit, and the former to the celestial tree endlessly producing jewel-like fruits. [12]

Bodhichitta produces boundless benefits. It destroys the negative karma we have created from beginningless time, just like the "great fire" will destroy the universe. According to the scriptures, one great eon is made up of eighty eons: twenty during which it is created, twenty during which it endures, twenty during which it is destroyed, and twenty during which it is empty. The phase of destruction will be brought on seven times by fire and then by water, and these phases alternate seven times themselves. It is the fire at the end of the universe, which will destroy it completely, that we call the "great fire."

The power and the advantages of bodhichitta are enormous, and they were taught by Maitreya to the bodhisattva Sudhana. [14]

In the *Bodhicharyavatara* it is said that compassion is very important at the beginning, just like the seed of a plant. It is important in the middle, where it is like the water that allows the plant to grow. And it is important in the end, where it is like the fruit the plant bears. The difference between a Mahayana practitioner and other practitioners is precisely this point of having developed bodhichitta.

Having attained enlightenment, the buddhas do not remain in perpetual absorption in bliss but work instead for the benefit of all sentient beings. The arhats of the Hinayana path are lacking this motivation, however, and remain absorbed in the ecstasy of nirvana. The infinite attributes of a buddha and his profound knowledge of all the methods to liberate every sentient being are due chiefly to the power of bodhichitta.

There is a difference between the mind that aspires to awaken and the mind that ventures to do so. [15]

The first mental attitude is the *bodhichitta of aspiration,* which is equivalent to the wish to go to a certain place, and the second is *bodhichitta in action* (or *engaged bodhichitta*), which corresponds to actually going there. The *bodhichitta of aspiration* is equivalent to knowing the six paramitas without having embarked on the actual practice, while the bodhichitta of action is equivalent to actually beginning to practice them in order to awaken. Both minds are driven by the aspiration to benefit others, but only the bodhichitta of action is based on real activity.

The mind that aspires to awaken, the bodhichitta of aspiration, is like a small diamond sliver; the venturing mind, the bodhichitta in action, is like a whole diamond. They are both more precious than the mind of a Hinayana arhat, which in this context is compared to gold.

The bodhichitta of aspiration will not only bring all the qualities and attributes of bodhichitta to fruition in the future, but it may also bring numerous benefits in this very life, although not as many as the bodhichitta of action. [17] Those who develop the bodhichitta of aspiration are called *bodhisattvas,* a name that we cannot ascribe to the Hinayana arhat.

A bodhisattva, having realized the necessity of attaining the state of a buddha for the benefit of others and having decided to practice that way, creates boundless merit even when unconscious or asleep. [19] The attributes of bodhichitta have been explained by the Buddha himself in the sutra requested by Subahu in order to encourage practitioners of the lesser vehicle to follow the Mahayana path. [20]

We might think that following this path is too burdensome a commitment, considering that beings are so varied and numerous, that it is impossible to help all of them, and that there are those who might hinder us in our task. Furthermore, we might think it impossible to actually attain the state of a buddha, and that it would be more reasonable to seek refuge in nirvana, or personal liberation. It is necessary to explain the benefits of bodhichitta to people who hold this conviction. It is only through bodhichitta that we can attain the state of a buddha.

If the simple act of giving a pill to a sick person is praised, what should we say of a bodhisattva acting for the benefit of all beings, wishing them to be free from suffering and the cause of suffering? [22]

This being will be worthy of immeasurable praise, and gain equally immeasurable merit. A benevolent intention is common to Brahma, to gods and sages, and to fathers and mothers, but their compassion does not equal the compassion of a bodhisattva. [23]

All of us, like these beings, do not possess such an attitude even for our own sake, so how could we ever cause it to arise for the sake of others? [24]

The ultimate aim and concern of bodhichitta is to benefit all beings, but at the moment we do not even have compassion for ourselves. A verse praising the bodhisattva of compassion, Avalokiteshvara (*Chenrezig* in Tibetan), states that our compassion for ourselves is equal to a thousandth, or even less, of the compassion he feels for us. How then is it possible for us to generate this attitude toward others? Without bodhichitta, we have no interest whatsoever in other beings, but after we develop it, we will be more concerned about them than about ourselves.

Bodhichitta is something extraordinary—it is a higher level of mind; it is a miracle. We must try to generate this precious mind, this jewel, within ourselves. It is the remedy that alleviates all suffering, and it is the cause of every joy. Since we are unable to fully appreciate the depth of this virtuous mind, we must exert ourselves and pray to the Three Jewels in order to obtain it. [25–26]

If merely a benevolent intention toward a single individual is meritorious, what of the merit of a bodhisattva who aspires to solve all problems for countless beings, and who strives to reach enlightenment for this purpose? [27]

Where there is mind, whether human or animal, there we find the desire to eliminate suffering and to find happiness. All beings pursue these aims. Those who are acquainted with and believe in the Dharma, although they might lack the direct realization of future lives, entrust themselves to trustworthy individuals and try to find a solution to their problems that goes beyond this life.

Christianity explains that if one does good deeds one will go to heaven. In the same way, according to Buddhism, those who create the causes in this life, producing positive karma, will gain a good rebirth. The more we are able to create such causes, the better our conditions will be in our future rebirths.

Jesus Christ was concerned for the welfare of all beings. He taught people to avoid negative actions and cultivate positive actions in order to gain favorable conditions in the future. Teaching this, Jesus was concerned not only with Christians, but with all beings. In the same way, Buddha did not give teachings merely to his followers, but to all those who wished to eliminate the causes of suffering and an unfortunate rebirth and to those who wished to obtain favorable conditions in the future. It is possible for Christians to take what is useful to them from the teachings of Buddha. In a similar way, Buddhists are also following the teachings of Christ when they eliminate their negative karma and engage in positive actions.

We are mind and body together. When this lifetime is over, the mental continuum goes on, linking itself to another body, and then to another, and another, and so on, until the causes of further rebirths are eliminated.

The practitioner of the lesser vehicle seeks to establish the causes for a better rebirth. At the middle level, the practitioner seeks to eliminate the causes of any rebirth in samsara, and to enter nirvana. Being born in Italy into a particular family, for example, or becoming old and sick is not dependent upon will—we have no choice in the matter since we are not free from mental afflictions. Eliminating such conditioning as well as its causes and freeing ourselves from this situation means achieving liberation, or nirvana. This is the motivation of the practitioner of the middle level.

On the higher level of spiritual practice, the practitioner's main concern is the welfare of others. We begin by realizing that others, too, are subject to various kinds of suffering, and that they wish to be free from it just as we do. Our aim then becomes the best way to help them achieve this purpose.

Such desire is a great aspiration, but by itself it does not bring any practical benefit, because in order to be truly helpful to others, we must first achieve the state of a buddha.

This kind of mental attitude is bodhichitta, but in order to develop the intention to embark on the path leading to enlightenment, we need to know the advantages that derive from generating bodhichitta. And this is precisely the subject matter that the first chapter of the *Bodhicharyavatara* presents.

The virtue generated with the bodhichitta of aspiration is incomparable. It is much greater than the merit we would gain from making offerings to the buddhas of the ten directions for countless cosmic eons. If this simple aspiration alone is the cause of countless merits, then what of the merit gained through the bodhichitta of action? Even just to worship the precious mind of the bodhisattvas is incredibly meritorious; in fact, it is only by holding them in high regard that we will try to imitate them.

The amount of negative karma we have created since beginningless time is enormous. The only antidote, and the only cause of happiness, is generating bodhichitta. A sick person must take the prescribed medicine if he wishes to become healthy. No one can do that for him. Similarly, since we are suffering, we must personally ascertain the causes of our suffering so that we can eliminate them. No one can practice the Dharma for us, or force us to do it. A physician will give us medicine and advice, but if we do not take the prescription in spite of having understood its importance, we will not become healthy again. He cannot force us to follow his instructions.

It is true that we show our interest in the Dharma, but this alone is not enough. We must put the teachings into practice in order to receive their benefits, become happier, and suffer less. First of all, we need to develop the attitude of judging others in a more favorable light. If we look at others' shortcomings, we will become accustomed to seeing only the negative side, and this will make us feel unhappy and constrained. However, a child who sees only his mother's good qualities will reciprocate her love with equal affection. If, after having become acquainted with the Dharma, we are able to appreciate the good qualities in others, then we can say that the Dharma has brought about a transformation within us.

A mother loves her only child deeply and wishes that he will never experience suffering. This is compassion. However, for the mother, this feeling exists only in relation to her child. We must try to extend this attitude to relatives, friends, and all beings, regardless of the category to which they belong—whether we like them, whether we do not like them, or whether we feel indifferent toward them.

In the beginning we must address our love and compassion for those we love, such as relatives and friends. Then we must consider our feelings for people that we perceive as strangers, for those toward whom we feel neither love nor aversion, and finally toward those we consider "enemies." In this way they will all be the objects of our love. This is in keeping with the mental training of bodhichitta, in which we continue this internal process by including all beings little by little, until the most difficult moment comes—the moment when we ask ourselves how it is possible to hold even the people we hate in a positive light.

These people were not always our enemies. They only became so from the moment we projected enmity upon them. Our present enemies might have been our friends until yesterday, and our relatives or even our mothers in a previous life. Naturally, it should be very clear to us that our present lives are not the only ones we have lived, and through reasoning we should reach the conclusion that in the past we have had numberless lives and numberless mothers. On the one hand, the number of mothers is infinite, and all beings have been our mothers and have been kind and loving to us in the past, including those we now call "enemy." On the other hand, the people we now call friends have also been our enemies in the past. Both our friends and our enemies are perfectly equal, since they have appeared to us in both roles. Our feelings of friendship or enmity are unreliable, and discriminating between friends and enemies is a mistake. Someone who has been very helpful to us in the past and now greatly mistreats us is no different from someone who has harmed us in the past and is now helping us. After careful consideration, we will realize that there is no logical basis for discrimination between friends, enemies, and people we are indifferent to.

Having developed love and compassion for all beings, the desire to help them be free from suffering will arise spontaneously within us. This attitude is said to be extraordinary.

Only a buddha can benefit all beings, and we say this not only because we are Buddhists, but also because a buddha is by definition a being who has eradicated every affliction, accumulated every virtue, and developed every positive quality. We are not able, at present, to comprehend everything correctly—our perception is clouded by many obstructions due to mental afflictions, and by many obstacles preventing omniscience. A buddha, however, is capable of perceiving every single phenomenon. Just as we cannot see a precious jewel if a cloth is covering it, in the same way it is impossible for us to perceive the true nature of phenomena due to our obstructions. By exerting ourselves, however, we will be able to remove the two kinds of hindrances and become enlightened beings.

Our mental continuums do not possess intrinsic existence, and it is for this reason that we have the potential to develop our minds until we become buddhas. It is the natural right of a newly born prince to become the king, and in the same way, we possess the seed that gives us the natural right to become a buddha. If a king has two children, and the first one is ignorant and indolent, whereas the second is intelligent and full of goodwill, the succession to the throne should naturally go to the latter, even if he is younger, because he deserves to hold power. We can compare ourselves to the first son—we have the natural right, the seed of enlightenment, but we have not progressed since we have made no effort in this direction.

We must avoid idleness, take advantage of the precious human birth we have acquired, and thus attain enlightenment as soon as possible. We might think that an individual's task is to think solely about himself, and that there is no need to be concerned about others, but this way of thinking is wrong. A mother concerned for her child's happiness will do her best to create favorable conditions for him. In the same way, having a slightly deeper understanding of what must be abandoned and what needs to be cultivated, we must help others do the same.

The bodhisattva's task is to try to satisfy all beings—they all desire happiness and wish to avoid suffering, but they do not know the specific causes of suffering since their perception is clouded by ignorance. Helping them eradicate ignorance is the most virtuous act of a bodhisattva, who is therefore our best friend. We usually appreciate a person who repays a kind deed; even more so, we should hold those who are altruistic without having received anything in high esteem.

We generally honor those who give food and drink to the needy—how great our appreciation must be, then, for the bodhisattva who performs good deeds for numberless beings for an infinite length of time! He helps them not only by offering material goods, whose value is limited, but by showing them the way to enlightenment, a permanent and invaluable gift. One truly cannot say in words how worthy of praise a bodhisattva is. [33]

Enlightenment is a state in which we experience permanent happiness, and in order to attain it, we must complete the two accumulations of merit and wisdom, starting by following the teachings and verifying whether a transformation has occurred. Even if a transformation does not take place, at least we will have more knowledge. It is crucial to dedicate as much time as possible to the Dharma and, once we have understood the advantages of developing bodhichitta, to build a strong motivation to attain the state of a buddha for the benefit of all beings.

Bodhisattvas are those who have chosen the Mahayana path and have taken the vows to enable their minds to evolve and attain enlightenment. For this reason they are honored and considered "Buddha's sons." If we bear an evil thought against one of them, we create extremely negative karma that will eventually ripen as intense suffering. In a flash all positive karma we have accumulated throughout an entire cosmic era will be destroyed. [34]

On the other hand, by cultivating a virtuous attitude toward a bodhisattva, we generate positive karma just because of the qualities of the object. A bodhisattva never generates negativity, not even if his own life is at risk, whereas he accumulates positive karma even while asleep. We must prostrate ourselves to one in whom such a precious mind is born. [36]

Generally we try to take revenge if we have been harmed, but this is not the case with a bodhisattva, who, in exchange for an evil action, performs a good deed. In the *Guru Puja* there is a verse relating to this that praises the bodhisattva's patience. It states that even if the beings of three thousand worlds attacked him and tried to harm him, he would always try to benefit them, without ever resorting to any form of revenge.

Let us pray that we may be able to develop such qualities.

∾ 2 ∾

THE DISCLOSURE OF EVIL

IF WE WISH TO ENTER the Mahayana path, whether through sutra or tantra practices, we must develop the mind of awakening, bodhichitta. That is the only gate of access. We all know that generating bodhichitta is not easy, but to be able to appreciate and rejoice in such mind we must first understand what it is—only then will we gradually create the conditions for its development. Furthermore, we need to increase our positive karma and eliminate our negative karma. When we invite an honored guest, we adorn and clean our homes first. If we wish to generate bodhichitta in our minds, we must first purify and beautify them.

The second chapter of Shantideva's text discusses refuge, the purification of negative karma, and the acknowledgment of negativity—hence the title. We must acknowledge our negative karma before we will be able to purify it.

Once we have generated bodhichitta, our negative karma will weaken, our positive karma will increase, and we will gain a more fortunate rebirth in the future. This precious mind is a wish-fulfilling gem. Just as a beggar who by chance finds a jewel can have all he desires from that moment on, through bodhichitta we will succeed in putting an end to most of our suffering by eliminating its causes. We will also be able to develop the transcendental perfections—generosity, for example—to the point where we will joyfully offer our own body to others.

First of all, it is necessary to lay down positive imprints by increasing virtuous karma, and to such an aim we begin by addressing the Three Jewels: the tathagatas (the enlightened beings), the Dharma (the stainless jewel), and the sons of Buddha (the arya bodhisattvas, oceans of excellence). [1]

A buddha has eliminated the obstructions caused by contamination and mental afflictions, which are temporary and not of the same nature as the mind, as well as their imprints. Bodhisattvas have purified their minds only to a certain degree and are on the path to the complete eradication of mental afflictions. Having completely cleared any obstruction is one of the aspects of the awakened mind.

We address the Three Jewels in order to create merit, but we can also make offerings and dedicate our virtuous actions to all sentient beings. These beings must certainly be the objects of our love and compassion.

On the altar in this room are many representations of the Three Jewels and various offerings—drinking water, water for ablution, flowers, incense, light, perfume, and food. We can offer the same objects at home and in this way create good karma. If we have some good karma, the money in our pockets will not disappear so fast.

We can offer anything we value, at any time, as soon as we see it. We can offer what we eat and drink to the Three Jewels. If we offer gold, silver, or precious stones, we gain merit in proportion to their value. We can offer the cool shade that we enjoy on a hot summer day. We can offer gold-encrusted mountains or, as in the offering of the mandala, the entire universe. We can visualize quiet and joyful places, fields of rippling wheat, trees bedecked with flowers, lakes and pools adorned with lotuses, or the beautiful cries of wild geese. If we offer our neighbor's gardens and flowers, we need not worry, because the Three Jewels will not take them—they have no use for them. We do all this to accumulate merit.

We start by offering our possessions. We offer not only this earth, but also the paradises within the limitless spheres of space. At the end, we ask that everything we have offered may kindly be accepted. [6]

In the practice of guru yoga we make an offering in which everything is contained, including good karma, generated as an object worth offering.

It is not possible to obtain the precious mind of bodhichitta in a short time and without a big effort. If, high in the mountains, there is a wonderful place that is inaccessible, we will generate the desire to go there only if we know of the pleasure it will bring us. In the same way, it is only by knowing the benefits of the mind of awakening that we will cherish the desire to possess it and commit ourselves accordingly. We need to prepare our minds, making offerings and gaining merit, while at the same time purifying our negative karma and revealing it to the Three Jewels.

It is not enough to scatter a few seeds and water them—we must first prepare the soil and remove the weeds and stones that are obstructing the growth of the plants. Likewise, we must cleanse our minds, eradicating any hindrances, in order to cultivate the bodhichitta plant. In other words, we must purify our negative karma.

Purification takes place when we apply the *four opponent powers:*

1. Acknowledging the negative effect of our nonvirtuous actions and atoning for those committed in the past
2. Determining to refrain from committing these actions in the future, and requesting the blessings needed in order to achieve this
3. Using the strength of the object. Bad karma is constantly generated toward sentient beings or the Three Jewels—to counteract this we make offerings to both and dedicate ourselves to meritorious actions
4. Purifying bad karma through specific antidotes, among them: reciting the one-hundred-syllable mantra, making prostrations, and meditating on emptiness

We must use the correct antidote to counteract the particular mental affliction that caused us to create a particular bad karma. For example, if the affliction was attachment, with the support of the one-hundred-syllable mantra we generate the antidote to desire. If the affliction was hatred, we generate the antidote to hatred to purify it.

The implementation of the opponent powers is the main aspect of purification. It gives immediate results without a great effort. Therefore, we can and must apply it straightaway.

If, when we have time, we clean our rooms, meditate, and then get up and go out, we will realize that something in our minds has changed. This will be a tangible experience. Doing the same every morning for five minutes, we might then extend the time and make it habitual, until, if one day we do not sit and meditate, we will feel the lack of it, together with a certain unease.

Buddha has purified all obscurations and attained all virtues. This did not happen in a day or in a year, but gradually. We can do the same. Even meditating for a short time in the right way is a step forward toward the transcendental perfections, and if we gain positive karma and purify negative karma, we will have created the causes of a happier rebirth.

And we can't rely on the buddhas and bodhisattvas to create positive karma on our behalf. If you do not personally generate the karma that will cause the enjoyment of a particular result, you will not be able to experience it. Take the case of a group of positively motivated people who create a Dharma center. Those who attend need to possess their own positive karma if they are to make use of it. If you do not generate the karma, you will not experience the results. Once we do create positive karma, unless it is destroyed by hatred, we will experience its result. The same applies to negative karma—unless we apply the four opponent powers and purify it, we will definitely experience the result.

The process of purification continues until the moment of awakening. We can differentiate various stages within it, and from one particular stage onward there is no longer any danger of falling into cyclic existence. There are five so-called "paths" in the Mahayana tradition, which correlate to stages in the journey to enlightenment. The first is the *path of accumulation,* during which we accumulate merit. This is not yet a stable path. The second is the *path of preparation,* which is divided into four levels; from the third level on, there is no longer any danger of falling back into unfortunate rebirths. The third path is the *path of seeing,* the fourth is the *path of meditation,* and the fifth is the *path of no more learning.*

There are five paths in the Hinayana tradition as well, and although their denomination is the same, they do not produce the same results. In order for a Hinayana practitioner to no longer be subject to cyclic rebirth, he must reach the last stage of the fifth path, which coincides with nirvana.

Until a Mahayana follower has attained the first *bhumi,* or ground, which coincides with the beginning of the third path, he will continue to be reborn due to the force of karma and mental afflictions. From the third path on, however, he will be capable of choosing his next rebirth with the circumstances most favorable to enable him to be of greater help to all beings. This is possible because he is no longer accumulating *projecting karma,* the karma that forces uncontrolled rebirth within cyclic existence, although he remains in cyclic existence until he attains the eighth bhumi, due to karmic accumulation in the past.

If we desire happy minds, we must create the causes for lasting happiness. If we resort to temporary solutions, such as going to the movies, the seashore, or the mountains, we will experience a kind of relief, but it will be brief and ineffective. One cause of lasting happiness is making offerings.

When making offerings, if you possess few material goods, you can imagine giving away everything that does not belong to anyone, such as the lakes and mountains, and ask the buddhas to accept them. Milarepa had nothing, but he offered his practice, and it proved to be a constant offering. What the buddhas and bodhisattvas appreciate the most is our commitment to the path, our accumulation of positive karma, and our purification of negative karma. In Lama Tsongkhapa's *Lamrim Chenmo* it is written that the best offering to one's master is the commitment to spiritual practice. If we practice, there is no need to make extra effort to let the buddhas and bodhisattvas know about it. They already know, and they rejoice in our good deeds, since their only desire is that we create the causes for our own happiness. If we possess nothing, we can offer our bodies and behave according to the wishes of buddhas and bodhisattvas; this will also please them, just as when someone offers himself as a servant of another. The aim of the buddhas and bodhisattvas is solely to benefit all beings, and we must help them without fear of rebirth in cyclic existence.

When we receive an honored guest we clean our homes, we offer food, we show him the bathroom, and we give him soap and a towel. Likewise, we can mentally offer the buddhas sweetly scented bathing chambers with brilliantly sparkling crystal floors and exquisite pillars ablaze with gems. Offer the objects you consider most beautiful, visualizing yourself in the act of offering vases filled with scented waters, or manifesting in attractive form, dancing, singing, and playing music. We dress the buddhas with fragrant garments of suitable colors after having anointed their bodies with perfumed oils, and place the used clothes in boxes on the altar. We can also offer jewels, necklaces, rings, and earrings without avarice. [12]

We do all of this in order to train the mind, and while meditating we give these mental offerings, remembering the names of the aryas Samantabhadra, Manjushri, Avalokiteshvara, and all the others. [13]

When we are angry, we may insult others by saying, "Go to hell!" or "Die!," and we feel satisfied, thinking that we have really harmed the other person. In reality, we have simply created negative karma for ourselves. When we make offerings in the ways described, we might think we are not doing anything at all, but in fact we also produce a result—we give ourselves the possibility of becoming acquainted with positive thoughts.

When we insult an enemy, if he is stupid he will be offended, but in reality nothing has happened to him, whereas we have created bad karma. If, however, we are used to wishing the best for others, thinking, "May this person realize what he desires," even if our wishes do not come true, we have familiarized our minds with positive thoughts and we have created virtuous karma. The same thing happens when we visualize the most beautiful objects during our offerings.

In the *nyung-ne* practice the meditation instructor pours water on a mirror and visualizes the largest possible offering. During one of my visits to Italy someone commented on this ablution ritual, saying that it seemed like a child's game. But that person did not know the mental process behind the ritual. If we know how to do it, it is meaningful and beneficial, otherwise it truly is a child's game.

We are human beings, and the time allotted to us on earth is very brief. We have already experienced this type of existence many times before, and we will do so again in the future. Many of us have already lived twenty, twenty-five, or forty years of our lives, and sooner or later we will have to say goodbye to our bodies and take on new rebirths. We will be unable to choose them because this depends not on will, but on action, and since we have created more negative than positive causes, it is likely that our future will be unpleasant.

We must try to create the greatest possible number of positive causes. This is possible in our human condition because we possess the intelligence that discriminates between good and evil. In a different realm, the animal realm or worse, this would be a very difficult thing to do.

Death is certain, and it is good to take it into account since we will definitely have to face it without any possibility of escape. Impermanence is intrinsic to our nature. Since it is not one of our desires, we must ask ourselves each day, "Do I wish to be reborn into an inferior realm?"

No one can say who or what we will be in the future, but it is nevertheless possible to look at our own minds and weigh up our positive and negative karma. If they are in balance, then the mental state we find ourselves in at the moment of death will affect our next rebirth—if we are feeling hatred or attachment, we will gain an unfortunate rebirth; if we have a virtuous state of mind, the outcome will be a fortunate rebirth. If we have many positive imprints, and some negative ones, the mental state at the moment of death will also be crucial. Hence, we have to purify our negative karma, even if only a little bit at a time, in the same way that we wash our dirty clothes. If someone has a clear conscience and the police summon him, he will go unperturbed. If we have accumulated good karma, we will face death with serenity and confidence. We will feel as if we are going home, as if we are young again and starting anew. If there were a chance to become young again, we would no doubt give any amount of money to do so. Bodhisattvas do not have this problem—they can always start anew. They say farewell to life with no regret in their hearts.

Deciding that from now on we will not do anything to harm others is practicing morality. Even taking the five vows—refraining from killing, from stealing, from lying, from sexual misconduct, and from taking intoxicants—for the length of our lives is practicing morality and will certainly bear fruit. If it is difficult to take these vows for our entire lives, we can begin by taking them for a year, a month, a day, or at least one morning. Training our minds slowly, we can eventually lengthen this amount of time. This is only a matter of habit; if we find it difficult at first, by and by it will become easier, much in the same way that someone who is learning how to drive will eventually be able to do it automatically.

What do we mean by negative karma? Negative karma is any action done under the stimulus of our mental afflictions.

A Tibetan proverb says, "If we think beforehand, we are wise; if we think afterward, we are foolish." And another one I like to recall says, "If we do not want to do what needs to be done in the morning, we will have to do it in the evening." In other words, if we do not practice the Dharma when we are young, when it is easier and our bodies and minds are more flexible, we will regret it in old age.

If we want to experience the outcome of certain actions, we need to gather merit. If the parents work hard, accumulate great wealth, and then leave it to their children who do not possess the adequate merit to enjoy it, some difficulty or other will prevent those children from benefiting from it. Also, a sick person will become healthy again only if he has the karma to do so.

I've already explained that one of the ways to accumulate merit is by making offerings to the Three Jewels. After having bathed the Buddha, offered him clothes, and visualized his body as luminous and golden, we then offer scented oils, the lotions and perfume we use ourselves. Then we offer garlands of various flowers and imagine sending forth clouds of incense. We offer jeweled lamps and celestial delicacies, as well as food and drink, visualizing ourselves in a luxurious, decorated environment. We offer jeweled palaces, imagining that they resound with exquisite, melodious hymns sung and played by female deities. [18]

Let us remember that we make these offerings to the Buddha, who has the nature of compassion, and who has realized the mind of awakening, bodhichitta. There are two types of offerings: conceivable and inconceivable. Those described above are conceivable, due to the fact that our mental capabilities are limited.

Imagining ourselves manifesting in bodies as numerous as all the atoms within the universe, we wholeheartedly prostrate to the Three Jewels, to the bodhisattvas, to all the places where Buddha appeared, to the mind of bodhichitta, to the stupas containing the reliquaries of buddhas and bodhisattvas, to the master who gives us the teachings, and to the Dharma practitioners. [25]

We then set forth our requests. We address the buddhas of the ten directions, disclosing our concern, "Throughout beginningless existence in this life and in others, I have unknowingly committed evil deeds and ordered others to do them. Overwhelmed by the deceptions of ignorance, I rejoiced in what was done. But now, seeing these mistakes, from my heart I declare them to the buddhas. I openly declare that whatever harmful acts of body, speech, and mind I have done in a disturbed mental state toward the Three Jewels, my parents, my guru, and others, and all the grave wrongs I have committed, so that I can purify all negative karma from this very moment on." [32]

No one seems to care about death, but we must purify ourselves, and in order to do so swiftly and successfully, we ask for blessings and protection.

"The lord of death does not wait for our work to be finished; he might catch hold of us whether we are sick or healthy. Our life and time are fleeting and consumed moment by moment. [33]

"At the moment of death, we will have to leave everything behind and depart alone. Not having understood this, we have committed various kinds of evil for the sake of friends and foes—but they will be unable to accompany us. [34]

"For me, on that day, all my enemies will disappear, and so will all my friends. I will also become nothing, and everything will disappear from this world. [35]

"As when awakening from the most beautiful dream or the most terrifying nightmare, only a faded memory remains. In the same way, anything beautiful or ugly I have experienced will become a memory, a dream that will never return. [36]

"I have experienced many things since birth, and these experiences will not be repeated. Friends and foes will not return, but the negative karma I have committed toward them or for their sakes remains ahead of me. [37]

"Thereby, not having realized the impermanence of my nature, or the fact that my life lasts but a brief moment, I have committed great evil, and now I understand this mistake." [38]

In order to eliminate suffering, we must first extinguish its causes—our negative habits—and change our attitudes. Upon close examination, we can see that the solution to our problems is found solely in the spiritual teachings. If we are not satisfied with our lives, we must also be concerned about what will happen to us in future lives. What we experience now is due to causes we have created in previous lives, and if we wish to find ourselves in good circumstances in the future, we must create the appropriate causes right now. Our mental continuum does not end with the dissolution of this physical body, but carries on, taking on other forms.

Karma is neither a hypothetical idea nor an invention. It is a fact that we cannot deny and that we need to take into account, because negative actions born out of our body, speech, and mind produce negative results, whereas good deeds produce positive results.

At our level it is perhaps difficult to understand that after the death of the body we will take on new rebirths that will not necessarily be human, or that, even if they are human, might exist in Africa or Asia, and not necessarily in Europe or America. The truth is, we cannot choose the kind of existence we will acquire in our next rebirths. And if we cannot tolerate the problems of our present lives, what of the problems we might encounter in a lower realm?

Even if we cannot envision a vast framework of time, we are able to see that in this very life someone who is miserly, angry, proud, or very attached is not loved or praised by anyone, but is in fact despised. We know that these are the afflictions that we must do away with, and we also acknowledge the fact that we have within us the aspiration to become the best person in the country or in the world. Such a person is not necessarily the wealthiest or the healthiest, but the one with a positive attitude and a good heart. We will find that not only would we like to be such a person, but also that, if we become such, others will then admire and cherish us. We must therefore change our minds!

When we think of the future, it seems so far away, but day and night, second by second, life is always slipping by—our lifespans diminish minute by minute, second by second, and cannot be lengthened. Our deaths are certain—the body will die. The moment comes closer and closer and cannot be postponed. [39]

As I mentioned above, some people believe that it is not appropriate to talk about this subject because it is unpleasant. But it is far better to know what death is so that one can be prepared and face it with joy, or at least with a peaceful mind. It is certain that this body will dissolve; this is a reality that we cannot hide in any way. When we realize this, we will proceed accordingly, purifying our negative karma and accumulating positive karma. With such strength in our hearts, why should we be afraid of death when the moment arrives? From the outside we can see that the situation of one who, having prepared himself, will acquire a human rebirth is better than the situation of one who, unprepared, will be reborn in a lower realm characterized by intense suffering.

If we do not succeed in purifying the negative karma that we have already created and accumulate positive karma, then as we lie in bed at the moment of death we will suffer, and we alone will experience it. No one else will suffer on our behalf. [40]

When seized by "the messengers of death," what benefit will friends and relatives be able to provide, even if they are surrounding us? Our merit and virtues alone will protect us then, and if we do not possess any, we will not have any protection. [41]

At that moment we will cry out, "Unaware of such a terrible situation as this, I have accumulated only negative karma." [42]

Imagine how petrified a person would be who has broken the law and is being led to a torture chamber. Or let us identify ourselves with one who, having created nothing but negative karma during his life, is seized by the frightful messengers of death, who act as guardians of the law of karma. [44]

Just as someone sentenced to death seeks help and, not finding it any-where, cries out in despair, we will look for protection in every possible direction but will not find any simply because we have not created it within ourselves, as positive karma. [46]

What will it be like? We will be utterly desperate, with no help or protection. Realizing this, we must seek protection and refuge right now, by accumulating positive karma and purifying our negativity. We must understand that we have every opportunity to create positive causes—we are intelligent human beings, and at present we find ourselves in favorable circumstances and in command of our mental faculties. We must use them in order to generate the causes for the best possible future.

We've talked about future lives, but one might ask whether they truly exist. To affirm their existence with certainty, first we'd need to ask our-selves whether there have been previous lives.

We are composed of body and mind. The body is made of atoms, of matter, whereas the mind is made up of formless mental factors, each of them possessing its own cause and origin. We can differentiate between two kinds of causes: a substantial cause, which transforms itself into a specific effect of the same substance, and a circumstantial cause, which is an environmental or secondary cause that helps the substantial cause turn into its effect. For example, in order to have an apple tree we need the substantial cause—the seed—and the circumstantial causes—the soil, sun, and water. Without these we cannot produce the apple tree.

Mind, too, must arise from two kinds of causes. Since it is not made of matter and it is unlike a body of atoms, it needs a substantial cause that shares its nature, and logically this can be traced only to the mind of a previous moment. A mind born out of the blue, autonomously, cannot exist.

After careful examination, we notice that each moment of the mind belongs to a mental continuum. Today's mind is the result of yesterday's. The mind of an adult arises from the mind of a young person, which in turn arises from the mind of a child. The mind of a child arises from the mind of a newborn baby, which can be traced back to the mind at the moment of conception, which itself must reasonably arise out of another mind. This mind therefore can be logically identified only as the mind of the former life. The physical body arises from the meeting of the male seed with the female egg, but we cannot trace the mind back to the minds of our parents. It can only be traced back to a previous mind sharing the same mental continuum. If we understand this, we can trace our mental continuum back to a former life through which we came to our present life. By the same reasoning, we can assert that we will experience another life in the future.

Mind's causes are of a mental nature, and the mind finds shelter in a physical sheath, such as the mother's womb. Before this meeting, there is an intermediate state, the *bardo*, where one retains a mind and a physical body, both very subtle. This continuum searches for a new life, which is determined by the karma of one's former lives and by particular karmic ties with the future parents. When the mind in the bardo finds the circumstantial cause—the new mother ready to conceive—it takes on a new rebirth.

If we retrace one of our former lives and from that perspective examine our present existence, we will see that the life we are now living is the future rebirth of our former life.

There is a formula in the Buddhist texts on logic that indicates the reason that we affirm the existence of former lives. It reads, "The mind of a baby when conceived must have a mind that precedes it, because it is mind." According to some philosophical schools, mind does not need to be preceded by a mental cause because it arises from the physical body. If this were true, we could ask whether a corpse has a mind, since it is, after all, a physical body. If you share this materialistic view, ask yourself this question.

Furthermore, if mind arises out of a physical body, that same body should then host many minds, since the body is made of many atoms. This could be a second argument. Another proof that mind arises from a former life is the observation that children of the same parents such as twins, or individuals who share a similar background, often have different attitudes and different levels of intelligence. This is due to the fact that each of them created different causes for their experiences in their previous lives.

There are some meditation processes that enable us to see our previous lives as well as those of other people. It is possible to know what we were, and many examples support this. We can look at the life of the current Dalai Lama, believed to be the reincarnation of his predecessor, the Thirteenth Dalai Lama. There is a sacred lake in Tibet in which the future can be seen by anyone who looks into it. When the moment came to look for the fourteenth reincarnation of the Dalai Lama, the regent at the time looked into the lake and saw a small, precisely defined valley reflected there. He also saw three Tibetan letters: *a, ka,* and *ma.* Predictions were made and various expeditions were sent out in search of the valley. One of the various expedition groups found the place—it was in the province of Amdo, and the meaning of the three letters was then understood. *A* stood for Amdo, *ka* were the initials of the local monastery, and *ka* and *ma* together were the name of a special retreat place in the area. The house where the future Dalai Lama lived was also recognized. His Holiness was three at the time, and upon being found he picked out articles that had belonged to the Thirteenth Dalai Lama from among various similar objects. He also recognized the true identity of a great lama whom he had known in a former life and who had now come to see him in disguise, dressed as a servant.

We can also ascertain the link between the current Dalai Lama and the previous one by considering his profound wisdom, intelligence, and great qualities. His extensive biography is widely available, and reading it will give us a more accurate picture.

Nothing in the universe is self-generating. To be produced, every phenomenon needs a cause, and this is why things manifest in particular moments and under certain circumstances. The fact that there are indeed particular moments shows that when the cause is operating, an effect is produced, and when the cause is not operating, no effect is produced.

Mind can be a *circumstantial* cause for the body and vice versa, but one cannot be a *substantial* cause for the other, since mind and matter have different natures. The being in the bardo and the being in the next rebirth both possess mind and body. The mind of the former is the substantial cause of the mind of the latter. The current mind has a connection with the mind of the bardo being, and this in turn has a connection with the mind of the being in the previous moment. All of these are causal ties.

Your body and your mind will separate at some point. Your body will dissolve, but your mind will not disappear; it will exist in the bardo and subsequently in a new rebirth, and it will continue in future lives unless you eliminate the causes that make this happen. It is as if you have climbed onto a train—wherever the locomotive is heading, you are going there too. Karma and mental afflictions will lead you everywhere, and you will have to follow them. If you succeed in purifying karma and eliminating mental afflictions, you will be able to jump off the train, take your own car, and go anywhere you please. You will be totally free to choose your next rebirth.

There have been many former lives, and there will be many future lives. Various testimonials and logical arguments support this theory. On the contrary, the only argument against former lives is the fact that we do not see them; but such an argument is not based on logical reasoning.

Some people practice a certain path because they have faith, and others, not having faith, do not practice. Those who do not believe in religion, who do not have faith, will not generate the causes for their future lives and will not prepare for them. Those who are religious, on the other hand, will perform good deeds in order to improve their situation and enjoy the results.

Whether we believe in them or not, the fact remains that we will experience future lives as well as the amount of good fortune we have created. If we believe in future lives, we will prepare ourselves in the best possible way. If we do not realize their reality, sooner or later we will see that we have been wasting our time, and there will no longer be a chance to prepare ourselves.

There are two ways of discerning phenomena: through *direct perception* and through *perfect reasoning*. There are many things that we cannot perceive directly, and they must be deduced by perfect reasoning.

In our present circumstances we are not capable of seeing directly into future lives. Perhaps we are not even able to understand their existence through perfect reasoning. Through meditation and practice, we may reach a level in which we attain clairvoyance, or the "divine eye," and through its aid see what particular rebirth a being will have after death. At present, however, it is crucial to listen to those who have experience and are able to guide us.

Why isn't it possible to remember our former lives? First of all, memory is such that we cannot recall everything that has happened to us. Moreover, moving from one life to the next is a big jump. Even in daily life we may go out and leave the oven on and burn our lunch. It is reasonable to assume that there could be gaps in our memories. We cannot say that just because we do not remember them, former lives are a fantasy. We were all born from our mothers' wombs, but we do not remember. I myself do not remember, but there are people who do. And some people can also remember their previous lives.

I heard the story, told by His Holiness the Dalai Lama, of an Indian child who remembered his previous life and did not much like his current mother and father. As he grew up, he began to recall his former parents and the fact that he had died young in an accident. He remembered the place he had lived and recognized his old parents and their home. All of us have surely heard similar stories.

From an Indian magazine I also learned of a woman who said that in one of her former lives she had also been a woman. She had married a man who did not love her and who, together with his lover, had killed her and put her in a trunk that was later thrown off a bridge from a moving train. She remembered this and recognized her old husband too. When she was two or three years old, she had already begun to remember, and said that she wanted to see her old parents. Her mother and father thought she was hallucinating, but the little girl insisted that she had had other parents. At the time she lived in a village that was far away from her previous family's home. When she was eight years old she named the place, and they took her there. Although she had never been there before, she clearly recognized it. When the Dalai Lama heard about this he was intrigued and sent out some people to verify it, and they confirmed the whole story.

Another meaningful episode concerns Lama Chusang Rinpoche, who, while traveling in northern Tibet, was no longer able to keep his cattle and other objects he had with him, so he left them with a Tibetan family. The head of the family took some wool from among these things and replaced it with some wool of poor quality. He also sold some yaks and said he had lost them. Lama Chusang Rinpoche came back after some time and was asked to give a long-life initiation, and I was present too. After the initiation ceremony many people went to visit Rinpoche, among them a woman who was possessed by a spirit. As soon as the spirit was close to Rinpoche, it told him that it was the deceased head of the family. The spirit apologized for having stolen the wool and having sold the yaks and asked to be forgiven. It also begged for water, since it had not had anything to drink for a long time. After drinking three jugs, the spirit said it was very happy. I had provided the water and considered giving a blessing as well, and recited the mantra *Om Ah Hum,* but at that point the spirit was no longer able to finish its drink.

We need help in our situation and must seek refuge in protectors who can lead us to complete liberation. These protectors are the awakened beings who act for the sake of others and the bodhisattvas who have attained higher levels of understanding. Let us also take refuge in what their minds have realized—this is the real refuge, because if we achieve these qualities ourselves, we will experience true protection. We will be able to free ourselves from the suffering of cyclic existence and attain perfect enlightenment, the final aim. [48]

When we take refuge, we are not doing it just for a day, but until we become buddhas.

We establish our refuge on the basis of its causes. The first is the fear of being reborn into cyclic existence, particularly into those realms where the most suffering is experienced. Even when we are human, we experience plenty of suffering, but there are lower rebirths within cyclic existence that we must be very careful to avoid. The second cause is faith in the Three Jewels, which can free us from suffering or, more precisely, show us the method that will allow us to be free from it.

We take refuge in the Three Jewels, but they can in fact be condensed into one: the Dharma, which is our realization along the path. Without this, the other two, Buddha and Sangha, are pointless. The Dharma is the true refuge. Although the Buddha is endowed with powers, he can only show us the way, as an expert traveler who has already made the journey. He can neither transfer his wisdom to us nor take away our mental afflictions.

When we generate the wisdom enabling us to discern the non-intrinsic nature of phenomena, we will be able to eliminate mental afflictions and achieve permanent happiness. The Buddha can save us by expounding the true nature of phenomena.

We must think that thanks to the Three Jewels, we engage in positive actions. Out of disrespect for them, as well as out of a state of affliction, we have performed evil deeds, thus creating suffering for ourselves.

When faced with unpleasant situations, we must pray to the Three Jewels; in this way we create positive karma and the help we need will be provided. Children often cry and ask for their mother, and in the same way the spiritual practitioner should pray to the Three Jewels. If we have nightmares and immediately we take refuge, this shows we are already on the right path of mental development.

I will tell you a story. A tailor named Kunchung went to see a woman whose husband was away. Her husband came back, and she, frightened of the possible consequences, hid the tailor in a basket and put it in the cellar. At night some thieves broke into the house. They saw the basket and, thinking that it contained precious goods, took it away. After a while, the tailor could no longer suppress the urge to pee. The rogues, who were convinced that they were carrying an inestimable treasure, noticed him and became furious. One of them, who was a devotee of the Indian deity Ishvara, told Kunchung, "You didn't tell us you were inside this heavy basket. We did all this hard work for nothing, so now we will sacrifice you to Ishvara." The tailor knew all too well that in a human sacrifice his head would be cut off. There was nothing he could do, but from the bottom of his heart he took refuge in the Three Jewels. At that moment the Buddha appeared as Ishvara and told the thieves, "Today I do not want a corpse offered to me, but a living body." The bandits obeyed and the tailor escaped with his life. This story is found in the scriptures and I myself heard it from a Rinpoche. There are many more stories like this.

If we observe the cause of any form of happiness, we will find that it is the Three Jewels. Whether we pray to them or not, they will try to protect us and help us in any possible way. Perhaps we do not believe in the Three Jewels, but if we have obtained this precious human rebirth it is thanks to our own good karma. We have accumulated this positive karma thanks to the Three Jewels. We might think that suffering is also their doing, but this is not the case—suffering is the result of our mental afflictions.

You will not remember all of what has been said, but it is crucial to keep the essentials in mind at least, and at home, in your room, reflect upon them and then put them into practice.

This is the Tibetan for the refuge prayer:

Sang gye cho dang tsog kyi chog nam la
Jang chub bar du dag ni kyab su chi
Dag gi jin sog gyi pai di da ki
Dro la pen chir sang gye drub par shog

[In the Buddha, Dharma, and Sangha
I go for refuge until I am enlightened.
Through the merit from practicing the six perfections
May I become a buddha to free all sentient beings.]

The first two lines mean that we entrust ourselves to the Three Jewels, not only for one day, but until our enlightenment. The next lines say that if we do not have the happiness we desire, it is because we have not created the right causes for it, and in order to create them we must perform virtuous actions—that is, the six *paramitas,* or transcendental perfections. These are the sources of positive karma; through them we will harvest the fruit of happiness.

Taking refuge in the Dharma means listening to—and following—the advice of the awakened ones, the buddhas. Taking refuge in the Sangha means taking refuge in the followers of the path. It is very difficult to practice the Dharma by ourselves, but we will feel encouraged and inspired if we share it with other practitioners. We can learn a lot from them. It is as if we wish to visit a faraway place—the company of a friend on a long journey makes us feel happier and more assured. If we embark on it alone, our enthusiasm may disappear. Confiding in the Three Jewels, praying so that they may show us the way to enlightenment—this is the meaning of taking refuge.

An evil action is one that brings suffering to oneself and others. The consequences of evil actions are manifold—some can be harmful immediately, while others are harmful only after a long time.

We must use our own experience to examine the nature of harmful actions. If someone strikes us, we feel pain and unhappiness, two sensations we prefer to avoid. We can deduce that what causes others to suffer is exactly these same things. We can therefore look to our own experience if we want to know what is harmful and what is not.

Let us also look at something that may appear unpleasant right now but may nevertheless be beneficial in the future—practicing the spiritual path and overcoming its difficulties. If someone were to suggest, "Let us forget about practice and just have some fun," that would be pleasant in the moment but harmful in the long run, since it would produce negative results. It is the same with drugs. Those who crave instant happiness gain a pleasant experience at that particular moment but create the causes for serious problems in the future.

If we look carefully we realize that we cannot find our bearings within the maze of cyclic existence all by ourselves. We need to find a guide who, using the right methods, can help us become free from it. The methods are stated in Buddha's teachings, but these words are not a magic cure—we also need to be clear ourselves about how things are. If we begin to observe how reality works, we will realize that one of the main laws of the physical world is the law of causation. We will also realize that the very same law operates within our mind.

We must analyze our suffering and our problems. We must recognize their causes and differentiate them from those that generate happiness. In this way we can establish the actions that we must practice and those we should avoid. If someone is helpful to us, we are very happy, so why not do the same for others? Benefiting others is positive karma, which means that it produces happiness.

In order to follow the right advice we need to act, not just pray and hope. This is also true of our worldly affairs, but with one big difference. When we work in a factory diligently, we generate profit not only for ourselves—by earning a salary—but also for the factory owner. In spiritual practice, however, we are the only beneficiaries.

A mother who loves her child will teach him to do only what is right.

She will explain that in order to have a satisfying life, he will have to study. Everything she says will be directed toward the welfare of her child who, unable to understand the advantages deriving from it, may interpret everything she says as a limitation on his freedom and as a restriction on his pleasure. In the same way, we are not inclined to engage in positive actions, whereas we do enjoy negative ones, not realizing that by doing so we cause suffering. We are not able to follow the advice of the buddhas and bodhisattvas, who relate to us like a mother to her child.

A beginner with some interest in practice should get up early in the morning, settle down in a suitable place, and practice meditation. He will soon realize that this brings peace and happiness to his mind and will find that these are the results of his spiritual practice. Once we experience its flavor, no one will be capable of deterring us from it, as when we taste a new type of food—if it is exquisite, we will want to taste it again. Once we have enjoyed our meditative experience, we will try to repeat it.

Teachings in Buddhism are given in accordance with the various levels of practitioner, just as a young child is given an education appropriate to his age rather than a university syllabus. Generally, three levels of teachings are discussed.

The first level of teachings focuses primarily on avoiding bad karma, purifying negative karma that has already been produced, and accumulating positive karma. These activities create the causes for happiness in the future, and are typically associated with the wish to achieve a more favorable rebirth in the next life.

The next level addresses not just the next life but tries to get at the root causes of suffering—our mental afflictions. The six main afflictions are anger, desire or attachment, envy, pride, doubt, and wrong views. Let us investigate them individually.

Hatred produces unhappiness. We experience something we do not like, and yet we cannot avoid it. If we have enemies we wish to harm and are not able to do so, we suffer. If we feel peaceful and happy and someone tells us something unpleasant, we feel aversion, and our minds become turbulent and negative. On a geopolitical scale, hatred is the motivation behind any declaration of war.

Attachment arises when we see something we like and we nurture the wish to possess it, thus experiencing unhappiness and agitation. We will do anything in our power to have that object, but even when we do manage to possess it, our problems are not over. From then on, the fear of loss and the fear of being separated from the object of desire arise.

Hatred and attachment are the basis for all conflicts, among both individuals and communities, and the cause of many forms of suffering. They generate tension and arguments between children and parents, between husband and wife. Where there is love and compassion, happiness reigns in the home; the same applies to nations.

Envy is the negative mental factor that arises when someone has something better than we have, such as a more beautiful house or a newer car.

Pride creates suffering every time we think of ourselves as superior to others in some way—as more knowledgeable, healthier, more beautiful, or wealthier—and when we feel that our superiority is not being properly recognized.

Doubt arises when we ask ourselves whether former and future lives, the Three Jewels, or the law of causation and so forth exist at all. This particular affliction creates confusion in our minds. We can sew perfectly well if we use a needle with one tip, but if the needle has two, it is impossible. A double-tipped needle is useless, and so is a mind always oscillating between two possibilities, unable to decide between one course of action and another. This generates unhappiness, and we never achieve the results we desire. For example, if we doubt that good karma creates happiness, we will not try to accumulate it. If we doubt the existence of former and future lives, or the objects of refuge, we will not eliminate our bad karma, we will make no effort, and we will not achieve anything whatsoever.

Holding on to *wrong views* means having the notion of an unchanging, self-existent *I*. We start thinking, "I must have all the happiness that is possible, I must not suffer, I must experience pleasure despite the needs of others." Clinging to this fundamentally wrong view is the root of all our problems. We have created this solid sense of *I* as separate from *others*. We have also created divisions among these others—between those who are dear to us, whom we call friends, those who harm us, whom we call enemies, and finally those we feel indifferent toward, whom we call strangers. We feel unhappy when we cannot benefit our friends adequately and unhappy when we cannot destroy our enemies. Concerning the third group, we remain ignorant.

Fortunately, these six mental afflictions can be removed, and doing so will change our attitudes radically. There are essentially two methods by which we do this—a temporary or provisional method, which prevents the manifestation of mental afflictions to some degree, and a stable one, which eradicates their very seed.

Let us look at the temporary method in relation to hatred. If our parents reproach us and slap us, we become very angry. But after some reflection, we realize that it was only a brief episode and that our mother and father have loved us and taken care of us for a long time, and our hatred subsides.

In relation to attachment, we learn not to cling to the positive experiences we might have had in the past. For what is left of them? Everything has already passed. Besides, if we experienced physical pleasure, we certainly accumulated a great deal of negative karma because of our attachment to it. While experiencing such pleasure, we were not creating good karma, and furthermore we have gone against our master's advice.

If pride arises because we are wealthy, we can consider that many people are wealthier than we are. If our pride is due to possessing great knowledge, we can think that, since we have not achieved the state of a buddha, there are many beings with greater levels of realization and understanding. Even if we are arhats, we still are not endowed with bodhichitta and complete awakening.

If we are proud of our youth and our good health, we can meditate on impermanence and death, reflecting upon the fact that we might become sick any moment, and that in any case we will definitely become old if we do not die first.

We must ask ourselves whether we are free from cyclic existence. Understanding that we are not, we will see that people we feel superior to now may be reborn in conditions more favorable than ours in the future. This also counteracts pride. Furthermore, who are we to judge someone who may in fact possess far more good qualities than we do? Whatever the case, we have many shortcomings. As when fighting an opponent, we must engage in the battle with pride as wholeheartedly as we can, using our capacity for logical reasoning.

These are all short-term ways to combat the mental afflictions. If we want a long-term solution, however—if we want to eradicate hatred and attachment completely—then we need to examine the nature of the objects of our hatred and attachment. We normally think that the objects of our feelings have a solid, self-sufficient existence outside of us, and that they do not depend upon the mind's projections or on anything else. With investigation, however, we can ascertain that this is not the case—these objects are indeed dependent on our minds. When we begin to understand how all phenomena lack such intrinsic existence, this understanding becomes the single most powerful antidote to all mental afflictions.

Say, for instance, that we think of Losang Dorje as an "enemy." Let us analyze where this enemy-ness might be located—is it in his head, in his feet, or in his mind? Having done this, we will see that this enemy is not *truly* there; it is merely a name given to that object by the mind. If we proceed in this way, hatred and unhappiness will both disappear.

If we are attached to Losang Dorje and try to establish where his attractiveness might reside, whether in his hair, head, or feet, we will soon realize that there is nothing in particular we *truly* like. Where is the appeal then? It is not there; it is merely a function of our projections.

Examine all this with great care, and establish valid reasons in your mind, opposing the mind of wrong views with the mind of correct views. In so doing we will completely eradicate the seeds of the afflictions.

Let us look closely at the way both hatred and attachment disappear as soon as we understand that objects do not exist in the way we believe them to. From afar we see a scarecrow resembling a man. If we are afraid of it, we feel aversion; if we like it, we feel desire. As soon as we get close and realize it is nothing but a scarecrow, both aversion and desire for the imaginary man disappear. Both hatred and desire for this "man" are products of our minds; we created both. Therefore, phenomena do not exist independently of various factors and circumstances, whereas normally we perceive them as solid and independent from everything else. The way they appear to us and the way they exist in reality are two different things.

Since objects of our hatred and attachment lack intrinsic, solid existence, how is it possible for us to experience them? At times even a single object can be the basis for both attachment and hatred. It all depends on what we project onto it.

Objects of hatred and attachment do not exist intrinsically; they are the result of our projections and of our ascribing a name to them. We could say that they are entirely our own creations. However, we can change our mental attitudes when we discover that they do not exist except as objects of our mental afflictions. Once we realize this, we can automatically eradicate them. This way of thinking is new to us, and we cannot therefore expect to exercise it immediately, because at the moment we believe exactly the opposite concerning the nature of phenomena. We need to reflect on it until it becomes for us a natural mode of perception, a realization.

The emptiness of intrinsic existence of phenomena is their real and ultimate mode of existence. With this realization we will achieve complete liberation, and the happiness we experience will be incomparable. Out of our wrong views we sometimes create positive karma and sometimes negative, and therefore we sometimes experience happiness and sometimes unhappiness. If we succeed in generating the correct view of phenomena, however, we will no longer produce the causes for suffering but only the causes for happiness.

Thus mental afflictions can be eliminated, but it is a gradual process, not a sudden transformation. Until the moment we succeed, we must avoid any opportunity for afflictions to arise, because they inevitably produce wrong views. We must behave as we would with a dangerous and violent madman who is confined to a room until he is completely cured, or who is tied up for fear that he might hurt himself.

Recognizing our mental afflictions and trying to free ourselves completely from their grip is what we call the "middle level" of Dharma practice. As you recall, the lower level is the wish to achieve a more favorable rebirth in the future. Finally, the highest level of practice consists in committing oneself to the path having generated the mind of awakening, which aspires to buddhahood for the sake of all beings.

We must make effort in each of these three levels of practice and create the causes to attain these three aims. If we want to go someplace, we need to ask directions and then make the journey. Listening to the teachings on the three levels is equivalent to asking directions, whereas the actual practice is equivalent to reaching the goal. There are several goals, but whichever we choose, we must begin by purifying our negative karma. Some negative karma is easy to purify and some is not, in the same way that some practices are easier than others. We must therefore devote ourselves to practicing what is most appropriate at our level, and gradually create the causes for higher forms of practice. As I said before, the second chapter of the *Bodhicharyavatara* addresses the purification of negative karma and the accumulation of merit as preparation for generating the mind of awakening.

Making offerings to the awakened ones who possess all positive qualities creates positive karma. The text says, "Out of fear of the consequences of negative karma, I offer my body to the bodhisattva Samantabhadra and the bodhisattva Manjushri, and ask for their protection." [49]

In the same way, we seek the protection of Avalokiteshvara, who is the manifestation of the compassion of all the buddhas. [50]

We then offer ourselves and seek refuge in the other bodhisattvas, such as Vajrapani, the sight of whom causes all the messengers of death to flee in terror. [52]

We seek protection and refuge in the eighth-ground bodhisattvas, who, although they are already buddhas, manifest as bodhisattvas for the sake of all beings. We seek their protection because we wish to purify the negative karma we have undoubtedly created so that we will not experience the suffering that inevitably ripens from it.

These invocations are based on our repentance for not having listened to the advice we have received. Realizing the gravity of our situation, we take refuge in order to be protected from the consequences of our behavior. If someone convicted of a serious crime knows that he can ask for mercy, he will surely wish to do so from his innermost heart. Likewise, considering the fact that our positive karma is little and our negative karma enormous, we must seek protection from and refuge in someone who is able to help us.

When we are sick we go to a doctor. Some of the cures he prescribes may be unpleasant, but hoping to get better, we will follow his advice. If we are prepared to act when frightened by a common illness, then why not seek the guide of an awakened being so as to avoid long-term suffering?

Hatred is a mental affliction that can cause destruction and suffering for many beings—no doctor on earth is able to cure such a serious illness. If we meet the "all-knowing physician" who explains how harmful hatred is and tells us what to do in order to eliminate it and how to become free from all mental afflictions, and at that point we refuse to follow his advice, we truly are unintelligent and worthy of scorn by all beings. [56]

We need to be careful even when walking near a small, ordinary preci-
pice. If we are not mindful when we are astride a much deeper crevasse, are
we not truly foolish? [57]

Even when we have understood the consequences of a negative karma,
out of laziness we think it is not necessary to purify it just yet, as we enjoy
thinking that today we will not die, and so we postpone the practice of
appropriate behavior. [58]

It is foolish to think that we will find more favorable conditions in the
future and not make the most of our current circumstances. We need to
do the right thing immediately, because we have no idea when we will
depart from this body.

Our ignorance has not allowed us to be conscious of the specific consequences of our actions until now. Now that we are aware of them, we
seek refuge in the true protectors, ask for their blessings, and disclose our
negative karma so that it can be purified.

There are two kinds of moral transgressions: those relating to ethical
discipline (for example, the precept "do not kill") and those relating to
particular vows we have taken (for example, the vow to refrain from drinking alcohol). In order to purify our negative karma, we must recognize
each of our transgressions in the presence of visualized enlightened beings
with a respectful attitude and make the appropriate offerings. Then let us
determine not to commit them anymore. [65]

It would be good for each of us to observe every action that we perform
during the day and assess whether it is positive or negative. It would also
be very useful to count the positive actions, and in this way review our
progress. We should be able to evaluate and protect ourselves from evil
deeds, much like a soldier defends his country.

If we create only positive karma, we will die peacefully and joyfully.
But if we create a lot of negative karma, at the time of death we will be
worried, unhappy, and restless. Creating negative karma will also cause us
to be unloved, while people will appreciate us if we create positive karma.
Such considerations can help us to be honorable and just.

If we have gold mixed with impurities, by removing the latter we will
be left with pure gold, and it will remain so whether we dip it in water or
throw it in fire. In the same way, if we purify our minds by eliminating
our mental afflictions, only the pure mind will remain. We will experience

constant happiness because we will possess only the cause of happiness and will have eliminated the cause of suffering.

The gross physical form is the basis of all our problems. We have created the causes for our gross body; we were forced to take it. If we uproot its causes, we will obtain a subtle body in the future, and we will experience lasting, satisfying happiness.

Upon reflection, we realize that even at birth we endured great suffering. We encountered many problems while growing up, and we will experience more in the future. This is all due to the body, which requires so much for its sustenance. As soon as we get up we need to drink, eat, and get dressed. We need a home and a shelter. All these things require effort and are necessities for our body's well-being. And yet, even when we possess many things, we are still not happy—the house we live in is not enough for us, we are disappointed in the country that we live in, and we go abroad looking for something else.

In the Buddha's first teaching, given in Sarnath, he spoke on the four noble truths. The Buddha explained that we must begin by acknowledging the *truth of suffering*. Then we have to understand the *truth of the origins of suffering*. We need to follow the *truth of the path* in order to actualize the *truth of cessation*. This is the process to follow in order to effectively extinguish suffering.

The antidote to the mental afflictions is to follow the path. Having learned that the physical body is the foundation of all suffering, we might be inclined to think that death would put an end to it. If that happens, we should recall that our mental continuums will go on endlessly, moment after moment. We cannot achieve liberation from our physical bodies by destroying them, but only by trying to free ourselves from the causes that bring them about so that we are not forced to take similar forms in the future. If we purify them from mental afflictions, they will be pure minds, while right now they are confused—a mixture of negative and positive mental factors. If we unburden our minds from mental afflictions, we will acquire a pure mind and a pure body, a "final" body, by means of which we will be capable of experiencing the highest happiness.

Mental afflictions stand as an obstacle between ourselves and reality; they veil correct perception. When we achieve the state of a buddha, a state in which afflictions are no longer present, we will be in a position to know reality directly, as clearly as we see an object in the palm of our hand.

A buddha has various manifestations, or "bodies" (*kayas*). The *dharmakaya*, which is actually the mind of a buddha, is the body that has completely eradicated all obstructions and mental afflictions and has realized all positive qualities. The awakened mind is a mental continuum that has completed both the purification of negativity and the accumulation of virtue. However, the dharmakaya can be perceived only by another awakened being. Therefore, a buddha manifests as a form body (*rupakaya*) in order to benefit other beings as well. A form body is a mental body too, but it appears on a gross level so that we can perceive it and benefit from it. The form body has two manifestations: the *sambhogakaya* and the *nirmanakaya*. The former can be perceived only by higher beings or aryas, those who perceive emptiness directly, while the latter can also be perceived by bodhisattvas on the lower levels of the path and by ordinary beings.

When Shakyamuni Buddha came into this world, everyone was able to see him because he manifested as a nirmanakaya. However, Shakyamuni Buddha can also take other forms—that of a friend or a master—according to the needs and the capacities of various beings.

In order to realize all this for ourselves, we must achieve the state of a buddha. To this end, we should cultivate bodhichitta, the loving mind of awakening that aspires to enlightenment for the sake of all beings, and we should practice the six transcendental *paramitas,* or perfections.

The first perfection is *giving,* which is not discussed specifically in any chapter of Shantideva's text, although we find it mentioned in general in the first, second, and ninth chapters. The second is *ethics.* The fourth and fifth chapters of this text are exclusively devoted to the discussion of ethics. *Patience* is explained in the sixth chapter. *Enthusiastic effort,* the joy of accumulating positive karma, is expounded in the seventh chapter. The paramita of *concentration* is explained in the eighth chapter, and *wisdom* is discussed in the ninth chapter.

The *Bodhicharyavatara,* in which all six paramitas are presented, is therefore a manual for those who aspire to practice the Buddha's path so that they may attain the same state for the sake of all sentient beings, which is the ultimate aim of the Dharma.

∾ 3 ∾
FULL ACCEPTANCE OF THE AWAKENING MIND

WE ACCUMULATE MERIT and purify negativity through the *Seven-Limb Prayer*. The seven limbs are as follows:

1. Prostrating to the buddhas and bodhisattvas, the antidote to pride
2. Making offerings, the antidote to greed
3. Confessing nonvirtues
4. Rejoicing in the positive karma created by ourselves and others, the antidote to jealousy
5. Requesting teachings
6. Requesting the masters to not abandon us but rather to remain in samsara as long as it exists and continue to guide us
7. Dedicating the merit generated in the past, present, and future to the attainment of buddhahood for the sake of all sentient beings

In the first two chapters, three of these practices were explained: prostration, offering, and confession. The third chapter begins with the discussion of the fourth branch: rejoicing, or joyful appreciation.

We delight in positive karma, in our own happiness and that of others, and in the happiness that, like a peaceful interval between long periods of suffering, can also be experienced in unfortunate samsaric states. [1]

Let us rejoice in this positive karma, in the gathering of virtue, in the causes that allow liberation from samsara, and also in the merit accumulated by the *shravaka* arhats, the *pratyekabuddha* arhats, and the *aryas*—the higher beings—who have gained final freedom from the miseries of cyclic existence. [2]

The desire of the buddhas is that all beings may be free from suffering and attain the final state of complete awakening; hence their virtue is a boundless ocean. Let us rejoice in it. [3]

Let us gladly rejoice in the bodhisattvas' virtue; in the merit needed for a more favorable rebirth; in positive karma, the cause of nirvana; and in the virtues leading one to enlightenment. [4]

Buddhas and bodhisattvas are the source of every kind of happiness and merit we possess because they teach us how to practice, how to accumulate good karma, and how to put an end to suffering. They practiced numerous and fathomless paths, such as the path of the six transcendental perfections, in order to help all beings. Let us rejoice in all this. Rejoicing is appreciating virtue in others. It prompts us to create more positive karma ourselves, and itself accumulates merit. Delighting in our negative karma and that of others, however, creates more bad karma.

The fifth branch is requesting the buddhas to turn the Dharma wheel. [5]

It is not enough that there are buddhas and bodhisattvas, that there are teachings, and that we wish for happiness and not for suffering; we need to learn how to become free from suffering and actually achieve happiness. In order to learn this, we must first create the conditions that will allow us to receive teachings and then follow them under the guidance of enlightened beings. We are shrouded in darkness and ignorance, and for this reason we cannot find the true path. We need the lamp of the Dharma and that of the spiritual master, just as when searching for something in a dark room it is necessary to turn on the light. Thus, we need to request those masters to teach.

The sixth branch is pleading the buddhas and bodhisattvas to continue to guide us for as long as possible so that we may find the right path, since at present we are like blind people wandering in the darkness of samsara. [6]

The seventh branch is the dedication of virtue collected through previous practices. We dedicate the virtue accumulated in the past, present, and future to the attainment of enlightenment for the sake of all beings. [7]

The seventh branch is a kind of insurance, for even if we have created a lot of positive karma, it might get destroyed. We preserve it by dedicating our positive karma to others.

These seven practices are performed in the presence of the buddhas and bodhisattvas visualized in front of us. Doing this, we accumulate merit and eliminate the potential for evil. If we invoke the enlightened beings to receive our offerings and listen to our prayers and requests from our inner-most hearts, they will certainly come. This is not just imagination. The buddhas and bodhisattvas can go anywhere simply by wishing to do so. The speed by which they move is like the speed of light moving through space. They have no need for ordinary transport as we do, but can move instead through aspiration or the power of meditation.

In the biography of the great yogi Milarepa, there is a story about how he met a shaman from the non-Buddhist Bön tradition who was skilled in magic. Milarepa and the shaman faced one another in a contest, the challenge being to reach the top of Mount Kailash by the fastest possible means. The winner would take over the mountain. The shaman left that same night, riding on a circular drum, but Milarepa slept soundly. As soon as it was daylight, however, he awoke and rode on the rays of the sun, reaching the peak of the mountain in an instant.

In lamrim texts, bodhichitta is discussed toward the end, but Shantideva expounds this subject right at the beginning, because the *Bodhicharyava-tara* is intended for those who already possess the capacity to undertake the direct path to enlightenment, the Mahayana.

It is important to understand that the chief method by which all enlight-ened beings help us is through expounding the Dharma. The teachings given by Shakyamuni Buddha were collected in numerous volumes and commented upon and condensed by various Indian masters. They were then brought to Tibet, where they were translated, studied, and sum-marized by Tibetan masters. Later on, some of the teachings were then brought to the West, the so-called outside world, where they were trans-lated, and from them we have learned how to achieve peace, improve cer-tain aspects of our lives, and develop bodhichitta. Having achieved these realizations, Westerners themselves are beginning to spread the teachings. Therefore, it is evident that we can receive real benefit from the original teachings, even though they are ancient.

Thinking of all beings as patients in need of a cure, let us continue our aspiration, wishing to be doctors, nurses, and medicine until all beings are completely healed. [8]

The text continues by explaining the training necessary to transform the mind into the form and attitude most able to benefit others. With such mental inclination, focused solely on benefiting others, all of our own problems cease as well.

Let us dedicate our positive karma, so that it may become a rain of food and drink descending to clear away the pain of thirst and hunger, and let us pray that we ourselves may during times of famine be changed into food and drink. [9]

There will be a particular cosmic era in which beings will experience this type of suffering.

We can resolve, "May I become an inexhaustible treasure for those who are poor, and may those who are destitute find from me everything they need. May I be beside them, so that they will not find it hard to acquire necessities." [10]

On the airplane from India to Europe, I can look down on the Middle East, in which some areas are almost entirely desert. The people of these lands discovered oil there, and so even though their countries lack other natural resources, they still enjoy a certain amount of prosperity. This could be the result of a bodhisattva's dedication. We can view this as an example of the way that a being can offer all of his energy to others in such a way that wherever the need arises, an appropriate solution may be found. Let us begin by training the mind and then commit ourselves to actions, unfathomable at present, by which we will effectively succeed in satisfying other people's needs.

Without any sense of loss, we then dedicate our bodies and enjoyments, as well as all our past, present, and future merit, for the sake of benefiting all beings. [11]

By offering everything in our dedication, we will achieve the final realization, the state of a buddha. Offering everything to the various beings is a sensible thing to do for two reasons. The first is that, just as we usually invest what we have in order to make a profit, so we could dedicate our merit to the attainment of a more favorable situation in the future, or, even better, to the attainment of nirvana, the cessation of suffering. But this is still inferior when compared with the maximum investment—the dedication of all merit to the attainment of the state of buddha, the highest realization, for the sake of sentient beings.

The second consideration is that at the moment of death we will have to leave behind our bodies, which are so dear to us. Is it not better to offer them now, achieving such great benefit by doing so, than have to abandon them later without purpose? [12]

"Having given this body up for the pleasure of all living beings, it is no longer my concern if they insult me, abuse me, or kill me, since it already has been given for their benefit." [13]

Having offered our bodies to others, we should not be concerned about what they will do with them, even if they beat them, despise them, or deride them. A mother gives a toy to her child, and the child does what he wants with it; a father does not insist on checking up on a car he has given to his son—to do so would mean that it was not truly a gift.

"May others use my body any way they wish, as long as this does not cause any ultimate harm to myself or to them. Since I have completely offered myself to others, may they find in me all they need, and may I never be useless to them." [15]

We should not impose limitations in offering ourselves to others. This does not mean, however, that we should be instrumental in killing someone or that we should lay ourselves open for others to kill us. Instead, by this practice we test our determination to offer our bodies completely, and to be ready to sacrifice them if in so doing we will be able to benefit others and ourselves.

One might think that in donating our bodies to others and allowing them to be derided, one is building a basis for negative karma to be created. We need discrimination in offering our bodies. We must act wisely in each situation, considering whether our gift will be beneficial or harmful. If the benefits amount to more than the harm, then it is appropriate to do it; otherwise, it is not a good idea.

If we were about to create a great amount of negative karma and someone, in order to prevent us from experiencing its consequences, killed us, we must be prepared to endure this. An episode from one of Buddha's former lives, when he was a bodhisattva, illustrates this very well. The bodhisattva was returning home from seeking treasure in the company of five hundred other merchants. They had amassed great wealth, and the bodhisattva learned that one of his companions planned to kill all the others and flee with the riches. The bodhisattva tried to dissuade him, but was unsuccessful. With great compassion, and to avoid great suffering, he killed the merchant. This action brought great benefit and, as it was motivated by compassion, did not produce negative karma.

The text mentions being prepared to allow oneself to be killed but does not specify the benefit derived from such action.

The text goes on, "May I always relate with every being who encounters me in such a way that, whether faith or anger arise in him, it becomes the source for fulfilling all his wishes." [16]

"May all those who mock and insult me, or cause me any other harm, have the fortune to fully awaken, and may I be the cause of their awakening." [17]

"May I be a guide for all travelers and a protector for those without one. May those who need to be led on the journey to enlightenment, or even only through the ordinary world, find a guide in me. May I be a bridge, a boat, and a ship for all who wish to cross the water." [18]

"May I be an island for those who seek rest. May I be a lamp for those who are in darkness and look for light. May I be a home or a shelter for those who need one, and a servant for all who want one." [19]

"May I be a wish-fulfilling jewel and a magic vase for all who have various needs."

"May I acquire all the powers of tantric practice and become a perfect practitioner, so as to satisfy all those who need to be cured and freed from suffering, and so that I too may obtain what I need." Through puja to Tara, we can produce everything we need as well as sow the seeds of virtue in others. We can also use wrathful action in certain circumstances for their sake.

"May I be mantras." Mantras are powerful formulas that we recite in tantric practice.

"May I be powerful medicine for all the suffering in the world." Here the reference is to pills made of flower essence, blessed by the recitation of mantras, giving health and longevity.

"May I become a wish-fulfilling tree." It is a tree found in the Southern Continent, so big that its roots reach down to the lower realms while its trunk is in the human realm and its foliage in the realm of the gods.

"May I be a cow of plenty for the world." [20]

If we ask ourselves where such a tree and cow might actually be, we could not answer specifically; but if they do exist somewhere, we wish to become these two sources of joy. Right now we cannot find that tree or manifest these wishes, but if we simply create good karma, on that basis we will be able to enjoy happiness.

"Just like space and the great elements—earth, water, fire, and air—may I become the same precious support for the lives of all the countless creatures." [21]

"Until they pass away from pain, may I also be the source of life for all the realms of varied beings that reach unto the ends of space." [22]

Someone once said to His Holiness the Dalai Lama, "Bodhisattvas' prayers are so sublime that it seems unlikely that they can become reality. What is their purpose?" The Dalai Lama answered that although it is impossible to realize most of them, these prayers expand the mind of the bodhisattvas and encourage them on the path. Training one's mind is important, and a bodhisattva will do it so completely that he will later on acquire the attitude of being able to do anything.

The last few verses present the dedication of our bodies, our virtues, and all that we possess as gifts so that we might be able to face any difficulty we might encounter in our practices on the path to perfect awakening. All this is part of our mental training.

Now we come to the presentation of the active bodhichitta, the mind of awakening. Previous buddhas have reached this stage only after having generated this mind and subsequently practiced the vows and the bodhisattva's commitments to adhere to the six transcendental perfections exclusively for the sake of all beings.

To achieve the state of a buddha we need its seed, bodhichitta, the attitude that enables us to personally take responsibility for the welfare of all beings. The mind that aspires to enlightenment for the welfare of all beings must arise spontaneously and not artificially, as is the case for us now. Its foundations are love and compassion. *Love* is the mind that wishes happiness for all beings, while *compassion* is the mind that, seeing their suffering, wishes the cessation of that suffering.

It is easy to generate love and compassion for friends, relatives, and people dear to us, whereas it is very hard to do so for our enemies or for people that we consider harmful. Generating these feelings toward those we feel indifferent to presents a medium degree of difficulty. However, we must direct our love and compassion toward every being, be they friend, enemy, or stranger. When we are able to include everyone within the scope of our affection, we will have obtained the realizations of these virtuous mental states.

Among those we love, our mothers are closest to us. We must visualize all beings as our mothers and, furthermore, come to the understanding that they have, in fact, actually been our mothers. If we were to try to logically analyze a starting point in the sequence of our lives, it would be impossible to establish a beginning. The continuum of our lives is without beginning. They are countless, and in each one of them we have had a mother. Thus, it is reasonable to posit that all beings have been our mothers at some point, and that they have thus done all they could for our welfare. We must return this kindness to each one of them. Even if we do not completely succeed in our task, we should at least nurture the aspiration to do so.

There is a logical progression to the seven-point contemplation below. Recognizing, first of all, that our lifetimes are without beginning, we consider the following:

1. We have had countless mothers, and therefore each being must have been our mother at some time.
2. As our mother, each being has been infinitely kind to us.
3. A desire to pay back this kindness naturally arises.
4. All beings appear dear—we feel affection toward them—and on this foundation love arises, the wish that they may be happy.
5. Compassion arises, too, the wish that they be free from suffering.
6. As a consequence, we develop the extraordinary aspiration that wishes to take personal responsibility for their welfare.
7. Bodhichitta, the mind of awakening, arises.

The first six points listed above are the causes of the final point, bodhichitta, and for this reason, this meditation is called "six causes and one effect." This particular explanation belongs to a lineage of oral teachings. On the basis of the six causes, the aspiration for bodhichitta arises, which includes the determination to stabilize this mind firmly until our enlightenment.

We must proceed like the bodhisattvas of the past, who first generated the aspiration to realize complete enlightenment and on that basis traveled the five paths, practiced the six paramitas, and finally became buddhas. The aspiration comes first, and what follows is actual practice.

Evaluating the advantages of bodhichitta, we aspire to generate it and take the bodhisattva vows. Stanzas 22 and 23 of the third chapter, recited three times, are one formula for receiving the bodhisattva ordination. Having first generated the aspiration to attain enlightenment for the sake of all beings, we commit to the bodhichitta of action or practice, stating, "In order to attain enlightenment, I will also follow gradually the practices of the bodhisattva."

The bodhisattva vows refer to the bodhichitta of action. Developing bodhichitta is a very demanding task. We succeed only with unwavering determination. Understanding various logical reasons and understanding the benefits involved, our resolve becomes firm. We vow to keep this type of mind until enlightenment.

Since this is a very positive and important step, once we have taken it, it is meaningful and necessary to congratulate ourselves, saying, "Having obtained this human existence, now my life has borne fruit and has been used in the best possible way: having generated bodhichitta I have been born in the family of Buddha, I am one of Buddha's sons, I have within me the seed to become like him." [26]

While we recite this praise, the joy of having generated such a mind is equal to the joy of a young beggar who has been chosen by the king as successor to the throne. Having generated bodhichitta, we have become princes of the Buddha's family, we are on the path to buddhahood, and for this reason our happiness is beyond comparison.

Whatever we do from now on must be in accord with the family of buddhas. [27]

We do not expect a prince to behave like a child; in the same way, now that we are part of the lineage of the buddhas, different behavior is expected of us than of ordinary people.

Perhaps you have already developed bodhichitta, or perhaps not. But since we trust that bodhichitta is the substantial cause of attaining enlightenment, we must at least experience the joy that comes from appreciating such a mind.

We have now understood how unpleasant both unfortunate rebirths and any conditioned existence can be, and we are acquainted with the methods that will enable us to free ourselves from this situation and achieve the following: more favorable rebirths; the cessation of all suffering, or nirvana; and the state of a buddha, or enlightenment. This shows that we have reached an understanding of the gradual path, which is in itself worthy of praise and appreciation. The texts say that even just comprehending the various stages of the gradual path is superior to possessing the *eight ordinary powers* and the *five eyes*. These are special powers, such as invisibility and clairvoyance.

We are acquainted with the path of freedom from unfortunate rebirths, with nirvana, and with complete awakening. We have made great efforts to receive these teachings and to gain the favorable conditions that enable us to receive them. This is all due to our keen interest and to the feeling of trust we feel for the effectiveness of the teachings. We are very fortunate, are we not? When death knocks at our door, even if we have all the wealth in the world, we will still have to leave everything behind. We will not be able to take even a needle with us. But nobody can take from us our knowledge, especially the knowledge of the gradual path.

Buddhas and bodhisattvas explain that negative causes produce negative effects but that we can nevertheless purify our negative karma. If we believe the first half of the statement, we must necessarily believe the second half. It is illogical, feeling squashed by the sheer weight of our negative karma, to assume that it is impossible to purify it—buddhas and bodhisattvas show us the means of purification, which are within our reach. Through them we can erase our previous negative karmic imprints. If we pray and generate the aspiration to be able to do so in the future, it will certainly happen. Even hearing the name of a buddha or a bodhisattva is enough to purify eons of negative karma.

We are on the path, and there is no reason to feel sad or hopeless. If we look back, we will see many who are not as fortunate as we are! However, if we think we are exceptional or special, we must look ahead and realize that there are surely many people who are better than us. This will subdue our pride.

If we are able to generate bodhichitta, or even just appreciate this precious mind, we will naturally feel happy and joyful. To have come across the teachings of bodhichitta is a fortuitous occurrence that arose due to particular circumstances, like a blind man discovering a jewel in a heap of rubbish. [28]

Bodhichitta is like ambrosia, the supreme nectar that overcomes the tyranny of death. [29]

When a bodhisattva teaches emptiness, sentient beings can realize emptiness and eliminate their mental afflictions, negative karma, the power of the elements, and therefore death. When we reach that stage, we will not need to rely on a coarse physical body. We will then possess a subtle mental body, and our lives will be much easier, without all the problems related to our present conditions. We will have no need to rely on a fan, a car, a train, or food. As in Milarepa's case, without the food of his samadhi, he could not possibly have sustained himself on a diet of nettles alone. Without having developed *tumo*, or inner heat, his simple garment of cotton could not have sheltered him from the cold. Through right effort everyone can reach the same extraordinary realizations.

When a bodhisattva reaches such levels, he will try to acquire ordinary rebirths so that he can be of more help to others, for with an extraordinary body he would not be able to interact with common beings.

It is not enough to simply accept these matters as logically credible; we must reflect deeply and internalize them until they become part of us, otherwise they are useless. It is likely that many of you do not spontaneously have the aspiration to study the Dharma in order to reach the state of buddha for the sake of all beings. It is a good thing, however, to generate it at least artificially, hoping that one day, out of habit, this altruistic thought may arise naturally.

When we come to realize that a future life is a reality, we will be concerned and begin to act accordingly. At present we are human beings; we live with certain people in certain circumstances, and this is the fruit of karma accumulated in former lives. We were fortunate not to have been born as insects, fish, or cows grazing in the fields. We are endowed with a human condition and various favorable characteristics; we are able to think and perform various acts. This is a gift of our previous actions, but now we must try to obtain a better gift for our next life. It is in our hands—we can be our own saviors or our own destroyers. We will become our own saviors if we create positive karma, and we will become our own destroyers if we create negative karma.

Bodhichitta is the inexhaustible treasure that eliminates all poverty in the world. It is the supreme medicine that cures the world's diseases. It is a refuge in which all beings can find solace and restore their strength in this very life. Like wanderers traveling through a wild, arid, and dangerous area who find a leafy tree that gives them shelter, bodhichitta is the shelter for those of us who are wandering on the path of conditioned existence. [30]

It is the support and the bridge for all beings who seek a solution to the problems of cyclic existence; it alleviates suffering like the radiance of the moon dispels the fever of certain illnesses. [31]

As mentioned earlier, there are two obstacles to enlightenment: the mental afflictions, which can be eradicated by the mind that realizes emptiness, and the obscurations to omniscient mind, which can be eliminated by bodhichitta. Bodhichitta removes obscurations like the sun dispels the darkness. By the churning of milk we extract butter, which is quintessential milk; likewise, through study, reflection, and meditation, we extract the essence of the ocean of Dharma—bodhichitta. [32]

All beings, human or otherwise, possess buddha nature, the absence of intrinsic existence of the mind. This lack of intrinsic existence makes perfect enlightenment possible, but we must apply the methods that will lead us there.

In order to attain this human body, a male seed and a female egg were required, and in order to become a buddha, we must possess bodhichitta, the altruistic mind, together with the wisdom that realizes the actual nature of phenomena. Bodhichitta and wisdom are the substantial causes that allow us to attain the state of a buddha. They are like the two wings of a bird— both necessary if the bird is to fly. We and all beings wandering in samsara are looking for happiness and the means to achieve it; bodhichitta is truly the source of both. A traveler will gladly stop when he finds food and shelter; in the same way, bodhichitta is the best solace and refuge for those who wander in samsara. [33]

How can bodhisattvas, who possess the mind of awakening, be the source of happiness? They know that negative karma is the cause of suffering and that positive karma is the cause of happiness; they will teach all beings, and these beings will listen to their advice and achieve happiness in their own right.

In the last stanza of this chapter, the new bodhisattva, who has generated bodhichitta mind and the determination not to abandon it until the attainment of complete enlightenment, and who has promised to succeed in his task for the sake of all beings, invites all beings to this banquet of temporary and ultimate happiness. [34]

"Temporary happiness" refers to the fact that bodhisattvas can help beings attain fortunate states of birth as gods or humans. "Ultimate happiness" refers to the fact that beings can also achieve liberation from samsara and the state of perfect awakening, where happiness is complete.

◠ 4 ◠
CONSCIENTIOUSNESS

HAVING FIRMLY GENERATED the mind of bodhichitta and the aspiration to practice the bodhichitta of action, we need to effectively practice the path of the six transcendental perfections. A bodhisattva, a "*conqueror's son*," must seize this mind unshakably and never forget his promise or neglect the practice of the six perfections and the four methods enabling him to guide sentient beings on the path. [1]

Generally speaking, if we have promised something that is beyond our capabilities and later realize that we are not able to keep it, it is possible for us to pull back. With bodhichitta, however, even if we did not fully evaluate its validity and our abilities, since these have been examined by the great wisdom of the buddhas and the bodhisattvas, we cannot withdraw from fulfilling our promise to attain enlightenment for the sake of all beings. This is no ordinary promise, but an extraordinary one. Not keeping such a promise means deceiving every living being. If we act like this, what kind of future rebirth can we expect? [4]

It has been taught by the buddhas that if someone has generated the intention to give even one small thing and then clings to it with greed, he creates the cause to be reborn as a hungry ghost. If this is true for changing one's mind over small things, what will happen if—after having promised all beings from our innermost hearts to help them attain complete awakening—we do not translate our promise into action? [6]

There are twenty-two levels of bodhichitta. At the first level bodhichitta can still be abandoned, but by the second level it is no longer reversible. In any case, how would this even be conceivable once we understand that other beings suffer as much as we do, that they also long for happiness, and that each of them has been our mother?

Having generated the aspiration to attain enlightenment for the benefit of sentient beings and having started our journey on the bodhisattva path, if we then consider that sentient beings are infinite, and that some of them, in spite of the help we give them, could cause us harm, we may become discouraged. We may wonder how we can possibly be of any help to them at all; we may feel tired, incapable of attaining enlightenment, and we may want to quit. But doing so would be abandoning bodhichitta and breaking one of the eighteen root vows of the bodhisattva.

There are beings, however, who have attained liberation even after having abandoned this mind. Shariputra, for example, was said to have generated bodhichitta and subsequently, due to particular circumstances, abandoned it—but he attained nirvana all the same. How is it possible, having broken one of the eighteen vows, to attain liberation anyway? The explanation lies in the particular karma of these beings, something that can be comprehended only by the omniscient mind of a buddha. [7–8]

Some of us may have generated bodhichitta and may be practicing the bodhisattva path. But if this is not the case we must prepare ourselves by accumulating as much positive karma as possible and purifying our negativity. The easiest way to accomplish this is by trying to help others and refraining from causing them harm. We will be loved as a result, in the same way that we love those who help us and do not harm us. Though bodhichitta mind is extremely precious and beneficial, developing it may not be easy since it requires time and commitment. In the meantime, we can benefit others and not harm them, and we can practice accumulation and purification. These practices are essential for the followers of the path.

You might worry that if you offer so much to another person you will end up being taken advantage of. If someone asks you for a hundred dollars and you know that later on he will ask for more, give him the money and tell him that in the future you won't be able to do so again. The fundamental point is to strive to do your best, even with your material resources, knowing full well that you will never be able to satisfy the countless wishes of all beings. Nevertheless, although we cannot manifest the ultimate benefit for all beings, we must offer them a deeper understanding of reality, and this is possible once we ourselves have reached that understanding. To help others optimally, we need to attain complete enlightenment. There is no other way.

Consider someone whose material resources are limited. He is aware that even giving all he has, he can satisfy only the basic needs of very few people. If, however, he uses his possessions to nurture his practice and through it attain high levels of realizations, he might have left some people hungry and thirsty in the process, but he will have generated many more positive causes, thanks to which he will be able to give them much greater happiness in the future. Milarepa, the famous Tibetan saint who lived and meditated in the mountains, had no material objects to offer, and if asked he would have not been able to give anything at all. Both courses of action—using one's resources in order to help others and practicing the Dharma—become causes of happiness for anyone who undertakes them.

As a car runs smoothly only if its engine has been properly maintained, so too we attain the state of a buddha only if we have generated bodhichitta and the wisdom that perceives emptiness.

The deeds of a bodhisattva are done for the welfare of all beings, and should we hinder one of these deeds even in the slightest, we will accumulate a great amount of negative karma and be reborn in lower states in the future. [9]

If this is the result when we destroy the joy of even one ordinary creature, our negative karma will be proportionally greater when we hinder the work of a bodhisattva. [10]

If we abandon the mind of awakening once we have generated it, we will fall into the lower realms, or we will remain in samsara for a long period of time. It is possible to regenerate such a mind, but we will have wasted much time reaching an objective that we had previously achieved. [11]

Bodhichitta is precious and rare and we must not abandon it, even at the cost of our own lives.

It is said in the texts that when one becomes a buddha one is able to benefit all beings, and that in the past there have been countless buddhas. We could then ask why it is that we are still suffering, and numberless beings with us? [13]

We are suffering because of our own misdeeds, not Buddha's. We have not followed the path shown to us. He is available to guide all, but his teachings will be understood and followed only by those who are prepared to receive and practice them. If a blind man is taken to a supermarket, he will not see anything for sale. This is not because the store is empty. We cannot see the buddhas directly, but there are texts and teachings available. If we make the effort to practice, we will finally succeed in creating the conditions that will allow us to perceive them.

If we are happy with our lives at present, we must remember that we will have to face suffering and difficulties both in this life and in future lives. We might think that since we have attained a precious human rebirth and may attain another one in the future, there is no need to make too much of an effort right now. This is wrong, because at present we find ourselves in a situation in which Buddha's teachings are available and we have faith and keen interest in practicing virtue. If we had none, the mere existence of the teachings would be worthless. It is not enough to achieve a human form—there are billions of human beings, but only a few are interested in spiritual practice.

The arising of a buddha, faith in his teachings, the attainment of a human body, the attitude for cultivating virtue—all of these conditions are rare and precious. How can we hope to sustain them if we do not practice the Dharma right now? [15]

Right now we are in good health and find ourselves in favorable circumstances. We must make the most of this opportunity, since there is no guarantee that we will obtain a human rebirth again. Even if we do, there is no certainty that we will have all the favorable circumstances. Besides, we cannot rely too much on this body of ours; it is like an object on loan, and at any moment we might have to give it back. [16]

It is good to examine the preciousness of our human rebirth in depth. The lamrim texts state, "Death is certain," since nobody who has taken on a physical form has lived forever. They also state, "The time of death is uncertain."

Our situation is like that of a candle in a storm—its flame can be extinguished at any moment. The conditions for life are few, whereas the conditions for death are numerous. We know all too well that life's duration is uncertain: some children die in their mothers' wombs, others when they are very small, and others during adolescence. We are not guaranteed to live to a ripe old age.

At the moment of death, nothing and no one will be of any help—not relatives, not friends, not wealth. The only things we will carry with us are positive and negative mental imprints. There are two kinds of people: those who try to realize their desires materially and those who try to realize them by practicing a spiritual path. The former build beautiful houses for themselves and accumulate all kinds of comforts, but at the moment of death they have to leave everything behind. Those who practice a spiritual path, in contrast, devote themselves to sound and beneficial conduct, and at the time of death they find themselves with a wealth of positive mental imprints generated through Dharma practice. If we were completely certain that we were not going to die, be reborn, or experience any problems in future lives, then there would be no need to practice.

We often talk about meditation; we have a keen interest in it. Well, these are precisely the subjects we should meditate upon. We should reflect on how long our current life might be, how long we will enjoy our physical form, and what rebirth we are likely to take in the future based on our present actions. If it will be an unfortunate rebirth, what kind of suffering will we endure? How can we avoid this and gain a favorable rebirth?

Our lives, although fortunate, do not satisfy us completely, and at times our discomfort seems unbearable. What to say, then, of unfortunate rebirths—that of an animal, for example? The suffering related to this realm is much more intense than any we experience now. As humans, we do not experience the continuous anxiety of being harmed for no reason, but animals live in constant fear of being suddenly killed or wounded. This is not an unreasonable fear; it is likely, in fact, and this is because in former lives they created the causes to experience such an outcome.

Those acquainted with a spiritual path know which causes produce happiness and they try to cultivate them—to sow the seeds—and refrain from accumulating the causes of suffering. If you believe that material means are better, and that the spiritual path is not valid, you should investigate clearly to see if possessions and sense pleasures really do bring lasting happiness.

It is relatively easy to understand intellectually that the practice of virtue is the best practice, but translating this understanding into action is difficult. It is not so easy to comprehend deeply the law of cause and effect, which pertains not only to the coarse, physical world, but also to more subtle phenomena, like the mind. There are phenomena in the physical world that are sometimes difficult to understand, even when seen with the naked eye. No wonder, then, that trying to understand karma, which is of a mental nature, is far more difficult. First of all we must familiarize our minds with repeated listening, with reflection, and with meditation. But this is not enough—we also need the support of accumulated merit and prayers to the buddhas and bodhisattvas. Such prayers prepare the mind for a deeper understanding of what we are about to receive. In Tibet, in the four-hour teaching sessions, one-third of the time was devoted to prayers such as these in order to purify negative karma and accumulate positive karma. Elderly people can pray to the enlightened beings so that they may achieve a fortunate rebirth in their next life and have another opportunity to practice the Dharma.

Even though the teachings say we have the potential to become buddhas, it will take some time before we can fully realize our potential. For now, evaluate your situation, compare it with the time before you encountered the teachings, and realize that you have made some progress that is due to the Dharma. Most of us can affirm that the meaning of our lives changed after encountering the Dharma.

When we are told that we must perform good deeds and avoid negative actions, we think that it is too simple, too obvious, and not interesting enough. In fact, these things are essential. We desire happiness and seek to avoid suffering, and this is determined by our positive or negative actions. Christianity has similar teachings, and these ethics are of great importance. Christian or Buddhist, if you abandon evil deeds, you eliminate the causes of suffering, and if you nurture positive actions, you create the causes of happiness.

All nations, imagining the possibility of war, prepare themselves for the future, spending huge amounts on defense so that they can meet with any threat. Likewise, if we prepare adequately we will be able to face challenges boldly and effectively. We must therefore make the necessary preparations for the moment of death, reflecting on what has been previously explained. We might find many of these things arduous, but it is helpful to make an effort to focus on them because they will bring benefit in the long run.

As human beings, we have the capability to avoid actions that are harmful to others and perform those that will help them. In our world, many humans follow various spiritual paths, but no animals are able to do so. It is very difficult for animals to create positive karma and very easy for them to create negative karma. We can see this by watching their actions—they kill and eat insects, attack other animals, and so forth.

Compared to animals, the number of people in the world is very small. That is because the causes for a human rebirth are difficult to create, whereas it is easy to be reborn in the lower realms. We might think that human beings are numerous, reaching the levels of overpopulation, but if we count the nonhuman beings living in a small village, we can easily say that they outnumber the human population of the entire country. Furthermore, most of our planet is made of water, and the number of beings living in the ocean is immeasurable. But even if we just look at humans, few are inclined to spiritual practice or prepared to persevere and listen diligently to the teachings. Few are interested in a path, and even fewer are prepared to follow it. Fortunate beings are rare, and so is our precious human birth, the condition that allows us to best take advantage of our potential.

It is very hard for beings in the lower realms to accumulate positive karma and consequently find a way out of their intense suffering; for them it will be rare even to hear the words "happy life." [19]

The difficulty of acquiring a precious human birth after having fallen into the lower realms is demonstrated in the story of the blind turtle that lives at the bottom of the ocean and surfaces once every hundred years. On the surface of the vast sea is a golden yoke moved about by the wind. The chance of this turtle inserting its neck into the golden yoke is equal to the chance of gaining a precious human rebirth once we have fallen into the lower realms. It is nearly impossible for the turtle to succeed, and in the same way it is unlikely that all favorable circumstances will be assembled for us to attain a higher rebirth. [20]

If we review our past, we realize how scarce and feeble the positive karma we have created actually is and how abundant and powerful is our negative karma. If a small negative action can cause us to spend an eon in a lower realm, what need is there to mention the result of the evil gathered since time without beginning? In the lower realms we will not only experience suffering, but we will also produce more of it, and it will therefore be nearly impossible to find a way out. [22]

Right now we find ourselves in a very favorable situation, with freedoms and opportunities. If we do not make use of it by creating positive karma, purifying negative karma, and so acquiring a better condition in the future, it will be the greatest folly and ignorance. [23]

This would be similar to a merchant who arrives at a treasure-filled island after a long and difficult journey and leaves taking rocks and stones with him rather than jewels.

What do we need to do in order to accumulate positive karma and purify negative karma? We must try every day to do something beneficial for others and avoid causing them harm, by and by strengthening this kind of practice. Generating repentance, determining to refrain from negative actions, and nurturing the aspiration to attain enlightenment for the sake of all beings—all of these purify negative karma.

And if, having understood that the outcome of negative karma is great suffering and that positive karma is the cause for happiness, we still continue to be indolent, then when the hour of death arrives we will feel tremendous regret, but it will be too late. [24]

And if falling into the lower realms, where we will experience the most unbearable suffering, we ask why we are in such a situation, we will know that we alone have caused it, and we will be seized by unimaginable remorse and will experience further mental suffering. [25]

We are acquainted with the causes of happiness and the causes of suffering, yet we are not yet capable of acting accordingly. It is as though we have been hypnotized and are under a spell. [27]

In any case, if we have accumulated negative karma, it is pointless to remain paralyzed. Instead, through faith in the Three Jewels and through the other opponent powers, we can purify it. We might think it impossible to destroy all the negative karma we have accumulated since time without beginning. At a certain point on the path, however, it does become possible. The process is equivalent to having filled a whole room with glasses over a great length of time and then smashing them all into pieces in an instant.

We need to be aware of karma. Many more future lives await us; hence, before each action we must analyze our true motivation. Examining every action before we do it, if we can see that it will be beneficial and not harmful, we should perform it. If we see that it will bring immediate harm but great advantage later on, it is still a positive action, like a surgical operation—painful now but beneficial in the long run. We must refrain from doing what is pleasurable in the moment but harmful in the future, and also from doing what might benefit few and harm many. We must act, however, if in so doing we harm few but benefit many.

We must avoid performing acts that are beneficial to us but harmful to others and not shy away from doing the opposite. A spiritual person is entirely devoted to others and to their welfare, to future lives, and to positive actions. If we act in this manner, we can call ourselves good people. I personally appreciate people who conduct themselves in this way.

Although it is not impossible to attain awakening in one lifetime, for most of us it would be very difficult, and so it is good to prepare ourselves to do so in a future life. A precious human rebirth is not easy to acquire, and consequently we need to do our best to ensure that we attain one. We must also be vigilant about the possibility of rebirth in the lower realms, where it is almost impossible to practice Dharma and accumulate positive karma. However, someone who has generated bodhichitta, perceived the actual nature of phenomena, and developed samadhi can achieve his aim even in one lifetime by following the tantric method. The practice of tantra is very swift indeed, but in order to complete it we need these qualities in our minds. If we want to cook a good meal, it is not enough to have flour and rice; we also need salt, butter, vegetables, and all the rest.

A good vehicle for practice is essential. If we travel by sea, we take good care to embark on a safe ship so we don't lose our lives in a shipwreck. Similarly, on an airline flight, the crew makes sure that everything is in place—many lives are at stake and the plane is very expensive too. Since our objective is to attain the state of a buddha, we too should make certain that we take advantage of this precious opportunity and that we acquire fortunate rebirths in the future, so as not to experience difficulties during this long journey.

A legendary character in Tibet once said, "Can't have a good horse, don't want a second-rate horse, so I'll go without a horse." In modern times we could say, "Can't have a good car, don't want a small car, so I'll walk." The meaning is that practices such as developing wisdom and samadhi appear too elevated, whereas purifying nonvirtue and accumulating merit appear too ordinary, and since we feel we are in the middle, we end up doing nothing at all. Unable to practice the higher teachings and thinking those that are suitable to be too ordinary, we remain stuck at the beginning. Likewise, if a penniless person, thinking that bread and cheese are not good enough for him, stays hungry wishing for a lot of money to buy excellent food, he is being foolish. In the same way, we should be glad to practice whatever practice is within reach and be satisfied with it.

When we rise early in the morning and sit down to pray, we should think, "Now I have obtained a precious human rebirth. It is impermanent, so I must not waste it. I must try to acquire similar rebirths in the future in order to achieve liberation and the state of a buddha for the sake of others."

We should become used to doing whatever we can right away. If we keep postponing our activities until tomorrow, next month, or next year, we will end up saying, "I will do it in my next life." But if we fall into the lower realms it will be very difficult to come out of them, and nearly impossible to create good karma, which is a difficult thing to generate even during the course of a precious human rebirth. We must be determined to practice as much as we can during this lifetime and give up the idea of waiting for the next.

We might think of postponing Dharma practice until we have accomplished the many things we must do. But this way of thinking is also not right, since ordinary commitments are endless and we do not know if there will be time left for the Dharma once we finish them. We must therefore start our practice as soon as we make the decision to do so.

Our minds might bring up another doubt: "Do we possess the ability to practice?" In answer to this, we must convince ourselves that we have all the advantageous conditions: we are intelligent, we have a suitable place, we have the wish to practice, and we have teachers. Realizing that we have all we need, that the Dharma provides us the tools, and that this life is fleeting, we must commit ourselves to practicing right now and not wait until we finish various undertakings.

Once a student in Tibet wished he could go on a picnic. His teacher promised that they would go when they completed their work, but the work was endless and they never found the opportunity to go. The student was really upset about this. One day while they were together, the teacher and student came across a corpse. The teacher asked his student whose it was, and the student replied angrily, "One who has finished his work!"

Forever waiting to finish our chores before we start our spiritual practice is foolish. Death could come first. However, it is reasonable to practice the Dharma and continue to do our work at the same time.

If we try to destroy a poisonous plant by regularly eliminating its fruits, new ones will invariably grow with each new season. The only way to destroy it is to eradicate the plant itself. Similarly, the karma we consciously or unconsciously create is the result of our mental afflictions. Hence we must first try to control them and finally eradicate them.

In the panorama of global relations we have several opposing groups: Israel and Palestine, India and Pakistan, Tibet and China. As spiritual practitioners, our specific enemies are our mental afflictions, which cause us boundless harm. We call them enemies because they create problems for us just as our physical enemies do, even though they have neither arms nor legs and are neither courageous nor wise. How then have they been able to use us like slaves? [28]

Because we have allowed them to enter our minds and do what they please! The result is that we create karma that will cast us into the lower realms. This is not the time to practice patience and endure these enemies within our minds. It is appropriate to practice patience toward other sentient beings, not toward internal enemies; but up to now we have done the opposite. [29]

We must learn how to defeat the mental afflictions by applying their antidotes. Many tangka paintings depict wrathful deities, but the hatred they manifest is directed against all mental afflictions and not at us.

Even if all the gods were to rise up against us, they still could not lead us to the extreme suffering of the lower realms, a feat that our more powerful inner enemies can accomplish. These disturbing conceptions have such power that they can cast us into flames capable of turning Mount Meru into ashes in an instant. [31]

The afflictions have been with us from time without beginning. They have always caused us harm, and they will continue to do so in the future until they are eliminated. All other beings are incapable of remaining our enemies for such a length of time. At times they are enemies for less than one human lifetime, and never for all of our former and future lives. [32]

Our external enemies and ourselves cause mutual harm, but we can make peace. This is impossible with the mental afflictions. Even if we were to offer them our friendship, they would continue to harm us relentlessly. They are our perpetual enemies and they are the cause of all the suffering we experience. Hence, we must make every effort to eliminate them completely. As long as they dwell in our minds, we will never be joyful or free from fear. [34]

Cyclic existence is like a prison, and the mental afflictions are the wardens; as long as they are present, we will not find our way out and experience happiness. [35]

The afflictions have tormented us in the past, and they continue to torment us, but we must not give up until we are certain that they have been completely destroyed.

When we have an enemy in the world, we plot against him in response to his affronts, and yet the harm he causes us is only slight and short-lived. Nevertheless we waste much energy and lose sleep over it. [36]

Even if our external enemies have very powerful weapons and can kill, defeat, or wound us, why do we make so much effort to fight them, knowing they will die of natural causes and will live no longer than a hundred years? Instead, why not fight relentlessly against our inner enemies, who will not die of natural causes? [37]

Any harm we receive in life has its cause within us. We should consider whether this is true or not! This point is crucial. If we realize it, we will be able to understand most of our problems.

If someone insults us and we do not react by becoming angry, then what has been said did not harm us. If, on the other hand, we feel angry and keep thinking about it, we make ourselves miserable. If we are no longer worried about what has happened, the case is closed. This might be a new way of thinking for some, but Tibetans did not invent it.

The *Bodhicharyavatara* was written by Shantideva, an Indian, and he himself explains at the beginning, "There is nothing here that has not been explained before. I am only saying it in a different way." He refers to the uninterrupted lineage of teachings going back to Shakyamuni Buddha, who learned all this by his own effort to acquire understanding over long eons. The Tibetans received these teachings from India and have tried to practice them. They have now reached the West, and those here must do the same. I do not know this text in great detail, but I am trying to explain what I have understood.

A cancer patient thinks of his doctor as kind and benign, even though the cancer he fears so much can only damage him in this life and in this body. The teachings are the medicine for the mental afflictions, and we must consider them more precious than the medicine that cures cancer!

What we are discussing here is not without logical foundations. These matters, though difficult to realize, prove to be real once we possess the right understanding.

The right motivation for our aspiration to attain the state of a buddha is the wish to do so for the sake of others, not for our own happiness. There is a difference between hoping to receive a reward for ourselves and expecting it for others, and thus a difference between aspiring to nirvana and aspiring to full enlightenment. The former is a selfish attitude because we assume that nirvana is enough, whereas there is no selfishness in wishing to attain the state of a buddha for the sake of others.

It is easy to see how hatred creates suffering, for we never encounter someone who is happy when he is angry. However, it is more difficult to understand how attachment produces suffering.

Attachment creates needs: an object appears more beautiful than it is, and we want to own it and never be separated from it. When an object is not the way we want it to be, we are unhappy, but if it fulfills our desires, we are afraid to lose it. In both cases we suffer. If we have no desire for an object, we are not in the least concerned about whether it will satisfy our expectations. We might feel happy when engaging with an object of desire, but our happiness is always mixed with suffering. Here are a few examples.

If we drive a car on a long journey, we are happy and comfortable at first, but sooner or later we tire of being inside the same car.

If we sit on a cushion, we are comfortable initially, but then we become uncomfortable.

If we go for a walk we find it pleasant, but if we continue for a long time we get worn out.

When we are hungry and begin to eat, we are satisfied at first, but if we eat too much we feel ill.

When we are cold, we look for a place to sit in the sun and feel better. But after a while we get hot and look for shade, only to begin feeling cold again.

These examples show the various remedies we apply in order to eliminate dissatisfaction and bring joy to the mind. Generally, we say the result is happiness, but in fact its nature is the suffering of change. Any sense pleasure we experience in this life will never satisfy us completely, since our bodies are the bedrock of suffering, and as long as we have them, no matter what favorable condition we achieve, we will never be completely happy. How could we be with the mental afflictions, our inner enemies, always present?

The root cause of the mental afflictions is the mind that has the wrong perception of phenomena and clings to their supposedly concrete existence. In reality there is no objective world that is self-existent or possesses intrinsic, independent existence—each phenomenon exists solely in relation to the mind that conceives it. A table is not a table by itself. It becomes a "table" as soon as we give it this name. Similarly, if a person who has helped us in the past hits us with a stick today, and another person does the reverse, which of them do we call a friend and which an enemy?

I will give another example that might sound a bit strange. Someone hits us with a stick and then hits a bodhisattva. We would consider that person our enemy, but the bodhisattva would see him as a most precious friend, because thanks to that being he is able to practice patience! This shows that the person has no intrinsic nature.

It is not easy to understand the fact that phenomena are without intrinsic existence, because the concept of an intrinsically existing reality is rooted very deeply within us. This subject has been widely discussed among Indian scholars. Among Buddhists we find four schools that each hold different views representing gradual levels of learning. The view of the first school is the first level and presents a more limited view when compared to the second, and so on. However, we must begin with the first in order to reach the last, the highest view, which states that phenomena do not exist in an objective, natural, concrete, self-existing way, but only as the result of having given a valid name to a valid basis. This is a very important subject in philosophical debate; in fact, it is a solution to the problems of the entire world.

There was a yogi in India named Lampopa who had realized emptiness. The local king, having heard of the great siddha, invited Lampopa to teach him. Lampopa did not use perfect skillful means when he explained to the king that reality is empty of existence. The king misunderstood and interpreted this to mean that there is no objective reality and consequently no basis for positive or negative actions. He became very angry with the mahasiddha and had him beheaded. After some time, however, either as a result of receiving further teachings or as a result of accumulating positive karma, the king comprehended Lampopa's meaning and realized that he had misunderstood. He atoned, made many offerings, and did purification practices.

We do not say that phenomena do not exist at all—we use the terms "truly," "intrinsically," and "with a self-nature" to qualify this. Therefore, we are not denying the existence of things; rather, we are denying their intrinsic, self-existent reality.

Before we venture into trying to understand what "void of intrinsic existence" means, we need to establish the way a self-existent phenomenon would hypothetically exist. A self-existent phenomenon would exist independently of any condition, factor, and any of its constituents—that is, it would exist from its own side. In reality, however, a phenomenon depends on its parts for its existence. A tape recorder's existence depends on its various parts; a recorder independent of those parts does not exist. Phenomena come into existence only after they have been conceived by a mind, and they exist mainly *because* they are conceived by a mind.

For example, when we are on top of a hill we call it "*this* hill," whereas the hill in the distance is "*that* hill." These labels are dependent on our own position. If we move to the other hill, "*that* hill" becomes "*this* hill," and vice versa. We are not saying that there are no phenomena but only that there are no independent phenomena.

I will give another example. When seated in a room, we have the clear concept that we are seated in a room. But if we look for "the room," we see that it is not the wall, the floor, or the door. No part of the room is the room. Analyzing in such a way, we no longer find the room. Thus we realize that the room does not exist independently. But the room does exist as soon as we give a name to the collection of its parts, and this kind of relative existence functions perfectly.

We sometimes encounter difficulties while studying the Dharma, and even if we have understood, we sometimes find it hard to practice. Surely there are obstacles on the path, but we should bear them as something useful, since they cause us to reach our goal of happiness. As Dharma practitioners, we should be happy to face our problems. When we are wounded in battle by our enemies, we wear the scars on our bodies as ornaments, and in the same way we must also wear the difficulties of practice patiently, knowing that they are useful and that their purpose is great. [39]

There are people who, having lost an arm or a leg during the Second World War, display their mutilations with great pride to show how much they have done for their countries. We should be even prouder since we are doing so much more. We usually feel proud when we possess something, but in the case of Dharma practice, we must be proud because we are pursuing a great objective.

Milarepa was one of the best-known Buddhist meditators. He was renowned because he possessed nothing. Many wish to obtain a state similar to his, even though he ate only wild plants and had no clothes. If we tell a buddha or a bodhisattva that we have abandoned our possessions they will be happy, whereas if we say the same to ordinary people they will only think we are crazy.

In the world we find fishermen, hunters, and farmers who endure great difficulties merely for their livelihood, so why can't we, who want to attain the state of a buddha, bear any hardship in studying and practicing the Dharma? [40]

If we want to achieve enlightenment, we must first eliminate our mental afflictions. This is the way to reach nirvana. This might seem to contradict our initial purpose of achieving complete awakening for the sake of all beings, but in fact we must think of the eradication of mental afflictions as a stage in reaching our objective. If we are not able to destroy our disturbing conceptions, we cannot possibly think of helping others to do the same. We need to trust that we are able to do a certain thing ourselves before we can help others do it as well.

What is the difference between the Hinayana arhats and the Mahayana bodhisattvas in terms of trying to eliminate the mental afflictions? Arhats wish to do so for their own happiness, while bodhisattvas do so for the sake of others.

If in eliminating mental afflictions we are prompted by a right motivation, it is not wrong to treat these afflictions as our enemies and use the relevant antidotes against them. Such an attitude is not in itself another mental affliction because it does not create suffering, given the particular nature of the object. [43] We must never encourage mental afflictions or give them an opportunity for victory—it would be better for us to lose our lives than to be forever bowing down to disturbing conceptions. [44]

Even if we are killed, we lose only our current lives, but by surrendering to mental afflictions we suffer for many lifetimes and end up in the lower realms.

We never completely defeat ordinary enemies—if we expel them from one region, they will settle somewhere else, recover their strength, and mobilize against us. It is not the same with disturbing conceptions. When we have completely defeated them through perfect wisdom, they will have nowhere to go, and they will disappear because they cannot exist outside the mind. [45]

If it is true that, once eliminated, mental afflictions will not return, why haven't we already eliminated them? Because our minds have always been feeble, and we have not generated enthusiastic effort or the wisdom that enables us to eliminate them completely! [46]

We might doubt that we can eradicate mental afflictions because we do not see that they arise from our minds but rather perceive them as true, real, and self-existent. However, despite the fact that afflictions can be said to exist conventionally since they cause us agitation, harm, and suffering, if we seek them through analysis, we will never be able to find them. They are, therefore, like illusions, for although they possess conventional existence they do not exist independently. And once they are completely eliminated from our minds, they lose even their conventional existence.

Thinking that the mental afflictions exist intrinsically fuels the fear that we are stuck with them. Knowing that this it is indeed possible to eradicate them, we must joyfully generate the aspiration to do so. Why would we freely allow them to cause us to suffer and be led by them into the lower realms? [47]

Having received the bodhisattva vows means we want to achieve complete awakening. We must, then, examine the various points discussed here and try to understand them well. Everything the Buddha said is for our benefit, and for that reason we must follow his advice. He meditated for eons on love and compassion, and it is inconceivable that he might have wished us harm. Having reached perfection for himself and others, there is no reason that he should not expound what has profound weight and meaning. We may be unable to understand and practice some aspects of his teachings immediately, but we must practice what we are able to right away.

The fourth chapter of the *Bodhicharyavatara* states that we must refrain from accumulating negative karma and that we must eliminate mental afflictions from their root. Furthermore, having developed the mind of bodhichitta, we should maintain and increase it. If we are not able to do so, we should pray that we will be able to in the future, and in the meantime practice what is now within our ability.

✌ 5 ✌

DISCRIMINATING ALERTNESS

So far we have studied the advantages of generating the mind of bodhichitta, the way to prepare ourselves so that we are able to generate it, and the way to effectively generate this mind. Finally, we have taken the bodhichitta vows. Now we must preserve these vows; otherwise we will be unable to protect our practice. [1]

We preserve our vows by controlling the mind. This is crucial. If we do not, we will be harmed, because an uncontrolled mind is like a wild and crazy elephant, although even the damage caused by a wild elephant is definitely less than the damage our minds can cause. [2]

If an elephant is firmly bound he will cease to cause harm, and so it is with the mind when we bind it with the rope of mindfulness. Mindfulness must always be present in everything we do, moment by moment, and, as the bound elephant, the mind disciplined through mindfulness will not cause fears to arise and will accumulate only virtue. [3]

First, we need to discern good from bad, and subsequently exert control over our minds. If our minds suggest a positive course of action we should act accordingly, but if they lead us to behave in a negative way we should stop them. We must not allow the mind total freedom, but instead set boundaries by using mindfulness.

If we fear tigers, lions, elephants, snakes, cannibals, spirits, or any other thing, it is because our minds are out of control as a result of the negative karma we have accumulated. There are thousands, even millions, of these frightening beings, and it is impossible to bind all of them securely. What we can do, however, is tame our own minds, since by doing so these enemies will also be subdued. [5]

If we succeed in training the mind, everything done by others will seem beneficial to us. Otherwise everything will be a source of problems. If we generate love and compassion toward others, they will love us. This is the equivalent of saying that they are tamed. The Buddha has no enemies because he has subdued his mind, whereas we meet those who harm us because we have not yet succeeded in doing so.

The Buddha explained that all fears and forms of suffering originate in our own minds. In the hell realms there are trees of thorns on top of which women and friends appear to us. Desperate to reach them, we climb the thorny branches and wound ourselves. Once we arrive at the top, we see that our loved ones are now beckoning us from the bottom, and the entire process begins again. The hell realms were not created by an external source, nor were the experiences we suffer there. All these things are merely the function of the negative karma of those who perceive them, which in turn was caused by a confused and afflicted mind. [8]

Westerners may or may not believe in the hell realms, but they are mentioned in the text. I was asked in Italy once whether the hell realms truly exist or whether they were invented to urge people to perform good deeds, and I replied that the hell realms do exist—but nobody can make a phone call to double-check!

If we do not believe in the hell realms, we also would not believe in the existence of those spirits called *pretas,* nor would we believe in gods or demigods, since we cannot see them. However, we cannot deny the existence of animals. In the desire realm, to which we belong, there are six levels of gods, and in the form and formless realms there are many more. Should we say that these beings do not exist just because we do not see them? And can we truly assert that millions of universes present in space do not exist just because we are not able to perceive them directly?

Buddha appeared two thousand five hundred years ago, and there has been no fundamental change made to his teachings, whereas in the realm of science, theories are constantly changing, and the latest is always thought to be the most accurate.

When we talk about the atom bomb, everybody is afraid of its effects, and indeed it was created by scientists without their knowing for certain whether it would be beneficial for humanity or not. If it were not dangerous, however, people would not demonstrate against the proliferation of nuclear power. If even great scientists were unable to foresee whether their work would bring benefit or harm, how can we expect to establish the existence of the hell realms with certainty?

However, we believe in things that scientists have told us without having verified them directly. They have discovered many things that have proven useful and invented machines that solved many of our problems. In Tibet we still rely on animals for transport, and we have to carry our luggage on our shoulders, but in the West, thanks to various inventions, we do not have the same difficulties. For example, in the West people no longer use oxen to work the fields, whereas in India and Tibet they do. Therefore, we can definitely say that there are positive aspects to science.

In the three realms of samsara—the desire, form, and formless—we need to control our minds, because they can cause us considerable damage and suffering. Since both pleasant and unpleasant experiences are their creations, we must encourage the mind to act on what is sound and prevent it from doing what is unsound. Now let's have a look at what positive deeds the mind is able to perform, particularly in terms of perfecting generosity.

But what is the perfection of generosity if it does not succeed in alleviating the world's poverty? It is the attitude of offering everything we have, and hence it is also a mental creation. [10]

Generosity is not so much the act of giving as it is developing the desire to give to the highest degree in our minds. This entails completely forsaking avarice. The Buddha helped beings not so much by offering material goods, but by explaining how to purify their negative karma, how to accumulate merit, and how to achieve the highest levels of happiness.

It is very difficult to benefit beings, but it is not impossible, and our aim is to achieve buddhahood so that we can actualize that aspiration. This is the reason we study the Dharma. It is possible to reach this goal by developing positive qualities and eliminating all negative traits, and when we have done so we will truly be able to help all beings. We need to nurture this aspiration. Generating this mental attitude is a little difficult at first, but it becomes easier with time and practice.

First, we need to ground ourselves in the logic of the actual reality of former and future lives. If this is not an easy task, we start by generating faith in the teachings and in the masters who have realized them before us. On the basis of this kind of trust we will then be able to reach some understanding on our own. At first it will be a rational understanding, but as we familiarize ourselves with these concepts, we will be able to clarify them naturally and spontaneously.

The foundation of Dharma is faith, and if we do not have any faith, we will be unable to accumulate merit. But faith alone is not enough for realization—we need to use logic through reasoning, thinking, "Right now I am an intelligent human being, but it has not always been so in the past, nor will it be so in the future. My future depends on the karma I create. If I have accumulated positive karma I will achieve a higher rebirth; if, instead, I have accumulated negative karma, I will be reborn into a lower rebirth." We must be conscious of this and engage ourselves with the practice. The immediate result of doing so will be that we suffer less and are happier, and in the long run, we will benefit from circumstances more favorable for the attainment of buddhahood, thanks to a fortunate rebirth.

Above we discussed how difficult it is to accumulate virtue in the lower realms, and how in that condition one only generates negativity. With a precious human birth, however, it is even possible to attain buddhahood.

We should start to reflect in this fashion, which is not so hard to do, thinking, "Why should I create good karma, refrain from generating more evil, and purify the negative karma I have already accumulated? Because I aspire to happier rebirths and I have no desire to be unhappy." We should not be satisfied, however, with achieving a more favorable rebirth, since we have already managed to acquire a good rebirth without being able to eliminate our problems and achieve the complete happiness we aspire to attain. We should aspire to develop the need to be free from samsara altogether, since this is the only way we can be free from suffering.

These teachings derive from the lamrim, the gradual path. If we do not train the mind through the gradual path first, it will be very difficult to do so through the *Bodhicharyavatara,* which represents a much higher level of teachings. In this text we find the teachings on bodhichitta as well as explanations on the bodhisattva path that are intended for those who have already renounced samsara and generated aversion for cyclic existence, and who have love and compassion for all other beings.

At present we do not even possess a strong desire for a happier rebirth, so for most of us it will be difficult to talk about bodhichitta. We must first nurture the desire to attain a more favorable rebirth, and then, realizing that this is not enough, and that as long as we remain within the cycle of samsaric rebirths existence will always be unsatisfactory and full of problems, the desire to be free from it will arise naturally.

We must remember what samsara means—we continually die and are reborn not by our own volition but by the power of karma and mental afflictions. We must understand that as long as we are forced to wander in samsara we will not experience the happiness we aspire to, but will suffer instead as animals, humans, or gods, and that we will be liberated only when we are able to choose our next rebirth. This understanding, together with concern for our condition, brings about the generation of renunciation.

What is the vehicle by which we go from life to life? The physical body. What is the place where we take a new rebirth? The various realms of existence, from the highest, the formless realms, to the lowest, the hell realms—the levels of which are determined by the particular intensity of our karma and mental afflictions.

In our endless wandering from life to life we experience several kinds of suffering, even though we may acquire a good rebirth. This is why we need to generate the aspiration to be completely free from all the suffering of samsara. The difference between life in samsara and liberation is akin to the difference between living in prison and living at home. In prison, life is extremely regimented—we must follow the timetable and eat what is given to us—whereas at home we can go out whenever we want and eat what we please and when we are hungry. Similarly, life in samsara is a state of imprisonment from which we naturally want to escape.

Any form of material pleasure we find in cyclic existence must sooner or later be abandoned. As human beings, if we have a beautiful home we will have to leave it behind, and it is the same with loved ones, relatives, friends, and so on. We already experience great suffering at the moment of birth. After conception, we must stay in our mother's womb for several months. We are nourished by the food she takes in, and if the food is boiling hot or too cold or if we don't have enough, we suffer. The physical environment in which we find ourselves during this time is not at all desirable; in fact, it is truly unclean. If we are on a solitary retreat for just one month we find it difficult, but in our fetal state we are stuck there for nine months and ten days! Then, as newborn babies, our condition is similar to that of a worm. Later on, while still small, we continue to depend on our parents to feed us, clothe us, and all the rest, since we are not able to discriminate what is good from what is not good.

Reflecting upon these matters, we will also come to understand how kind our mothers have been to us and how much they really cared for us. Without them we would not be here at all.

In youth we experienced many problems—we had to study and take exams, we did not find what we desired, we had to face what we did not like, and we were unable to defeat our enemies or help our friends. Now that we have reached adulthood, we experience other kinds of suffering. If we have jobs in any field we must overcome various difficulties, and if we do not have jobs we worry because we do not know how to use our time, and we have problems falling asleep at night.

Soon, we will have to face the suffering of old age. When we are old we may wish to speak to a young person, but he or she will not pay any attention to us since the young are not interested in old people. If we have not accumulated any positive karma, we will start worrying about the effects of our negativity on our future lives.

In other words, we live in suffering all the time.

Observing our physical bodies, we can see that they are not unlike bags of rubbish—anything that comes out of them is dirty. It has already been explained that our bodies are collections of impurities and that we have obtained them because of our karma and mental afflictions. We must therefore refrain from generating attachment toward them, as well as toward the bodies of others, but until we have eliminated the causes that determine rebirth with this type of physical body there is no way that we can avoid getting one.

Our minds are full of mental afflictions—the causes of all suffering—but in the same way that there are extremely strong and opposing powers on a political level, there is also an immensely powerful antidote against the mental obscurations—that is, the wisdom that knows emptiness. Once we possess this type of wisdom, we can eradicate our mental afflictions, and we will no longer possess a body like the one we have now. Negative karma, if there is any left at all, will not ripen, in the same way that rice seeds bottled in a jar without soil, sun, and moisture cannot sprout. Among the conditions that allow karma to ripen is the desire to be reborn and take on another life-form.

Mental afflictions are enemies that deprive us of our freedom; we discuss them in order to generate the desire to be free from them and to understand reality, not in order to feel discouraged. If we were not able to eliminate them, then talking about the mental afflictions would make us feel depressed and would be pointless. If, however, we are suffering and experience discomfort, with the understanding that these mental afflictions are a form of illness that arise due to our disturbing conceptions, we will be able to cure them and eliminate the suffering that accompanies them.

First, we must closely examine our own conditions, since it is natural to be concerned about ourselves. Later on, we need to extend our concern to others, who suffer just as much as we do, and keep their situations in mind. If we are able to recognize that all beings experience suffering, we will be concerned about the welfare of each of them. Love and compassion will arise, and with them the extraordinary wish to do something for others.

We must understand that it is possible to realize a state in which all mental afflictions have been eradicated and all positive qualities have evolved. We must also understand that this is something not just for ourselves to realize, but for all beings. Once we do this, we will then desire to reach that state in order to help others do the same. Without this inner development we will experience difficulties and become discouraged. Once we have realized wisdom and compassion, it will be our natural capacity to think of others!

When presidents and prime ministers were schoolchildren, they could not imagine how they could become world leaders. How did they reach that level? First, they went to school and learned whatever they could. Then they took humble jobs and slowly realized that they could do better. Others also noticed that they were talented and encouraged them. Gradually, they acquired the necessary knowledge, and as a result they eventually achieved these roles. No one becomes a prime minister just after finishing school, but only gradually.

Likewise, on the spiritual path, we first generate the fear of being reborn into unhappy rebirths. We extend such fear to all of cyclic existence. We continue by nurturing the desire that *all* beings may be free from cyclic existence until we develop the aspiration to achieve the state of a buddha for their sake, the highest aim of someone who practices the Dharma.

We need to begin by generating love and compassion for our friends, relatives, and loved ones, then move on to generating love and compassion for those toward whom we feel indifferent, and finally for our enemies. In this way we include all beings. We will then be able to generate the extraordinary aspiration to save all beings, although we will soon realize that we are not capable of doing so unless we reach buddhahood. The mind that generates this desire is bodhichitta, a mind present in all buddhas and bodhisattvas. If it were not possible to benefit all beings, there would be no buddhas or bodhisattvas.

In our minds, there are two kinds of mental obscurations: the obscurations to omniscience and the obscurations caused by the mental afflictions. These obscurations are impermanent and changeable. They have antidotes, and there are people who understand them, as well as related teachings. It is possible for all sentient beings to generate aversion for these afflictions because no one wishes to experience unhappiness and therefore everyone will try to avoid it. As soon as the aspiration to achieve liberation arises, and with it the knowledge that there are methods to obtain it, we will do everything possible to know them and practice them. On the one hand there are buddhas and bodhisattvas who have attained liberation, and on the other there are sentient beings who desire it, and so a communion arises between them. If someone is ill, even with a doctor nearby, the doctor will be able to cure him only if the sick person has the desire to recover and has made the effort to see the doctor.

It is definitely possible to attain the state of buddha and help all beings do the same. The nature of the mental afflictions is the same for everyone. It is not true that only some people are able to eliminate them whereas others cannot, and it is as possible to help all beings as it is to help one of them. In the *Bodhicharyavatara* we read that even flies and insects possess the seed of buddhahood and can attain this state through right effort. Why then can't we do the same, endowed as we are with intelligence and the ability to discern what is good from what is not?

We read in the scriptures that if we fall into the lower realms, we cannot create positive karma. How then is it possible for a worm or a fly to attain buddhahood? The explanation of this statement is that the worm or the fly may not achieve buddhahood while in its animal form but can attain it at some other point in the cycle of rebirths. At times we reach the peak of the rebirth cycle, and at times we fall into its depths, but when in our wandering we acquire favorable conditions and manage to use them, the opportunity for enlightenment is present, since we carry the seed for buddhahood within us.

We do not find a single being about whom we can say that his mental afflictions and his karma cannot be purified and eradicated, since everyone has a mind and this mind does not possess intrinsic existence. The root of all obstructions is our belief in a self-existent nature of phenomena, and out of this wrong view all other mental afflictions are born. When we have eliminated the mind that grasps concrete existence, we will also have eliminated the cause of the afflictions. Knowing the genuine nature of phenomena, our wrong views will dissolve, and once we have realized the empty nature of the mind, the idea of its intrinsic existence will disappear.

Why do we say that beings have the same nature as buddhas? Those who have attained enlightenment are well acquainted with the path and are familiar with the methods used to reach that goal. We can receive valuable help from them and, by following their advice, reach the same state. This process of mental development is possible for all because of the empty nature of the mind, and this is why the empty nature of the mind is buddha nature. Just as one who is of regal descent can become a king, likewise we who belong to the ancestry of the buddhas can in turn become buddhas. It is good for us to become acquainted with teachings so as to develop clarity with regards to this point, but without foundations it will be difficult to understand.

However, even a buddha cannot benefit all the various beings in a short time. Someone who owns a shop can try to make a little profit every day but will have earned enough money to reinvest only after several years.

Previously, we talked about the perfection of generosity, and now we will discuss the next part of the text, the perfection of moral discipline. Moral discipline means the determination to refrain from causing harm to anyone. This should be understood not as an effort on our part to prevent all beings from causing harm to one another, but instead as the maximum development of this attitude in our own minds. Consequently, this entails restraint from negative actions of the body such as killing, taking what does not belong to us, and having sexual relations if one is a monk or indulging in sexual misconduct or adultery if one is a layperson.

There is a difference between simply non-killing and the resolve not to kill. In the first case, not having a particular motivation, we will not produce positive or negative karma, whereas if we refrain from taking life after having resolved not to do so, we create virtuous karma.

Similarly, in terms of the negative actions of mind and speech, if we resolve not to crave other people's possessions, even if there is no chance of obtaining them, we create a positive imprint in our minds. And if we eradicate malevolence, we will gain from it whether or not we actually have the opportunity to harm others.

When the Buddha was asked about mental discipline, he replied, "Mental discipline is the resolve to refrain from negative actions." This is not a difficult method to actualize. It can be put into practice even in our daily lives. Neglecting it and going in search of more complicated methods is chasing after illusions—if we know the secret of the Dharma, we will see that it is very simple.

There is a difference between one who refrains from negative actions, follows the spiritual path, and goes to the seaside and enjoys himself, and one who stays in his room for an hour without generating that same resolve. The first attitude is far better!

Going to work while respecting the Dharma, we gain the double benefit of generating positive karma and earning money as well. When working in a factory, we can accumulate merit by being committed to our work and thinking that in this way we also benefit our bosses.

Therefore, even while at work we can practice the perfections of generosity and morality, and if we endure the toil we are also practicing the perfection of patience. In this way, thanks to our positive motivation, we accumulate merit as well as money. If, however, we do our job solely for profit, it will only be hard work.

The objects of our hatred are as unlimited as space, and it is impossible to destroy them all, but if we eliminate hatred from our minds through transforming them, it is equal to destroying all external obstacles.

To change all beings is impossible, but if we limit ourselves to transforming our own minds, it will be easier and moreover we will have solved the problem. [12]

If we think that we can protect our feet from getting cut by covering the entire surface of the earth, we will never find enough leather or carpets to do so. If, however, we find enough leather to cover our feet, we will be equally protected. [13]

In the same way, we cannot control the course of external events, but if we exercise control over our minds, there will be no need to control all the rest. [14]

Two equal actions, whether physical or verbal, are differentiated by the mental motivation accompanying them. In fact, even a single instant of concentration can cause rebirth with the state of Brahma. [15]

If we pray from the depths of our hearts, our prayers become very powerful, whereas if our minds wander, the prayer will be merely a verbal action, and not very effective. The Buddha said, "If you are on retreat or on a fast without a valid motivation, the effect of these actions will be worthless, and it will be the same if you sit in meditation with your mind dwelling on the objects of the senses and of desire." [16]

When meditating or reciting mantras, we must be fully concentrated on the activity, and the mind must not get distracted or fall asleep. Then many results will be gained from it.

Those beings who are not capable of comprehending the secret of the mind, in itself the most meaningful phenomenon, will wander aimlessly in samsara. Such a secret is understanding the emptiness of phenomena. [17]

In order to eliminate our mental afflictions, we must remember what is valid and what is not. Then, we must be constantly aware and keep the mind in check so that we are able to do what is right and abstain from what is wrong. These two mental factors, discriminating alertness and mindfulness, are extremely important in disciplining the mind. Discriminating alertness is the mental factor that is able to judge what the mind is doing at any given moment, and mindfulness is the factor that keeps this observation constant.

While driving, we must be conscious of speed, of the other drivers' behavior, of the road, and generally keep an eye on everything. In the same way, if we want to control the mind, we must be conscious of it moment by moment, and if it has positive intentions we must praise ourselves, whereas if it has negative intentions we must stop and refrain from translating them into action. Other disciplines are of no use if one is not able to control the mind. This is one of the fundamental practices. [18]

We desire happiness and do not want suffering, and since what determines karma is the mind, we must be like sentries who control what the mind produces. Whether we act through the body or through the speech, the main cause and motivating factor at all times is the mind, and this is why it is so important.

If we have a very sensitive wound and find ourselves in a group of people, we will move cautiously so as to avoid being hurt. In the same way, when we are with people, we must pay attention to our minds so that they do not lead us into wrong behavior. If we are so careful with a physical wound, why not be careful with our minds' wounds, which can cause us the enormous suffering of descent into the lower realms? [20]

If we are able to control our mental actions, and if we have developed discriminating alertness, there will be no problem with living in the midst of unruly people or among women, who can become objects of desire even for a monk. Even if he finds himself among them, if he is aware of the body's impermanence and of its impurities, and he knows emptiness and the antidotes to desire, there will be no danger. If he has defeated hatred, he will not be harmed by anyone. [21]

It does not matter if we do not have wealth or honor, if our body is declining, or if we have only a few means of sustenance—it is better to let these things deteriorate than to allow the virtues of the mind to decline. [22]

It does not matter much if we let outer qualities deteriorate, but deterioration is very dangerous with qualities of the mind, particularly bodhichitta.

"I beseech with folded hands those who want to guard their mind," Shantideva says, "to always be vigilant over mindfulness and discriminating alertness!" [23]

Even if our minds possess these characteristics, we must first establish the knowledge of what is correct and what is not. For, just as ordinary sickness weakens the body, which is then unable to do anything useful, so the mind diseased and weakened by ignorance will decrease in energy and will not be able to produce anything of value. [24]

If we lack mindfulness, whatever action we undertake or whatever we meditate upon will be like pouring water into a leaking vase—nothing will be retained in our memory and all will have been in vain. [25]

Even if there are those who have much intelligence, faith, and enthusiastic perseverance, if they lack mindfulness, they will only accumulate negative karma and make mistakes. [26]

Without discriminating alertness, following the decline of our mindfulness, our mental afflictions will steal all merit away from us like thieves, and we will proceed into our next lives empty-handed. [27]

Here's an example. When we have accumulated merit through virtuous deeds, hatred could arise due to our mental afflictions and lack of awareness, and thus destroy that positive karma. But if mindfulness is there, we can detect hatred as it arises and stop it, and thus preserve the merit we have previously gained.

Our mental afflictions are like a gang of thieves—they will pursue us, waiting for the opportunity to steal our virtue, and they will find it, since we lack discriminating alertness. In this way we will end up in the lower realms in our next lives. [28]

In everyday life, too, our enemies are constantly lying in ambush, ready to strike us. In the same way, our mental afflictions are ready to catch us unaware so that they can lead us to do what they want, which is to perform nonvirtuous actions. If we want to control the mind, we must perform only meritorious actions without allowing mindfulness to leave the doorway of the mind. Even if this does happen, we must immediately recognize the situation and bring the mind back. For example, if we perform a positive action and realize that we are being diverted from it and are turning it into a negative one, we must recognize this process right away with discriminating alertness and re-establish mindfulness. [29]

In order to maintain this kind of mind successfully, it is better to keep good company, such as that of masters or practitioners, for then we will be afraid of being criticized when we do not behave correctly, and we will have the opportunity to receive instructions from the abbot. [30]

We must therefore at all times remind ourselves of our vows and remember our spiritual masters, feeling ashamed of what they would say to us if we were to transgress our vows. This can help us proceed on the right path. Buddhas and bodhisattvas are omniscient and perceive everything without any hindrance, and consequently we must do what they expect of us. We must always be mindful of the fact that positive karma brings happiness and negative karma brings suffering. If we have developed a sense of shame for wrong deeds and a sense of respect for our teachers, we will perform no evil deeds, and recollection of the Buddha will often occur. [32]

What happens to our karma when, thanks to discriminating alertness, we see hatred arising and stop it? If we are able to block hatred, which, among the ten types of negative karmas is among those produced by the mind through malevolence, then we prevent suffering from being generated in our mind. This is called the discipline of abstaining from malevolence.

Ours is the best condition for the practice of the Dharma, and we must therefore constantly create the causes for obtaining precious human rebirths in the future by deciding not to perform negative actions, not giving in to the temptation of killing, stealing, committing adultery, and so forth, and by observing ethical discipline effectively.

Human beings at times have difficulty in finding the means of survival, and in this situation practicing the Dharma is also difficult. Chandrakirti said that beings' happiness is connected to their various possessions, and that in order to obtain these things we must create their causes through practicing generosity. Nagarjuna said that practicing generosity yields the karmic result (in a human rebirth) of riches and morality.

Making offerings to the Three Jewels and to sentient beings are practices of generosity. If we practice moral discipline we will obtain a precious human rebirth in which we will be able to hear the teachings and follow the Dharma. If we practice generosity in addition to this, we will not have problems of sustenance. Also, in order to obtain a divine rebirth, we must practice both morality and generosity, both of which are needed in order to reach the final goal.

The practice of the six paramitas can produce various results, depending on the motivation. If we practice them in order to avoid lower rebirths or to reach nirvana, we will obtain only that. If, instead, we practice them in order to obtain the state of buddha, this will be the result, and it is the best result. Depending on the motivation, the same practice can produce different results.

We must meditate on the various types of suffering and realize that even the better forms of life are nothing but a succession of these sufferings, and consequently renounce samsara. It is the same for those who want to reach nirvana and for those who want to attain enlightenment. But while the concern of the first type of person is to reach liberation only for himself, the other, having realized that all beings suffer and that the motivation of wishing to reach nirvana is egotistical, wishes liberation for every being.

Just as a mother who has much love and compassion for her children will always desire their well-being and wish that they may not suffer, we too must try to develop this same attitude toward our parents, siblings, relatives, friends, and gradually even people toward whom we feel indifference and those who have harmed us—in other words, all beings.

It is very important to have compassion, because compassion is the seed, the fundamental cause, of the state of a buddha, of every happiness characteristic to that state, and of bodhichitta. Compassion is also the circumstantial cause that prompts a bodhisattva to practice. Although he must strive in many ways in order to attain enlightenment, he is spurred on by the concern he feels for all beings. The arhats of the Hinayana path remain in samadhi for eons, enjoying this blissful state without concern for others, whereas buddhas do not cease to benefit others even for a single moment. Compassion differentiates the two.

If we have compassion, we will help others and we will not harm them. Even if we do not actually benefit them, if the desire and aspiration to do so are present, we will possess the essence of the Dharma. For all these reasons we consider bodhichitta to be precious.

If a person serving the government possesses compassion, he will try to perform only for the good of the nation, and there will be no reason for others to complain. One never speaks evil of those who possess such an attitude, but we consider those without it to be bad. Whether or not we are religious, if our minds are concerned with alleviating the suffering of others, people will say good things about us, and even dogs, cats, wild animals, and birds will love us. Children love their mother whether she is young or old, beautiful or not so beautiful, because she is always compassionate.

We have already discussed that it is possible for all beings to attain buddhahood and that it is also possible for a buddha to benefit all beings. Why haven't we reached this state yet? The reason is that we have not generated compassion. Therefore we must strive to obtain it through developing two mental attitudes. The first attitude that we must develop is the understanding that all beings suffer. However, this alone is not enough—in fact, we already possess this attitude on a rational level. In addition to this, we must strive to develop the attitude of seeing all beings as our mothers, and therefore perceive them as dear to us, wish that they do not suffer, and generate bodhichitta.

If our friends are sick we suffer for them, but if we hear of ill people that we are not acquainted with we do not feel anything at all. We might even feel joy at the pain and suffering of an enemy. Why is it that, although the condition of these three types of people is one and the same, there is a difference in our response to them? The reason is that we are unable to see them as equal.

We must consider our enemies in the same way that we consider our loved ones, and the same applies to strangers, since all of them have benefited us and have been our mothers many times in former lives, and since our past lives are numberless. If we want to get an idea of their number, we can reflect on the fact that every person we see corresponds to a single lifetime—including not only the people present here, but the entire world population. We can also consider that they are like the number of drops in the ocean, or even more than that. Furthermore, we are unable to determine the first moment of our existence in our minds, because it arose from time without beginning. Since we cannot count our former lives and since the beings in the universe are countless, we can say that every being has no doubt been our mother—not just once, but several times. Let us consider the kindness of the mother we have in our current lifetime, and think about the many worries she has endured for our sake, and then let us extend our reflection to the kindness all beings have shown us in the past.

Both our mothers in this life and our mothers of former lives have behaved with so much kindness. We must be grateful to them and try to repay them. Reflecting in this way, we will feel that everyone we meet has been our mother and it will be natural to have a loving attitude toward each person.

If one of our hands is wounded, we do not neglect it, but try to heal it. In the same way, we must care for all beings as we do ourselves, without discriminating, since they all possess the same aspiration to reach happiness and avoid suffering.

Normally if someone benefits us, we perceive him as a friend; if he does not relate to us, we feel indifferent toward him; and if he harms us, we perceive him as an enemy. However, the correct attitude is to place all three at the same level. Differentiating between the three is wrong since it is not founded on logical reasons.

It is unlikely that a mother would discriminate among her children, desiring happiness for some and unhappiness for others. Nor should a doctor be partial, wishing to cure only a few among a hundred patients. Likewise a head of state should not favor a particular social class at the expense of another but instead should be concerned for the welfare of the entire population. This equanimity is the basis for love and compassion, which then leads to the generation of the extraordinary attitude of wanting to personally liberate all beings.

Among those who seek a solution to suffering through the spiritual path, the attitude of those who strive to do this only for their own benefit is very limited and reveals a narrow mind. On the other hand, the motivation of those who seek liberation for the sake of others is a great motivation. These teachings are Mahayana teachings, and a Mahayana follower is one who is concerned about all beings. The aim of the Hinayanists is the attainment of nirvana, whereas the aim of the Mahayanists is complete enlightenment. The foundation of the practices of the latter path is compassion. Since we have not yet developed compassion, we cannot call ourselves Mahayanists. There is a big difference between those who wish to be on the Mahayana path and those who are truly on it. We can think of ourselves as Mahayanists only from the moment we generate the mind of bodhichitta.

The aspiration that others may attain the happiness they desire is typical of the Mahayana practitioner, and so if someone who has such an aspiration finds himself working in public office, he will work gladly and with great energy. If he is a teacher, this aspiration will serve him better than if he did not possess it. If he is a doctor, he will perform his duty responsibly, whether or not he earns money. And if he is a nurse, he will perform his work with more care and attention. Every person who is full of compassion will be able to give his very best, become more dignified, feel better about himself, and be loved by everyone. The goodness a person possesses cannot be found in his clothes or his wealth, but dwells in his heart.

However, generating bodhichitta alone is not enough. It is also necessary to strive in the practices of the three aspects of the bodhisattva's discipline:

avoiding any negative action, practicing virtue, and *benefiting others.* The text is now considering the first aspect.

We must analyze the motivation behind each action we are about to perform. If the motivation is hatred, we must immediately eradicate it. However, we should support the positive mind, and not allow it to be tainted by mental afflictions. [34]

As we walk to our destination, we must not allow the mind to wander in all directions, but instead keep it focused on an appropriate object such as the Three Jewels or sentient beings. We must look ahead of us at a meter's distance, proceeding with a resolute mind. [35]

Naturally, if we are keeping mindful while driving, we should not look ahead at a meter's distance, or else we will end up crashing into another car!

We might feel tired after a while, so we should rest our gaze around us in order to relax. If we see someone, we should not keep our concentration but instead behave normally, greeting that person and talking to him. When walking in this fashion, we should have a smiling face and refrain from looking at others with hostility, and when meeting a layperson we should tell him about the Dharma. [36]

It does not happen in the West, but in Tibet when someone was coming from afar one would invite him home, offer something, and engage in conversation with him.

When walking, we should be aware in order to avoid dangers, and, gathering our possessions after a stop, we should look carefully around so that nothing is left behind. [37]

This advice was given to bodhisattvas who traveled carrying their possessions, since in those days there were no buses, cars, or trains. All the same, we should remember not to leave anything behind when getting off a train!

When walking on a path we should make certain that there is no danger anywhere and then proceed. We must be aware at all times that our actions of body, speech, and mind are done for the welfare of all beings. [38]

When we leave for a particular destination we take all the things that might be useful with us. In the same way, for every action we wish to perform, we must think of the way to do it and then be aware of every phase until we have brought it to completion. [39]

Our mind is compared to a crazed and wild elephant—it must be controlled and tied with the rope of mindfulness, so as not to cause any harm. [40]

When we train in concentration, we must keep the mind fixed on the object. We then maintain this concentration constantly using mindfulness, and subsequently keep the mind from wandering through discriminating alertness. [41]

When training our minds in concentration, we must use the two important factors of mindfulness and discriminating alertness. The mind chooses the object on which to concentrate, mindfulness maintains concentration, and alertness, like a policeman, checks that we maintain that concentration. If the mind is distracted or sleepy, the mental factor of alertness brings our mental attention back to the object of concentration.

In a dangerous situation, or if we are performing rituals or ceremonies, it is possible to relax our concentration.

Morality is not more important than the practice of generosity. [42]

A monk is forbidden to touch a woman because of his vows, but if a woman is, for example, drowning, he must save her. This is a form of generosity. It is as if he were offering life to this woman, and while he is doing this he can relax the practice of moral discipline. At times, when involved in a virtuous action, it is not possible to apply both types of practice at the same time. So we commit ourselves to the practice with more affinity to the action we have decided to perform. In the particular case of the drowning woman and the monk who saves her, since there is no time to think about whether to observe the discipline of morality, the practitioner must act first and resume the interrupted practice later.

It can happen that we meditate on impermanence, and that at some point the thought arises that it is better to meditate on bodhichitta instead. Then we change again and meditate on emptiness and on other subjects. It is not important to establish what is better, but we should dedicate the necessary time to the practice of a chosen subject, moving from one to the other only after having attained some results from the previous meditation. Otherwise we will not succeed in achieving anything in any of our meditations. [43]

Meditating on the path, gradually we familiarize ourselves with the thoughts of future lives, total liberation, and bodhichitta. But even if the explanations of the entire path are available to us, we must begin with the meditation that is the most suitable for our minds. Studying the Dharma, we will improve our thinking. If we realize that the mind is prey to mental afflictions and is giving in to them, we must then apply the specific antidotes. [44]

It is no good spending time reading novels, following idle talk, or listening to songs and entertainment. If we do participate in these things, we should not do so with attachment. [45]

We must also interrupt any useless harmful activity toward other beings as soon as we become aware of it—for example, killing worms while digging the earth. [46]

When we want to go somewhere or speak to someone, we must examine our motivation and act only if it is positive. If it is influenced by hatred or attachment, we must not proceed. [47]

A tree is not influenced by hatred or attachment; it is simply rooted in the soil. It simply exists, and we should do the same. [48]

In the same way, when our minds are distracted, wish to mock others, are proud and consider others inferior, wish to cheat others, are eager to be praised, or desire to criticize others, recognize these mental afflictions and remain still and unshaken, like a tree. [50]

Whenever we desire gain, fame, and honor or wish to be served, recognize these defects and remain like a tree. [51]

When our desire to work for others wanes, or when we are tempted to say only what creates gain for us, we must remain like a tree. [52]

When we do not tolerate others' opinions or are lazy in our virtue or driven to engage in senseless talk, we must remain like a tree. [53]

If mental afflictions push the mind toward meaningless striving, we must apply the appropriate antidotes. Just like a hero defeats a cowardly foe, we must lean on these antidotes in order to be victorious. [54]

It is necessary to possess a good understanding of the teachings, positive faith, and delight and enthusiasm for the meritorious actions we are about to perform, thinking of their usefulness. We must be kind, respectful, polite, and peaceful toward others, persevering in our effort to make them happy. [55]

We should not refrain from doing good for someone who makes himself useful, even if someone else suffers jealousy as a result. We should reflect that his jealousy is a mental affliction, and continue with our good deed. In the same way, we must not react if someone becomes angry with us but instead respond with compassion, since that person is under the influence of mental afflictions, and we should never create the opportunity to fall prey to them ourselves. [56]

If we create positive karma, we should not feel proud of it, because this feeling too is a mental affliction that defeats us, and we must prevent it from arising. We must not think that we are the only ones who perform good deeds, or that we are doing something "truly" good that "really" exists. [57]

Having understood the value of our precious human rebirth, the type of existence that allows us to reach all objectives, we must, motivated by this certainty, create positive karma. [58]

So far we have explained the first type of practice: the practice of abstaining from creating negative karma through stealing, killing, committing adultery, and so forth.

The second group of disciplines for a bodhisattva refers to the accumulation of positive karma and the purification of the negative karma already accumulated. Since it is not possible to apply ourselves to the first practice if we have attachment to the physical body, we must begin by eradicating this mental affliction. In Tibet, when a person died, the body was taken to the mountains and offered to the birds, and the bones would be ground and mixed with barley flour and given to animals. Animals dying in the mountains are also eaten by birds.

If, once we are dead, our minds do not feel aversion for the vultures, greedy for flesh, who drag and toss about our bodies, why are we so hostile to those who harm those same bodies now? [59]

There is no reason that we should be attached to our physical bodies, and furthermore, this attachment causes suffering. We might protest that we should take care of our bodies because they are useful to us, but we think this only because we are incapable of reflecting correctly, otherwise we would know that we are slaves to our bodies. In spite of our attachment to the body, we still have to leave it at the moment of death, when it will be of little help to us. Another possible protest is that we have been with this body for a long time and casting away our attachment is not an easy thing to do.

Our ignorant minds establish the existence of an "I" on the basis of the body, considering it to be its physical expression and not what it really is—an assemblage of impurities. It is for this reason that attachment to the body arises, rather than attachment to a piece of wood, which is cleaner and has more qualities. [61]

Thinking of our bodies as bags of rubbish, we can then imagine skinning them, seeing what is underneath, and removing pieces of flesh and bone. We will discover that there is nothing there worth being attached to, and that it is only because of our ignorance that we consider our bodies pure.

Having reflected in this way, we will discover that there is no essence in the body to which we can cling, and that it is an aggregation of various impurities, not even good enough to be drunk or eaten—for blood and intestines cannot be used for these purposes. Why then do we care for it so much? [65]

Perhaps we wish to protect and save this body for the feast of vultures, jackals, and worms?

Thanks to this newly developed understanding, we must use our bodies only to accumulate positive karma, which will be useful to us in the future. [66]

While practicing Dharma, we need a convenient means to eliminate suffering, and the body is precisely that. Therefore we need to take good care of it without attachment. The body can be a thousand times more useful than the money that we hoard jealously, and the need to protect it is even greater.

This physical form, characteristic of a human rebirth, is compared to a wish-fulfilling gem because it allows us to attain various aims: liberation from lower rebirths, nirvana, and supreme enlightenment. We might not be able to do everything right now, but we must do our best to practice what we can. Even if we cannot succeed in eliminating all the types of suffering that we have discussed, we must begin with those within our reach, and pray that in the future we might be able to eliminate the others as well. We must first ascertain what the various types of suffering are, discovering them for ourselves or learning of them from others, and then we must gradually try to eliminate them without feeling discouraged.

If someone has an enemy but is strong and brave himself, he can succeed in defeating that enemy. We should feel the same on the spiritual path, and face all the problems we encounter in life squarely. We speak of suffering only in order to find the methods to eliminate it. A doctor does not send his patient to have examinations, x-rays, and analysis in order to remind him of his physical problems and make him feel depressed. On the contrary, the doctor wishes to learn everything about his illness so that he can find a remedy.

When the Tibetans reached India, many were seriously ill and the Indian doctors advised them to undergo x-ray examinations, but they did not want to because they did not understand their importance. I myself refused several times, until one day I was forcibly taken. The x-ray technician was not there, and I was happy about it, as no one had explained to me that x-rays were nothing but a means to diagnose an illness!

Westerners behave in the same way when they are told about suffering. Not understanding that suffering is explained in order to encourage us to find a solution, they react negatively. If we know suffering, we can eliminate it with the methods learned through the Dharma, which therefore must be considered an inestimable treasure. If we are not able to do that, it is because we did not strive to do so in the correct way.

The teachings are applicable to our lives, and right now we can begin with those that are within our reach. With regards to knowledge, we must learn all methods, but as far as practice goes, we must work with those that we can manage—a supermarket has many items, but we buy only those that are necessary.

We must be skillful when receiving the teachings. In Dharma practice there are many possible things to do, but we should choose those that we can practice effectively right now, without being intimidated by the entire scope. It is difficult to know the essential points of the Dharma in a few days. First we must dedicate ourselves to listening, then to studying and reflection, and only afterward engage in meditation.

The proactive system of diminishing suffering by eliminating its causes is a method that can be used not only within the spiritual domain but in the material world as well. Shantideva wrote that although we desire happiness, we behave as if it were our enemy! How is this possible? This happens because we do not create positive karma or, even if we do create it, we then proceed to obliterate it through hatred and negative mental factors, in the same way hail destroys the harvest. We must begin by accumulating the causes of happiness and then not allow any space for negative states of mind such as anger or wrong views to arise, so that the positive karma we create is not destroyed and we may enjoy its outcome.

If we plant the seed of a fruit tree, taking good care to provide all the necessary conditions that will aid its growth, such as fertilizer, water, and soil, even if we might later decide that we do not want it anymore, this will not prevent its growth. If we create positive karma and do not destroy it, even if we do not wish to experience the happiness that it will bring, this desire—the request "May I not experience happiness"—will not prevent positive karma from bearing fruit and allowing us to have a taste of that happiness. At present, having obtained a human rebirth, we are enjoying its privileges and comforts, whereas dogs and animals in general cannot do so since they have not created its causes, regardless of what they are doing now or what they might do in the future.

A person who lives in an affluent family enjoys the effects of causes he has created in some former life, but one who is born into a poor family, in spite of having a human rebirth, does not have the advantages of wealth, since he has not created its causes.

If you take two people who attended the same school and the same classes and received the same final grades, it might happen that one lands a good job and the other does not. This is because the former created its causes whereas the latter did not accumulate enough positive karma.

Observing traders and businessmen investing their money, we will notice that some will make a profit whereas others will only pile up enormous losses—this is due to different causes created in former lives. Furthermore, for some people it is extremely easy to find friends and favorable situations, while others find only hostile environments and unfriendly people who harm them.

For all these reasons it is important to study the Dharma, and this is why we have come here through considerable effort. Our resolve will bring results. A person who has learned the various aspects of the Dharma must subsequently apply them in order to be called a spiritual practitioner. If he does not apply them, in spite of having excellent knowledge, he is like someone who knows medical science but does not take the medicine necessary to cure his illness. Knowledge alone will be useless to eliminate it.

The difference between a religious and a non-religious person is that the former considers future lives to be more important than the present one. Because of this conviction, he will create positive karma. We can examine our own attitude to ascertain if we are religious.

When we plant corn, the main objective is to produce grain, but in addition there will be other parts of the plant that we can use in various ways. In the tantric texts it is said that a person who accumulates positive karma for future lives is able to enjoy happiness in this life as well.

If we think of others as more important than ourselves, we can consider ourselves Mahayana practitioners. If we think future lives are more important than the current one, it makes no difference whether we are ordained or lay—we can call ourselves spiritual practitioners. And finally, if we consider future lives more important but continue to create more negative than positive karma, we must pray that in the future the opposite might become possible for us.

If we recognize these three attitudes in ourselves we are truly good people, noble and praiseworthy, people who can be admired by others. When we say someone is "good," we are not referring to his healthy body, his nice clothes, or how cultured he is; the difference between a good person and one who is not is in the quality of the mind. We would all be happy to become such people, but we must know how—we must understand the importance of studying the Dharma!

In Tibet there were three great monasteries—Sera, Drepung, and Ganden—renowned for the profound level of Dharma studies that they encompassed. Understanding this, many Western people recognize their importance. The Chinese people, however, destroyed many Tibetan monasteries, ignorant of the activities going on there. They considered the monks social parasites and considered their lifestyles harmful. If they knew that I were giving these teachings, they would think that I am cheating people! Despite this, even the Chinese must admit that others are more important than oneself, since others are so much greater in number. A person who understands that this is the essence of the Dharma will appreciate it and try to study it. The Chinese can be excused for their behavior because of their ignorance. If they had known that the Dharma teaches that an individual should have more respect for others than for oneself, they would not have tried to destroy the Dharma but rather would have sought to protect it.

These things have been said in order to give you some idea about the subject matter, but the main point is to change our egoistic attitudes, eliminate all mental afflictions, and destroy their root causes—ignorance, attachment, and hatred.

Attachment to the body derives from a wrong view based on the fact that we consider it to be clean and desirable. However, once we have understood its real nature, this attachment will fall away.

How does attachment to the body arise? The external appearance of the body is skin, so let us try to understand what kind of skin creates such strong attachment. Is it the skin on our hands, on our back, on our face? Our body has a bone structure, and these bones are affixed to internal and external layers of muscle and skin, but which of these creates attachment? Which bone do we favor—a bone in our head, in our legs, in our feet, in our chest? Reflecting upon it, we can ascertain that no part of the body attracts us and that there is no valid reason to justify our attachment. In order to eliminate this kind of attachment, we can do this type of meditation, taking ourselves as the object. In the case of attachment to the body of another—of a man for a woman or vice versa—we use that particular body as the object of meditation. At this point, all of the reasons for clinging will fall away.

This is the antidote used to eliminate attachment to the body. However, we must continue to take good care of our bodies, just as we do the garbage bags toward which we do not cherish any attraction, but that we buy and use since they are useful to us.

If we think that having a lot of attachment is wrong but that we could perhaps afford to have a little of it, let us state right away that we should not have any, not even a tiny bit!

The teachings of Buddha are truly vast—there are 108 volumes of discourses recorded in the Kangyur alone, and in the *Bodhicharyavatara* Shantideva has condensed them, extracting from them this small text that I am now commenting upon.

Next, the disadvantages of having attachment for the body are explained. If, in spite of everything, you continue to dedicate a large part of your time to the care of this body, what will you do when death comes and snatches it away and gives it to the birds and dogs? At that moment you will be unable to do anything, or protect it from this destiny in any way. [67]

Like a servant who leaves us when we can no longer pay him, this body which has been given so much care and treated as the most precious thing will abandon us, even if we beg it to stay! Why then be so attached to it? [68]

What we must do is use this body in the best way, just like the owner of a factory who demands that his staff performs adequately in exchange for their salary. Those who endeavor according to his expectations will be provided with incentives—perhaps an extra vacation—and he will threaten to reduce the salaries of those who do not. In the same way, if our bodies behave well and perform their function of supporting the practice of Dharma, we will praise them, nourish them, clothe them, and give them all the small things they desire. Furthermore, we should offer ourselves the advice we usually give others.

At night, examining whether we have used our day correctly, it would be good to praise ourselves if we have done so, and reproach ourselves if the opposite is true.

We pay wages to our employees and then somehow use their expertise; and from our bodies, too, which we clothe and nourish, we should elicit a gain. And if, rather than carrying out their duty and performing virtuous deeds, they persist in laziness and wrongdoing, then we should not give them anything. [69]

The practice of Dharma, aimed at achieving permanent happiness and the possibility of attaining buddhahood, is based on this physical body, which is therefore important. Shantideva compares it to a ship we use to cross the ocean of suffering and reach the shore beyond. In spite of the body's crucial role in acquiring definitive happiness, we should not desire to possess a coarse body in our next rebirth, as this is a cause of suffering. Instead, we should strive to create the causes for acquiring more subtle forms, which do not produce suffering. The type of bodies that we have are the basis of suffering and we should not, therefore, be too pleased with them.

Arhats, who have attained the ultimate realization of the Hinayana path, have obtained their bodies because of their direct perception of emptiness and their elimination of the mental afflictions. Unlike buddhas, they possess still the imprints of ignorance, which are not a cause of suffering.

The bodies of bodhisattvas derive from their compassion and their prayers, and unlike ours they do not create new causes for suffering.

The body of a buddha, finally, is of a mental nature. We may think, "But if a physical body is no longer present, how can we possibly exist?" My suggestion is not to worry about this, because we will have other, better forms on which to base our existence in the future. At present our concern is to set ourselves free from a coarse body. When we obtain a subtler one, which will not be a cause of suffering, it will no longer be necessary to worry about ridding ourselves of it.

We should think of our bodies as boats, as simple vehicles for coming and going, and transform them into wish-fulfilling gems for the benefit of others. [70]

In order to benefit others, we need to free ourselves from the control of our afflictions. When we are under the influence of anger, we speak the first words that come to mind, throw anything that happens to be within our reach, and are totally beside ourselves and out of control. It is the same when we are under the influence of attachment. It is therefore necessary to free ourselves from both of these afflictions.

We must always be aware of our state of mind, meet others with a smiling face, offer advice and friendship, and instill a sense of trust in people so that they become familiar with us and are able to confide in and feel friendly toward us. [71]

We should not act inconsiderately, moving objects noisily or opening doors violently, but instead be glad in humility. [72]

When we go to someone's house it is good to be polite and kind rather than being like a policeman who demands to know everything and makes his authority known! The stork, the cat, and the thief move silently and carefully, and we should do the same. [73]

We feel happy when we receive benefits from others because we have gained something, whereas a bodhisattva overflows with gratitude when he can make himself useful. We should be guides, give advice to those who wish to practice the Dharma, and offer our help, and if we see someone who behaves in this way we should praise that person, respect him, and consider him our master. We should act as if we are everyone's pupil and disciple, gladly and with gratitude accepting any good advice we are given and not behaving as if we know better. [74]

We should welcome anything that is said to us with words such as "Thank you," "Well said," "Welcome," and so on.

While praising people who perform good deeds and help others, our hearts should be glad for their altruistic qualities. If we hear someone being praised, we should not point out that person's defects but instead join in the praise, though not necessarily in his presence. In fact, it is better to do so when he is not there so that we do not cause pride to arise in his mind. [75]

For example, if we hear that Losang Donden is good we should praise him too, but we should not chime in when he is criticized!

If someone enumerates our good qualities, whether we possess them or not, we should think that those who delight in others' accomplishments are truly excellent people. [76]

Everything we do must be for the sake of other people's joy, and even if it costs us money, it is worth it! When we do something useful for someone, he will not be envious of us, because people are envious only toward those they do not like. If we benefit someone, he or she will like us.

We should feel glad and rejoice when someone is engaged in spiritual practice. [77]

Since we are doing all we can for the good of others, we will obtain what we desire effortlessly—when we act positively, someone will always be there to ask us whether we need anything, and in our future lives too we will surely experience happiness.

A few days ago, some people who live nearby invited me over for tea. A woman named Carla was their guest, and they were all very happy with her because she was helpful and kind to them. Their positive judgment was the result of Carla's correct behavior. If she had been angry or acted rudely, they would not have been pleased to have her in their home. Those same people observed, "You are Buddhists and we are Christians, but now we realize that Buddhists after all are not so different from Christians."

Acting under the influence of hatred, attachment, and ignorance, we will make others and ourselves unhappy. [78]

When talking to others our words should be understandable, sensible, and devoid of negative motivation; we should not assail them by speaking of personal matters, because that would tire them. [79]

When we look at someone, we should think that it is thanks to this person that we will attain buddhahood, and therefore generate a feeling of openness and love toward him. [80]

We should not perform a great number of virtuous deeds for a short time and then abandon everything.

There are three "merit fields," or sources of merit and wisdom, and therefore three objects of our virtuous actions: *the objects of refuge,* which constitute "the excellent and superior field," *parents and teachers,* which constitute "the field of benefit," and *sentient beings,* which constitute "the field of suffering," particularly when we consider those who are in need or ill.

We must make offerings, perform good deeds, and extend our help to these three fields. [81]

By caring for our parents, who have benefited us and showered us with kindness, we will gain great merit. This will also be the case if we help those who suffer just because they need our help. When we offer donations in order to build a hospital or improve the conditions of an already existing facility, we do so bearing in mind that it is a beneficial institution designed for those who are ill. When we support a school, we reflect on the fact that it will be useful for those who are deprived of knowledge. Helping monks is also an extremely meritorious practice because they are "sources of quality."

What if you strive to help someone who then thinks that your intervention was of no help? Was your deed negative or positive? If your intention was to do good, then it is valid, and if that person did not understand it, you are not the cause of his suffering. Even if he does not comprehend that yours was a positive action, the fact that you performed it benefits him and does not harm him in any way, so it is correct to act in this way.

In other instances, if we continue to help someone but our help is then used for something that is not useful, we should ask ourselves whether our actions were truly beneficial. Better still, we should act in such a way that he might learn how to behave responsibly.

In the practice of the six perfections and in Dharma practice in general, we must make progress day by day, month by month, and we must refrain from betraying a great virtue for a small merit! We would not spend ten dollars in order to buy one dollar; in the same way, we should not neglect a great virtuous action in order to perform a small one. It is positive, however, to avoid doing a small virtue in order to perform a greater one. For example, it is senseless to neglect the welfare of a hundred people in favor of one.

For the happiness of future lives it is good not to be concerned about the present life, and it is not appropriate to neglect the happiness of future lives in pursuit of it in this one. For the welfare of others we must renounce our own welfare, and in order to realize our own, we must not neglect the welfare of others. [83]

A Mahayana follower acts for the good of others, so if we consider ourselves to be practitioners of this spiritual path we must do the same, forgetting our own interest.

The ten negative karmas, or the ten paths of nonvirtue, are always forbidden to the followers of the Hinayana path, the *pratyekabuddha* and *shravaka*, whereas a bodhisattva is allowed to engage in the three of body and the four of speech if they procure benefit for others. [84]

For example, if a bodhisattva knows for certain that someone intends to kill a hundred people, he can kill that person—naturally, if there are no other means to stop him—since there is no way to avoid the fact that the person determined to carry out a massacre will accumulate much negative karma and that many people will suffer and lose their lives.

If the opportunity arises, we must share our food with beings (such as animals who have fallen into the lower realms), with those who are in need, and with spiritual practitioners. As for ourselves, we should eat only what is necessary for our sustenance, and only two-thirds of the stomach's capacity. According to the practice of generosity, a monk must give all that he has except the three robes, and if he has a spare one, he should give that away too. [85]

Since we must give away everything, if someone were to come up to us and ask for our bodies, we should analyze whether there is an important reason for giving it. If there is not, we should refuse. Instead of donating our bodies for a small reason, we should use them to practice the Dharma, by which we can attain buddhahood and be of benefit to all beings, helping them attain the happiness they desire and eliminate the suffering they do not want. [86]

It has been said that this body is the basis of all suffering. If, however, we use it for practicing the Dharma with the aim of attaining complete liberation for the sake of all beings, it will be of immense service. It has also been said that the body is like an enemy, since like an enemy it causes us to be unhappy. If, however, we succeed in using it for a great purpose, then we transform it into a friend, because as long as we have these human bodies we are able to eliminate negative karma and create positive karma.

There are instances in which a bodhisattva can donate parts of his body or even his entire body, but this can be done only when the bodhisattva has reached the necessary level of maturity. We must not practice generosity with our bodies if we are not yet able to tolerate the suffering that will arise from such an act and if we do not yet harbor authentic compassion toward the particular being to whom we wish to make this type of offering.

On the other hand, if our mental development is so advanced that we are able to rejoice mentally in spite of physical pain, and if we have compassion and we will not regret it, we can perform this type of action.

When there is no trace of greed left within us and when we have accumulated great merit, then we can offer even our very lives! [87]

There are four types of generosity: the generosity *of the Dharma,* the generosity *of offering material objects,* the generosity *of giving love,* and the generosity *of protecting from fear,* or protecting life.

In relation to whom should we practice the generosity of teaching Dharma? Not in relation to those who are disrespectful toward it. We should not teach the Dharma to someone who wears a hat, unless that person is ill, or to someone who holds an umbrella, a stick, or a weapon. We should not teach the Dharma to someone who is asleep, or has something over his face, or to someone who is lying down or wants to relax. [88]

All this means is that we should not teach the Dharma to those who do not have respect for or interest in it. We should also not teach the Dharma to those who are sitting on chairs while everybody else is sitting on the floor, unless they are elderly, or people who cannot sit cross-legged.

It is good to refrain from giving advanced teachings to someone who is not intelligent enough, because we could confuse him. Also, a fully ordained monk must not teach a woman who is alone or unaccompanied by a man. We must not discriminate among the teachings by saying that some are Mahayana and others Hinayana and on this basis have more respect for the higher teachings and less for those we consider inferior. Instead we must have the same respect for all. [89]

We must not give lower teachings to people endowed with great ability. For example, we should not give Hinayana teachings to someone who possesses a Mahayana aptitude, but rather we must give teachings according to the inclination of each individual.

We must never abandon the moral discipline of abstaining from non-virtuous actions, thinking that we will be able to purify them later through the recitation of mantras. [90]

At times bodhisattvas manifest as ministers, heads of state, and so on in order to prevent beings from committing negative karma and keep moral discipline. Through their position, they rule through laws that forbid murder, robbery, and so forth, by which means they practice the Dharma and encourage others to practice it.

The teachings belonging to the Vinaya Pitaka must be observed by a bodhisattva too, and even if he is a layperson, he must avoid what might cause loss of faith or loss of respect in others.

Referring to the example in the next stanza of the text, a twig used as a toothbrush should be covered with earth when thrown away, and the same must be done with saliva when spitting. This is irrelevant in the West since here you already have the good habit of using a paper tissue, which is then thrown into a basket.

We must not urinate and so forth in water or on dry land used by others, or in clean places. Besides being unhygienic, this can also upset the "lords of the places," the beings who rule over those areas. [91]

We should not eat noisily, or with our mouths wide open, or fill them up to the point where we cannot move our tongues. In the West this does not apply, since usually people eat with a certain dignity, but with Tibetans it is different! In monasteries, discipline demands that we eat without making any noise, and this is how the monks are trained. We should not eat with an open mouth or chew in an inappropriate manner. We should not be like cows chewing grass!

Another thing we should not do when receiving teachings is sit with our legs outstretched, although we can relax from time to time if we are not used to sitting cross-legged. Also, we should not rub our hands together. [92]

A bodhisattva, layman, or monk must not ride a horse with another man's wife or sit near her or stay in a room alone with her, so that his behavior does not cause others to lose faith and respect. If we do not know what is appropriate and what is not, we must ask, and having asked, behave accordingly. [93]

People in Tibet used to wash rarely because of the cold and the high altitude, and it was common to have lice, but this was not considered serious or important. In the West, on the other hand, a monk with lice would be judged severely, and he could lose people's respect. In India nobody pays attention to someone who constantly picks his nose, pulling out the mucus, but in the West people consider this highly inappropriate. We should behave in accordance with the customs of the place in which we live and do at all times only what is considered appropriate.

If we wish to call to someone, we must do so in a gentle tone, without clapping or waving our left hand, because this shows lack of respect. If we are asked for road directions, we must indicate the right way respectfully and with the entire hand, not just one finger, since the latter would show lack of respect. [94]

When monks walk on the road, they must not swing their arms wildly or let them simply hang. They should allow a slight movement of the hands, without producing any useless sound. [95]

Why is it necessary to behave in such a controlled way? It is necessary because it helps to maintain discipline.

When we sleep, we should take the position in which the Buddha reached parinirvana—that is, lying on our right sides with the left leg resting on the right, our right hands under our faces with one finger closing the right nostril, one closing the right eye, and one closing the right ear. Then we should arrange our bed sheets properly, and turn our minds to emptiness and bodhichitta and to the fact that we have been able to create positive karma and practice the Dharma, and above all we should think that tomorrow we will be able to do better. [96]

People in Tibet used to go to bed very early and get up very early in the morning, whereas in the West it is just the opposite. A practitioner should awaken in the early hours of the morning, because at that time both mind and body are more refreshed. Those who wish to create positive karma, perform virtuous practices, and meditate will be more successful in the morning and their task will be easy.

If we do not rest, the body weakens, so we should fall asleep with the motivation to protect the body and keep it healthy so that we can use it for the practice of the Dharma. We must also remember the Three Jewels and our master. Now that we have learned this new method, we can begin to practice it. Sleeping in this way will protect us from many hindrances, ensure that there will be less chance of having to meet with obstacles, and help us have good dreams.

Whether or not we believe in a spiritual path, a person who is more interested in others than in himself is considered to have an elevated mind, just as a head of state who is concerned about the welfare of his citizens will be praised, whereas if he is concerned only about his own interests he will be considered an egoist. There is also a difference among people who possess altruistic attitudes. Between one who is concerned solely about his own country's welfare and one who holds the well-being of the whole world dear, the latter will be more respected. In the same way, on the spiritual path a Mahayana practitioner who seeks liberation in order to benefit all beings will be praised more than a follower of the Hinayana path, who seeks liberation for himself alone.

It often happens that some politicians announce their intention of working for the welfare of the entire nation to the voters and that the people, with faith in these promises, vote for them. Once elected, however, the politicians only look after their own interests. Dissatisfaction arises because they are not trying to help others but instead sacrifice the welfare of all in favor of their own gain.

His Holiness the Dalai Lama became the head of the Tibetan people at the age of seventeen, and he has tried ever since to do solely what is beneficial for his people and never for himself. In this way he has never caused any reason for complaint. He receives a token salary from the Tibetan government, and this is enough for him; the donations and offerings he receives are completely devoted to the benefit of others, with whom he is constantly concerned.

We must pray that we might also have an altruistic attitude, since this is useful to others and to ourselves, and for this reason is praised by everyone. The first chapter of the *Bodhicharyavatara* deals with the advantages and benefits derived from such a precious mind. In order to develop this we must purify our negative imprints and accumulate positive ones through the *Seven-Limb Prayer,* as explained in the second and third chapters. Having received the bodhisattva vows, we commit ourselves to the solemn promise not to create any more negative karma and to accumulate positive karma. In this way, we generate the determination to work for the welfare of others, taking good care that such determination does not degenerate, as explained in the fourth chapter. Finally, to check whether we are doing what must be done, we rely on the mental factor of vigilance, which is what the present chapter describes.

Among all the practices that a bodhisattva can do, the most important is the training in disciplining the mind, and each person must strive to practice what has been mentioned here, even if he is not able to practice everything right away. [97]

Negative karma does not require any effort on our part—it accumulates spontaneously in our minds, like dust settling naturally in the house where we live. As we need to clean our homes daily, the same applies to our minds—day by day purifying the negative karma that we create because of our mental afflictions. To do this, we can use *The Sutra of the Three Heaps*. The three heaps are purification, joy, and dedication. Through this brief text, which we recite three times during the day and three times at night, we will be able to purify negative karma. [98]

If we learn this by heart, we can combine it with the six-session guru yoga so that we will be adding the superior bodhisattva motivation to it as well. Entrusting ourselves to the Three Jewels, generating the altruistic mind of bodhichitta, and applying the four opponent powers with firm determination, we will purify our negative karma.

In any situation we must stay vigilant, ensuring that we are practicing what is right and constantly employing mindfulness. [99]

There is nothing a bodhisattva learns that he does not put into practice. As his intention is to benefit all beings, he must know the different methods appropriate to each of them, and having learned them, he does not neglect any of them.

For such a bodhisattva there will never be an occasion upon which he will accumulate negative karma, and he will always produce meritorious karma. [100]

If we wish to help others, learning a foreign language is very useful. We can notice this here and now, seeing that the work of one person is instead performed by three—myself teaching and two other people translating. As far as I am concerned, I think I am too old to do it because I might not have many more years ahead of me—only two or three perhaps—and so I would waste this time that would be better employed in purifying negative karma. For this sole reason I do not have the desire to learn languages, but perhaps this is a wrong view! In Italy someone once told me, "You have lived in this country for one and a half years, and not only have you not learned Italian, but you have not even learned to eat properly. I used to have faith in you, but now I have lost it a little!"

We must never do anything that is not beneficial to others, directly or indirectly, and we must dedicate the merit of anything positive that we do to the attainment of buddhahood solely for the welfare of all beings. [101]

We should never abandon, even at the cost of our lives, the master, the spiritual friend, the one who wisely indicates the Mahayana path and at the same time practices what he is teaching. [102]

As we can learn from the biography of Shrisambhava Bodhisattva, we must practice devotion toward our master and behave accordingly. Whether the master is good or not, what matters is how we see him—it is totally up to us. We must always look at his positive characteristics and try to emulate them. [103]

A Tibetan proverb says that if one possesses good faith, even the tooth of a dog can emanate light! In the story this proverb refers to, it is said that in an eastern region of Tibet called Kham, far from Lhasa, where communications were scarce and it took a long time to reach the capital, a woman asked her son who had to travel to Lhasa to bring her back a sacred relic so that she could make some offerings. The son went to Lhasa but forgot his mother's request and returned home empty-handed.

After a while, he had to leave again for the capital, and his mother again requested, urging him not to forget a second time. Instead, this is exactly what happened, but this time he remembered just as he approached home, and he thought of something so as to not disappoint his mother. He looked around and saw a dog's corpse, so he pulled out a tooth, cleaned it well, wrapped it in a precious cloth, and brought it to his mother, telling her that it was a very sacred relic.

The woman put it on the altar and generated intense devotion toward it. She made prostrations and offerings, praying fervently, until one day she saw light emanating from the dog's tooth. This happened because of her great faith, even though there was nothing sacred or extraordinary about the object itself.

In the same way, how we perceive the master is up to us. He may be wise and have deep knowledge, but if we have no faith, we will attain nothing. To understand the correct way to evaluate him, we can use the example of a mother who, observing her son, judges him to be an excellent, strong, and brave child, even though his qualities might be a little bit coarse. This shows how differently we can look at things. Loving someone for his qualities is different than being attached to him; for example, we love the attributes of the Three Jewels, but we do not possess any attachment toward them.

If we dwell on what is not right, aversion and anger will arise naturally, and consequently unhappiness. We must read all the texts pertaining to the bodhisattva's discipline and learn what they advise us to do and not do, and then apply their counsel in our lives.

The collection of sutras describes everything that is in accord with the bodhisattva's conduct, and therefore we should read them, starting with the *Akashagarbha Sutra.* [104]

In the Shantideva's *Shikshasamucchaya (Compendium of All Practices),* we find many instructions related to the bodhisattva's practice, such as how to generate an appropriate motivation, the various ways of practicing the path, and how to dedicate the merit accumulated. [105]

Sutras are truly vast and complex, and if it is not possible to read them all, we can study the *Sutrasamucchaya (Compendium of All Sutras),* also by Shantideva. We can also examine two other compendiums bearing the same titles that were composed by Nagarjuna. [106]

It is good to follow the instructions that these texts provide with regard to what is virtuous and what is not, and we should practice what is advised and strive to do what is not unbecoming to a bodhisattva. A bodhisattva must act in such a way as to protect the minds of ordinary people, through impeccable and inspired actions. [107]

For example, if a person lives high in the mountains or alone in a cold place, he can refrain from washing because this does not cause him any harm. If, on the other hand, he lives in society, he should wash out of consideration for other people. The essential meaning of all this is that we must constantly observe the state of our bodies and our minds, examine our physical conduct and our mental states, and then act according to circumstances.

The defining characteristic of discriminating alertness is to constantly observe and examine the actions of our three doors. [108]

Everything we learn must be transformed into the practices of the body, speech, and mind, otherwise mere knowledge and discussion are pointless. [109]

If someone does not believe in the spiritual path, he must still live in a noble and virtuous way, and in so doing will be practicing the Dharma even though he might call himself a non-religious person.

The Dharma provides the method to live a meaningful life, and if we live in a right and correct way we will be happy, and our friends, relatives, and all those around us will be happy too. In a family, if a husband and wife lead this type of life, they will be happy even if their means are limited. If, however, they practice wrong conduct, they will not be joyful, although they might be wealthy. If students in a Dharma center are practicing, visitors will find it a relaxed and supportive environment, and when they come there they will feel happy.

ᢍ 6 ᢌ

PATIENCE

W E ALL KNOW that hatred causes suffering, and that is why we have a great desire to listen to the teachings on patience. On the other hand, it is harder to recognize the harm caused by attachment, which can be compared to a person who appears calm and peaceful on the outside but is malevolent within. Such a person will create problems for us without us realizing it, acting quietly. Therefore, we must learn what mental afflictions are and how they work, and then apply the relevant antidotes. If we do not actively eliminate them from our minds, they will not go away of their own accord. Similarly, if we do not strive to accumulate positive karma, it will not come to us on its own.

Samsara, which is dependent on causes and conditions, is also called cyclic existence, since living beings move through the cycles of birth, old age, and death infinite numbers of times. What forces us to follow these cycles? Mental afflictions and the karma we create under their control. In order to understand this in detail, we now refer to what is taught in the *twelve links of dependent arising*. The twelve links are:

1. Ignorance
2. Karmic formation
3. Consciousness
4. Name and form
5. Six sense sources
6. Contact
7. Feeling
8. Desire, or attachment

9. Craving
10. Becoming, or existence
11. Birth
12. Aging and death

These twelve links are the factors that bring about continuous rebirth in cyclic existence. The wheel of life, a traditional Buddhist depiction, portrays these twelve links through images. It shows the twelve links and the six types of samsaric beings within a wheel, which is held in the jaws of Yama (the sovereign of death), and presents pictorial symbolism related to the twelve links.

The first link, *ignorance,* is depicted by a blind man walking with a stick. The second, *karmic formation,* is shown by a picture of a potter at work. The third, *consciousness,* is represented by a monkey hopping around in a house, as consciousness wanders through the six senses. The fourth link, *name and form,* is represented by a boat carrying two people. The fifth, *the six sense sources,* is depicted by an empty house with open windows. The windows represent the sensory organs, through which we perceive external phenomena. The next picture is of a man and a woman embracing, which represents the sixth link, *contact,* referring to the contact that occurs between the sensory organs and the external world. Through contact arises *feeling,* the seventh link, which is represented by a man with an arrow sticking out of one eye. He is certainly experiencing strong sensations in his current situation! The eighth link, *attachment,* is represented by a picture of a man drinking and becoming intoxicated with wine. Attachment grows stronger and develops into the lust of *craving,* which is the ninth link, represented by a monkey plucking fruits from a tree. The tenth link, which is called *becoming* or *existence,* arises from a previous desire to take a particular physical form, and is depicted as a pregnant woman or as a couple copulating. The eleventh link is *birth,* represented by a woman giving birth. The twelfth, *aging and death,* is depicted by an old man with a corpse. This is a brief presentation of the twelve links as depicted in the wheel of life.

Now I will explain the twelve links individually in terms of how they actually function. Let us consider the first link, ignorance. Ignorance leads us to believe in a truly existing "I," which is the root of our innate desire to experience happiness and not experience suffering. As a result of this preference, we create positive and negative karma, and the actions by which we do so constitute the second link.

Actions performed on the basis of ignorance leave an imprint on the consciousness, which is the third link. The third link is followed by the eighth link, desire, which refers to the desire to obtain a physical form. This is followed by the ninth link, craving, which occurs as desire intensifies into craving at the possession of this form. Attachment and craving act as cooperative, circumstantial causes and bring about the ripening of a karmic seed that becomes the substantial cause for the tenth link, existence. "Existence" in this case, however, does not refer to factual existence, but rather to karma that has the potential to manifest in a concrete form—in other words, karma created in relation to future lives, in which its fruit will ripen fully.

The Tibetan terms *dochag* and *sepa* are both translated as "attachment." *Dochag* is the mental affliction, included among the six root afflictions, that makes one stick to the desired object. The attachment, or desire, corresponding to the term *sepa* is referred to mainly in relation to the eighth of the twelve links of dependent arising, and it can be of three types: attachment to objects of desire, attachment in the sense of not wanting to be separated from objects one possesses, and attachment to the acquisition of a particular form of existence—for example, wanting to be reborn into a rich family.

Links one, two, three, eight, nine, and ten—ignorance, action, consciousness, attachment, craving, and becoming—are all created within a single lifetime. In one lifetime we have the basis of ignorance in our minds, through which we create karma, thus accumulating the imprints of attachment, craving, and existence, which lay the groundwork for future lives that will be determined by the karma that we have created in this one. We speak of karmic formation, the second link, which can also be called *action,* as a substantial cause. However, this is not true of attachment and craving, which are in fact circumstantial causes that cause karma to ripen and produce the tenth link, that seed of existence that will bring about the eleventh link, actual rebirth in a particular realm. In each life we create millions of these links.

The eleventh link is the time of conception in the mother's womb, when the fetus begins to take shape into the five *skandhas,* or aggregates, which are present in the fourth link of name and form. "Name" refers to the four nonphysical aggregates and "form" to the aggregate of the body. Then the fetus develops until the sensory organs take shape, which is the fifth link, and when the sensory organs come into contact with external phenomena, the sixth link of contact is produced.

Once consciousness has come into contact with external objects through the sensory organs, feelings are generated that can be pleasant, unpleasant, or neutral. From the second instant after conception until the final moments of life, we experience aging and death, which are both included in one link because they constitute one continual process.

The causes of the life we are living now are ignorance, action, consciousness, attachment, craving, and existence—all causal links accumulated in previous lives. This life began with conception in the maternal womb, the development of the fetus, the subsequent development of the sensory organs, and contact. From contact, feeling came into being, and now we are experiencing the process of aging, which started at the beginning of life and will end at death. Thus, the seeds of our current lives are a group of six causal links that are bearing fruit in the present. In this life, too, we accumulate more of them for future lives, but in the meantime we experience those fruits, the other six links, which we call effect links. Again, these are the present birth, name and form, sensory sources, contact, feeling, and aging and death.

The third link has two aspects: the cause and the effect. The causal aspect consists of being a support to the karmic imprint, the second link; the effect takes place at conception, the moment when the eleventh link is produced.

The twelve links are commonly listed in the order presented at the beginning, in relation to the wheel of life, which is an order of cause and effect and not a sequential, chronological order.

Again, each of the twelve links are present in each life, but the six "causal" links of our current life were accumulated in a previous existence, whereas from the six of the same type we are creating now we will experience six "effect" links in future lives. To summarize, in one lifetime all twelve are present, but they exist in combinations of links belonging to different chains. When the causal links of feeling, attachment, craving, existence, ignorance, karmic formations, and consciousness are present, all twelve links will be created. Following another feeling, we start all over again from attachment, and six new causal links are created for a future existence. All this goes on millions of times in a single day.

Thus, we are living this life because we have created the six causal links (or rather five plus half of the third link, consciousness) in some former life, and we are at present experiencing their fruit, the six effect links (or rather six and a half). At present we are experiencing the twelfth link, aging and death. The other five effect links have already passed, and we can trace their cause to the six causal links created in some former life.

Because of ignorance, we continually create actions that leave imprints in the mind in every instant, whatever we do. The eighth link, attachment, and the ninth link, craving, constitute the intensity of these actions, built over a long time, whereas there can be only one of the tenth, existence, also called actualizing karma, in each lifetime. This is because even though we have so many potential seeds for our various rebirths, only one is activated at a time. It is as if we have many seeds in a glass, but only one of them is planted in the soil and, if cultivated, will grow. Therefore each tenth link that is created, one for every lifetime, will set off the next existence.

Now, if, on the one hand, we have the ignorance that leads us to create projecting karma, which leaves its imprints in our consciousness, and going through the other causal links we reach the ninth, existence or becoming, this will produce the next rebirth. If, on the other hand, we possess the first few links but do not possess craving, a very intense desire, then the actual maturation of the karmic seed in a specific rebirth will take place in some later life.

Because of ignorance, we have many karmic formations and imprints in our consciousnesses. Attachment and craving, however, exist in relation to a specific rebirth. For example, although we might not necessarily be conscious of it, we can have a particular feeling of craving, the ninth link, to obtain a certain form—a human, deva, or even an animal form. This link will then fasten itself to the tenth link with one of the many karmic seeds already present, and activate it. From among all karmic formations, craving chooses one and activates it through the tenth link, the actualizing karma, and thus completed, produces the eleventh link of birth and all the other links in the lifetime that immediately follows.

The aspiration to obtain buddhahood or a precious human rebirth does not necessarily have to be mixed with attachment. Aspiration acts in order to grant us the results of buddhahood or a precious human rebirth based on the pure observance of moral discipline together with the practice of the paramitas. It might be mixed with attachment for us, and perhaps we do not realize it, but it should not be so. The eighth and ninth links, attachment and craving, however, exist in relation to the wish to obtain a particular form of conditioned existence.

Ignorance is the basis of the twelve links—it is the general of their army. But through the wisdom that sees emptiness we can fight off this commander and destroy it, and as a result we will not have the karmic formations or their imprints on our consciousness, nor will we have attachment, craving, or the subsequent conditioned existence. Conditioned existence is caused by ignorance and by action, and the power is on their side, but now we must try to gain control over them.

Since we desire happiness, we are trying here to learn ways to obtain it. Since we do not desire unhappiness, we are also trying to understand its causes and learn the methods to eliminate it. At present we cannot choose how we will be born, nor can we choose—no matter how much we may wish to—not to become old. But in the future the opportunity might arise to allow us to overcome this state of complete impotence and instead have the ability to decide. If we do not have this freedom right now, let us look for it!

We have just discussed how a person lives and wanders in cyclic existence through the chain of dependent arising. Because of the twelve links, we experience conditioned existence, and we cannot avoid the suffering implicit in it. If we assemble the twelve links according to the truth of suffering and the truth of the cause of suffering, then ignorance, karmic formations, the first half of the third link (consciousness as cause), attachment, craving, and existence constitute the truth of the cause of suffering. The other six and the second half of the third link, consciousness as effect, constitute the truth of suffering.

The Buddha himself, in his first teaching at Sarnath on the noble truth of suffering, said that the psychophysical aggregates, the sensory organs, contact, feelings, birth, and aging and death are themselves the truth of suffering that we must recognize. He also explained that whoever has these as a foundation will necessarily experience suffering, and that because we wish to be free from this, we must understand the cause of suffering itself.

ple. From the moment we are born to the moment we die, we depend completely on others—we are in no way able to procure everything we need by ourselves.

Also, if the country we live in has not been invaded, we owe it to the effort of other beings. The Chinese have invaded Tibet, but my coming here from India to speak to you of the Dharma—we owe all of this to them.

From the food we eat to the clothes we wear and even to the praise we get—all this comes from the kindness of others. If, having concluded that all beings have been, and still are, extremely kind to us, we are still incapable of cultivating love and compassion toward them, this is our mistake alone.

Usually we divide people into three categories: friends, people we feel indifferent to, and enemies, or those who give us trouble. What makes us think of some as friends is the fact that they have been both kind to us and in some way beneficial. But since we have just concluded that in the course of countless rebirths all beings have benefited us in many ways, it should be possible to include people whom we now feel indifferent toward and even those toward whom we feel aversion in the category of friends. This will be easier if we think that all beings have been kind to us in both our present and former lives.

If the criterion we use in judging someone as kind is the fact that he has just benefited us, then we could not say, for example, that my grandmother is kind, because right now she is not even here! Aren't those people who were kind to us in the past considered kind? A person who was kind to us when we were small is also a kind person!

At this point we could think, however, that others have harmed us too—but harm or no harm depends on us. For example, if someone hits us with a stick and, generating patience, we do not become angry, then this person has benefited us instead of harmed us. We must see that person as our master, teaching us the practice of patience. If everything we usually define as harm is in fact a benefit, then it will not be possible to say that only what are conventionally called benefits are benefits!

Even if we have succeeded in refraining from harming others, by practicing morality we owe our success precisely to those who served as objects of our practice. It is likewise necessary to have an object—other beings—that will allow us to generate the qualities of love and compassion, and the same applies to bodhichitta, the perfection of generosity, and all the other transcendental perfections.

Recognizing the kindness other beings have shown us, as well as the suffering that they are now experiencing, we will be able to generate love and compassion, we will have an appropriate motivation, and we will practice the Dharma and so indirectly benefit ourselves. On the other hand, if we remind ourselves how much others have harmed us, we will only feel hatred and more suffering. By succeeding in cultivating love and compassion and by seeking to hold the mind steadfastly on these two points, we avoid generating negative thoughts and malevolence toward other beings.

If someone says unpleasant words to us, rather than reacting angrily we could try to be patient and reflect in this way: "Even though he is being rude, I must not become angry, because his words are nothing but sound, and if I do not worry about it, I will not be harmed in any way. The only reason that they make me suffer is because I give them weight and I think about them, but if I do not do that, they will have no effect on me whatsoever." Reflecting in this way, our hatred will naturally diminish.

Words in fact do not have the power to cause harm. If, looking in the dictionary, we find, for example, the word "crazy," we do not feel any emotion when we read it. However, if someone says to us, "You are crazy," we become angry. In reality, the word as such does not truly have power over us—if it did we should become angry when we see it written down!

Learning the various methods of mental training is an excellent thing to do, but it is necessary to know which technique will be the most useful and which is actually within our reach, just as when we decide to paint a tangka. We start by making an outline in black, and then we begin to use a different color, then another, and in this way a good painting will result. If we were to use all the colors at the same time, we would get nowhere. We must therefore understand the right order of the practices we are committing ourselves to.

To be able to ride a motorbike, we must first learn to ride a bicycle. In this way we avoid accidents. Likewise, if we do not know the right sequence of spiritual practices, we could become discouraged and disappointed, since it would be hard to practice the very advanced ones as beginners.

There is a big difference between a spiritual person and a materialistic one. The point of view of the latter leads him to seek personal gain, whereas the chief aim of one on a spiritual path is to benefit others and tolerate difficulties on their behalf.

If we are able to be the losers—in other words, to let others gain—we will, in fact, be the true winners. Nobody wants to lose, neither ourselves nor others, and so conflict, struggle, and physical confrontation are born. If we really do not want to lose, let us try at least to generate the desire to not harm others, and let us do our best to see that they are not defeated. When two people confront each other, naturally each wants to have the upper hand since no one fights in order to lose. However, it is certain that one of them will lose, and, if possible, it would be better that it be us, because in doing so we will gain advantages and benefits as a result of our practice of patience.

It is difficult to put all this into practice, but starting gradually, renouncing being the winner once, then a second time, then a third, and so on, we will eventually succeed in becoming better people.

The deeper our understanding of the spiritual path, the bigger the reward in our lives. We have obtained human forms, minds gifted with intelligence, and we are capable of discerning what is good and what is not; we are lucky! It might be hard, however, to commit ourselves to Dharma practice in the same way that Milarepa did, with the same kind of effort.

A monk, a *gelong,* who dedicates his entire life to the practice of the Dharma will depend solely on begging and the food offered to him, but he does not die of starvation and manages to survive. Perhaps it is not possible for a layperson to dedicate himself totally to the practice without working; however, it is wise to dedicate all the free time you have available after work to the practice, or, if that is also not possible, even some of this time. Truly, we should dedicate most of our time to the practice of the Dharma, leaving a small part for earning our means of sustenance. But since this is probably a difficult thing to do, let us at least make sure that a certain amount of time is dedicated to it.

In the beginning it is not easy to believe what we are told, but if we reflect on it, we will slowly begin to understand. Milarepa abandoned worldly life and every enjoyment to dedicate himself completely to the practice of the Dharma, thus succeeding in attaining enlightenment, and he is now renowned throughout the whole world.

In his text Shantideva describes the way we must proceed in training our minds and what a bodhisattva must do in order to attain the final stage of complete enlightenment. Although we are not yet bodhisattvas, we will gain enormously by learning what bodhisattvas must do.

In our present condition we are dissatisfied with the way we are and with how much we have, so we continually seek something else. We strive to obtain what we desire at work, such as a better salary, and at home, by asking our parents for more. We try in every possible way to acquire other people's help, or to achieve something other than what we have, but we do not reach the objective we longed for in spite of all our efforts, and with the means we currently use, we will never succeed.

At this point we might ask ourselves whether any other means to eliminate suffering exist. So far we have not been able to comprehend the origin of this suffering and the true enemies who create misery for us—for if we were to recognize them, we would be able to stop our suffering by eliminating them.

Geshe Chekawa, a lama from the Kadampa tradition who lived in the twelfth century, explains in his *Seven-Point Mind Training* that the true enemies are not outside but inside ourselves, and that these are the negative emotions present in our minds, which we must learn to recognize.

To work for the sake of others is also the cause of our own happiness, and if actualizing it is not easy, let us remember that in any case trying to make others happy is a positive thing.

If someone harms us, it certainly does not make us happy; likewise, if we harm another, that person is not happy. We must therefore learn to stop when we are about to create suffering for others. If we give in to the urge, we harm ourselves. When two children quarrel, if one hurts the other slightly, his friend will hit him harder, and the altercation will escalate. The same happens between two nations—if one nation is harmed by another, it retaliates with greater strength. But if a country has been treated kindly, it instead tries to show its friendship, and both countries benefit. Through these examples we can comprehend that when we do something positive we will gain in return; otherwise there will only be disadvantages.

If we think that someone has been kind to us, it is natural for us to try to pay back that kindness. For example, if one of two children recognizes their parents' kindness, he will strive to repay it, whereas the other child who does not feel any gratitude will not make any effort whatsoever.

How can we truly recognize the kindness of others? Tibetans have been deprived of their independence by the Chinese. In this country, on the other hand, people enjoy freedom and a high level of development. They find what they need and there is not so much crime—this is all due to the kindness of those who worked in order to create these conditions, to the kindness of the heads of state and the people in the government. Also, we have clothes, various tools, and means of transport, and this is all due to the kindness of those who work in factories and of shopkeepers. Farmers are also kind to us, because of what they produce, and dairy farmers, for providing us with milk. Everything we enjoy from the moment we get up in the morning is due to the kindness of others, not just to our own effort.

Our parents have been and still are kind to us. When we were born we looked like little worms, incapable of telling what we could or could not eat. If someone works for us for a day we have to pay him a particular sum, and if he works for us for a month we have to pay him a proportionately greater sum—but our parents worked for us for years, and we have not given them anything in return. Had they not cared for us in our infancy, we would not even be able to enjoy this human existence. If we remember their kindness, trying to repay them will only be natural, and in so doing we will accumulate positive karma.

If we have a store of positive imprints, we will be able to enjoy what we desire, we will not have any difficulty in our lives, we will have good friends, and everything will be favorable.

If we desire better conditions for ourselves in the present, we need to refrain from harming others and try to benefit them. If we do not think of ourselves as spiritual but nevertheless help others and refrain from harming them, we are in fact spiritual people, because the essence of the spiritual path is nothing more than trying to help others and not create suffering.

We must remember the kindness of all beings and recognize the fact that our true enemies are our mental afflictions—principally ignorance, attachment, and hatred.

Hatred is an attitude that causes suffering not only for others but also for ourselves, and it can destroy our merit in an instant. The sixth chapter of the *Bodhicharyavatara* presents the practice of patience, which is the antidote to hatred, but first it explains the disadvantages of harboring this hatred.

The strength of hatred is such that in an instant it can destroy the merit accumulated through the practices of generosity, discipline, and the other perfections over three cosmic eras as fire destroys a whole forest. [1]

In Venice there are many glassmakers' workshops in which you can see fragile objects on display that took a long time to produce. If you were to go in with a stick, you could easily destroy all those precious things in an instant. Hatred is exactly like this.

There is no greater negativity than hatred, and there is no better virtue than patience, if we succeed in practicing it. [2]

It can be difficult in the beginning, but it will gradually become simpler and more familiar, in the same way that learning how to drive is at first complicated but later becomes natural through habit, and all difficulties are overcome.

How does hatred cause suffering? If we are relaxed, peaceful, and at ease, and someone approaches us saying unpleasant things, unhappiness and aversion will suddenly arise in us, and before we know it our tranquility will be lost.

When we are angry we cannot even sleep—we feel unsettled and we throw anything within our reach at others. If a mother is angry, she will slap her child even if he did not do anything. When we are angry we simply cannot stay calmly seated, and we even wish to harm those we usually love. [3]

Our friends, seeing our anger, will change their opinions of us and we will lose their friendship. If we are angry and we offer something, others will not want to be near us and they will not feel grateful for our gifts. It is very unlikely that a person who is enraged would say, "I am happy because I am angry." [5]

Hatred is no ordinary enemy, because it causes suffering not only in this life but also in future lives, and those who strive to destroy it will find happiness not only in this life but in future lives as well. [6]

What are the causes of hatred? Hatred is supported by the feeling of unhappiness that arises from the fact that others are not doing what we want, or are doing what we do not want, or are creating obstacles to the attainment of what we desire. [7]

This mental distress acts like food for our hatred. If we feed it, hatred develops and eventually defeats us. Therefore, the first step is to eliminate such harmful food. [8]

We must not feel unhappy when someone seems to hinder us, or when we do not obtain what we desire, or when something happens to us that we do not like. Unhappiness and mental distress destroy our inner peace and joy, and we must strive in every possible way to make sure that this does not happen. There is no usefulness or advantage to anger, because in any case it does not grant us what we desire, but only unhappiness and the destruction of our accumulated merits. [9]

When we are annoyed by something, we must look for the cause by analyzing the situation. If it is possible to redress the problem, we must strive to do so. If that is so, what is the point of becoming angry or feeling unhappy? For example, if we are thirsty we simply need to drink, and if we are sick we remedy this by taking medicine. However, when we cannot remedy our unpleasant situation in any way, becoming angry or feeling unhappy is purposeless. [10]

If we have cancer and doctors cannot be of any more help, it would be pointless to be unhappy. Instead we should try to live in the best possible way, without further depression. If a person who is seriously ill understands his condition, he will suffer physically but not mentally. If he does not understand it, he will suffer both physically and mentally, because, knowing that he has cancer, he will worry about his imminent death. In reality we all must die. Death may even happen soon, and yet no one reflects on it.

We want no suffering, no poverty, no disrespect, and no bad reputation for ourselves, our loved ones, or our friends—however, we do want all these things for our enemies. [11]

Hatred, our enemy, will bring us all of the above, and besides which it will also destroy what we cherish: happiness, wealth, praise, and fame. So, practicing the Dharma, we must generate forbearance. When someone harms us we must develop the moral fortitude and the necessary patience required to endure the difficulties.

It is very important to learn how to endure unavoidable suffering because there are many situations that bring us suffering. If we learn how to tolerate them, our lives will be more serene and more agreeable. Happiness is uncommon since its causes are rare and accidental and also since ours is a conditioned existence whose nature is suffering. However, suffering can remind us of our unlucky situation and prompt us to seek liberation. Suffering is important, because without it there is no renunciation. [12]

Usually people who follow a spiritual path have experienced such acute suffering in the past that, in order to escape it, they have sought various solutions and finally have encountered the Dharma.

If we succeed in enduring the suffering we experience, then we will not be unhappy and depressed. For example, consider people who endure great difficulties for small objectives. In order to win a bicycle race and gain a little fame, someone will train intensively, and those who ski endure both the cold and strenuous activity. Yet if they were ordered to go into the deep snow against their wishes, they probably would not do it. It all depends on one's way of thinking.

If we are able to endure hardships joyfully while pursuing meaningless objectives, even more so should we endure the hardships we encounter when practicing the Dharma in order to attain ultimate happiness, which is a valid objective. [13]

We must become accustomed to enduring small hardships and difficulties, so that in the future we will be able to endure greater hardships. [14]

It is hard at first for beginners to sit cross-legged for even five minutes, but day by day the time they are able to do this can be prolonged. We can easily tolerate the bites of insects and snakes, as well as hunger and thirst. Why then would it not be possible for us to learn to practice patience when facing adversity? [15]

If we are impatient with heat and cold, wind and rain, illnesses and being beaten, our suffering will increase, but if we are patient, that same suffering will diminish. Complaining also cripples the mind, so we should refrain from doing this as well. [16]

There are those who are wounded in battle who, at the sight of their own blood, become braver, but there are others who, when they see the blood of others, faint and fall unconscious. [17]

Our reaction does not therefore depend on the specific circumstances—in this case, the sight of our own or other people's blood—but on our mode of thinking, on the way we handle the situation.

We must develop more courage as we face the various hardships in life, and not allow them to defeat us. One who dedicates his whole life to

the Dharma will have to overcome difficulties and will not possess many
things, but if he is able to endure it, he will succeed in improving his
mind. Wise people and practitioners of the Mahayana have clear, unperturbed minds, even in the face of various physical hardships and suffering,
and therefore they will not experience too many problems in attaining the
goals they have set for themselves.

We are waging war on our mental afflictions and will certainly encounter hardships and suffering, but we must bravely endure what befalls us
and continue our struggle. [19]

Ordinary warriors kill only bodies, since everyone is destined to die.
Our mental afflictions, however, will not die of their own accord. It is a
brave warrior who goes to battle with these enemies instead. [20]

We have seen so far how we must endure and bravely face our suffering
and difficulties. But suffering also possesses some qualities—it destroys our
pride and allows us to understand the suffering of others so that we are able
to generate love and compassion toward all beings. Furthermore, suffering
induces us to seek the teachings of the Dharma and the methods of practice, to recognize the fact that we have obtained both a favorable physical
form and an intelligent mind, capable of discerning between good and evil.
Finally, it prompts us to make use of these favorable circumstances. [21]

What are the causes of suffering? Our inner enemies, the mental afflictions. They have no legs or hands, they are neither wise nor strong, and
they possess nothing whatsoever that makes them truly dreadful. It is we
who allow them to cause us harm and suffering.

These enemies have been with us since time without beginning, and
they will continue to stay with us for a long time to come, until we destroy
them. We must therefore succeed in doing so, even if we have to endure
severe hardship.

The text now moves from diagnosing the problem to providing antidotes to anger.

We need to train ourselves in the three types of *patience:* the patience
of *enduring the suffering we encounter in life,* the patience of *not taking
revenge* but instead joyfully enduring the harm brought on by others, and
the patience of *accepting difficulties in Dharma practice.*

With regard to the first type, the patience of enduring suffering, if we
experience problems such as sickness, hunger, and cold, we must simply

look for solutions without becoming unhappy. If we do not find solutions, we should avoid adding mental suffering to the physical suffering we are already experiencing, since doing so would bring no advantage.

The second type of suffering is the patience of joyfully enduring the harm brought on by others. It has been explained that when we find ourselves in situations in which we are harmed, we must not become angry, and yet we might think that when someone harms us it is right to generate hatred. We say, for example, that we become angry with some people because they caused us harm, which then caused us suffering, but by the same token we should then be angry with our bodies too, since they are the cause of the greatest suffering! We do not think like this, however, but say instead that it is not the body itself, but the causes and conditions of suffering—an illness, for example—that make us suffer. The same argument must then also be valid in terms of the harm brought on by others, since it is also brought about by causes and conditions—the mental afflictions that arise in these people. [22]

We do not become angry with our bodies when they grow sick and when we suffer because of an illness, as we understand that illness is determined by particular causes and circumstances. In the same way we must not become angry with those who harm us, because they are under the influence of mental afflictions. Just as our bodies become ill without our wish, so do mental afflictions arise in our minds, unwanted. [23]

If we really must become angry with someone, we should become angry with the mental afflictions themselves, the true cause of harm we receive. We must understand and remember these teachings, and apply them each time we are about to become angry.

Hatred is born out of discomfort and mental unhappiness due to particular circumstances, and easily transforms into rage even if we do not want it to. The same happens to others. They do not think, "Now I will become angry, now I will cause harm." Hatred and anger arise spontaneously, urging them to cause harm without any choice. [24]

All evil that comes from others, all the negative karma brought to fruition, all suffering, everything unpleasant that we experience arises when the proper causes and circumstances are accumulated—nothing is born by chance, without a cause, independently. [25]

Those same causes and conditions also assemble dependently and have no intention to create suffering, but the mere fact that they assemble together means that suffering and unhappiness are produced. [26]

If someone harms us, he has no choice at that moment. He is not harming us voluntarily, but is driven instead by certain conditions and mental afflictions, and he is helpless.

If someone dear to us, whom we consider a good person, suddenly goes mad and tries to harm us, we understand that he is driven by a disturbed mental condition. Therefore we are already applying the same type of thinking that I have explained above to our everyday lives. No one will try to repay the injury suffered at the hands of a madman—everyone would condemn such a person! Wishing to avenge ourselves against someone who harms us is similar, as that person is prey to mental afflictions, just as the madman is prey to his mental illness.

In the text, as we have mentioned, it is said that all produced phenomena are born out of causes and circumstances and that no phenomenon is independent. But the non-Buddhist Indian philosophical school of the Samkhya maintains, in contrast, that some phenomena are entirely independent and arise as a result of their particular nature. [27] This school declares that there is a principal creator of the entire universe, and that all existing phenomena have been created by a certain type of energy—different, however, from the energy of atomic particles.

Other philosophical schools state that Ishvara is the creator of everything. In Buddhism, however, it is maintained that everything that exists derives from mind itself—there is no creator but the mind. A positive mind creates positive things, while a negative mind produces negativity, and all effects can be separated into these two categories

It is said that all the positive things we experience are due to the buddhas and bodhisattvas, which means that we have learned from them that in order to obtain positive effects we must plant positive causes, and vice versa. If someone gives us a piece of land, he will encourage us to cultivate it and explain how to do so, and the fruits of our labor will be obtained thanks to him and his instructions. When a child goes to school he might not know much, but little by little he will learn various things and finally become an educated person, thanks to the kindness of his teachers.

Putting the advice of the buddhas, bodhisattvas, and our gurus into practice, we will obtain happiness. It is indisputable that all the valid things we possess are due to them, and that all that is incorrect is due to our mental afflictions. If it were the buddhas and bodhisattvas that caused our suffering, we should eliminate them. However, this is not the case. We desire happiness and do not desire suffering and problems. If we depend on the buddhas and bodhisattvas we will have the first, and if we depend on mental afflictions we will have the second.

The non-Buddhist school of the Samkhyas states that all that exists depends on a primal independent substance that produces the various phenomena enjoyed by a self, or soul, that is both devoid of parts and permanent, and that does not depend on causes and conditions. But since there are no produced phenomena that exist without depending on causes and conditions, there cannot exist a substance or a primordial force of that sort, nor can there be a permanent self that learns and takes delight in the various phenomena. This primal substance presented by the Samkhyas cannot even possess the motivation for creating something, and since it is not produced itself, it cannot produce in turn, because it is permanent. In fact, any effect can arise only out of particular conditions from a substantial cause, which in turn derives from another cause.

Non-Buddhist schools believe in the existence of a permanent self or "I," whereas Buddhists believe that the self is impermanent. By "permanent" we mean something that is not subject to any kind of inner change.

If there were a soul or a permanent self that had the experience of a particular object, it would have to experience that object at all times.

If we had a permanent self and were enjoying food, we would have to keep eating without ever stopping, the characteristic of immutability being permanent. Instead, we continuously change our activities—we eat, sleep, and walk. [28]

If a permanent self existed, it would be like space, devoid of action. But there is no such thing as a primal substance endowed with volition and able to create, nor does there exist a permanent self. The Samkhyas say that the primal substance is permanent, but that it is able to create by encountering particular circumstances. Now, something permanent cannot come into contact with any circumstance or condition, since nothing can modify a permanent phenomenon, whose nature is definitively unchanging.

What influence can any agent have on this hypothetical primal substance whose nature is supposed to be permanent? None whatsoever!

Nothing can modify or benefit a permanent self, because self and object could not relate, and would not be connected. [29]

Fire and smoke are of different natures, and yet fire has an effect and an influence on smoke. If there were a permanent self, nothing could influence it.

Relationships between various phenomena can be of two kinds: of the same nature, or cause and effect. "Of the same nature" refers to two characteristics of the same phenomenon, such as being produced and being impermanent, or warmth and light, two characteristics of fire. The "of the same nature" argument is invoked after denying the possibility of acting on something permanent. The Samkhyas defend their position by stating that there is an additional type of relationship by which a permanent self can interact with other objects. In reality, however, the only relationships that exist are the two previously described, in which phenomena relate mutually. If one phenomenon were permanent, it could not relate with the other!

In order to speak of causal relationships between phenomena, there must be an effect. For instance, if we are ill and become healthy again after taking medicine, we can say that we were cured as a result of the medicine.

Since a permanent phenomenon cannot ever change, any action or influence on it will not produce an effect. The Samkhyas consider the objects of the world to be impermanent and the self to be permanent. This permanent self should then enjoy impermanent objects—but this type of relationship is completely absurd. For if one phenomenon is permanent and the others are impermanent, it is possible for neither a same-nature relationship nor a relationship of cause and effect to exist between them. [30]

Nothing is produced independently, and each phenomenon is therefore like an illusion. We should understand things in this way and not generate aversion toward the unpleasant things we encounter. [31]

Since everything exists because of causes and conditions, and nothing exists independently, we must not become angry at conditioned phenomena. Even wrong deeds performed by our enemies arise because of causes and conditions.

Anything that may happen or appear to us is like an illusion, and we must not become angry at illusions, or be attached to them. In this way we will no longer create negative karma, which is the cause of suffering. In order to understand how phenomena are illusory we need to understand their real nature—their lack of intrinsic, independent, and true existence.

Likewise, we must regard one who harms us to be illusory—a madman or a sick person—because he is under the influence of his mental afflictions. If we are able to reflect in this way, even though we might not succeed in changing the external situation, there will be an inner change in the way we see things. Although they might still appear harmful, we will no longer be affected by them. We might even be abused and insulted, but we will not be touched by it.

Usually we become angry if someone makes us suffer directly, and we think it right to react in such a way, but the result is that because of this we suffer even more. It is wrong to believe that it is right to be angry at those who harm us, since that person is influenced by mental afflictions and not acting of his own accord. Hatred, and with it all the mental afflictions that induce someone to cause us harm, are born out of causes and conditions and for this reason do not possess independent existence.

Since everything is like an illusion, both hatred and the objects of hatred, one might then ask why we need to apply its antidotes. Hatred, the illusion, could not be eliminated, and there would be no need! In truth, it is not wrong to use wisdom as an antidote to ignorance, even though both wisdom and ignorance are devoid of intrinsic existence. By developing the wisdom that realizes the authentic nature of phenomena, we will eliminate ignorance. By eliminating ignorance we will eliminate the mental afflictions that it causes, and by eliminating mental afflictions we will no longer create negative karma, and therefore not experience suffering. [32]

Understanding that actions derive from causes and conditions, we will be able to remain in a happy state of mind even if someone harms us. [33]

Furthermore, let us reflect on the fact that it is impossible for things to happen always and only in the way that we wish them to happen. We all desire only happiness and would not choose to suffer. If we could achieve happiness freely, we would certainly never suffer. [34]

Some people, in order to eliminate their problems, seek a way out through suicide—they shoot themselves, they throw themselves from a cliff, they jump in front of a train, or take poison. Others, obsessed by the desire for riches, even suffer hunger to obtain them. But in so doing they create negative karma, which will be the cause of further great suffering in the future. [35]

We become angry at others because they harm us, and we suffer injury because of their actions, but if people behave so violently toward themselves, it is no wonder then that they harm other living beings as well. They do not behave this way, however, as a result of free choice, and it is unreasonable to be angry with them. We should try instead to feel compassion, because they are under the influence of the mental afflictions, of wrong conceptions, and of the negative emotions that drive them to kill themselves or harm others. [37]

If we cannot feel compassion, at least we should not be angry. [38]

Even if it were in the nature of those who behave childishly to cause harm, or if an occasional mistake were committed by one who is normally trustworthy, it would be unreasonable to be angry. This would be the same as being angry at the fire that burns our hand after placing it on a flame, or with space or sky for allowing smoke to arise. [40]

It is wrong to think that we have the right to be angry at others because they have directly harmed us, but if we truly believe that, then we should be angry at the stick used to hit us, since it caused us direct harm. Now, we say we cannot be angry at the stick because it would not have ended up on our head without someone's aid. But then we cannot be angry at the person either, since he himself was urged to act by the mental afflictions, hatred in particular. We should instead turn our anger toward the afflictions themselves. [41]

Instead, we become unreasonably angry with the person who is in the intermediate position between the hatred and the stick. What we should do is, seeing the harmfulness of the anger in the other person's mind, eliminate the same anger from our own mind. The wrathful deities, full of compassion for beings whose minds are full of mental afflictions, have a terrifying appearance directed precisely at those mental afflictions.

When someone harms us, we must think that every suffering and difficulty we encounter is due to the fact that in our current life or in a former one we have created its causes through injuring others, and that we are in this way not only experiencing the effects of those actions, but also purifying and exhausting that negative karma. [42]

When someone hits us with a stick, if we become angry we create more negative imprints that will cause us further suffering in the future. Besides, if we think that it is right to be angry with those who have caused us pain, then we should feel the same also toward our bodies, the basis of all suffering.

If someone cuts off an arm with a knife, both arm and knife are the cause of the pain. If the knife was the cause, then, say, if it strikes a rock, the rock should feel pain, but because of its very nature the rock does not. Therefore the responsibility for pain must be shared between the weapon and the arm, because it is in the nature of the physical body to be the basis of suffering. Since the body creates so much suffering for you, then you should be angry with the body. [43]

If our bodies are covered with sores and someone touches us by mistake, causing great pain, by understanding the mistake, and that it is because of the sores that we suffer, let us not become angry with that person. [44]

We must think that we do not suffer merely because of external causes, but mainly because of our bodies, which are very weak and not able to endure all the hardships we encounter in life. We are like children, and although we do not wish to suffer, we are extremely attached to the causes of suffering and continuously accumulate new ones. If we suffer, it is mainly our fault, and we must not therefore be angry with others, thinking that they are responsible. [45]

The guardians of the hell realms or the forests of razor-sharp leaves are produced by our karma, by our actions, and therefore there is no reason to be intolerant of these extremely unpleasant situations that we may experience. [46]

We can also reflect on the fact that, if we suffer because of the harm caused us by others, it is our karma that urged them to act in that way, and that they are in fact its instruments.

We become angry because a person harms us, but in reality, if we look closely, we come to realize that we are the one harming that person. He acts under the impulse of hatred, and this will be the cause of his falling into the lower realms, whereas if we practice patience toward him, it will become the cause of our happiness. [47]

Through the practice of patience we can purify much negative karma and accumulate many positive imprints, whereas the person harming us has hatred toward us, and we thus become the indirect cause of his descent into the lower realms. [48]

That person is extremely kind to us, whereas we are the cause of his future suffering. Rather than being angry, we should therefore feel compassion and gratitude toward that person. [49]

We are the instruments through which he accumulates negative karma, but since this is not our intention, we do not create any for ourselves.

Trying to repay the harm inflicted is not useful in terms of either protecting ourselves or protecting others. It will only impair our practice. If, on the other hand, we practice patience, we will maintain the purity of our vows and improve our practice, and in this way we will protect ourselves. [51]

By these reflections we do not mean that we should not try to elude suffering. When unwanted, unpleasant circumstances happen to us, we should definitely try to avoid them.

If our parents ask us to be kind and help them, we must not refuse them. We should analyze their requests and, if it is within our capacity, do all that we can to fulfill them. If, however, they tell us not to listen to the teachings and not to practice the Dharma, we must not obey, although we should act wisely and tactfully. It is very important to be on good terms with one's parents. I did not have a good rapport with mine when I was little, before I started studying the lamrim, but growing up, my attitude changed, although by then my parents had died.

We must be clear with our parents and explain what we are doing, so that they might comprehend the meaning of the Dharma. We must treat them with kindness and love. Parents must realize that their child is enhancing his or her qualities through the practice of the Dharma. We must provide proof of this through our actions and our behavior, and if they are Christians we must explain to them that, as in Christianity, in Buddhism too one tries to refrain from committing negative actions.

It often happens that parents think that their son has gone crazy if he follows a spiritual path—it is up to that son to show that, instead, he has made an improvement. By having a good rapport with our parents, we will be successful in what we do, we will be happier in life, and we will have made good use of that field of merit. Equal merits are created by offering butter to the Three Jewels or to one's parents, and thus both are fields of merit. If we have a difficult relationship with our mother, we must begin by making peace with her. If we are the object of her complaints, we must reflect, and if her complaint is justified we must accept it and no longer behave as before.

Then there are situations in which we cannot be understood or make ourselves understood—try to avoid them! The important thing is to have a positive heart and a positive mind. Other people's actions also depend on those
they come into contact with; therefore the way we act is very important.

We all know that hatred and anger are truly negative, but we do not
know how to eliminate them or how to change our mental attitudes.
Hatred is the cause of every conflict, of every separation between husband
and wife, parents and children, friends, within groups of the same country, and between countries themselves. Even if a person possesses much, he
cannot be happy if anger resides in him. Our experience tells us that anger
causes unhappiness. Is there anyone among us who is happy when angry?

Peace in the world is thwarted by hatred. His Holiness the Dalai Lama
is held in high regard also in the West because he shows the way to peace,
saying that we must not cause harm to others in any way, but instead live
together in harmony.

If we stop harming one another and try instead to help each other, it
will bring peace. If a house is in flames, we can put out the fire and the
damage will not be too serious. If we do not do this, the house will burn
to the ground. Likewise, there are methods to control and destroy hatred,
and if we do not apply them, hatred will annihilate us.

Since our mind is not physical, it cannot be harmed. We say that evil
caused by others harms our body, but harsh speech, lack of respect, or
what others do does not provoke physical pain, so why do we become
angry? [53]

If we are quick-tempered, it will cause us to be unloved by others who
will be afraid of us, avoid us, and not be our friends.

It is far better to die than to have a long life in which our means of
survival are acquired by cheating others. [56]

The best way to leave this life is free from the weight of our negative
karma. We must therefore use the methods that allow us to purify negative karma and accumulate positive karma, so that when we die we will
be happy and serene as a result of practicing the Dharma. The happiness
of future lives also depends on this, as we will find if we obtain a happy
rebirth; otherwise we will experience suffering.

If a person dreams of having had a hundred years of happiness, and
another dreams of having had only one day of happiness, upon awakening

their happiness will be only a memory, and at that moment there will be no difference between the two. The same applies to someone who has had a happy life for fifty years and another for one year only—at the moment of death, happiness will not return in either case. [58]

Although a person may live happily for many years as a result of having obtained a great deal of material wealth, at the moment of death he will not be able to take anything with him, just as if he had been robbed by thieves. [59]

If a person accumulates many possessions, justifying it with his good intentions of using the opportunity to accumulate positive karma and purify negative karma, but then becomes angry in order to obtain those riches, he will destroy the merit he has generated and collect new negative imprints, and it will all be meaningless. [60]

We live in order to enjoy various benefits, but if we then destroy these same benefits, what is the point of living? The life of one who commits himself to the Dharma by eliminating mental afflictions and practicing what is good will be very useful, but one who, instead, performs evil deeds, will only create harm for himself. A life spent in this way is pointless. [61]

Bodhisattvas pray that those who commit much negative karma will not live long and so will not have the opportunity to go on creating many causes for their own suffering.

It is wrong to think that we have the right to be angry with someone who slanders us and keeps away the people who used to hold us in high regard. If we become angry and relate the facts to others, we are also keeping his friends away from him, and behaving exactly as he did. Likewise, it is pointless to become angry with someone who is disrespectful toward us, while patiently tolerating injury perpetrated against others. In both cases disrespect is caused by the arising of disturbing conceptions. [63]

Furthermore, saying that we are tolerant of harsh words directed at us but not of those directed at God, at buddhas, at our lama, and at the Dharma, and feeling authorized to become angry, is an unreasonable way of thinking, because these beings will not be affected by those insults in the least—no one can harm them. [64]

Instead of anger we should feel compassion toward those who speak in such ways, because they are accumulating negative karma.

When we become angry we always have many reasons to justify it, but if we examine them closely we find them to be illogical. If someone wrongs our master or our friends, we should think that this situation has arisen because of a specific karma. [65]

Objects that can harm us are of two kinds: animate, possessing a mind, and inanimate, devoid of mind. Usually we do not become angry with the latter, but with the former. Why is that? If we are crossing a river and the strong current takes us away, we do not become angry with the current, but instead we think that we have not been strong and steady enough. And if, while climbing a mountain, there is a landslide, we do not become angry at the stones. Why then, if we do not become angry with things devoid of a mind, do we become angry with those who possess one? If there are good reasons for our anger, we should experience rage for both types of phenomena. [66]

Yet again, what we are trying to stress is the bias in our reasoning, and its inconsistency.

We should also refrain from being angry when someone does wrong or makes mistakes. He does so because of ignorance, and if we become angry also because of ignorance, who is at fault? Who is without fault? [67]

When we become angry we never think that we are wrong. If someone hurts us, it is because we ourselves have committed negative actions of that type in the past, and therefore we must not feel resentful, but think instead that what is happening to us is the fruition of these actions. If we do not want to suffer, we must ask ourselves, "Why have I created all this negative karma?" [68]

Therefore we should generate only loving thoughts toward all beings and do exclusively what is meritorious and what will cause happiness. [69]

Those who cultivate love and compassion cannot generate hatred. Hatred is a destructive power that is as strong as an atom bomb. In fact, there are much bigger objects that exist in the world that do not have this same destructive power. However, faith and a correct attitude possess enormous virtuous strength, and a single moment of faith can produce a great amount of positive karma.

The four opponent powers, when applied intensely, can purify all our negative karma, no matter how much we have accumulated in the past and for how long. Whatever problems and unpleasant circumstances we find ourselves in, we must train ourselves to endure them. When we meet someone who harms us we must be tolerant, reflecting that he is influenced by mental afflictions, that it is all due to our karma, and that others are but karma's instruments—we ourselves are the real cause of our suffering.

If we consider that someone who harms others or ourselves is wrong, then we must, for the same reasons, consider our wish to repay the harm to be wrong. If instead of becoming angry we generate patience, those who see us will think that we are acting correctly and will judge us positively. When someone abuses us and we analyze the facts, we realize that his insults do not harm us physically, and therefore we are capable of enduring them and being tolerant.

Usually we do not become angry with someone who harms a stranger, but we certainly do become angry if the insult is directed at someone dear to us. This is because of our attachment, which is not, however, a good justification for our anger. In this case the feeling of hatred arises from our attachment and expands, just as a fire grows stronger when it touches straw or wood. Therefore, as soon as we are aware that we are becoming angry on this basis, we must remove hatred from our minds. [71]

When the sentence of a man sentenced to death is mitigated to the mere amputation of his hand, this is considered a fortunate outcome, even though normally this is certainly not the case. Likewise, we must consider life's sufferings to be our good fortune, because they prevent us from experiencing worse sufferings in the future. [72]

If we are incapable of enduring relatively small sufferings such as those of the present, why not eradicate anger from our hearts, as it is the cause of far greater sufferings in the future? It is truly sensible on our part to avoid creating causes of greater misfortune. [73]

If in practicing patience we experience difficulties, it is worth facing them, considering that in former lives we have endured enormous suffering for no reason at all. [74]

At present, however, we possess a good reason. What we have endured in the past has not been useful to us or to others, but now we must allow the sufferings of our current life to bear fruit and meaning for the benefit of ourselves and other people. We must therefore accept them gladly and experience them. [75]

When someone praises us or our dearest friends we are happy—why then don't we experience the same feeling if our enemy is being praised?

The person praising another enjoys it greatly, finding good qualities in that person. Why aren't we joining in the praise, and thus making our minds happy? [76]

The pleasure we experience when praising others is genuine, and it is appreciated by the buddhas. [77]

Having a loving attitude is the best way to make friends—if we love others, they will like us and we will be loved in return, whereas this will not happen if we are full of hostility.

If we do not want to experience the joy of praising others because it makes only them happy, then for the same reason we should not pay our workmen, because it makes only them happy. If we think like this, in the end we will be the ones to lose out, because we will no longer have any employees and we will have accumulated negative karma, which will be the cause of future sufferings. [78]

If we do not wish our enemies to be happy, we should feel the same about everyone. If someone sings our praises we feel delighted, not intolerant, and this is due to both the joy we ourselves feel and the joy from the person who praises us. When, however, an enemy is praised, we cannot tolerate the happiness experienced by the one who praises, or our enemy's happiness, and this is a contradiction. [79]

The one who praises our enemies is happy, otherwise he would not do so, and our enemies are happy to be praised. Why then not rejoice in the happiness of these two people? We have already generated bodhichitta, the mind that aspires to enlightenment for the benefit of all beings, wishing to fulfill the desires of all beings one day and to spare them all that they do not want. If someone obtains something that makes him happy without our effort, why should we be angry? [80]

We say that we desire the greatest happiness for all beings, and that we wish them to be free from all suffering, but then when they secure the smallest happiness we become angry—this too is absurd.

If a child in our care succeeds in becoming self-reliant, we are delighted. Likewise, when others succeed in attaining happiness by themselves we should be happy, even though we have vowed to assume personal responsibility for the happiness of all beings. [82]

If we are unable to tolerate the little happiness that beings procure for themselves without our help, how can we say that we aspire to possess bodhichitta and attain enlightenment in order for all beings to achieve this state of awakening? [83]

If a person becomes angry at the small happiness of another, he does not possess bodhichitta.

When our enemy receives help from a benefactor, we are not happy about it, but there is no reason to be unhappy or jealous since, whether a gift is given to our enemy or whether it remains in the benefactor's house, in either case it is not in our possession. [84]

If we receive fame and riches we are happy, but if our enemy receives them we feel angry and envious, and as a result anger destroys our merits and the very causes of obtaining fame and riches. We should be angry at ourselves for having thus destroyed the causes capable of causing us to realize our wishes. [85]

If we are poor and feel envious and angry toward the rich, these feelings will not make us rich—instead, they will destroy any possibility of future wealth. We must therefore avoid those negative mental factors that deprive us of the causes of wealth. If someone is rich we must understand that this is thanks to his merit, and if we desire wealth for ourselves we must be inspired by this and in turn accumulate merit of our own.

Obtaining wealth from the practice of generosity is a valid relationship of cause and effect. It is written that people will find happiness in the wealth derived from the practice of generosity, and the Buddha explains that it is important to put this into practice. We all desire happiness and wealth, but not everyone who makes an effort in this direction succeeds, because they both depend on virtuous accumulations.

If we want to obtain a precious human rebirth in the future we must observe morality, and if we desire wealth we must practice generosity. We like to hear about the human realm and the realm of the gods because these are fortunate conditions, but we are not fond of descriptions of the lower realms, although they are only meant to protect us from falling into them. Accordingly, we will avoid creating their cause, which is negative karma. If we have not produced any negative karma, we will never be reborn in a lower realm.

Shantideva is a bodhisattva whose sole concern is the happiness of all beings, and he has written this text solely for the purpose of fulfilling that happiness. If we accumulate negative karma all our lives, since we will die one day, we will certainly fall into these unfortunate states of existence, even though we have never heard of them. Positive karma, however, will cause rebirth in fortunate realms. There are various levels of existence in the deva realms, such as the realm of desire, the realm of form, and the formless realm, and each of them can be divided into subgroups. The same is true for the lower realms, but I will not talk about them because I think you might not like it. However, maintaining that there are no such things as hell realms and deva realms is like saying no nations exist besides your own!

Although we may not believe in the hell realms because we do not see them, we cannot deny the existence of the animal realm. Let us consider ants—they want something to eat, and if we leave out some sugar or honey they rush to it in large numbers. They do not wish to suffer, and when it is cold or rainy they hide underground—not because they like it, but because they are forced to do so. Animals suffer as a result of not being able to find shelter, food, and drink, and so do we. Both their suffering and our own depend on the negative imprints that have been created, and it is therefore possible that the hell realms do exist, because if there are beings who must experience these types of suffering, then places of this kind will automatically come into being. In any case, if we do not create negative karma, but only positive karma, we need not be concerned about the hell realms, even if they are a reality.

Right now, however, we are human beings, and we possess intelligent minds that are capable of discernment.

The entire world can have happiness or suffering because of the mind—being satisfied or unsatisfied depends on the mind, which is therefore powerful and helpful and must not be wasted, but instead used correctly. Since we all desire happiness, we must create its causes, and since we do not want suffering, we must avoid the causes that bring it about. By accumulating only positive karma, we will reach the point where we will only experience happiness.

Among the practices that are taught in the Dharma, we must first of all choose those within our reach and then slowly, as we obtain results, we can keep doing a little more, until we are able to practice them all.

When our enemy suffers we are happy, but it is not our desire for him to experience difficulties that causes him to suffer problems and grief. [87]

And even if these wishes of ours were to come true, what would we gain from it? We can answer that we gain nothing from our enemies' suffering, and that nevertheless we feel pleased. This is the reasoning of a wretched mind, and an attitude that will damage us. [88]

This attitude derives from our mental afflictions. They have cast the hook and we bite—we are like fish seized by the fisherman's bait. The fisherman is our mental afflictions, the hook is our karma, and we are the fish. Seized by mental afflictions, we will be thrown into hell's cauldron, where we will cook! [89]

To delight in our enemies' suffering is a despicable attitude and is equal to enjoying our own suffering. We may think of becoming angry with our enemy because he destroys our fame and honor, but are praise and honor really that important? They do not turn into merit, they do not lengthen our lives, they do not give us strength—nor do they free us from illness or provide any physical happiness. What is it about them that might justify the accumulation of negative karma through anger? [90]

If we maintain that fame and praise give us a little mental happiness, then we should devote ourselves to drinking and gambling, but these are not considered methods for achieving happiness. [91]

Fame and praise are but words and they bring no advantage whatso-ever—when we die, to whom will they give pleasure? [92]

Children cry when their sandcastles are destroyed, and we do the same when our fame vanishes. [93]

Words of praise produce nothing at all—they are only sounds, and have no intention in themselves of praising us. In praising us, someone perhaps shows us in a better light and is happy about it, but what do we gain from his joy? [94]

The fact that others feel happy while praising us does not bring about anything for us, because we cannot have a slice of their happiness. If we say that we are happy because the bestower of praise is happy, then we should also be happy when someone praises our enemy. This does not happen, and therefore ours is not a good reason. [96]

To be happy in receiving praise is a childish attitude. Besides, praise distracts our minds, undermines our disillusionment with cyclic existence, and allows pride to arise, with the result that we forget that we are merely beings roaming in cyclic existence. We no longer remember others or cultivate compassion and a positive attitude. Envying the good qualities of others, we then destroy our virtue and merit. Praise and fame, therefore, are solely harmful. [98]

Not only should we not be angry with the enemy who destroys our fame, but we should be grateful to him because he protects us from falling into the lower realms. [99]

Since we desire liberation, we should be grateful to our enemies for depriving us of material gains and honors—these are the chains that bind us to cyclic existence. Our enemies cut these chains by destroying our fame and prevent our entering the house of the most atrocious suffering. [100]

Those who wish us harm are like buddhas bestowing waves of blessings. We should not be angry with those who close the door to the lower realms. [101]

We could argue, on the one hand, that fame and praise are worldly things, but that, on the other hand, it is right to be angry if we are hindered in our practice of the Dharma. This is also wrong, because there is no better opportunity for accumulating merit than the practice of patience. Since this might be a rare occurrence, let us not waste these opportunities that are being offered. [102]

If someone harms us and we are not able to practice patience, it is entirely our error if we do not take advantage of the situation. If in these cases we let our anger explode, we ourselves are creating obstacles to the accumulation of merit. The enemy is not the impediment to our practice of patience, but rather the cause. [103]

The suffering we feel is not caused by our enemy—even if he harms us, if we do not become angry we will not be unhappy. Until we familiarize ourselves with this way of reasoning, it will be natural for us to feel anger. However, if we turn an enemy into a friend, there is no danger of friends becoming enemies instead!

All beings, even those appearing to be people who cause us trouble, are kind to us, and we must therefore abandon the mind that feels distant from enemies and close to friends and realize equanimity, so that we are able to eliminate hatred for the former and attachment to the latter.

Before considering that all beings have been our mothers, we must develop this attitude of equanimity, which is also the basis for the other method of generating bodhichitta, exchanging oneself with others. In order to build a house we need good foundations, and in this case equanimity is the basis for the development of the Mahayana attitude.

It is good to have been able to reflect on how our enemies are in fact our friends. At present we succeed in seeing our enemies as friends only through reasoning, but with practice we will spontaneously succeed in seeing even those who harm us as friends.

In this way Shantideva's purpose in writing this chapter has been fulfilled. Even though he wrote it a long time ago, we have come across it, and benefited from it, only now. We must pray to the Three Jewels, purify our negative karma, and accumulate positive karma. In this way we will make good progress. If we do not make an effort gradually, we will not improve.

As the abbot and the other monks help us to receive ordination and become monks ourselves, so an enemy is not a hindrance to us but is instead a support in the practice of patience. [105]

Usually it is not difficult to find someone toward whom we can be generous, since there are so many people in need, but it is hard to find someone who can act as the object of our practice of patience.

Generally no one harms us if we ourselves have not caused harm, but if we do find someone who harms us without any provocation, a good opportunity is upon us, and it has arisen without any effort on our part. [106]

In the *Eight Verses of Mental Training* it is said, "May I consider as my best friend and most precious master he who unreasonably, in exchange for good received from me, repays me with harm."

If we were to discover a treasure in the house we would be extremely happy, even though jewels are not that important since we can use them only while we are alive. If, however, we were to meet an enemy and succeed in practicing patience with him, and were thus able to perfect it, this would be one of the factors that would allow us to attain enlightenment. [107]

"And if the enemy is the cause of my perfecting of patience, and this in turn is the cause of my enlightenment, I will have to give the first fruits to him, who has urged me toward the practice." [108]

We could object that our enemy has no intention of being the cause of our development of the perfection of patience and that therefore there is no reason to repay him in this way. But the Dharma also has no intention of benefiting us. Why then do we venerate it and make it the object of our prayers? [109]

One aspect of the Dharma is the cessation of suffering, which is a permanent phenomenon, and a permanent phenomenon cannot affect us. The truth of the path has no mind and no will but is nevertheless a cause for the achievement of enlightenment. We must therefore make offerings and pay homage to the Dharma, because it is worthy. Even for these particular teachings, in the form of texts, we normally have respect and veneration. Should we not have such because they do not possess a mind? The objects of our offerings are statues and images that represent the body of the Buddha, scriptures that represent his words, and stupas that represent his mind. We could say that they have no intention to benefit us, and also no intention to harm us, unlike our enemies. But if our enemies only wished to benefit us and had no intention to cause us harm, how could we practice patience toward them? They would not be enemies, and we would have no chance to refrain from being angry. [110] Precisely because they harm us, they can be the objects of our patience, and we should practice not only patience, but the whole of the Dharma. [111]

We must make the most of the precious opportunity we have to reflect on these matters by learning from others, such as the buddhas and bodhisattvas. Using them as an example, we must practice in the same way ourselves. There are two types of benefit that we can obtain: temporary and long term. As far as temporary benefits go, since we are in samsara, we must obtain the best of them, but in the long term we must try to dedicate our entire energy to attaining buddhahood. The Buddha taught that there are two objects for generating merit: the Three Jewels and sentient beings. The enemy who is harming us is a sentient being, and if we become angry with him we misuse this opportunity and accumulate negative karma. If, on the other hand, we practice tolerance toward him, we accumulate positive karma, which is the main purpose of a follower of a spiritual path.

We respect and have faith in the Three Jewels, and understand that they are a basis for the accumulation of merit, but we do not consider how this also applies to sentient beings. What reason do we have to think like this? [113]

Since they are both fields for accumulation of virtue, we must generate the same respect for the field of sentient beings that we do for the field of the Three Jewels. We could object, however, that sentient beings are not equal to the buddhas, whose qualities are infinite, whereas the qualities of beings are not. But what we must understand is that they are equal as a basis for generating positive karma, which is the cause of attaining enlightenment. [114]

We accumulate merit by generating love and compassion toward all beings, as well as faith and respect toward the Three Jewels. Besides which, we must have respect for all beings, even if their good qualities are only a minute fraction of those of the buddhas. [116]

If a person possesses even a tiny amount of virtue compared to the buddhas, he is worthy of receiving all the universes as an offering, because he plays a role, even if it is a small one, in allowing us to obtain the supreme qualities of a buddha. [118]

The Buddha is not biased in granting his help, and to repay his kindness we must respect all sentient beings, who are the objects of his benevolence. He has obtained this state by concerning himself with their happiness, and also, when he was a bodhisattva, he took them as the object of his bodhichitta.

The best way to repay the buddhas, therefore, is by serving and taking care of sentient beings, to whom the buddhas have dedicated their lives. [119]

Buddhas have offered their lives many times and have remained in samsara for an infinite number of eons with the sole aim of helping all beings, and we too, in order to show our gratitude, must treat them with respect, even if they harm us, turning this into an opportunity for the accumulation of merit through the practice of patience. [120]

Buddhas have been concerned about the welfare of all beings even at the cost of their own lives, whereas we, full of pride and self-importance, ignore them. We must not behave in this way any longer, but instead think of dedicating our lives to them. [121]

Buddhas are happy when beings are happy, and if we harm beings, we indirectly harm the buddhas. It is as if we wanted to please a mother, while at the same time we harmed her son. A mother loves her son, and if we help him she will be delighted, whereas if we harm him she will suffer. Likewise, the buddhas, who dedicate themselves completely to all beings, will be pleased if we too benefit them. [122]

If we were to offer delicious food to someone whose body is ablaze with fire, surely he would not be able to appreciate it. Likewise, if on the one hand we make offerings to the buddhas, wishing to please them, while on the other we neglect beings and have no compassion toward them, this is a contradiction, inappropriate behavior, and we must correct it—we must pay homage to the buddhas by taking good care of all beings. [123]

A king asked Nagarjuna, "How is it possible that I have so many obligations and responsibilities in ruling my kingdom and have no time to practice the Dharma? What is your advice? Since I have made the buddhas unhappy by harming and neglecting all beings, now I confess and purify these wrong deeds of mine. May I be forgiven for any pain I might have caused the buddhas and for having acted thus. Since helping all beings definitely pleases the buddhas, I will endeavor to benefit them, to become their servant, and having promised this, even if they were to beat me, I will endure the injury. May the buddhas be delighted in my practice." [125]

The buddhas have so much compassion that they constantly think of alleviating suffering and procuring happiness for everyone, and this sense of responsibility is their own, in spite of the fact that they do not conceive themselves as truly existent "I." [126]

I have no doubt that there is an altruistic and compassionate attitude in you as well.

We must try to please the buddhas by making ritual offerings of flowers, light, and prayers, but also, we must not neglect compassion for all beings and helping them. If we succeed in doing so we will also make the buddhas happy. Besides, making others happy alleviates their suffering, and therefore it is necessary to put this method into practice. This is in our own interest, since it is the cause of attaining enlightenment. [127]

If the ministers or the members of a royal family harm others, and if those harmed are farsighted, they will not avenge themselves, because if they do they will provoke the king's wrath. In order to avoid this, they will endure the injury. In fact, by turning against the king's men they would be indirectly turning against the king himself. [128]

Just as we must endure the harm caused by the men of a despotic king because we know that he might cause us further harm, likewise we must endure the mischief of malevolent beings. [129]

We must not underestimate a defenseless person or someone who harms us, because these weak beings are supported not only by the buddhas, but also by the guardians of the hell realms. [130]

However, at most a tyrant might harm us physically, but he cannot send us to the hell realms. If, on the other hand, we avenge ourselves for the damage we suffer at the hands of others, we will later have to endure the suffering of rebirth in the lower realms. [131]

If we please the kings we will not obtain buddhahood, but if we please sentient beings we will get it, and in our own life too we will meet favorable circumstances and find friends, because the people we are benefiting now will help us sooner or later. [133]

Many expressions of love, however, are not necessarily pure Dharma, and it is likely that they will be mixed with attachment.

We must see other beings as guides, because thanks to them we will succeed in attaining buddhahood. These are valid reasons.

The Buddha said that dying is not in itself a great occurrence, nor particularly important, but dying without having spotlessly maintained ethical discipline is something that we should feel is unendurable. We can understand the meaning of his words by reflecting on the fact that if someone harms us, we can practice patience and accumulate considerable merit and, because of this, obtain a more fortunate rebirth. If we do not endure the harm and instead avenge ourselves, it will prompt a negative reaction in the other. He will try to harm us again in turn, and we will have accumulated a considerable amount of negative karma, which we will carry with us at the moment of death, and in future lives we will have to endure more suffering.

If someone insults us we become angry, but if we examine the matter closely we can see that their offensive words have no power whatsoever and that, if we feel unhappy, it is solely due to the way that we perceive them.

If we practice patience, the other will change his behavior. In Dharamsala there is a restaurant run by a married couple. For a long time the wife treated her husband badly, but he never reacted, until finally she became tired and stopped insulting him.

Intolerance always fosters disharmony. If we are prey to anger we are not able to sleep, and even if we eat a delicacy we cannot enjoy it. Patience, on the other hand, will banish both insomnia and the inability to enjoy food.

Practicing patience, not only will we attain buddhahood, but within cyclic existence we will possess an attractive physical form, live a long, pleasurable, and comfortable life devoid of illness and pain, and even become universal kings. [134]

It might be hard at first to practice patience, but the right effort will bring results. A person who teaches it might not be able to practice it himself, because teaching is easy but practicing is a great deal harder— however, even just the thought of being patient is beneficial.

Because of ignorance we destroy happiness and its causes as if they were our enemies. We cannot practice patience, and so we dissipate the positive karma already accumulated. The same thing happens with wrong views, with disbelief in the Three Jewels and in former and future lives, and with ignorance about the way phenomena exist.

The remedy that eliminates mental afflictions at their root is the wisdom that realizes right view, emptiness, and, understanding its importance, we must try to develop it.

Right now we have a small amount of love and compassion for friends and relatives, but in order to increase it further we must first of all generate equanimity for all beings. We feel sorry when our loved ones go through difficulties, but we are not sorry if strangers do, and even less so if the same happens to our enemies—in fact, if our enemies suffer, we even feel joy. But the person who now appears to us as an enemy has not always been so—in former lives he was not only our friend but even our mother. Besides, our friends and relatives and the people we feel indifferent to have also been our enemies in former lives. We can thus comprehend that all beings, whether friends, enemies, or strangers, are equal and that there is no reason to be attached to some, hate others, and be indifferent to others still.

In another sense, too, beings are the same—they all desire happiness, because they are deprived of it, and they do not wish to suffer.

If ten beggars were to ask us for food, it would be unreasonable to give it to only one of them and leave all the others starving, since they are all equally in need. Now, every being desires happiness and does not wish to suffer, but we discriminate between friends, enemies, and strangers, repaying some with love and our attentions, others with contempt, and others still with indifference. This attitude of ours is unreasonable.

A doctor who cares only for some patients and neglects others is himself in the wrong, and his patients, who all need his care equally, are not.

All beings are equal in their condition as "sick people," in desiring happiness and wanting to avoid suffering, and it is we who are in the wrong when we discriminate. Besides, they are all equal to us, since they have all benefited us in former lives, and we should therefore feel an impartial gratitude toward them.

There is one more reason for cultivating and extending the love and compassion we feel for friends and relatives to all beings, which is that with such an attitude we can develop our mind to the point of thinking that on our own, we ourselves must assume the responsibility for benefiting all beings. Since in our present situation we are not able to do so, and only a buddha is, we will feel the urgency to attain buddhahood, and therefore generate bodhichitta.

The source of happiness, even of the smallest kind as experienced by an animal, is previous positive karma. The cause of the smallest suffering can be attributed to negative karma. We must therefore make the greatest effort to purify negative karma and accumulate positive karma.

Another motive to reflect upon is the fact that all happiness derives from benefiting all beings, whereas all problems derive from harming them and not being kind to them. We must therefore help them, and if we are not able to do so at present we must at least try to refrain from causing them harm. If we are not capable of virtue we must at least avoid creating negativity, otherwise in spite of possessing material wealth we will nevertheless be unhappy.

All the happiness we desire can be obtained solely through spiritual practice; we must therefore commit ourselves to it.

There is a big difference between two people suffering harm if one of them is a spiritual practitioner and the other is not. The former will not feel anguish because he understands that whoever is harming him is clouded by his mental afflictions, whereas the latter will be very unhappy, not being able to practice patience. So although the harm is the same, the result will be different. Encountering adverse circumstances, one who practices the Dharma will be able to endure them by understanding that they are the result of his negative karma, whereas one who does not practice will experience much mental anguish, not knowing how to generate patience.

Unfortunately all of us must work for a living and it is hard not to take that into account, so we must continue to do our work for that purpose, as well as practice on the spiritual path so that it might bring us happiness. If, by ignoring the Dharma, we concern ourselves only with possessions and worldly pleasures, we will be greatly harmed.

It is important to realize that there are many types of beings in the sea, on land, and in the sky, and we are among them. But why are we more intelligent than others—than animals, for example? Why do we experience more happiness? Why do we possess the tools that allow us to obtain even more? Why is there so much difference? The answer lies in the fact that we have previously generated much more positive karma and that now we are experiencing its result, whereas animals do not experience happiness because they were not capable of accumulating the appropriate causes.

Material means can bring only short-term benefit, whereas spiritual practice can bring us long-term benefit. Its fruit will never abandon us. Material means give us a brief, ephemeral happiness; the Dharma provides us with a greater and more lasting happiness. It is necessary to put much more effort into the practice of the Dharma, the final results of which are personal liberation and the state of complete enlightenment, but which also brings benefits within cyclic existence. If there is something worth channeling our efforts into and worthy of our devotion, it is the spiritual path.

⌁ 7 ⌁

ENTHUSIASTIC EFFORT

W E NOW BEGIN THE SEVENTH CHAPTER, the discussion of enthusiastic effort, also known as joyful perseverance, or the appreciation
of virtue.

If we can practice patience and endure the suffering and harm caused
by others, we also need to have the desire to attain enlightenment for their
sake. Therefore, we generate enthusiastic effort, without which we would
not succeed in our task. [1]

In order to light a lamp, the right conditions are needed—for example,
the absence of wind—and the same applies to virtuous deeds and the creation of merit. These things could not be brought about without joyful
effort—the mind that delights in committing itself to meritorious practices and whose nature is the appreciation of positive karma and virtue.

Working and being committed to our business is not enthusiastic effort.
By enthusiastic effort we are referring exclusively to the practice of making
effort toward positive deeds. The obstacle to this practice is laziness, which
prevents us from appreciating merit and virtue. [2]

A lazy person will not be able to practice the Dharma or study profitably; nor will he eat well, because he will not even be able to prepare his
own food.

There are three types of *laziness.* The first is the laziness of *being
attached to worldly activities,* or the laziness of being interested in negative
things and unconcerned about things that are worth accomplishing—in
other words, the practice of the Dharma. This kind of laziness is characterized by the attraction to nonvirtuous actions, which do not result in
ultimate happiness.

The second type of laziness is *tiredness*. In spite of the fact that we understand that the Dharma involves a lot of practice, we feel devoid of the necessary strength required for the task. On the Mahayana path we must consider all beings to be more important than ourselves. This is a rather difficult, advanced practice. Thinking that we do not possess the necessary energy to pursue it is the meaning of this form of laziness.

The third aspect of laziness is *not feeling adequate,* not having a good opinion of ourselves, being discouraged, and thinking that we do not possess the skills or the intelligence to fulfill certain commitments.

The causes of laziness, the opponents of enthusiastic perseverance, are wanting to enjoy the happiness that is most easily achieved, not wishing to make any effort, attachment to and craving for sleep, not understanding one's own suffering and, because of that, not feeling aversion to the suffering of cyclic existence in general. [3]

When we realize that the nature of samsara is suffering, we will generate repulsion and contempt for it, and thus we will succeed in eliminating laziness. On this basis, by observing all beings, we will understand that they too, like us, find themselves in a situation of suffering and wish to be free from it.

The majority of beings on this earth are not aware of the spiritual path, and even those who are do not practice it. Some do not feel comfortable with it, and others, although they acknowledge the fact that they should pursue it, postpone doing so in order to finish whatever it is that they are doing. In this situation, although they are acquainted with the path and its methods of practice, they are unable to bring it to fruition.

Why aren't we able to devote ourselves completely to the Dharma from this moment on? Because we do not have strong determination.

It is mainly the awareness of impermanence and death that can prompt us to bring our mind back to practice. Also, we should consider our good fortune in having obtained a precious human birth, together with the awareness of possessing a good combination of body and mind which, if not employed right away, will be hard to obtain in the future.

Thanks to this precious human birth we can know and practice the Dharma, whose value is far greater than even a vast quantity of jewels. The most precious among them could not free us from samsara, nor help us obtain buddhahood, and in any case we would have to leave the jewel behind at the moment of death. On the basis of this precious human rebirth, however, by applying the necessary effort, we can practice in order to obtain liberation and also enlightenment.

If we realize this and still do not practice the Dharma now, then when will we ever do it? Just as an animal caught in a trap by a hunter will certainly die, it is the same with us, caught in the trap of the mental afflictions. We are already in the mouth of death but do not realize this danger, and so if we do not succeed in understanding it now, when will it happen? [4]

Most of us are not truly even conscious of the fact that death, in many places and precisely at this moment, is taking away many human beings. How many, young and old, unaware of death, have placidly gone to sleep and had life snatched away from them? We are also on the verge of death and cannot be certain as to when this will happen.

We are able to say all of this with words, but it is not yet part of our minds, because if we truly understood it we would not be wasting time and we would be doing something useful in every moment. Death is certain and the course of life is very uncertain—we know this, but we do not exactly understand what we must do. We behave like the buffalo who, in spite of having seen the butcher kill other animals, continues to graze placidly. [5]

We are not conscious of what is happening and we waste time, and so every passing moment is a wasted moment. We can be certain that we will die—the route has already been marked. The lord of death comes nearer and nearer, and while we still indulge in eating and drinking, he approaches closer still. [6]

How can a person condemned to die enjoy food and sleep in the little time left to him? If he did this, it would certainly look absurd to us, and yet we behave in the same fashion. With death approaching closer and closer every moment, instead of finding a way out, we continue to enjoy various pleasures. Instead of this, we must use the time left to us to engage in positive, virtuous deeds. In the West most people do not appreciate talking about death, but if we do not understand the uncertainty of life, impermanence, and the certainty of death, we will not be able to devote ourselves to spiritual practice and defeat laziness. Mindfulness of these things is necessary to encourage us to use our time profitably. Taking future lives into consideration, we will work for them.

If there were no rebirth after death, there would be no need to worry, but this is not so—mind carries on, and after this life there will be others, the quality of which will depend on previously accumulated karma. If we want happiness we must prepare ourselves.

We will be separated from this body, obtained from our parents, at the moment of death. If we want better circumstances in the future we must create positive karma. If instead we are indolent, we will obtain unfortunate rebirths as cats, worms, or even worse. As human beings or gods we will experience less suffering and more happiness in relation to other beings. If we obtain a favorable human form again, we then have the hope to improve, to be able to practice the Dharma, and eventually to succeed in eliminating all mental afflictions, and finally obtaining liberation and enlightenment.

If we do not possess the ability to create positive karma in this life and avoid negative karma, it is likely that we will be more unhappy in our next lives. For example, we will be born as animals, and then it will be difficult to have the opportunity to practice the Dharma. In this type of existence, instead of progressing, we will increasingly worsen our situation.

Just as we must plan well for a holiday to be successful, so too must we plan well for our future lives, and then there will be no uncertainty as to the results. If we do not plan well, our situations will be very precarious indeed. Now we are in good health and we have time at our disposal. But what will we be able to do when we are ill or on our deathbeds? In spite of our good intentions, we will not be in a position to do anything at all, nor will we have the time. [7]

Death comes suddenly—it does not wait for anyone—even if we have begun a task that must be finished at all costs, even if we still have many projects for the future. [8]

If we practice the Dharma and death comes unexpectedly, we will have no regrets and we will die serenely. If we do not practice, we will be prey to remorse, knowing that we did not perform the necessary good deeds or purify our negative actions. At that moment, the faces of our relatives will flow with tears and their eyes will be red and swollen with sorrow and, because of our negative karma, we will be tormented by terrifying visions. [9]

We will hear the horrifying sounds of hell, our bodies will experience terrible pain, and we will become incontinent. How can we do good in such a critical moment? [10]

As fish caught and thrown onto the hot sand shake convulsively, seized with anguish and pain, we too, remembering our unwholesome deeds, will suffer. [11]

How can we remain relaxed and not worry about anything, knowing that we have accumulated so much negative karma? If our bodies cannot endure boiling hot water, how can we even imagine being able to endure the tremendous heat of the hell realms? The pain we will experience in the lower realms will certainly be greater than that of our present life. [12]

A burn on an adult's hand is painful, but a burn on a child's is even more so. Likewise, one who has generated more negative karma will suffer even more intense pain.

Having created all the causes that will result in suffering, how can we be at ease?

We certainly cannot expect to have the things we desire if we do not put the necessary enthusiastic effort into obtaining them. We have experienced death many times, and it is approaching closer and closer; nevertheless we are convinced that our lives will be long and that we will continue to live for many more years. This thought defeats us, and it will cause us suffering. [13]

Now we possess a precious human life and we can obtain anything we want, even liberation from all suffering, if we know how to put it to good use. Anything we desire is within our reach, and if we want to obtain favorable circumstances we must strive to create positive karma—it is up to us.

Suffering and unhappiness have causes, otherwise there would be two alternatives—either they would be constant, or they would not be there at all. This is not the case, because suffering does exist. However, because it is impermanent, we can see that it arises from causes. These causes are negative mental imprints, which can be removed through purification.

Right now we are in samsara, which is like an ocean of suffering, and in order to cross it and reach the other shore we have a boat, our human life. Since it will be very difficult to obtain a rebirth as favorable as this one in the future, we must not waste time and squander it by falling prey to sleep and ignorance, given that now we can realize any aim. [14]

Our minds have existed from beginningless time and our mental afflictions have constantly traveled with them. We cannot establish a moment when they began, a moment before which there was nothing.

It can be difficult for us to establish how a particular cause has a certain effect, but we can surely say that a positive cause produces a positive effect and vice versa. Only a buddha can know the particular effects produced by specific causes, and that in order to obtain the form of a human or a deva one must practice moral discipline, and in order to obtain the comforts and pleasures of these types of existence one must practice generosity. Any suffering we experience is caused solely by the negative karma we have created. Even cats or dogs who find food and a good master do so because of their previous good karma. These beings were born as animals because they did not observe moral discipline, and they enjoy favorable conditions because they practiced generosity. Among human beings, there are rich people and poor people—they are all human as a consequence of having been able to practice ethical discipline, but the person who is poor in spite of his efforts is so because he has not practiced generosity. Human rebirth is a consequence of the practice of morality and the condition of poverty is due to a lack of generosity. The relationship between cause and effect is definite.

Bodhisattvas are experts in the various types of morality, and all of their activities can be included within the six perfections.

When going to battle, one wears armor and carries weapons. Similarly, if we want to practice the Dharma, we must wear the armor of joyous perseverance and, instead of indulging in our discouragement, be supported by enthusiasm. Practicing with zeal, we must exert control over ourselves.

One who sees that all beings are equal in desiring happiness and not desiring suffering is considered a good person.

It is good to think about ourselves, but it is best to do so without forgetting others—in other words, allowing room for our thoughts to turn to them. If we enjoy some happiness, it is important to wish that others have the same, and if we experience suffering, it is important to wish that also others may not have to endure it any longer. If we are satisfied after a good meal, we should generate the wish that others might experience the same satisfaction.

Understanding the importance of fortunate rebirths, we extend this thought to others and wish that they may also obtain one, because it is selfish not to do so. If we have a healthy body, we develop the wish that everyone might possess one. Although these are only thoughts, in this way we can train our minds so that we might one day truly strive to actualize every altruistic intention.

We have said that all beings have been very kind and of great help to us. Therefore, we must develop the desire to repay them. In the chapter on patience we discussed the fact that our enemies, too, have been kind to us. If even they are of great benefit, how much more are those who help us. Therefore, we must repay everybody's kindness, and the best way to do this it is to try to liberate every being from suffering and procure happiness for others.

Through the two attitudes of love and compassion it is possible to develop bodhichitta, thanks to which one can attain buddhahood and therefore be of maximum benefit to all beings. All this must not remain on an intellectual or verbal level, for if we deeply absorb it we will be able to truly realize this type of mind.

Having developed equanimity, we must not remain content but go further and be able to exchange ourselves for others. Right now we feel more important than others, but by developing equanimity we will first bring ourselves to their level, and later we will consider them more important—that is, we will exchange self for others. [16]

Once we have developed this attitude, we will be able to sacrifice ourselves and be happy when someone else is happy, even if we are suffering.

Thinking of profiting from other beings or even of being able to sacrifice them in order to gain something is definitely incorrect, but this is precisely the way we behave. Fishermen go out to sea and catch many fish and crabs, and also sacrifice many worms in a single day, because they think that they themselves are more important than these beings. We are used to this kind of behavior, but we must nevertheless develop a radically opposite view and instead sacrifice ourselves for others, even at the cost of our lives. There are two ways of doing this—with or without the expectation of gaining something in the future.

Right now we only have the desire to benefit others, but once we have attained buddhahood, we will actually succeed in doing so. The fact that we will also enjoy much happiness is secondary, and an extra gain. The Mahayana mode of thinking is to be mainly concerned for others. Anything we may gain for ourselves is a kind of byproduct.

Likewise, if the purpose motivating us to practice Dharma is to obtain positive results in future lives, then if we gain something good in this life, it will be a secondary result. The Buddha has said that people who are concerned about future lives will obtain benefits in this life as well. When we cultivate corn we desire to have a good harvest, but we obtain straw as well, even though this was not our intention.

In the first chapter it was said that a person who has taken the bodhisattva vows and truly generated the mind of bodhichitta creates positive karma even while sleeping. Sleep is a neutral mental state, and it is made positive or negative in dependence on one's motivation when going to sleep. Therefore it is very important that this motivation be positive. We can fall asleep remembering the Three Jewels, or bodhichitta, or thinking about the non-intrinsic existence of phenomena. There are also numerous tantric practices, some of which we can practice even during sleep.

Truly understanding that the Dharma is the only thing worth practicing and that it is the Dharma toward which we should devote our efforts will help us avoid every type of laziness. Only a buddha is omniscient—in other words, a buddha knows all phenomena within and beyond samsara, and knows them with the same clarity with which we are able to perceive an apple placed on the palm of our hand. A buddha knows that only the Dharma will be of benefit at all times, and therefore teaches us the need to practice it.

We cannot escape death. If we are well prepared the moment that it arrives, we will not be worried and we will leave this life fearlessly; otherwise we will be scared of the future.

There are no logical reasons to assert that there is not a future life, and saying that we cannot see it is certainly not a valid reason. In Tibet it is very unlikely that one would find someone who would deny the existence of future lives, because people are used to this way of thinking, and also because many reincarnated lamas have been recognized. There are examples of dead people coming back to their relatives as spirits or in other forms, complaining that their families had not taken good enough care of them.

In any case, whether we believe in them or not, being well prepared is to our advantage—if future lives exist we will be all right, and if they do not, the positive deeds we perform will be useful to us during this lifetime.

Preparing for the future does not mean building a beautiful house or accumulating money in the bank, because we will not be able to take these things with us when we die. Instead, it means purifying our negative karma and accumulating positive karma. However, we must not be content with this alone, for if we are, we will obtain better lives but remain in the grip of karma and mental afflictions. Furthermore, until we are free from conditioned existence, we will not obtain anything worthy and important, and we will be born without choice, become old without choice, become sick without choice, and die without choice.

It is not enough to wish liberation for oneself either, because all beings are in the same situation that we are. Therefore, as spiritual practitioners, we must extend this wish of attainment to them as well, with buddhahood as our ultimate purpose.

We could think, "Enlightenment is certainly valid, but how can I succeed in reaching so difficult a goal?" We must never indulge in this type of laziness. [17]

The Buddha only speaks the truth, so we can believe him when he said that even flies, bees, and mosquitoes, developing enthusiastic effort, can obtain the unsurpassable state of enlightenment. [18]

If in the sutras it is explained that even small insects, with sufficient effort and vigor, can succeed in this, then it should be even easier for us because we have obtained a rebirth that is definitely superior, endowed as it is with an intelligent mind and favorable circumstances. [19]

In the past we have had many lives and we have certainly been mosquitoes as well, but now we have obtained a precious human rebirth. If in this life we succeed in developing bodhichitta and in practicing and obtaining buddhahood, it is proof that mosquitoes and other animals have the same potential. The Buddha himself was, before his enlightenment, an ordinary being like us. In some previous life he was an insect as well—therefore, that mosquito of a previous life has now become the Buddha.

A lay practitioner once went to Shakyamuni Buddha and asked him if he had previously accumulated some virtue. The answer he received was that many lives before in a certain region there had been a flood and near a small stupa a horse had dropped some excrement. At that time, that person was a fly who landed on the excrement, which, floating on the water, went around the stupa—and such a circumstance allowed the fly to accumulate positive karma. If even a small seed of virtue such as this, created unintentionally, can be the cause of liberation, how much more so does this hold true for what we do with intention!

If we are not lazy and if we generate the right effort, we will certainly obtain buddhahood. We have seen that in order to succeed we must develop all positive qualities, such as generosity, which also includes offering our own life and parts of our body. We may think now that we are not able to do this, but we must understand that "great," "long," and "difficult" are all relative concepts. [20]

In past lives we have endured incredible suffering and this has produced no results, whereas the small efforts that we can make now will bring huge results. We must reflect on the fact that everything is relative. For example, when we were reborn as cows in previous lives we were killed and butchered, and yet this suffering bore no fruit and did not procure buddhahood for us. [21]

The suffering we endure in order to attain enlightenment will have an end, because at a certain level the bodhisattva, though it might seem that he suffers, in reality does not suffer any longer, whereas the suffering experienced in cyclic existence is endless. [22]

We are prepared, in the case of an illness, to undergo even painful surgery—in other words, we accept this suffering, and the doctor himself advises us to do so in order to keep our condition from worsening. With a similar spirit we must be capable of enduring the suffering in our lives, with the motivation to not endure greater suffering in cyclic existence and to experience instead the great happiness of liberation. [23]

We must joyfully endure the suffering and the discomfort that we encounter in our practice of the Dharma, because the Buddha, the best of doctors in treating the greatest ills, is offering us skillful and effective means to defeat ignorance. [24]

The entire path, which is the means by which we can eliminate every problem of conditioned existence, is valuable and full of joy, so if we experience difficulties at the beginning we must endure them.

The Buddha first teaches us through well-founded reason, not forcing us to practice, but explaining the benefits of doing so. When we have subsequently understood them, we will naturally develop the wish to engage in the practice. The Buddha's method explains the advantages derived from our involvement in the spiritual path and then leaves the choice to the individual who, appreciating these points, will practice the Dharma and not become discouraged even if he has to practice for a long period of time. Without such understanding, it would be unbearable even to sit in this hall and listen to the teachings. If we were to strive all night to practice the twenty-one aspects of Tara for valid reasons that we recognize, we would have no difficulty completing the practice.

The Buddha's advice is not an order or a set of obligations, but a simple explanation that, once understood, will naturally engender the aspiration to practice. For example, when developing the profound attitude of generosity, in addition to the practice itself, simply hearing requests for help that we can satisfy will fill us with joy.

The Buddha does not suggest that we offer our bodies at the beginning of our practice, but suggests that we begin by giving objects of little value. We then gradually increase the value of the offerings—giving food, then money, then clothes, and so forth. When we develop the wisdom that understands the true nature of phenomena, we will understand that our bodies are ordinary objects and we will have no more consideration for them than we do for fruit or salad. We will then be capable of offering them in the same way that we would offer these things. [25]

Practicing in this way on the path of preparation, a bodhisattva still experiences suffering but has the strength to face it with joy. Once he has reached the path of seeing, he will no longer have to endure it. From this level on he regards his own body like food and has no difficulty giving it away. [26]

Such bodhisattvas are endowed with compassion and joy, and it is possible for them to choose their next rebirths. If they see that there is a purpose in doing so, they will offer their bodies as an act of generosity and will take on a new birth in favorable circumstances where they can be of greater help to all beings.

Nowadays there is no need to give away our bodies in order to be reborn in a different country so as to help others, since it suffices to board a plane and go to that country. But perhaps in the past a bodhisattva might have found the first method more convenient, with the added bonus of new parents to take care of him!

We are talking about vigor in practice and about the joy of performing virtuous deeds, the antidotes to laziness. Laziness binds us to actions that have no meaning or value, and prevents us from practicing the Dharma with the reason that it is too difficult or that we have many things to do, so that we feel depressed and incapable. This laziness is a wrong way of thinking and hinders us from striving in what is advantageous. We must stop giving it the opportunity to arise, and instead reflect on the fact that what is contained in the teachings has been said by the Buddha and so have trust in it.

We might think that buddhahood is not near at hand and that we will have to practice for eons and eons, and thus feel discouraged. But a bodhisattva must never lose heart in this way, because having purified his negative karma and developed virtue, he will not experience physical suffering and, having acquired wisdom, he will not lack joy. The mental unhappiness we experience is caused by our concept of a truly existent "I," and physical suffering is caused by the negative karma we create by clinging to such a false "I." However, a bodhisattva who has eliminated both of these causes will not experience problems of any kind. [27]

A bodhisattva must cultivate his mind and practice virtue for an incalculable number of eons. By releasing his grip on the "I" and the other mental afflictions, he no longer accumulates negative karma, which is the cause of suffering, and thus no longer experiences suffering itself. Consequently, it does not matter if it takes him a long time to attain enlightenment, since he no longer experiences any difficulties in cyclic existence. If we suffer mentally or physically, even a short stay in samsara will seem unbearable, but if we do not, there will be no problem remaining there for eons.

A bodhisattva has generated the mind of awakening and has promised to strive in the various practices for the benefit of all beings, and because of this he has accumulated much virtue, thanks to which he will experience only favorable circumstances. He has the wisdom that understands the real nature of all phenomena, and thus his mind is joyful. Furthermore, because of his great compassion, even if he has to remain in samsara for eons, he is not concerned. [28]

There is a story about a bodhisattva whose name means "the one who cries constantly." This bodhisattva, in order to be able to make offerings to his master, tried in many ways to accumulate wealth, even trying to sell his body.

The arya bodhisattvas who have reached the path of seeing can decide their existence freely and choose to be reborn where they will be of more benefit to beings. In order to recognize their reincarnations one must investigate and then seek the help of the great lamas who have the power to see the mind, and have trust in what they say.

As well as the reincarnation of the Thirteenth Dalai Lama and the current Fourteenth Dalai Lama, numerous other reincarnated lamas have been recognized in Tibet, and in other parts of the world there must also be many, even though they have not been identified. These bodhisattvas can appear in the guise of heads of state, or at any rate as guides, in order to benefit all beings, and it is precisely for this reason that they take on different forms.

There are surely many bodhisattvas who have appeared also in the guise of adherents of the various world religions in order to be of better help to others. Also among animals, as has already been said, there is no doubt that there are bodhisattvas who succeed in giving protection to others thanks to their particular form. For example, among some herds of deer are those who lead the others into protected areas where hunting is forbidden.

We must attain enlightenment for the benefit of all beings, with these beings and the buddhas as our basis. The Mahayana path is more profound and more sacred than the Hinayana because through this method a bodhisattva can purify a greater amount of negative karma and accumulate oceans of virtue. [29]

Understanding its importance, we must generate enthusiastic effort and relinquish discouragement and weariness, mounting the horse of bodhichitta and traveling the path that proceeds from joy to joy to the ultimate happiness. [30]

If we are told to reach a certain place on foot, we feel very discouraged, but it is another matter if we go there by car. Likewise, if we are urged to attain buddhahood by way of the path of joy, we will not feel depressed.

The task and the responsibilities of a bodhisattva are to help all beings by attaining buddhahood through the purification of all negative karma and the accumulation of all virtues. In order to accomplish this one needs support. The four supports that help a bodhisattva and aid the development of enthusiastic perseverance are aspiration, firmness, joy, and rest. [31]

Aspiration. The fear of suffering within cyclic existence generates the desire for liberation. In order to attain liberation, we must practice the three trainings, whereas in order to attain enlightenment we also practice the two methods: bodhichitta and the wisdom that perceives emptiness. We need to develop a deep understanding of the necessary requisites and then strive to attain them. If we are certain that through buddhahood we will be able to benefit all beings, the desire to attain it will arise in us spontaneously, in the same way that we naturally aspire to do something we like.

Firmness. This is the attitude of examining the advantages and disadvantages of a certain action and, if we find it appropriate, not abandoning the determination to perform it once we decide upon it. Therefore, before practicing the Dharma, we must consider whether there are any reasons for doing so, and what we will miss if we do not practice it. In this way we will see that there are many advantages, and we will strive without hesitation, with an unwavering mind, and without second thoughts. If we practice or listen to the Dharma because our friends do so, we are not going to have a strong foundation, and our practice will not be steady. Not having realized its importance for ourselves, our motivation will not be our own, but borrowed! Another unsound reason for attending Dharma courses is in order to have a vacation.

Joy. Children never tire of playing, and we should have the same type of enthusiasm and joy in listening to, and practicing, the Dharma.

Rest. This word in Tibetan also means "to relinquish." When we practice the Dharma, the intensity of the effort makes us tired, and it is therefore a good thing to rest in order to be able to start afresh and with renewed vigor.

We must generate enthusiastic perseverance and the four factors supporting it, and be mindful at all times of whatever practices we are engaged in. For example, if we are developing the wisdom that perceives emptiness, we must possess discriminating alertness, watching to see if our minds are involved in right effort, continually and unequivocally, in the direction that we have chosen. [32]

We have promised to become bodhisattvas for the benefit of all beings, thus we must first of all purify any error committed in the past. In order to eliminate just one mistake we have to use a great deal of energy, because we are so familiar with negative karma and not very familiar with positive karma. If we do not begin right away, how are we going to endure the suffering that will result? [34]

In order to attain buddhahood, we must also realize all the positive qualities, and each of them requires much time and effort. Given that at the present we do not possess even a fraction of all the virtues we must accumulate, how are we going to generate all of them if we do not start right away? [35]

Although we have acquired a precious human rebirth, we have not profited from it in the best way, and instead have wasted these favorable circumstances. [36]

Let us therefore generate repentance for having acted so foolishly.

"I did not make offerings to sentient beings and bodhisattvas, I did not act to support the Dharma, I did not accumulate much virtue, nor did I purify much negative karma. I was not able to give security and comfort to the weak and the sick. Although I made many promises countless times to attain buddhahood for the benefit of all beings, the only thing I have accomplished as a human being is causing great agony for my mother when I was born—this is what I have succeeded in achieving with my rebirth, nothing else." [38]

Here Shantideva reminds us that there are only advantages in practicing the Dharma, and that if we do not devote ourselves to this practice the only thing we will achieve in this precious human rebirth is the pain we caused our mother at birth.

If a child did not want to go to school, and spent all his time playing, what would the neighbors think and how would his parents feel? To the buddhas and bodhisattvas we are just like that child. And if a child did go to school, but once he finished his studies he did not seek employment but instead wandered about aimlessly, taking drugs, he would be an object of scorn. Likewise, if we study the Dharma but do not put into practice the teachings that will allow us to eliminate suffering and accumulate merit, it will be just like having led an unfortunate life, and the buddhas and bodhisattvas will be saddened.

To us, buddhahood seems remote, but if we were reborn into a lower realm, even a human rebirth would seem remote, just as enlightenment is right now. If we have no interest in the Dharma, we cannot even be certain that we will not be reborn into a lower state. But if we do have some interest, we must cultivate it and not allow it to die.

The interest is the bedrock of any virtuous deed, and therefore we must not abandon it, but cultivate it, recognizing the causes and effects of every action. We must understand that suffering derives from mental afflictions and therefore strive to eliminate them, developing a great aspiration for practice. [40]

Through material means we can obtain small relief from hunger and cold, but it is through the Dharma that we obtain alleviation of a greater kind. If we understand that the Dharma will succeed in providing us with what we want, pleasure and commitment to its practice will be born. Neglecting a great objective in favor of something of little importance is behaving foolishly.

We have come from faraway places with effort, and we have learned that happiness derives from positive karma and that suffering derives from negative karma. Our practice, therefore, must be devoted to accumulating the former rather than the latter. We understand this precisely because of the effort involved in coming to this center. We did not come here on holiday, but in order to improve our lives, and to succeed in doing so we must practice virtue, so that the objective that motivated us is realized.

If a person with a serious illness knows where there is a pharmacy with the medicines he needs and where there is a doctor who can cure him, and still he does not go there, it is his mistake, due to stupidity. Similarly, I have put all my effort into giving the teachings, but if you then do not understand the need to apply them, I can be of no further help.

Right now we have physical pain and mental unhappiness, and we are forced to leave what we are attached to. All this arises from the imprints of past negative actions. [41]

When we have eliminated malevolence and other negative mental factors and constantly strive in virtuous deeds, we find favorable circumstances everywhere we go. [42]

Everyone makes careful arrangements before a visit from an important person because they respect him, so if we want to be treated in the same way we too must accumulate positive karma, because every desirable thing is obtained as a result of the meritorious deeds we have performed.

Having created negative karma, wherever we go we will be overcome by unfavorable circumstances. [43]

Sukhavati is a pure land, vast and immaculate, scented with delicious fragrance, and when a bodhisattva is reborn into this realm, he is not born from a mother's womb but rather from a lotus opened by the light radiating from the head of the Buddha, and he is nourished by *amrita,* or celestial nectar, and not by ordinary substances like we are. He hears music and sounds possessing the sixty qualities of a buddha's speech, and his luminous body is supported by the samadhi focused on the real nature of phenomena. [44]

Sukhavati is ruled by Amitabha Buddha, in accordance with the Dharma, and one is reborn into this pure land solely as a result of the virtuous deeds one has accumulated. It is not possible to go there by airplane, or by any other material means. The practice of the Dharma can bring about such results, and for this reason we must undertake it.

There are different types of birth: birth from a lotus flower; from assisting factors, such as dampness and warmth; from an egg; or from a maternal womb. At the beginning of an eon beings are mainly born from a lotus or a flower bud, and they do not eat coarse substances but instead thrive on *manna,* a delicate food covering the earth that does not cause the production of excrement. Their bodies emanate light as a result of previous virtuous deeds. When the virtuous karma diminishes, however, these resulting effects start to fade and they must eat coarser food. From that moment on, with the need to expel excrement, the digestive apparatus is created, and then the genitals, with the division between male and female, and then birth through the womb begins.

The result of negative karma may be rebirth in a lower realm, where the guardians will rip our skin off, pour melted copper on our bodies, pierce us with flaming swords and daggers, cut our flesh into a thousand pieces, and then throw us upon a fiercely blazing iron ground. [45]

Because extremely positive circumstances exist, extremely negative circumstances must exist as well. Hearing about Sukhavati, we might wish to be reborn there, but it is unthinkable to wish the same when hearing about the lower realms, and the mere mention of them sounds very unpleasant to us.

Since we can obtain the positive effects mentioned earlier, we must generate the enthusiastic effort needed to create positive karma, meditating with respect upon actions and their fruits. [46]

On the other hand, understanding that negative karma can truly bring about the unpleasant results described before, the desire to refrain from generating it will arise spontaneously.

When the sun shines in the sky, not even the highest mountains can obstruct it, and so a bodhisattva, possessing infinite qualities, will never be discouraged by beings' negative actions, no matter how hideous they may be. Bodhisattvas have such great will and compassion for all that nothing and no one, not even those who do the exact opposite of what they have been advised to do, can succeed in discouraging them, and that is because they possess mental stability.

Another aspect of a bodhisattva's firmness is translated from Tibetan by the word "pride," which is to be understood not as the mental affliction but instead as self-confidence. Having examined what needs to be done, one must have the determination to bring the deed to completion, and in this case confidence is very important.

Generally, before we undertake something we need to establish whether we can pursue it or not, and if there are valid reasons for accomplishing the deed. If we feel capable, once we have started we must bring it to completion. On the other hand, if we do not find any good reason and also do not feel confident, we must leave it. [47]

"If I do not bring to completion some work that I have started, this habit will continue in other lives and negativity and suffering will increase. Apart from which other actions too, at the moment of bearing fruit, will be weak and incomplete." [48]

If we want to engage in the practice of the Dharma we must first analyze it deeply, see if we have sufficient reasons to apply ourselves to the practice and whether we possess enough confidence, and then undertake it. If, however, we do not find these qualities, we must try to acquire them in the future.

We must have a steady mind and the certainty of success in destroying the wrong views and the other mental afflictions by applying the antidotes. [49]

"How can those who give up trying due to faint-heartedness ever attain liberation?" [53]

Therefore, with firm faith in ourselves, we must try to avoid any slip in our conduct. If we fail in this, our determination to obtain all powers will become just an object of derision. [54]

It is said that a buddha is like a lion, superior to any other animal and the king of them all, the strongest, whom no one can harm.

A bodhisattva, a child of the conquerors, is also like a lion, because he can destroy every mental affliction and be proud of this. [55]

Whoever possesses such confidence will not be overcome by mental afflictions, whereas those endowed with ordinary pride—the self-importance that leads one to the lower realms—will. [56]

A self-important person is not loved by others and will be left alone, unlike a humble person. The result of self-importance is that in future lives we will experience slavery, we will be at the mercy of other people, we will be stupid, crazy, unloved, and despised by all. [58]

The self-important cannot be counted among the proud, among the "victorious heroes" who are able to conquer all of the other mental afflictions. Such heroes will be loved by humans and gods alike, and will fulfill the wishes of all beings. [59]

It is possible to develop much merit on the basis of enthusiastic effort. This merit, even if it is obtained through external, material factors, is the essential cause of our happiness. For example, two traders or two businessmen with the same education or the same commitment to work experience a different result depending on their positive karma.

How can we accumulate merit? By having faith in the Three Jewels and making offerings to them and by benefiting sentient beings motivated by love and compassion.

Enthusiastic effort is experiencing joy in the accumulation of merit. A person who cannot generate it will not be able to obtain the desired results, and a person who complains about each small difficulty will also suffer greatly.

There are many attractive things, but the most precious is the spiritual path, the source of all happiness, and it is wrong to neglect it in order to run after meaningless activities such as idle talk, laziness, and amusements. We must do without this laziness. In the beginning it is difficult to control the body and the mind, but we can succeed by using enthusiastic effort in our practice and by being diligent in the practice of equalizing and exchanging ourselves with others.

If we know how to practice the Dharma, we will certainly enjoy its results, which cannot be taken away from us. This is also the best method to achieve happiness.

The suffering we experience is caused by our own failings and not by those of others, and if we can eliminate them, we will also eliminate the causes of suffering and achieve permanent happiness. Then we will also be able to help others do the same by sharing our own experiences.

If we establish the habit of controlling our mental afflictions, we will not be overcome by them. But until we have achieved mastery over them, it is better that we avoid the objects that may activate them, and instead remain in an isolated place where there is no danger of coming into contact with them. However, if this is not possible, we must be as vigilant as when, finding ourselves in a place full of thieves and bandits, we hold on to our belongings, keeping them safe and carefully protecting them.

In circumstances in which it is likely for mental afflictions to arise, we must remember the relevant antidotes and be like the lion who has no fear of being overcome by other animals. [60]

For example, we might have reasons that lead us to become angry, and in this case we must remember that rage creates nothing but suffering and does not in any way harm our enemy, but harms us alone, and therefore avoid generating it.

We can also examine what happens when we start to become attached— to a particular person, for example. What makes our desire arise? The skin? The internal organs? Upon reflection, we will be convinced that no part of this person is worthy of our attention. Even if we find one part attractive, such as the skin, we must analyze and ask ourselves which area of the skin is so appealing. Is it a small one? A large one? Where is it? We will then see that no part of it is *truly* attractive. We can also imagine removing the skin and holding it in our hands, and ask ourselves if we would still feel attachment to it in this situation.

It is not enough to express the desire to eliminate the mental afflictions, which are responsible for our suffering. We must also examine the mechanism by which they develop, and analyze whether what we believe in really exists within the objects of the afflictions themselves, and then realize that what is there is merely an overevaluation on our part, and nothing, intrinsically, in the object itself.

When we are in danger, we instinctively guard our eyes as if they were the most precious thing. Likewise, when mental afflictions arise we should be mindful and hasten to protect our minds. [61]

It is better to be burned or cut into pieces than to allow our disturbing conceptions to enslave us. We must be mindful at all times of what we are thinking, saying, and doing, and if we realize that it is something unsound we should stop right away. [62]

With this we conclude the teaching on mental firmness, one of the forces that aid the creation of enthusiastic perseverance in the bodhisattva.

Children find pleasure in playing and are never tired; they enjoy themselves and want to continue forever. Likewise, we should be delighted in performing virtuous deeds and never have enough of them. [63]

We put a lot of effort into worldly activities, in business or at work, even though the resulting happiness is not definite, but we do not apply ourselves to the Dharma, where the results are certain. [64]

We experience great attachment to the objects of our senses—but they are like honey spread on a razor blade. If we try to lick it, we will most probably cut ourselves, and yet we feel that we can never have enough. It is certain, on the other hand, that the Dharma will provide us with authentic happiness—why then do we feel content, believing that we have already performed enough deeds that will ripen into happiness? [65]

The elephant, tormented by the heat of the sun and wanting to find relief by bathing in a lake, does not hesitate but plunges into the water. Likewise, we must have the same eagerness to perform continuously virtuous deeds, so that no one will be able to stop us. [66]

However, we must not strive excessively in the practice of the Dharma, in order to avoid feeling repulsion for the practice itself. We must begin an activity, then rest and start again later, using common sense. Especially at the beginning, we must leave the practice aside when we become too tired. When we rest we should do so thinking that in this way we will be able to practice better later, and so rest too becomes a virtuous deed. [67]

We already possess the spontaneous desire for better living conditions. Therefore, we must develop this aspiration into the wish to attain buddhahood. We must develop bodhichitta on a solid basis of aversion to samsara. If such repulsion has already arisen, we can begin our practice of bodhichitta right away. Wanting to build a five-story house, we cannot possibly demand to have the fifth floor built first, as this would be impossible. However, once we have finished building the first floor, we must not stop there, but instead carry on with the second and so forth.

One who is experienced in martial arts knows that he must simultaneously defend himself and strike the enemy, and that if he is disarmed, he must try to pick up the sword at once. Likewise, if even for an instant we lose the weapon of mindfulness, we must retrieve it, fearing that the mental afflictions will harm us and throw us into the lower realms. [69]

When a poisoned arrow pierces someone's leg, he might need to amputate it in order to protect his whole body, because a small quantity of poison spreading through the bloodstream can cause death. Likewise, if a small mental affliction remains in our minds, the danger is great, and therefore we must have control over even the tiniest delusion, otherwise it will quickly spread. [70]

We must be mindful in our practice, like a person who is forced by an enemy to carry a jar full of oil on his head, and is threatened with death if he spills just one drop. [71]

Seeing a snake on our laps, we do not get up calmly, but instead quickly push it away. Likewise, we must not indulge laziness and sleepiness, but abandon them quickly. [72]

If we discover that we are lazy, we must criticize ourselves and tell ourselves, "I have allowed this to happen until now, but from now on I will change." [73]

We must have control over our minds at all times, using mindfulness and intelligence, and if we meet a good teacher or possess a good text, we should try to follow the advice that is given. [74]

We gain advantages from the Dharma in general, and from the Mahayana path in particular, and therefore we must use our bodies and minds and let joy and enthusiasm for spiritual practice arise. If we do not make the most of these favorable circumstances, it will be a serious mistake. [75]

"A weightless piece of cotton is set in motion by even the lightest wind; likewise, joy must direct my mind, and then I can accomplish everything." [76]

We must utilize our present human condition by employing the three doors of body, speech, and mind, by which every virtuous deed is accomplished, in order to realize the state of perfect enlightenment in the shortest time possible. When we practice we must start with the simplest forms of practice and then gradually engage in the higher forms, as we do when consuming a meal, following a certain order through the various courses.

Upon waking in the morning we must remember our precious human birth, that it will end, and that we will take on another life whose quality will be determined by karma. In this way we will be determined to generate positive karma and eliminate the negative karma we have already accumulated. In the evening it is good to assess the deeds we have performed, developing the desire to improve them in the future, to attain liberation, and, extending our wishes further, to care for others as a result of the attainment of buddhahood.

When we clean our homes, we throw away what is superfluous and put the useful things back in their places, and we must do the same with our minds, eliminating what creates problems and protecting what will bring about benefits.

We are studying the Dharma in order to transform our mental attitudes. Right now we are attached to this life, and thus the first change consists of beginning to consider our future lives to be more precious than this one. Subsequently, we must aspire to liberation, and this is the second type of motivation. Finally, in accordance with the Mahayana teachings, if at present we are concerned solely with ourselves, we must transform this attitude, considering instead that others are more important. This is the third type of motivation, the highest motivation.

In order to attain buddhahood, we must practice the Dharma after having become acquainted with it, and it is for this reason that you are listening to teachings based on the *Bodhicharyavatara*. Do you understand? In any case, if you do not agree, you can get up and leave.

~: 8 :~
CONCENTRATION

THE TEXT SAYS, "Having developed enthusiastic effort in this way, I should place my mind in concentration, for the person whose mind is distracted abides between the fangs of disturbing conceptions." [1]

Concentration is the capacity of the mind to dwell for a long time on an object. Its opposite is distraction, which causes the mind to wander and prevents it from holding a single object steadily for even a minute. In such cases we will never succeed in keeping our mind concentrated and realizing samadhi, because both will be hindered by the various disturbing conceptions.

As a man bitten by a tiger will surely be devoured, so it is certain that the distracted person will fall prey to mental afflictions and will not be able to escape them. However, this will not happen if body and mind remain in solitude, which means, respectively, living in isolated places such as mountains, and not thinking of mundane things, but only of the Dharma. We must not give too much importance to food, clothes, and fame, but instead forsake those thoughts that keep us preoccupied in this direction, as well as all distorted views that make us unhappy, for they lead us to worry about the fact that others think or speak evil of us. [2]

We are very attached to this life, but we have to forsake desire and craving, for otherwise we will not even be able to practice.

As far as attachment to material things goes, it is not that we should not use them, for Dharma practitioners too need food and clothes, but we should not cling to them, in the same way that ill people do not cling to the medicines they take due to necessity. [3]

Disturbing conceptions can be overcome by superior insight combined with calm abiding, and it is this state of mental peace that we must strive to attain. The best samadhi is the samadhi that takes emptiness as its object. The realization of emptiness eliminates all mental afflictions at their root. The verses now state that we must acquire peace through the genuine joy typical of those unattached to worldly things. [4]

The main hindrance to such realization is attachment, which, when we are meditating, for example, provokes a particular distraction that manifests in the thought of having to do or buy a certain thing, so that our concentration vanishes.

We must not generate attachment to material objects, to people, to our bodies, to servants, or to friends, because all these things are by nature impermanent. Our bodies will become old, ugly, and undesirable, and in the same way everything will one day be harmed or destroyed.

If we become attached to something or someone, for thousands of lives we will not see that object or being again. [5]

You might wonder whether it is right to have attachment to the guru, the spiritual teacher. Attachment to the guru can have two meanings: devotion and out-and-out attachment. The former is a positive attitude, the latter is a mental affliction. Likewise, one can have two types of attachment to the Buddha.

We feel unhappy when experiencing unpleasantness and rejoice when experiencing pleasurable things—but then also in this case we endure difficulties because we are not entirely satisfied and continue to feel attached, and thus we never succeed in concentrating our minds on a single point. [6]

To conclude, in order to destroy our mental afflictions we must develop superior insight—*lhagtong* in Tibetan, *vipashyana* in Sanskrit—and to this end we must first develop meditative equipoise, or calm abiding—*shiné* in Tibetan, *shamata* in Sanskrit. We must not feel attachment to riches, to objects of the senses, or to sentient beings. In other words, we must not feel attachment to the container—the external world—or to its inhabitants.

This text explains how to practice the Dharma. If we do not do this, our lives will rest solely on our material possessions. It would be great if we could be happy simply by relying on these, but this is not the case, given that even rich people are not always happy. We want to eliminate suffering and attain every kind of happiness, but if we do not use the proper methods, the results we desire will not manifest by themselves. The sun rises with no effort on our part—we go to bed, and tomorrow it will come up in the east—but the same does not apply to the attainment of authentic satisfaction and the elimination of our problems. The right method is the Dharma.

Generally, even just watching a television show activates our mental afflictions. When our minds are seized by an object of desire, they lose their happiness, and so we must try to prevent this from happening. When we do not succeed in obtaining something, we suffer; when we have obtained it, we are still dissatisfied. When, finally, we inevitably must separate from it, our minds suffer even more still.

To meditate and attain mental peace, we must eliminate the hindrances caused by our distracted mind. Sentient beings are one of the objects of our attachment, and this attachment leads to the obscuring of the understanding of the authentic nature of phenomena. [7]

To be attached to this existence, to forms, and to the various kinds of well-being is an obstacle to the practice of meditation. To be pleased with oneself and one's appearance is self-deception, and it will prevent us from attaining liberation. At the moment we are satisfied with life, but because we will die and separate from the body, we will have to endure a great deal of suffering. Besides, being solely concerned with our current lives, we will end up wasting them for meaningless things, using them only to have money, comfort, and good food. In so doing we will be reborn into the lower realms, where we will suffer enormously. Our attachment to friends and relatives is also meaningless, because they are impermanent and one day we will have to leave them. This attachment is an obstacle to our practice of the Dharma. [8]

If we associate with childish or evil people who lead us to behave like them, who have no interest in the Dharma and do not practice it, and who are not as lucky as we are, we will fall into the lower realms. Being attached to them is therefore both pointless and detrimental from a spiritual point of view. [9]

If we relate to ordinary, childish friends, we will be on good terms in the morning, argue in the evening, and the next day make up again. This does not happen with aryas or superior beings. [10]

If in some way we benefit the first type of people, they are friendly to us, but if we cause them slight harm they become our enemies. It is difficult to please them, and if we give them good advice they become angry with us. If we are doing something good, like practicing the Dharma, they criticize us and tell us not to continue with our practice. If we do not listen to them they become angry and so they accumulate negative karma. [11]

They are envious of superiors, competitive with equals, arrogant toward inferiors, conceited when praised, and if anything unpleasant is said to them they become angry. Considering all this, there is no benefit in seeking the friendship of such childish individuals. [12]

The attitude of ordinary people is to belittle others and praise themselves, and by talking to them about the joys of cyclic existence or by slandering those we do not like we will create much negative karma. [13]

Associating with them, we will destroy the good fortune of both our current and future lives. [14]

If possible, we should seek the company of good friends. If this is not possible, we must at least avoid entrusting ourselves to evil friends. We possess both virtue and shortcomings—if by relating to someone, our positive qualities increase, then we are dealing with a virtuous friend, and it is good to keep his company. If, on the other hand, we realize that being in the company of a certain person is unhelpful to both parties, it is better to stay away from that person. If we happen to meet him, we must greet him with kindness, without, however, becoming too familiar. [15]

A bee collecting pollen from a flower to make honey has no attachment to its color or form. So, for example, if one has a benefactor in the practice of the Dharma, one must behave just like this insect, and have no craving. [16]

The next verse discusses arrogance and pride. If we look at ourselves as having much material wealth and honor, or as being loved by people, and we nurture too much self-importance, at the moment of death we will be terrified. [17]

Since we do not know the authentic nature of phenomena, we generate attachment and therefore negative karma, which will cause us misery a thousand times greater than the pleasures the sense objects can bring us. [18]

A thief must endure much suffering once he is caught, and he who is attached to samsara must endure incomparably greater misery. [19]

Even if we think, "I am rich, people respect me, everybody loves me," we must not be arrogant, or be attached to fame and possessions, because these things have no power to accompany us after death. [20]

If someone praises us, it is wrong to feel pleased, since elsewhere there are also many who despise us. However, we must not lose heart if someone despises us, because there are also people who praise us. [21]

If even the Tathagata, the Buddha who appeared on this earth, was unable to satisfy the various desires of all beings, how will we be able to do so? [22]

The nature of ordinary beings is such that they criticize the wealthy for certain reasons, and they criticize the poor for other reasons. [23]

Childish people are satisfied only if nothing goes against their interests, therefore we must refrain from seeking their friendship. [24]

When we practice the Dharma and when we meditate we must choose a quiet place, such as a forest, where there are deer, birds, and other animals that do not hinder us in our meditation. Living with other people, we hear their opinions and the mind becomes confused. If there are only animals and trees, we will not have distractions and it is then possible to train the mind in bodhichitta and emptiness. [25]

While dwelling in these solitary places, such as caves, empty shrines, or at the base of trees, we must not bring the mind back to the past, to places where we were before, but instead cultivate detachment. [26]

In such places not belonging to anyone, by nature vast and open, one is free to behave as one wishes and can therefore cultivate non-attachment to "I" and to "mine." [27]

We should aspire to possess only a begging bowl and the objects abandoned by others, and not wear costly garments but those that no one, not even thieves, are interested in. [28]

Living thus, with meager possessions and with only animals as our friends, we should then meditate on non-attachment, on the absence of self, on impermanence, and on our body's inadequacies—its impurities, for example. [29]

In Tibet, after someone dies, the corpse is cut into pieces and given to the vultures. If we had the chance to thoroughly contemplate this, we could cultivate detachment from the body.

At the moment our bodies are supported by our minds, and that is why we are alive, but when they separate the flesh will start to rot and not even

jackals will come close. Our bodies are similar to a corpse—the only difference is that at the moment our bodies are still supported by our minds. [30]

At birth we were alone, with no friends, and when we die our bodies,
which were given to us at birth, will be abandoned. It is therefore obvious
that we will also have to leave our friends behind, and the verses advise us
not to be attached to them.

Even at the moment of death, it will not be possible to share our pain
with others. What then is the use of having friends, who are obstacles to
the practice of the Dharma? [32]

I will give you an example: Traveling on a train and talking to someone
for a few hours, or even traveling on a plane and talking for more than a
few hours, is a pointless pointless activity. It is unwise to be attached to the
person with whom we have exchanged a few words. Likewise, since we are
traveling in samsara, it is unwise to be attached to those we call friends and
relatives. Friendship with traveling companions lasts a couple of hours, and
since we have had countless lives in the past and will have as many in the
future, our current life's attachments equal a few hours' acquaintance on a
train or plane. It is therefore unwise to feel attached to one's friends. [33]

It is better to retreat to the forest before our bodies are taken to the
cemetery by four gravediggers. [34]

If it seems difficult to you to live in accordance with these instructions,
you must aspire to become someone capable of doing so in a future life.
Milarepa abandoned attachment to the body, to material objects, and to
his parents, went to live in solitude, and attained buddhahood in that very
lifetime.

If we choose a solitary place to live, we wake up in the morning, we
have breakfast, and with no one else around, we have time to practice
the Dharma throughout the day, apart from the time needed for preparing food and eating. Then we go to sleep, and upon waking there is no
opportunity for chit-chatting. Even if we are unable to live in solitude,
when we have free time we must not waste it in idle talk, but instead use
it profitably by studying and meditating on the teachings.

The Buddha's advice is at all times to practice according to one's
ability and not more, making sure we feel at ease. When our practice is
good, the bliss it generates in our minds is incomparable to the happiness wealth can give, or to the taste of good food, or to the good feelings

we get from wearing wonderful clothes. Perhaps some of you have had the experience of spending a night practicing the *Praises to Tara,* and feeling more joy than if you had gone to the mountains or the seaside, with the additional benefit of feeling that you have done something virtuous. Likewise, there is a difference between spending an hour meditating and spending an hour in idle talk. If we experience happiness in the practice of simple spiritual activities, then the happiness we will experience by using all our time in the practice of the pure Dharma is beyond the capacity of our imagination.

If we choose a tranquil and solitary place as our dwelling, we will be dead to others, so when we actually die we can do so quietly, because there will not be anyone around us crying and lamenting, and we will have the opportunity to recite prayers, meditate on bodhichitta, and remember the kindness of the buddhas. [36]

We can find pleasant dwellings where it is easy to obtain food and water, and where it is possible to keep our body in good health and our mind at peace. [37]

Having detached ourselves from our family and friends, we should cultivate qualities such as non-hatred and non-attachment, and develop the wisdom that realizes emptiness. Meditating on bodhichitta and emptiness, we will become capable of separating the mind from the mental afflictions, and when we have cultivated both we will no doubt realize buddhahood. On the other hand, continuing to live where it is possible to generate attachment, we will have many problems even in this life—such as suffering a violent death or going to prison—and in future lives we will experience suffering due to craving sense objects. [39]

Someone wanting a spouse at any cost who commits evil deeds, tries to accumulate money, lies, and cheats, and even if in the end that person succeeds in finding a wife or a husband, it is no different than embracing a skeleton. It is therefore wiser to abandon sensual pleasures so that we can attain ultimate peace. [42]

The essence of this advice is to develop enthusiasm for the practice and not for the pleasures of the senses, having the attainment of the ultimate state of a buddha as our objective.

When getting married, one is at first shy and bashful. The wife does not show her face to the husband, who cannot wait to admire it. However, if she then dies and her face is devoured by vultures, it will be intolerable to look at. It is therefore foolish to be attached to beauty. [44]

If the skin is removed from the face, it is no longer attractive, but when the skin covers the bones we feel attached—let us try to think that there is no difference between these two. A man who is too attached to a woman, or a woman to a man, must apply these methods during meditation. As long as we live in samsara, it is not possible to attain ultimate happiness. We do desire this happiness, regardless, and must therefore strive to attain liberation, uprooting the three mental poisons by understanding their characteristics and the negative effects they generate.

These teachings are given to help us overcome attachment, and not in order to encourage us to despise others. If we reflect on them honestly, we realize that attachment is truly the source of suffering, and not of happiness.

If another man looks at your wife, you do not like it and try to defend her from his attentions, but will you do the same once she is dead? [45]

Caring for our bodies, we generally use powders, lotions, makeup, ornaments, and perfume, but what is the use of these things, since at the moment of death they will only be food for the vultures? [46]

A dead person does not move, and yet we are afraid of a corpse. Why then are we not as afraid of the living, who are like zombies, walking corpses? [47]

When our beloved's body is covered with clothes we desire it, but why don't we desire the same when we see it naked at the place of cremation? It is in fact unthinkable to have sex with a corpse, but it is the same thing with a living body, because they are both impure. [48]

The meaning of this is that if we feel attachment to the body of some-one who is alive, we should feel the same when the person is dead, because physically there is no difference. In the same way, if we desire to embrace someone who is living, we should also wish to embrace his corpse.

Shantideva has given these instructions on the need to be unattached to places, friends, and possessions because these are great obstacles to success in freeing oneself from conditioned existence and attaining lasting happiness. He explains through logical reasoning how, beginning with the eradication of our attachment to the opposite sex, we can eliminate all attachment.

We must analyze whether attachment brings us happiness or suffer-ing, and once we have understood that it brings problems and that it is a mental affliction, we must apply the appropriate antidotes to remove it. We must consider attachment an illness, and think that in order to cure it we must go to the doctor who will prescribe the right medicines.

Shantideva had a thousand times more love and compassion for us than we have, and has written this text to show us the path in order to help us eliminate inner obscurations and achieve happiness. But the mere desire for this to occur is not enough. In addition, we must strive effectively for this result. It is in the nature of phenomena that without an appropriate cause there cannot be a particular result. Mental afflictions are the only cause of suffering, and when they are completely eliminated we will live in perfect peace.

We take medicines to cure illnesses, and consequently our troubles are eliminated and we feel at ease. With the medicine of the Dharma we can achieve three types of a far greater happiness. The *smallest happiness* we will achieve is rebirth as a human being or a god. This occurs through the practice of ethical discipline and the six perfections. The *medium happiness* we will achieve is the attainment of nirvana, which occurs through the practice of the three higher trainings: ethics, concentration, and wisdom. The *greatest happiness* that we can attain through the Dharma is the attainment of buddhahood, which is the result of the practice of bodhichitta joined with the realization of emptiness.

The aim of the Dharma is to help others. If we are unable to do this, we should at least refrain from harming them, otherwise we will pay the consequences in the future. When we mistreat others they suffer, and eventually, as a result of karma, we will have to experience this suffering ourselves as well. If we benefit others instead, they will be happy and we will also experience happiness.

Upon waking up, it is very important to let the motivation to benefit others arise, or at least the motivation to avoid harming them. Those who teach, in particular, should think, "Today I will do my best to give good advice and explanations to my pupils so that they will have good opportunities in life." In this way even going to school becomes Dharma practice, and, since we must stay there for a certain amount of time, it is better to teach with a good heart. In this way our time will not be wasted and we will accumulate merit. There is a difference between one who understands

the Dharma and one who does not. The first type of person, if he is a
teacher, treats his pupils as his own children, with affection, whereas the
other person tries to pass the time as quickly as possible. Furthermore,
not being stupid, students understand the qualities of a good teacher, and
will love and think highly of him. If he is not a good teacher, they will
do the opposite. Likewise, a workman will do good work in a factory if
his motivation is to benefit others with his work, and a civil servant will
accumulate virtue by thinking that he is helping the state and its citizens.
Someone who works in a hospital and sees a patient who is ill and weak
will think, "May this person feel better." This aspiration alone is an accumulation of merit and the practice of the Dharma.

If we meet someone who is rich and beautiful, we must think that this
is because that person has accumulated merit in previous lives, and decide
to practice in the same way.

The text goes on, "We like to kiss our beloved and find joy in saliva, but
this arises from food, and so does excrement. Why then do we not feel the
same attraction to excrement? [49]

"Pillows and mattresses are soft to the touch, but we do not find any
sexual pleasure in them. Why then we do find pleasure in an impure,
foul-smelling human body?" [50]

Being attached to the softness of a woman's body and not to a pillow
is an error related to the sense of touch. If we feel attachment to softness
itself, we should also be attracted to a pillow, because it has the same
quality. If instead the body is the object of our attachment, in spite of its
impurities, we should reflect that it is made of bones tied together with
tendons, muscles, and flesh, like a house made of bricks held together by
cement, and covered by skin and hair. [52]

We generally take care of our bodies, even if they are filled with
impurities, but we certainly do not need to take care of other bags of
garbage. [53]

If we are attached to touching and gazing at flesh, then why not feel the
same for a corpse that has no mind? [54]

If we desire someone because he (or she) is kind and has a good mind,
we must think that this cannot be seen or touched. Anything that we can
see or touch is not a consciousness. [55]

It is not so strange that we do not understand the bodies of others to be of an impure nature, but it is truly incredible that we do not understand our own bodies to be so. [56]

The next verse states that if at some point we have forsaken even a young lotus flower unfolded by beams of sunlight, it is unreasonable to be still attached to a body, which is but a cage of filth. [57]

Since we do not like to touch places or things that are smeared with excrement, why do we enjoy the body from which it comes? [58]

The bodies we now possess were created in our mothers' wombs, an impure container, and have their origins in male and female fluids. Knowing this, we should not feel attachment. [59]

We do not like the worms we find in excrement, but we love the body containing the same excrement from which they come. [60]

"Not only should I not be attached to my body, for it is unclean, but I should feel even less attachment to the bodies of others." [61]

When food is on the plate, it is inviting and wholesome, but if we spit it out after we put it into our mouth, it is impure. [62]

If you fail to understand that your own body is impure for the above reasons, go to the cremation grounds and look at others' corpses—they are unclean, discarded heaps. [63]

If someone were to remove our skin and show us what is underneath, the view would be intolerable, so why then is this same skin now the source of our attachment? [64]

We anoint our bodies with perfume to which we then feel attracted, but why, since the fragrance does not belong to the body but to the sandalwood and so on? [65]

Making our bodies more agreeable by using lotions and perfume is pointless—scents do not arise from the body, but from its causes, which do not have its same nature. [67]

The body's natural state cannot be changed, and it is truly frightening. We can see this if we stop taking care of it for a while—hair and nails grow long, teeth become yellow, and the whole body will be coated with the odor of dirt. [68]

We are at present attached to our bodies because we do not realize their impurity, but as soon as we do, our attitude will change. Going to cemeteries and cremation grounds, we will see corpses with their organs coming out, and we will feel repulsion and understand that our bodies are like theirs, and that therefore we must not be attached to them. [70]

It is generally difficult to find a wife without paying a price, and in order to obtain her we might perform evil deeds that will consequently lead us to be reborn into lower realms. [71]

As a child one is unable to increase one's wealth, and as a youth one does not have enough money to afford a wife. Having become an old man by the time one succeeds in possessing money, how is one then going to enjoy a wife? [72]

Some evil and lustful people wear themselves out by working all day, and when they return home in the evening, exhausted, they lie down like corpses. [73]

Also, there are those who go to faraway lands to earn money without any chance of seeing their wife and children for many years, even if they are very attached to them. [74]

Some, too, due to their confusion, think that they will gain by selling themselves to others, but in this way they waste their time and have none left to dedicate to the practice of virtuous actions. [75]

To earn money and support a wife and children, some people sell themselves to others, but by allowing themselves to be exploited in this way, they do not even have the chance to see them, and when their loved ones are in trouble, who will take care of them? [76]

The meaning of the word "enemy" is "one who causes us harm." Our true enemies are our mental afflictions, which have caused us harm from time beginningless and will continue to do so for a long time to come. Before training the mind in bodhichitta, we must strive to reduce hatred and attachment, since this is the only way we will succeed in generating it. We are born as a result of karma and mental afflictions, and for the same reason we become old and one day die. We are called "samsaric beings" because we are under their domain. However, the Three Jewels exist as our protectors, to free us from this slavery. Medicine, and not the doctor, is the true antidote, and thus the Dharma is the true refuge, and the Buddha shows us the methods to put it into practice. We can consider the Sangha to be a gathering of patients who gradually improve thanks to the guidance of a doctor who prescribes the right medicine for each one. Likewise, people belonging to the community of practitioners are at first rude, self-centered, and difficult, but gradually, under the guidance of the master, they change and become kinder.

Of all the mental afflictions, ignorance of the authentic nature of phenomena is the most powerful. We fight this by developing the wisdom that correctly understands the way that phenomena exist. When we succeed in directly realizing the absence of a "true," self-existent, independent self, we free ourselves from samsara. This is the protection offered to us by the Dharma! And it is in order to listen to Dharma teachings that places such as this center exist, and for the same reason people come here even from afar. I am not a qualified teacher, but I do think that to listen to the teachings of the *Bodhicharyavatara* is good fortune for all of us indeed.

One who has never encountered the Dharma or whose mind is not directed toward it wishes happiness only for this lifetime. Now that we are acquainted with it, however, this motivation no longer suffices, because our minds have expanded and at least sometimes we must harbor the aspiration to help others. Before, perhaps, we might have thought that once we became rich and famous we would be happy. Now we understand that this is not so, because we cannot take anything with us when we die, and our main efforts must turn to the elimination of the mental afflictions in order to achieve true happiness for ourselves and for other people.

The text goes on to explain how attachment manifests and how one can pacify it.

Some fools who are deceived by desire, wishing to make a living and to earn money, become soldiers, go to foreign lands as spies, or become slaves in the service of others. [77]

Likewise, because of greed, some steal and rob even just to support their families. When they are captured, imprisoned, condemned, tortured, and beheaded, the suffering that ensues is nothing but the results of their actions. [78]

At times attachment arises for our bodies, or for the bodies of others, and at other times for one's house, for a place, or for our possessions. When the mind is free, it is at peace, but if the mind is overwhelmed, peace is lost. Concerning attachment and hatred, the former is frequent, the latter is rare.

The following verses discuss the need to be unattached to one's possessions.

Wealth too comes fraught with infinite problems. At first we must endure difficulties gathering it, and then we spend most of our time protecting it. Later we feel pain abandoning it, thus experiencing suffering at every stage. As long as we are slaves to this attachment and our minds are distracted, there is no chance to be free of samsara. [79]

Happiness obtained through desire is meaningless, and its disadvantages are enormous. This is similar to the condition of animals drawing carts all day, with no time to stop and eat but only to chew a few mouthfuls of grass found along the road. [80]

It is generally said that there is a great difference between human and animal life, in relation to both the body and the mind. But since even animals can obtain some joy in this life, if we spend all our energies in the pursuit of ordinary happiness, there is no distinction between us and them. [81]

We have obtained an extraordinary body and mind, not often acquired, and must therefore use them to obtain a new rebirth as a human or a deva in order to achieve nirvana and buddhahood.

In order to have power and wealth, usually people face great difficulties and contrive various strategies. Once they achieve them, they exercise great effort in holding on to them and in this way throw away the time that could instead be used in the attainment of enlightenment, which they then never achieve. [83]

When one has contemplated the miseries of hell, caused by mental afflictions such as attachment, it will be clear that such miseries cannot be compared to the harm caused by weapons, poison, fire, falling into ravines, or enemies. [84]

There are five sense objects that can generate attachment: attractive forms, fragrant smells, pleasant sounds, delicious flavors, and objects pleasant to the touch. Viewing them as true enemies and cultivating aversion to samsaric life, we should generate a love of solitude. [85]

If you are attached to the idea of having a family, you will spend all your time finding a home and furniture, and will be almost completely absorbed by these concerns, whereas by remaining alone you can lead an independent and satisfying life.

The happiness of the universal monarch, the king of the four continents, is not comparable to the happiness you might experience in solitude, where you are free from quarrels, frustrations, and the objects that generate hatred and attachment, and where the mind dwells in peace. You can even live in the forest, walking on large flat stones, cooled by a light breeze. In this way you are free from confusion and the activities of cities and you have much time to reflect on how you can benefit others. [86]

Solitary life leaves much room for the Dharma, and we cannot compare the satisfaction it brings with that which we might experience in a town, where even people who wish to devote themselves solely to spiritual practice cannot do so due to the many distractions, and therefore feel dissatisfied. If they choose a solitary place, however, they can instead devote all their time to spiritual pursuits and develop much joy.

In a solitary place it is not necessary to have a beautiful house—a few branches suffice to build a small hut. Nor is there any need to protect it. Because of this we feel free, and if we want to, we can move elsewhere without a care. [87]

Being content with the food we find and with enough clothes to protect ourselves from the cold and the wind, we can devote ourselves completely to the practice and experience a happiness unthinkable even for those who are powerful in samsara. [88]

The mind should dwell in solitude, pacifying disturbing conceptions completely. In order to meditate, we should choose a solitary place, not be involved in diverting activities, and keep the mind free from distractions so that we can train it in bodhichitta. [89]

Shakyamuni Buddha was at first an ordinary person like us, but later he transformed his mind by reflecting that it was pointless to strive solely for his own happiness, and began to think of the welfare of others. He began by developing a great love for others, desiring that all beings could be happy, and developing great compassion, desiring that they could be free from suffering. But mere intention was not enough, since alone it would not bring benefit, so he took one more step. He personally took responsibility for doing something that would help sentient beings effectively. Understanding, however, that he was not yet capable of fulfilling this great undertaking, and that it was first necessary to attain buddhahood by practicing the transcendental perfections of the bodhisattvas, he then spent three incalculable eons in this practice. He finally attained perfect enlightenment and was able to help beings by giving the teachings of the Dharma. With the first teaching on the four noble truths, he expressed the need to recognize suffering, its causes, and the path, thus coming to the cessation of suffering to which this path leads.

An analogy related to the first noble truth, the truth of suffering, is a water leak. As the water drips from the ceiling into this room, we feel uncomfortable, and so it is for suffering in general. Understanding the causes of the leak and finding its origin allow us to stop it. When we do this, the floor stops becoming wet and dries out. Likewise, if we recognize the causes of suffering and remove them, we will experience only happiness. As we find the source of the leak and seal it up with cement, so through the path we can eliminate the causes of suffering and achieve cessation.

There are several methods to achieve complete enlightenment for the sake of all beings, but none are for our benefit alone.

During these teachings I have advocated both practicing in solitude and also helping others, and this may seem like a contradiction. Actually, there are two kinds of practice. For those practitioners untroubled by hatred and attachment, it can be beneficial to be with others. However, if we suspect that hatred and attachment may arise in us, it is better to be alone, to seek solitude in order to pacify the mind. Similarly, a person with a fever is advised by his doctor to avoid meat and alcohol, but for someone suffering an imbalance of the internal winds, called *lung* in Tibetan, meat and alcohol are prescribed. This is not contradictory, because the advice in each case is tailored to the particular circumstances. The same goes for deciding which type of practice is appropriate.

Likewise, if a friend harms our Dharma practice, it is better to avoid spending time with him, though we should try to continue helping him in some way.

It is not possible to generate bodhichitta unless we have generated the desire to help beings eliminate their suffering. In order to be Mahayanists, we must develop this desire. We are equal to others because everyone wants happiness and does not want suffering, and so it is not right to work solely for our own benefit—there are no valid reasons to do so. [90]

The following verses show how to strive toward equalizing oneself with others.

Thinking that other people's suffering does not touch us and that we should not concern ourselves with eliminating it is a wrong conception that must be erased. This is equal to asserting that it is pointless to protect ourselves from the suffering we will experience when we are old, since it is not affecting us now, whereas we know full well that we must do so from a young age. We must protect others from suffering in the same way that we protect ourselves now from the suffering of old age.

The various problems that we encounter do not harm others, but only harm ourselves, and yet we strive to solve them. In the same way, although other people's miseries are not ours, it is right and good to eliminate them. [92–93]

When you are in trouble and go through many difficulties you need others, and in the same way others need your help so that they can overcome their difficulties. You feel happy if others help you, and likewise others will be pleased with you if you help them.

A doctor does not experience his patients' pain, but he is ready to alleviate their miseries. Although the suffering of children is not that of their parents, still the parents are always ready to help them.

We think of alleviating a headache, or pain in the legs or hands, because these are all parts of our body. We consider the previous example of the person who tries to solve his future problems of old age by working hard in his youth, or the case of a person who accumulates merit thinking of his next life, to be sensible attitudes because, even though our bodies change from rebirth to rebirth, our individual mental continuum continues. However, we do not find it sensible to work for others, because they have different mental continuums. [98]

The idea that other people's problems do not touch us is truly a mistaken conception. We must help others to eliminate suffering simply because it is suffering, and we must benefit other sentient beings as we do our own bodies, to which we give food, clothes, and so forth. [99]

The main obstacle to benefiting others is ignorance, the worst aspect of which is the mind clinging to the self. [100]

Right now we do not have the slightest concern for the suffering or happiness of others, but we have a tremendous amount for our own problems and pleasure. This is because our minds are self-centered and confused, and they grasp firmly and steadily to "I" and "mine." Consequently, we have the same concern for the suffering and happiness of our parents, relatives, or friends. In reality, "I" and "mine" do not exist independently, but are instead relative concepts, and therefore not self-existent.

We speak of aggregates, of various parts of the body, and of a mental continuum, but none of these exists independently or intrinsically. For example, a single bead is not called a "rosary," but a set of 108 beads strung together is. Likewise, a soldier is not called an "army," whereas a group of many soldiers together makes an army. And body parts, in the same way, make up a body. [101]

If the self does not "truly" exist, then also the self that "truly" suffers also does not exist, nor does the object "truly" experienced by it—in this case, suffering. Naturally, we must understand this in terms of ultimate truth, because at the level of relative truth, suffering, happiness, and the person experiencing them do exist.

When there is suffering it is pointless to differentiate whether it is one's own or that of others, because either way it is unwanted and must be removed. We cannot think, "I must dispel this suffering because it is mine, but I can leave the suffering of others alone." Such an attitude is inconsistent. [102]

We have such discriminating thoughts because at present we are accustomed to care only about ourselves, but we will succeed in changing these thoughts if we extend this loving attitude to other beings.

If we think that there is no need to eliminate the suffering of others, then there is also no need to eliminate our own. But if we cannot endure our own suffering because of the continual pain, then we should feel the same for others, because it is suffering itself that creates harm and discomfort. [103]

This mental attitude is compassion. Without this in our minds, we cannot consider ourselves followers of the Mahayana tradition, and we can never generate bodhichitta. Without bodhichitta, no matter what we practice—morality, generosity, patience, enthusiastic effort, concentration, or wisdom—for no matter how long or how intensely, there is no hope of attaining full enlightenment.

Now I am asking you whether you believe that you can seriously commit yourselves to eliminating the suffering of others. I would like to add that everyone can succeed in doing this since, in the case of the bodhisattvas who are on the paths of accumulation and preparation (the first two of the five main Mahayana paths), even though they have not yet completely uprooted the mistaken conception of a true "I," they are, however, concerned for the welfare of all beings. They are like a mother strongly motivated to solve her children's problems, in spite of still having the wrong view of an independent, intrinsically existent self.

We must not conclude that it is too difficult to help others and that we will never manage to do so, because then this desire will never arise. On the contrary, we must try regardless to develop this attitude in our minds, and by and by our courage will grow and we will truly succeed in doing something for others. As in our studies, we begin by aspiring to be more committed until the moment comes when we study in earnest. Likewise, by gradually generating the desire to help others, we will eventually succeed.

If even just thinking of having the courage to help others is too difficult for us, we should at least pray that we may fully develop it in the future, and then one day it will happen.

Consideration for the benefit of others does not manifest in a single instant. We should begin by trying to solve our own problems, being happy ourselves so that we can then extend that happiness to our parents, friends, acquaintances, those we are indifferent to, and finally our enemies. At night, before falling asleep, let us examine how many people we have benefited during the day, and let us decide to help more tomorrow. Also, let us consider how many people we have harmed, and motivate ourselves to no longer harm anyone in the future.

For monks it is quite easy to live in solitude and follow these points of advice, whereas for laypeople it is very difficult. Nevertheless you must live by practicing the Dharma, helping others as much as possible and abandoning malevolent attitudes. If you do this with sincerity and enthusiasm, then you will face the moment of death in a state of peace, with joy, and without regrets.

When someone is happy or experiences pleasure, we should not feel jealous or envious but instead help him increase it.

Since compassion is the mental attitude by which one cannot endure seeing others suffer, we could think that by developing it and being concerned about others, we will feel bad and lose our peace, and that it would therefore be better to refrain. But this way of thinking is wrong. In reality, this slight suffering in our minds will make it possible to destroy the suffering of many beings. [104]

We might feel uneasy, but we should accept this, because it will bring great results in future lives, such as liberation and the benefit of beings as infinite as space.

The text now refers to the story of Supushpachandra Bodhisattva, whose name means "the flower adorned by the moon." He knew that by going to see a certain king he would be executed, but also that because of this many people would gain numerous and substantial advantages. In order to not deprive them of this possibility, he went to the king and gave up his life. [106]

There is another episode I have heard about. During the British rule of India, the English proposed that three Indians, probably prominent people, be hanged in exchange for the independence of their country. They agreed, and when the moment of their execution came they were neither regretful nor depressed, but instead were singing songs of freedom. I do not know if the story is true, but according to the tale, those people gave their lives for the freedom of their country and signed a document declaring that they were extremely happy to die for the welfare of India. They were happy to sacrifice their lives, because a whole population would gain by their doing so.

Even though developing bodhichitta is difficult, if we do not neglect our commitment and our attitude of being concerned for and wanting to help others, the moment will come when all this will fill our minds with joy and we will be ready to endure any kind of difficulty for the welfare of others, even to the point of taking rebirth in the worst hell, Avici, the hell of uninterrupted pain. We will be as happy to do this as a swan or a wild goose plunging into a lotus pool. [107]

Although we are working for the benefit of others, we should not have any sense of pride or arrogance, nor should we have expectations. We usually practice generosity with the motivation of becoming rich in a future life or something similar. A bodhisattva, on the other hand, practices generosity with concern only for the benefit of others, and without the slightest concern for himself. [109]

If we help someone while thinking that in the future he might help us, our actions are contaminated by an egoistic mental attitude. But if what motivates us is the desire that the person experience less problems or solves them altogether, then it will indeed be an altruistic action, and the results will be a thousand times greater than those arising from the former motivation. For example, when engaged in business we always try to avoid loss and procure maximum gain. Likewise, by practicing bodhichitta, we do all we can in order to ensure that others do not experience suffering and instead experience happiness. [110]

If we strive in this direction, one day we will certainly succeed in developing this precious mind, just as we come to regard the bodies that we possess, which come from our parents, as exclusively our own simply through familiarity with this thought. [111]

Although it is difficult to extend the same love and care we have for our own bodies to the bodies of others, it is only a matter of training. By training well, these attitudes will spontaneously arise. This is part of the practice of *exchanging oneself with others*. [112]

Living in a neighborhood and remaining harmonious with our neighbors, being more concerned for them than for ourselves, is a small example of the meaning of this type of practice. If we do not care at all about them, the immediate result of our behavior will be the impossibility of maintaining good relations. In any place or in any society in which we live, in a community or in a family, if we are concerned only with ourselves, no one will love us, but if we do the opposite everyone will love us. If we are civil servants or government officials and we sincerely work for others, then we can truly say that we are at the service of the state, and we will be loved and respected. But if we put our own interests at the top of the list we will be chastised.

The first time I came to Italy I heard about a minister who had bought twenty defective airplanes from the United States for the price of new ones with public money in order to make personal profit. People later became aware of the fraud, and the minister was arrested. Anyway, apart from what happened, we must consider his story a failure due to the self-cherishing mind, which is laden with faults and shortcomings and is subject to all sorts of criticism.

Selfishness is the source of all unhappiness and suffering and must be rejected, whereas concern for others is the source of all happiness, and we must familiarize ourselves with this attitude. [113]

In a stanza of the *Guru Puja* one asks for blessings so that, having generated the aspiration to benefit all beings, and to lead them to ultimate and supreme happiness, even if they were all to turn against us and become our enemies, we may consider that altruistic attitude to be the source of every joy and more important than our own existence.

In the same way that we accept that our hands and so forth are all limbs of the same organism and for this reason do not want to separate ourselves from them, so we should consider all beings as branches of the same body, because they have helped us many times in the past. Then, unable to bear the thought that they might face difficulties, we should try to help them solely because they are sentient beings. [114]

At present we are concerned only about ourselves. It is not impossible, however, to change this attitude, to transform it completely. This is because the self does not intrinsically exist, but is only a nominal designation made on the basis of the five aggregates. Because of the familiarity we have created in all our previous lives with the thought that the self has an independent existence, this wrong conception arises spontaneously and with great force. In the same way, if we train ourselves to want to take care of others, the moment will come when we actually possess this altruistic attitude. [115]

Our minds will then be free from any pride and any expectation of reward, just as we do not have any pride when feeding our body. [116]

Just as we do not want to suffer and as we protect ourselves from the smallest unpleasant thing, we should do the same for others. [117]

From his great compassion for all beings, Avalokiteshvara blessed his own name, granting to it the power to dispel any type of fear or anxiety among those who recite it. [118]

So, if we have to give a public talk or speak to someone whom we find intimidating, or take exams, and we feel worried, reciting his mantra beforehand will help us gain control over anxiety and nervousness.

We think at first that being concerned about others is a difficult thing to achieve, and we conceive of it as a dangerous practice, almost as one of our enemies, whose mere name incites fear within us. As we familiarize ourselves with it, however, since our attitude toward him has changed, it will be almost as if our enemy has become an excellent friend, so that we even feel sad if he has to go away for a while. [119]

Once we have acquired the altruistic mind, we will behave as Buddha did in the stories of his previous lives. When he was still a bodhisattva and training in bodhichitta, the Buddha offered his body to a tiger. The place where this occurred can still be seen. Having more concern for others than for oneself is not unreasonable, and good reasons for this practice are explained in the following verses.

Those who wish to liberate themselves and others from samsara should undertake the sacred pledge of exchanging themselves for others, the holy or noble "secret." [120]

This pledge is something very profound, even burdensome in a sense, since it is not an easy thing for everyone to practice and achieve. On the other hand, the selfish mind, concerned solely with its own well-being, is the cause of all the suffering we experience.

Attachment to the self is the cause of every negative action sentient beings perform, and there are examples that show this. First they have attachment to the self, followed by attachment to the body. To protect it from hunger, thirst, or various types of illness, they end up killing fish, birds, and other animals, or attacking people in order to rob them. For their own profit, they might even kill their parents or steal what belongs to the Three Jewels. As a result of these actions, they will proceed to burn in the flames of the deepest hell. [123]

Some commit robbery and are caught by the police and put in jail. The sole root of all this is the attachment to the self. The same applies to an argument that degenerates and becomes so heated that it leads even to murder. In court cases, where each of the two parties claim to be right and want to win, or in arguments between parents and children, selfishness is once again the culprit. Couples' disagreements and separations, and conflicts between teachers and students or between gurus and disciples—all have their origins in a selfish attitude, which is concerned solely with and attached to personal benefit.

Every problem and every mistake is born out of wanting for ourselves every advantage. However, if we transform this attitude and no longer wish to keep what is pleasant for ourselves, but instead offer it to others, all difficulties will disappear. Whether or not we show a friendly face, whether or not we are kind, the right attitude is to benefit others. Usually it is a rarity to find someone in the world who behaves like this, but we have promised to practice the Mahayana teachings and tantra in particular, and therefore it is our responsibility to exchange ourselves for others.

We should strive enthusiastically to offer every pleasant thing to them, and this habit will gradually increase in our mind.

A wise man has no attachment or desire for his own body; he does not protect and gratify it. [124]

If someone asks us to give him something that he needs, and we think, "What will I be left with?" this type of mental attitude is similar to a demon's, and is called the "dharma of the pretas." But if in the same situation, with no hesitation and with a pure altruistic thought, we give the requested object, this is called the "dharma of the gods." [125]

If, in our own interest, we harm others, the result will be a rebirth in the realms of suffering, whereas if we experience difficulties in order to benefit others, it will be the cause of all happiness. [126]

Holding ourselves in high esteem and thinking of ourselves as wealthier or of a higher social class, we will find ourselves reborn in unpleasant realms, and even if we are born as humans we will be stupid. But if we reverse this attitude, we will instead acquire the joys of a higher realm and receive honors and consideration from all. [127]

Using others for our own gain will result in us having to serve in a future life, whereas putting ourselves at other people's service is the cause of being reborn into a higher social class, as an important person, or as a person in a position of power. [128]

In short, any happiness in this world derives from our concern for others. We are all enjoying a human rebirth, and this is the effect of a loving mind that has not caused harm but has been interested in and taken good care of others. Those who serve others will be respected and held in high esteem by all, will improve their social position, and, if one day they were to stand as candidates, they would be elected. Even the posts of prime minister or president therefore have consideration for others at their root.

On the other hand, every suffering, fear, problem, or difficulty derives from the self-centered mind. Without giving much explanation, it suffices to look at this typically childish behavior and compare it with that of the buddhas, who instead work for the benefit of others. [130]

The reason that we prostrate to, make offerings to, and worship any statue of Buddha, even if it is made of stone, is because his attitude was constantly altruistic.

If we do not exchange ourselves for others, we will never attain buddhahood, and in samsara we will have no happiness. [131]

Without elaborate examples and without speaking of future lives, even with small things and in this very existence, we can see this at work. If we are, for example, employed in a firm or within a family and work without diligence, our superior will not be happy and we will consequently lose the job or will not get paid. On the other hand, if we are the employers and fail to pay our staff who work conscientiously, one day they will leave and will no longer work for us. [132]

Therefore, even in order to succeed and obtain good results in this life, an altruistic attitude is important. Without it, we will not achieve our goals and we will face many problems in the future. What use is such a mind, concerned solely with itself? [134]

If we do not forsake egoism completely, we will never succeed in putting an end to our suffering in samsara. Just as we must move away from fire if we do not want to get burned, so the only way to put an end to and pacify our own and others' suffering is to abandon the egoistic attitude and substitute it with concern for the well-being of others. [136]

Also, in the six-session guru yoga, there is a verse that says, "I offer my body, my riches, and the accumulation of virtue of the three eons, without any sense of loss, to the benefit of all beings."

If we go to a wealthy person and ask him for a job, we promise that we will work diligently. Likewise, since we have promised to be concerned about others and to offer ourselves to them, we should forget ourselves, and all our senses must be at others' disposal and no longer focused on serving ourselves. We must therefore keep the promise of not using our bodies to harm sentient beings, and instead devote all we possess to their well-being. [139]

Continuing with the text's commentary, we differentiate three types of people in relation to ourselves: those who are superior, equal, and inferior. It might look at first as if the verses say that we should practice envy and jealousy toward people who are superior to us, competitiveness with those at the same level, and arrogance and pride toward those below us, but actually the verses deal with specific ways of eliminating these mental afflictions. [140]

Concerning the third type, we meditate by imagining that we put ourselves in the place of people we consider inferior, and give them our place. Now it is they who feel arrogance, and we who suffer the repercussions. Let us consider, for example, a teacher and his disciple—usually the teacher feels proud, superior to the disciple. What he should do is consider himself to be the disciple, and his disciple to be the teacher.

This is the actual practice. I visualize myself on the one hand as a bodhisattva and on the other as an ordinary being, and I imagine that a discussion takes place between these two simultaneous visualizations of myself. In my second role, I say to myself as a bodhisattva, "You are a bodhisattva, and everyone serves and honors you, whereas I, an ordinary being, have no one to take care of me, offer me help, or show me respect. You, as a bodhisattva, can obtain anything you need and can solve any problem, whereas I have nothing. You are praised and respected by all, whereas I am despised and criticized. You have all the happiness and I have all the suffering." And, continuing in my reproachful tone, I, as an ordinary being, say to myself, the bodhisattva, "You only rest, whereas I must work all day. You are renowned for your wisdom, whereas I am known for having no good qualities whatsoever." [142]

The conversation goes on and I, visualized as an ordinary being, finally make this promise to myself, visualized as a bodhisattva, "You have achieved wisdom and every good quality, thanks to your striving; now I shall do the same."

This practice is specifically for a bodhisattva who, as such, can at times generate pride. He will then visualize other beings reproaching him in the way described above. This practice is, however, useful at any level. For example, an educated person who has arrogance when meeting an ignorant person visualizes himself being challenged by the latter in the following way: "Why do you feel superior? I also, through striving, can attain your knowledge. Therefore, you have no reason to be proud."

The bodhisattva who feels proud may also visualize himself on the one hand as an ordinary being and on the other as a bodhisattva with the former reproaching the latter, as follows. "You feel superior because you are a bodhisattva, but in fact there are other bodhisattvas who are higher than you. You think that I am below you, but this is only in relation to yourself, for there are others who are below me, and in relation to them I am superior. It is of no use then to consider things in such a solid way, because superiority and inferiority exist only relatively; they are interdependent." [143]

And in the visualization, the dialogue continues. "You should not feel too proud, bodhisattva, of your morality or of your view, thinking that I possess fewer of these qualities. This situation is contingent, and if I strive adequately, I will become like you. I, a common person, am inferior to you, a bodhisattva, in morality and knowledge, and it is your task to help me improve. For the benefit of all beings, you should accept joyfully any privation. You are known as a person of great qualities and you should use them to help others; otherwise they are wasted." [145]

In the case of a good translator who feels proud, I would say to him, "You must not feel proud because you translate well, but must only strive to constantly improve your work."

During the day we commit various kinds of negative actions, even unconsciously, and we also harm others by despising them. So at night, reflecting on our actions and recognizing them to be wrong, we should reproach ourselves as the text describes, and resolve to no longer act like this in the future. [146]

One more example. If, say, the Italian prime minister realizes that he is not doing his duty, that he is not truly working for others, he can visualize himself sitting opposite and the citizens in his place instead. Then, as the citizens, he starts to criticize and highlight his own shortcomings and the various mistakes he has made while in office, saying to himself, "You are not truly working for the benefit of others, you are not doing your duty." In this way he generates the courage to change his motivation.

A bodhisattva criticizes himself in the same fashion, so that he can improve his practice and in order to be stimulated to enhance his qualities.

Now the text goes on to explain how a bodhisattva should handle competitiveness with an equal.

The basic visualization is like the previous one. I as a bodhisattva project myself outside, and imagine another bodhisattva, my equal, who says to me, "Now we will discuss our wealth, our fame, and our good qualities. I am going to work and earn more than you; I will study and become more educated than you. I will try to spread my good qualities and wisdom far and wide, and I will endeavor to hide yours as much as possible. I will try to hide all my shortcomings and reveal yours, and with every means I can, I will try to obtain veneration, offerings, and respect from everyone and create as many obstacles as possible for you, to prevent you from attaining the same. With great pleasure I have pointed out the mistakes that you, bodhisattva, have made in the past and are making now, and I will make sure that you become an object of scorn and derision." [150]

This is the competitiveness the text refers to. If people praise us and are happy with us, it is a cause for pride to arise, whereas being subject to derision helps us avoid it. Examining our mistakes is also useful to develop humility, whereas recognizing the virtues of others will engender our respect for them, and this is a good thing. To feel humbler than the lowest is one of the practices pertinent to the bodhisattva. In fact, a bodhisattva feels that the only thing that is lower than himself is water.

Now we approach the third aspect of the meditation. The bodhisattva practicing this visualizes a person higher than himself who speaks to him thus: "I am superior to you in knowledge, intelligence, beauty, standing, and wealth. You must not feel envious, but instead be delighted with these qualities of mine. Of what you have attained and gained, keep only what is essential to your survival and share the rest with others, otherwise you are not striving in the bodhisattva practice. Forget the comfortable life, indolence, and laziness, and instead work to help all beings." [153]

The meditating bodhisattva receives this advice from the projection of another, superior bodhisattva. Therefore it is he who convinces and exhorts himself to be at the service of others.

Egoistic mind, or a self-centered attitude, is what truly destroys happiness on a grand scale. Because of it we remain in samsara, and even if we have worked hard and tried with great effort through eons to achieve every happiness, the only thing we seem to have obtained is suffering. [155]

If we examine our habitual mental attitude, we can see that we always try to benefit ourselves and find a solution to our problems, and that this very attitude has actually been the cause of all our suffering. Having understood this, we must now strive to change and consider the egoistic mind to be our true enemy, and the altruistic attitude to be what speedily takes us to buddhahood.

Since the words of the Buddha are infallible, if we act according to them, purifying our attitudes and exchanging our self-concern with concern for others, we will certainly see positive results in the future. If we had done this in the past, we too would already be buddhas. [157]

We should thoroughly examine whether a particular deed is going to benefit a person or group, and then act accordingly. We should also deprive ourselves of what we own and give it to those who are in need. [159]

We should think, "I am happy but others are sad; I have a high standing though others are low; I have benefits, while others do not." Let us then be envious of ourselves, in order to be able to work in such a way that others will also be able to acquire what we possess. [160]

We must separate ourselves from our happiness and give it to others. We must take upon ourselves the suffering of others and during the course of our day examine our actions of body, speech, and mind, and when we find faults, reproach ourselves in order to do better. [161]

If someone hits us with a stick, rather than being angry we should pray that his negative action might ripen on us. If we have shortcomings or have made mistakes, it is better to openly admit them than to hide them. Revealing our faults is in itself purification. [162]

Furthermore, we must praise those who possess good qualities, and this will become an accumulation of merit.

We must also deliberately divulge the good qualities and renown of others, and let them outshine our own. We must consider ourselves to be the lowest servant, thus committing ourselves to do everything that others require of us. [163]

By considering the great quantity of faults we have, even if we do possess some good qualities—a little wisdom and so forth—we should not show ourselves off, but hide our qualities like a lamp inside a vase. [164]

A bodhisattva does not reveal his good qualities, but instead discloses his mistakes, whereas we hide our shortcomings and boast about our virtues.

Shantideva now presents a stanza that also appears in the *Guru Puja:* "Compassionate Guru, may all the evil karma and obscuration of every being ripen on me and bless me so that I might be capable of offering my virtues and happiness to others." [165]

Because of our egoistic attitude, we have created much negative karma in the past and must therefore pray that it might ripen now, so that we may free ourselves from its future results, and so that this may also be the cause of the benefit of all beings.

In our daily behavior we should be humble, free from aggressiveness, greed, and ignorance, like a young bride who is naturally bashful, timid, and restrained in her new home. [166]

When getting up in the morning, we must decide to perform only good deeds. In the evening, before going to sleep, we must examine our actions, and if we have done something wrong, we must resolve to refrain from doing it again the next day, so that we gradually bring improvement to our three doors. This is exercising active vigilance. [167]

The difference between one who understands the Dharma and one who does not manifests in two ways. A rich person, for example, with all the possessions and money in the world, will travel often, going each time to a new holiday destination, and will eat delicacies. Without an understanding of the Dharma, changing environments constantly and eating increasingly luxurious foods can cause great suffering. In contrast, one who is acquainted with the Dharma might have problems, might not be rich, and might not have many opportunities—in fact, he might be in dire straits. When experiencing such discomfort, however, he will find solace in thinking that suffering is the nature of samsara and that having to continually encounter problems is the very nature of cyclic existence. Consequently, he will try to generate the inner energy needed to remain mentally at peace and to face every difficulty with a relaxed mind.

The greatest misery one has to endure in life occurs at the moment of death, when one experiences many types of suffering, such as leaving behind one's loved ones, friends, possessions, and riches. This is true for an ordinary person with no understanding of the Dharma, but one who has internalized its essence will not suffer because he knows that in the future he will acquire a higher rebirth.

Between material advantages, which are limited to this life, and the advantages gained through Dharma practice, which reach beyond to future lives, the latter are infinitely superior.

I do not mean to say that we should forsake all our material possessions, for as long as we have a physical body we do need these things. But it would be a pity, having had this precious opportunity of a human rebirth, to waste all our energy and intelligence solely in the pursuit of material riches, and to completely forget the spiritual path.

In all situations, the more we pay attention to others the more we gain ourselves. If, on the other hand, we mistreat or harm them, we ourselves will suffer. By eliminating the egoistic attitude, we also destroy its function of causing suffering.

Addressing the egoistic attitude directly, Shantideva says, "Until now I did not know the harm you inflicted on me. I did not know you, but now I do, and I refuse to remain under your control. Your rule is over. I have unmasked your secret of forever pursuing exclusively selfish gain, and I have understood the harm you have caused me. From now on, I will no longer think that you are of help to me—therefore, stop your activity." [169]

We should determine to devote ourselves solely to others, to forsake all egoistic attitudes, and to work at all times and in every way for all beings, without ever becoming discouraged. [170]

If, having thus decided, we again become concerned solely with our-selves, it is equal to throwing ourselves into the hell realms. [171]

If we accept a job and pocket the money in advance but do not honor our commitment, we know the consequences will be unpleasant. How much more so if we betray our commitment to work for all beings.

"For ages you, egoistic attitude, have consigned me to the guardians of hell; you are my true enemy and I will now try to destroy you. Having understood the harm that befalls me if I follow you, from now on I will forsake you and no longer allow you to have power over me." [172]

So if we wish to have a long and peaceful life, and every happiness, we must cast aside our egoistic attitude and use all our energy and intelligence to protect all other beings from suffering as well. [173]

In order to help all beings, we need a precious human rebirth, and we need to take good care of our bodies, as we will not be able to help them if we do not protect our bodies from hunger and sickness. However, since our bodies find even the slightest pain unbearable, we should not satisfy every single demand, for the more they receive, the more they demand, and even if we were to offer everything on earth to our attachment, it still would not be satisfied. It is therefore much better to cease trying to achieve satisfaction and eliminate desire from the very beginning. [175]

This is referred to in the story of a certain king who had a vast kingdom and, not satisfied, acquired another, and then another, until he was the king of all four continents. Still dissatisfied, he ascended to the paradise of the thirty-three gods, and succeeded in gaining command of that kingdom, Indra's realm, as well. While still driven by his craving, however, his good fortune and his positive karma ended, and he fell to earth. He then finally understood, and said, "My dissatisfaction has been my greatest error." [176]

Our craving functions through the desire for more and more, and its byproducts are dissatisfaction and discontent, which in turn bring about impatience and unhappiness. We must therefore try to eliminate these by using the appropriate antidotes and ceasing to consider the objects of our attachment to be attractive when we come in contact with them. Desire is the attitude wishing to possess what we do not have, and dissatisfaction is the wish to enhance and increase what we have already. When we are free from both, however, we possess the true wealth of fulfillment. [177]

If someone who already has a house sees a better one and thinks, "My house is not as big and beautiful," as a result he will start to crave a nicer house. To solve the problem, the first possible solution is to buy a home of that kind, saving money if there is not enough. But if that person cannot find the money he needs and still cultivates the desire for what he cannot have, he will be unhappy. A second solution, then, is to block such craving by changing his mental attitude—for example, by thinking that any home he has grants him shelter and enough rooms to live in. Trying to be satisfied with what he has, the craving will start to decrease, and finally it will disappear.

Likewise, if we are not very rich and we feel discouraged because we see that there is nothing we can do to earn more, let us think that, whatever the sum we possess, we will never be satisfied. This is a sensible way of thinking, for what is the point of feeling sad if we cannot find more money?

Another way of thinking is the following: "Right now I want this lovely house, but what will be the use of it once I have to leave this world? And what will be the use of even the little house in which I now live?" Or, "What will be the use of the money I have? When I die, I will have to leave even this body that I have cared so much for and for which I have so much attachment." Indeed, at that moment, we will have to abandon everything.

If we try to think in these terms, our minds will start to evolve and move in the right direction. It is because we are unable to reflect in the right way that we feel attached to nonsensical things. But when we improve our way of seeing things and take on correct attitudes, we will gradually forsake desire, no longer being subject to the suffering it causes us, and we will feel more satisfied, more fulfilled. At the very least we will not feel unhappy.

This positive change in our attitude is the result of our mental training, or spiritual method.

Negative mental factors associated with hatred are very harmful, but at least we do not generate them very often, whereas attachment is continually with us. It is like scabies—it is relieved when we scratch, but by scratching it spreads. The more we try to satisfy our attachment, the more it grows, leaving imprints of suffering; therefore we must eliminate it.

This beautiful body of ours will eventually be buried, thrown in a river, cremated, or, as in Tibet, given to the vultures—in any case, we shall have to forsake it. It is made of flesh, bones, and skin, which ultimately are the causes of suffering. It is a machine for processing food, a pile of mud and dust, and there is no reason to be proud of it, because it is composed of impurities. [179]

Since our body is the source of all our suffering, we should not be attached to it. At the same time, however, we must not misuse it or waste it, but take care of it as a vehicle to practice the Dharma and attain personal liberation and enlightenment, thus finding ultimate happiness.

A body does not react when derided or praised, so there is no reason for us to do so either. [182]

It is wrong if, out of attachment, we praise our body, and out of aversion we despise or criticize the bodies of others. We must treat them in the same way. [183]

In order to benefit all beings we can also, with generosity, offer our body. [184]

This does not mean that from the beginning we must literally practice this way. We can, however, without fear of harm, offer ourselves completely, and we do not have to die in order to work for others. For example, if we go to see a wise, accomplished person and offer our body completely, we will then be supported by him and we will eat what he offers us, while at the same time being totally available. If we offer our body to the root guru and to the Three Jewels, from that moment on we will work for the benefit of all beings and to fulfill our master's wishes.

We offer our body to the buddhas by making it useful to all beings, and this pleases them, because their only wish and objective is that all might receive benefits. Offering one's body to the buddhas and making it available to all beings will also prevent us from any type of hindrance that might come from evil beings or spirits, and will protect us from catching contagious diseases.

We possess the courage and the desire to listen to the Dharma, and we must pray that this positive and useful attitude may continue, without thinking that we must practice it all at once, but gradually, little by little. When a strong rain falls on a steep slope, the water gathers and large rivulets are formed. Then, when the sun returns, it dries everything quickly, since all the water has fallen down into the valley. Our behavior must not reflect the sense of this metaphor, but instead we must try to progress day by day, year by year, and life after life, until we succeed in attaining the state of omniscience.

We must free ourselves from samsara, because it is nothing but suffering. But is it possible to do so? Certainly, because the conception of samsara existing intrinsically is erroneous, since no phenomena exist "truly"—that is, by their own characteristics or by their own nature. Nor do they exist without depending on their constituent parts, on a nominal attribute, or on their causes and conditions (for those that are impermanent).

In order to generate the discriminating intelligence that realizes emptiness, we must be capable of maintaining our meditation for a long time, and in order to maintain concentration, we must first practice ethical discipline, or morality.

We are kept as prisoners by mental afflictions but will be free when we destroy them. For example, the Chinese have deprived Tibet of freedom and independence, but when we Tibetans find a way to gain these back, we will again enjoy them.

In all the teachings of the Buddha and in all the scriptures of the masters there is full agreement on the fact that all the suffering in samsara, and the fact of having to be reborn into it without choice, arises due to mental afflictions and karma. Complete and ultimate freedom will be attained only after having destroyed their power. Both the Dharma and material wealth can help us in different ways, but we must choose which is the most effective.

It is like being asked to choose between gold bullion and the same quantity of iron—surely, even if both of them can be useful in different ways, we will choose gold, because it is the most precious. Likewise, it is far more sensible to strive in the practice of the Dharma, which is more helpful and more useful than material possessions.

If we devote our energy solely to spiritual practice without worrying about accumulating wealth, the indirect outcome will be that we will succeed in having material wealth anyway—even more, in fact, than we would have gained by thinking exclusively about it—and that we will not face problems related to poverty.

Since attachment and aversion hinder the development of meditative concentration, one has to abandon them and try instead to follow the practices of the bodhisattvas as well as their advice on conscientiousness. One must apply the antidotes to mental dullness. [185]

In order to fight this obstacle—if, for instance, we are meditating on an image of the Buddha—we must first try to visualize it as clearly as possible. Then, when the visualization is clear, we must apply memory in order to maintain our concentration on that image.

A second type of mental dullness is that which we may experience when lying in the sun. Still another hindrance to concentration, as we have seen previously, is the mental factor of distraction, which can manifest through thinking about our loved ones and friends, or about going for a walk, and so forth. While training in meditative steadfastness, we must also avoid the regret we feel when considering negative deeds we performed in the past. Allowing remorse to overwhelm us only becomes a new obstacle in such cases. We must also avoid any malevolent thoughts or doubts about the usefulness of our meditation. All the mental factors that have been described—gross and subtle mental dullness, distraction, remorse, and doubt—prevent the attainment of concentration and must be avoided.

We must also consider the need for developing the courage of buddhas and bodhisattvas in order to succeed in meditating and practicing day and night, reflecting on the fact that without striving in this way, the final result of enlightenment will not be attained. It is equally necessary to generate a firm conviction that great meditators have obtained results from their practices by overcoming various difficulties, and that we must do the same. [186]

We must therefore practice the common teachings of the Parami-tayana, the path of the sutras, and the extraordinary, uncommon teach-ings of tantra.

In order to attain individual liberation we must eliminate mental afflic-tions through the realization of emptiness, and in order to do this we must develop perfect concentration, avoiding the various disturbing factors that are a hindrance to meditation, and contemplate emptiness itself. [187]

QUESTION: How does one visualize the image of the Buddha?
ANSWER: The visualization must be clear. You can visualize the Buddha as he is described in the texts, or by referring to the details you see in various paintings. It is important that your mental image is not of a bronze statue or a painting, but alive, and endowed with the nature of light—nothing solid, only light, but with all those characteristics described or seen. When striving in concentration, you should never change the dimensions of the visualization once you have chosen them.

QUESTION: What happens when, during meditation, the visualization of the Buddha turns into the image of a normal person?
ANSWER: Probably what you visualize or see is a projection of your mental attitude. Usually it is difficult to have a clear visualization, and it is in fact hazy or cloudy, and we need to try to improve it and develop a living image. Once it is clear, we must place our concentration upon it.

QUESTION: It is said that we must control the body and the mind, but what is this "I" that must do so?
ANSWER: The "I" involved in this process exists, and it is the awareness observing what the mind is doing, together with the discriminating alertness that recognizes what is negative. Both develop greatly alongside *shamata*—in other words, meditating on one point, be it the mind or another object. We can eliminate all distractions and gradually control the mind, going from one minute of concentration to hours and days without being distracted.

If we add the altruistic mind of bodhichitta to the wisdom that realizes emptiness, we can attain buddhahood.

Thus we conclude the explanation of the eighth chapter, which chiefly contains the instructions on how to develop perfect concentration and how to use this to engender the love and compassion that is typical of bodhichitta. However, it is also possible for some practitioners to develop bodhichitta first and then samadhi.

Note to Chapter 9

Venerable Geshe Yeshe Tobden maintained that it was very important to try to provide the reader with a supporting framework for the ninth, or "wisdom," chapter of the Bodhicharyavatara. *He therefore asked me to elaborate on the four key points around which the entire content of this chapter is developed. The reader will find this further explanation in the appendix. Here are his comments about the explanation.*
—Fiorella Rizzi

"Thanks to this concise presentation," *he explained,* "even without having Shantideva's root text at your disposal, you will nevertheless be able to develop a clear general idea about the wisdom chapter, in the same way as you would recognize the main episodes of a person's life, from his birth through adolescence and adulthood, by viewing a film lasting only a couple of hours.

"Since the philosophical position held by the Prasangika-Madhyamikas on the emptiness of true existence is expounded with many different arguments, equally numerous objections to these also arise from the point of view of the lesser schools. Shantideva's intention in the ninth chapter is to present the Prasangika view, precisely clarify any misunderstanding, and refute the wrong assertions of the exponents of the lesser schools in general, and specifically those of the Chittamatrins, as the debate between them has been particularly detailed and ongoing."

↝ 9 ↜
WISDOM

IF WE EXAMINE OURSELVES, we will find that we always desire happiness, that we are never satisfied with the happiness we already possess, and that we never want to experience suffering. This is true for all beings, including animals. Since one of the main causes of our unhappiness is attachment, let us begin by considering its nature and the way it causes dissatisfaction in our minds, forever pushing us into wanting something more.

In order to eliminate attachment, the cause of so much suffering, we should analyze the nature of the object toward which it is directed at any given time and try to verify whether the object is able to satisfy us fully. Reflecting deeply, we will find that this object does not actually possess all the positive qualities that we ascribe to it. Realizing this, we will begin to understand the futility of our attachment and the desire we foster toward the object will gradually diminish and eventually disappear. At this point, even if we do not manage to possess that particular object, we will not be unhappy.

Let us take money as an example, and observe its nature. Money is an object that we yearn to possess, accumulate, and increase. At the beginning, we endure numerous difficulties trying to earn it. Once we actually possess it our difficulties continue, for then we experience the problems of having to keep it safe so that it is not stolen or lost. Despite all of this, money does not have the power to eliminate all of our unhappiness and suffering, nor is it able to procure for us all that we desire. Even if it does allow us to acquire something, money cannot grant us complete satisfaction.

Imagine that someone has been very involved in his work and has become rich and deposited all his money in the bank. When he dies, he will have to leave it behind. Therefore, all the striving and hardships he faced in order to accumulate it will remain with the money in the bank and he will be unable to benefit from them.

Then consider two people. The first is not concerned about wealth but is interested in the Dharma, purifying negative karma and accumulating positive karma. The second person has worked very hard to accumulate money. When they die, the first person will be able carry his good karma along with him, while the second person will leave everything on this earth behind and will not manage to carry a single cent.

Generally laypeople must work, as particularly in the West it is very hard to survive without doing so. In Dharamsala there is an old woman who says she still needs to exercise her trade in order to live but also that she needs to practice the Dharma, because sooner or later she is going to die. We have the same problem—in order to live we must work, but since we are going to die we must also practice the Dharma in a way that will be beneficial to our future lives.

A fortunate rebirth depends on good karma, and on this point Buddhism and Christianity agree. All religions state that by performing virtuous deeds, good results will ensue.

In order to solve life's many problems, the method used by a follower of the Dharma is to accumulate as much positive karma and eliminate as much negative karma as possible, in order to obtain more happiness and less suffering. The method of one who is not acquainted with the Dharma, in contrast, is to accumulate material wealth. Undoubtedly, positive karma ripens into happy experiences and negative karma ripens into unhappy experiences, in the same way that edible plants bear edible fruit and poisonous plants bear poisonous fruit. If a person is not acquainted with the Dharma, but nevertheless strives to do good for others and behaves in a non-harmful way toward them, he will attain more happiness, and experience less misery and problems.

If you try as much as possible to avoid harming others, you will find that you will have fewer and fewer enemies, and if you strive to do good and help them you will find that you will have more friends. A person who has more friends than enemies will not only be happier, but will also be praised by many.

For laypeople the best method to practice the Dharma is to have a job in order to earn a living, and then dedicate all one's free time to the accumulation of positive karma and the purification of negative karma. This is a good method for using one's precious time in an advantageous way.

Fully ordained monks, or *gelong,* and novices, or *getsul,* should strive as much as possible to attain nirvana, and beg for the food they need to survive. In this way they should attempt to actualize the meaning of their life choice. According to the etymology of the Tibetan word, *ge* means virtue (and ultimate virtue is in nirvana), and *long* means beggar.

Living in this way is still possible in countries like Thailand and Burma, where there are people who support the monks so that they are able to devote themselves entirely to spiritual practice. In India, as well, we can find examples of spiritual practitioners who live solely on the offerings they receive.

In Tibet those who wanted to devote their lives to the Dharma would beg for their food during the time following the harvest. The food that they collected would then be used throughout the entire year. Naturally these monks had a very simple lifestyle and the food they ate was barely enough for their survival! Others found benefactors who provided them with the essentials so that they could lead a monastic life. Moreover some monasteries owned land that was cultivated by peasants with whom the crops would be shared at the time of harvest, and the monastery's share would be distributed among its members.

Monks in the West can live with the help of their parents or friends and can also do jobs that do not contradict the Dharma. In this way, they can succeed in procuring what they need to survive. In any case they should devote as much time as possible to practice. Besides this, it should not be hard for a person truly interested in devoting his or her time entirely to the Dharma to recycle and use leftovers from hotels and restaurants—I once saw a lot of food being thrown away from a restaurant at the end of the day.

The great mahasiddha Luipa lived like this in India—he would stop near the place where fishermen cleaned their fish and threw away the entrails and he would gather the waste and then clean, boil, and eat it. This is how Luipa sustained himself.

Reflecting carefully, we realize that many of our concerns are related to the physical body—we must appease its hunger, clothe it, let it rest when it is tired, and so on. This must be considered "samsara," and until we are able to free ourselves from it we are bound to suffer.

Surely such liberation must not be pursued by adopting solutions like suicide and the like, but instead by uprooting the cause that drives us to continually take new rebirths within cyclic existence. The karma that will result in a rebirth in samsara is already present within our minds, but it is the conditions of desire and strong attachment, both generated by ignorance, that cause it to ripen. In particular, it is the ignorance that clings to a truly existent self that causes this karmic maturation. This ignorance can be eliminated only by the wisdom that realizes emptiness directly. Generating this wisdom, we will be able to destroy all negative mental factors such as attachment, hatred, and so on. Besides, since this body, the cause of suffering, is obtained on the basis of these disturbing mental factors, if we eliminate them we will no longer be reborn in samsara with an impure body. Someone might think erroneously that in this way we will merely obtain a state of darkness or nothingness, but this is not so, since there are forms of existence that are pure, clear, and made of light, and which are of the same nature as our minds.

When we become free from the slavery of the ordinary physical body, our mental continuums will not cease to exist, but will instead be characterized by unalterable happiness. This is why we say that the Dharma can eliminate all suffering and lead to happiness without end.

At present we are under the influence of laziness, and this is the reason we are unable to strive very hard in Dharma practice. If, however, we are able to generate the wisdom that realizes emptiness, we will be able to eliminate the causes of that disturbing emotion and put an end to the suffering of conditioned cyclic existence. Supporting the wisdom that realizes emptiness with the mind of enlightenment, bodhichitta, we will also be able to eliminate the obscurations to omniscience, and so become buddhas. In this way we will be able to help other beings eliminate all suffering and attain all happiness.

Let us take as an example the Tibetans who escaped Tibet in 1959 and retreated to India. If they had had to provide for their sustenance and solve the numerous problems that arose alone, they would have faced great obstacles. However, these issues were reduced because they had a very special karmic bond with the current Fourteenth Dalai Lama, their spiritual and political leader who guides them through the most difficult hardships to this day. The Tibetans who remained in Tibet under direct Chinese rule still have much faith in him and are not in any way deterred. In the last twenty or thirty years the Chinese regime in Tibet has forced Tibetans to criticize the Dalai Lama, and even persecuted them in order to obtain their disavowal of his political and religious position. However, the people, supported by a pure faith in his deeds and his view, not only refused to do this but have even increased and consolidated their bond with him. The reason for this special relationship between the Dalai Lama and his people is that he possesses the compassionate mind of bodhichitta, by which he devotes everything to others.

Dharma teachings speak of the need to develop love—the thought of procuring happiness for all beings—and compassion—the thought wanting to free them from all suffering. The Dalai Lama, since he has ripened these two mental attitudes, strives constantly with joy to work for his people. His Holiness also possesses an excellent knowledge of the Dharma, and it is for this reason that he is able to fully satisfy the spiritual needs, doubts, and questions of every being. Any quality that he has is not only the result of his striving in this life, but also derives from the positive karma accumulated in his mental continuum in previous lives.

The Dalai Lama does not have many opportunities to work for the Chinese, nor do the Chinese have many opportunities to know the Dalai Lama, but the majority of people in China think that he is able to do something positive for them, and this is due to his realizations, his bodhichitta. This is officially well known, and has been confirmed to me by a person who lives in Dharamsala, who had lived in Tibet and then in China for five years, where he saw and heard all of this.

Every time His Holiness has launched an appeal to the Chinese government, he has not done so thinking solely about his own people, but has pointed it out as a general principle, maintaining that it is everyone's natural right to seek freedom and peace. As the political leader of the Tibetan people, he should not make appeals in favor of the Chinese, but as a bodhisattva this is appropriate, notwithstanding the fact that the Chinese have invaded his land, ruled his people, and forced him to flee. This is due to the influence of Dharma teachings.

The Dalai Lama is an example of someone who, by working for others, has succeeding in bringing about improvements. There are certainly many cases such as these, which demonstrate how beings endowed with a good understanding of the Dharma possess skillful means in order to find solutions to problems and achieve true satisfaction. Those not acquainted with the Dharma think that the only possibility in this direction is the use of material or external means, but these in fact cannot achieve much.

Working during the day and meeting in the evening to listen to the Dharma, as you do, is a great thing, because it is a way to create positive karma, which will allow you to improve your practice and have more possibilities in the future.

As stated before, in order to eliminate the seed or the root of all afflictions, one must possess the realization of wisdom supported by method. The first five perfections, which constitute the support for realizing the perfection of wisdom, are explained from the first to the eighth chapter of the *Bodhicharyavatara*. In order to eliminate the obscurations to wisdom, the perfection of wisdom must be supported by the first five perfections.

Bodhichitta, the method, is the resolve to attain buddhahood, together with the aspiration to eliminate not only one's own suffering, but also that of all sentient beings. Those who possess such determination must realize the wisdom that sees emptiness. All this has been taught by Shakyamuni Buddha. [1]

It is necessary for a bodhisattva to fully comprehend the two truths—conventional and ultimate—which constitute the basis of the path. The path is the practice of method combined with the development of wisdom. The final result is the two bodies of a buddha. All Mahayana texts give instructions on these three points.

Ascertaining the Two Truths

In relation to the two truths, ultimate truth is defined as what is realized explicitly by a direct, valid perceiver without dualistic appearances. Conventional truth is defined as what is realized explicitly by a direct, valid perceiver with dualistic appearances.

In order to comprehend the two truths, we can simplify them in the following way. Every phenomenon that is not emptiness itself is conventional truth, or deceptive truth, since the appearance of phenomena makes them seem endowed with true existence, which in fact is lacking. The emptiness of every phenomenon is ultimate truth, or nondeceptive. The person and the physical and mental aggregates are examples of conventional truths. Their emptiness, or lack of intrinsic existence, is ultimate truth.

There are three kinds of dualistic appearances: the appearance of conventional phenomena, the appearance of the perceived object and perceiving subject, and the appearance of true, or intrinsic, existence.

The direct realization of emptiness is the perception of ultimate truth, free from these three kinds of dualistic appearances.

During the meditative absorption of a person who possesses the wisdom that realizes emptiness, there is no duality whatsoever—for example, there is no appearance of the perceiving subject and the perceived object. At the level of conventional truth, however, the object is perceived as separate or different from the mind that perceives it, and there is a twofold appearance. Ultimate truth cannot be perceived by a mind that perceives a dual appearance; it is the referent of the mind that realizes emptiness directly and cannot be the referent of the mind that sees things dualistically. [2]

It is not very easy to gain an understanding of emptiness; therefore I will give a few examples.

When a plant grows from a seed, it comes into existence because of that seed; its existence therefore depends on that particular cause. If this was not the case, the plant would be devoid of existence—in other words, it would not exist.

Let us take a wheel as an example. A wheel is made out of a rim, spokes, a hub, and so on. The wheel exists in dependence on its parts; therefore a hypothetical wheel that exists without dependence on its parts is devoid of existence. The wheel cannot be both a phenomenon that exists in dependence on its parts and a phenomenon that exists without dependence on its parts—it can be only one of the two.

It is easy to comprehend how external things come into existence in dependence on various conditions. The farmer knows that in order to have crops, seeds are necessary, as are soil, water, and so on.

Going back to the example of the wheel—if all its components are present, the wheel exists. What we commonly call "wheel" is dependent on its components, whereas a wheel that does not depend on them does not exist.

Let us consider a further example: a tape recorder. The two conditions of the name "tape recorder" and the mind that perceives the object as "tape recorder" make the existence of the tape recorder possible. Therefore its existence arises in dependence on the name and the mind that perceives it as a tape recorder, and without these two conditions, its existence would not be possible.

A tape recorder that depends on these two conditions and a tape recorder that does not depend on them cannot both exist at the same time; hence the tape recorder is empty or devoid of being a "true" tape recorder, independent of these two conditions. In the same way, if a statement is a lie, it is definitely not the truth; therefore a lie is empty or devoid of truth.

The statue of a man, although similar to him in appearance, is in reality empty or devoid of being a man. When we are watching television, the people appearing on the screen, although real, are devoid of being real people. All phenomena that exist in the universe depend on these two factors: the mind that perceives them and the name that is given to them by the mind itself. Therefore whatever depends on these two conditions is empty of an intrinsic existence, or true existence, or existence with its own characteristics, or existence by its own nature. All these terms are synonymous.

What makes us unhappy and miserable are our own mental afflictions, such as hatred, attachment, and ignorance. In order to eliminate these causes of suffering we should generate the wisdom that realizes emptiness.

In reality, no object exists "truly," or intrinsically, since this kind of concept or view is merely a mental construct. When something appears to us to exist in that sense, we are dealing with an erroneous view of our own mind.

Let us suppose that there is a Mr. A and a Mr. B. If Mr. A approaches us and says that Mr. B has bad intentions toward us, aversion toward Mr. B will arise in us, even if what we have been told is not true. In reality, Mr. B is not bothering us in the least, and the fact that he might want to harm us is merely Mr. A's invention, but if we believe it we generate a mind distorted by Mr. A's words.

Likewise, all of us at present have wrong conceptions with regard to many things. For example, we are very attached to our body, and because of this disturbing emotion we consider it beautiful and precious. In reality it is an assemblage of impure substances such as bones, flesh, skin, blood, and so forth. If we opened it up mentally and extracted the internal organs and all that it is made of, we might not like this beautiful body anymore. Therefore the way that the body exists does not correspond to our concept or idea of it. What makes this body "beautiful" is a wrong view, an illusory perception of reality, which fosters the arising of attachment to the body and consequently many other problems.

Attachment and hatred do not arise toward appropriate or correct objects, but always toward wrong, deceptive objects. We have desire for things for which we should not have desire, and hatred for that which should not generate hatred. This kind of deceit is due to the mind obscured by its own grasping at an intrinsically existent self. In the case we considered earlier, the scarecrow seen in the distance is mistaken for a man, and we start thinking that he might wish to harm us, or that he will be good to us, but as we get closer and realize that this man in reality does not exist, the attachment or the hatred we felt toward him vanishes.

Likewise, when we generate the wisdom that realizes emptiness—that is, the ultimate nature of phenomena—this wisdom is able to eliminate the ignorance that grasps at an intrinsic self, and simultaneously the mental afflictions born of this ignorance also vanish. Therefore, when we feel depressed or unhappy, the best antidote is the meditation on emptiness.

QUESTION: Is there a logical process that would allow us to understand in what way the mind of bodhichitta acts as an antidote to all mental afflictions? Or, in order to understand its function as an antidote, should we just trust and wait until we ourselves have realized it?

ANSWER: The direct antidote to mental afflictions is not bodhichitta, but the wisdom that realizes emptiness. Without the support of bodhichitta, however, this wisdom allows only the attainment of the Hinayana nirvana. On the other hand, if the realization of emptiness is supported by the mind of bodhichitta, then the former is not only the antidote to mental afflictions, but is also able to eliminate obscurations to omniscience, thus allowing the attainment of buddhahood. This process is sustained by logic.

The Hinayana arhats possess the wisdom that realizes emptiness, but only bodhisattvas, since they have also generated bodhichitta, are able to eliminate the obstacles to the attainment of buddhahood.

The Hinayana arhats have not attained buddhahood precisely because they do not have the realization of bodhichitta. Buddhahood, in fact, can be attained only through the practice that unites method and wisdom. In this context, bodhichitta is the method, and wisdom is the realization of emptiness.

The realization of emptiness is not in itself an exclusively Mahayana Dharma, but bodhichitta seizes the wisdom that realizes emptiness and directs it toward the objective of benefiting numberless sentient beings. In addition to this, it produces an unlimited amount of merit and good qualities.

The difference between the practice of generosity performed on the basis of having generated the mind of bodhichitta and the practice of generosity performed without the support of such a mind is enormous, and this is also true for the remaining five perfections.

QUESTION: If a bodhisattva's bodhichitta is only a motivation aimed at eliminating the obscurations to omniscience, which are actually overcome only through the realization of emptiness, why is it that the Hinayana arhat, since he also has such wisdom, is not able to eliminate the obscurations to omniscience?

ANSWER: If there are two of us fighting against one, we are stronger. The Hinayana arhat has a limited motivation from the beginning of his practice—he wishes to attain his own liberation, and once this aim is reached he stops, because he is satisfied. The bodhisattva, on the other hand, has a greater motivation—he wishes not only to attain his own liberation, but also that all other beings may be free from suffering and samsara; therefore he is concerned for the well-being of all.

Let us suppose that someone wants to go to Rome, whereas someone else wishes to go to India. The first will not necessarily need to travel by plane, but might use a car or a train, whereas the second will need to go by plane.

Another example is to consider the benefit that a sick person can derive by taking only specific medicines, without integrating the cure with other things such as vitamins, and compare this with the benefits for someone using both. Each person will obtain qualitatively different results. Also, when we drink tea we notice differences—think about how it tastes with nothing added to it, and then how it tastes with milk, sugar, or honey!

Therefore, with the support of bodhichitta, the wisdom that realizes emptiness is more powerful, steadier, and possesses a much wider scope.

Hence, even if a Hinayana arhat and an arya bodhisattva both possess this wisdom, during their meditation (*samadhi*) the presence or the absence of bodhichitta is the cause that differentiates the result of their respective final realizations.

There is no other method to eliminate all mental afflictions and misery, and generate all kinds of happiness, than the practice of the Dharma, and it is for this reason that it is necessary to become gradually acquainted with it.

To begin, we should create a sound basis of knowledge, and then try to deepen it until we reach the essence of the Buddha's teachings. We should refrain from trying to comprehend everything immediately, including the most profound and subtle meanings. Even at school, learning the syllabus happens gradually. Let us suppose that there is a course lasting ten years— first we will have to study the first part of the syllabus, the simplest and most basic, then later on, gradually, we will be introduced to the more advanced aspects, and finally we will study the most difficult parts. In this way, through progression, we will tackle the various levels of knowledge as we are ready.

We are now examining the ninth chapter, which discusses the wisdom that realizes emptiness. It has previously been said that the ignorance that grasps at the self is the cause of all mental afflictions, whereas the wisdom that realizes emptiness is its direct antidote. Therefore it is now necessary to understand what this wisdom is and how we can develop it.

Most of you are not new to Dharma teachings and now wish to know its more profound and subtle aspects, and for this reason I am trying to transmit to you the content of chapter 9 of the *Bodhicharyavatara*, although I do not think of myself as a qualified guide.

Among practitioners with the three types of motivation, the highest level is those who wish to attain buddhahood for the benefit of all sentient beings. To this aim, mental afflictions and their seeds must be eliminated, and so must the obscurations to omniscience. In order to perfect this attainment it is necessary to generate the appropriate antidotes, and paramount among them is wisdom. [1]

For this reason, we should at first understand the two truths, conventional and ultimate, which are the objects examined by wisdom and analyzed by two types of people: ordinary beings and beings possessing upper realizations (*naljorpa* in Tibetan, *yogi* in Sanskrit). These are beings who have listened to and studied many teachings, reflected on them for a long time, and subsequently developed perfect calm abiding and superior view, and unified these two attainments. By generating the wisdom that realizes emptiness, they are able to perceive that things exist in dependence upon their components, and that they do not exist inherently.

Unlike them, ordinary people erroneously believe that things exist of their own accord, without depending on causes and conditions, on their constituent parts, and on the mind that apprehends them.

Yogis possessing the wisdom that realizes emptiness have a correct and appropriate view with regard to the existence of things. They are therefore able to guide ordinary beings toward right understanding; for this reason it is said that their view is opposed to and invalidates the wrong view of ordinary beings. [3]

In Buddhism there are four schools of doctrinal principles: the Vaibhashika, Sautrantika, Chittamatra, and Madhyamaka. Among the practitioners of these philosophical schools, the Vaibhashikas possess the inferior view, whereas the Madhyamikas possess the supreme view.

Followers of the first three schools and of the Svatantrika-Madhyamaka, which is one of the subgroups of the Madhyamaka school, maintain that people and phenomena exist by their own nature, and we can therefore say that they have a form of grasping to the self of person and the self of phenomena.

Unlike them, the Prasangika-Madhyamikas, the followers of the other subgroup of the Madhyamaka school, maintain that no phenomenon exists of its own nature, not even conventionally, and for this reason their view is an antidote to all those of lesser schools.

The view of the Prasangika-Madhyamikas is supported by correct logical reasoning and thus invalidates the views of the other schools.

On each of the ten progressive grounds, or *bhumis,* from the path of seeing passing through the path of meditation until buddhahood, the view of emptiness is present. The view possessed by the bodhisattva on the second ground is deeper than that on the first ground, and so forth. Therefore it is said that the view of emptiness of the second ground supersedes that of the first. Just as sunlight overwhelms the light of a candle, the view of the yogis who are on the second ground eclipses and overcomes the view of the yogis who are on the first ground, for the former is a more profound understanding of the ultimate nature of phenomena.

Since phenomena are devoid of intrinsic self, the view in accord with this reality is correct and is supported by valid reasons. The view of ordinary beings cannot be supported by logic and is therefore invalidated by the correct view.

A useful example to explain this principle is that of a person who has seen someone stealing. If both people find themselves in court being cross-examined, the person who has stolen, even though he might lie in order to support his story, would never be able to back up his claim with valid proof. On the other hand, the person who has seen him steal can demonstrate his claim on the strength of what he saw. In this way his statements will invalidate the thief's arguments, which have no basis.

This text, which presents the two paths, belongs to the Mahayana. Among the four Buddhist schools, it supports the view of the Prasangika-Madhyamaka. It explains how phenomena do not exist by their own nature, independent of their causes, their components, and the name attributed to them.

When we begin to develop right understanding with regard to the nature of phenomena, wisdom will begin to take root and grow more and more. In contrast, the erroneous view that grasps at phenomena as existing by their own nature or as truly existent will begin to crumble, until we reach the point where the ignorance that perceives phenomena and clings to them as truly existent is totally eliminated. At that moment we will attain buddhahood.

The exponents of the other schools, such as the Chittamatrins, do not correctly understand the view of phenomena as expounded by the Prasangikas, and when the latter state that phenomena do not exist "truly," or that they are devoid of intrinsic existence, they assume that with such a statement the Prasangikas are also denying their conventional or relative existence.

For lesser schools, in fact, stating that phenomena do not truly exist is the same as saying that phenomena do not exist at all, yielding a view that falls into the extreme of nihilism.

Now, through logical reasons, the Madhyamikas in general and the

Prasangika-Madhyamikas in particular refute the various doctrinal principles of the other philosophical schools. The specific interlocutors that propel these debates will be introduced as the text continues.

Refuting Objections with Regard to Conventional, or Deceptive, Truths

Exponents of the three Buddhist schools ask, "You state that phenomena do not truly exist and that your view is an antidote to ours, but this is not acceptable, because there is no proof of the fact that phenomena do not truly exist."

The Prasangikas reply that such proofs exist, and in order to demonstrate them, they present examples that are commonly accepted by all schools: the illusory emanation of a magician, dreaming, and so forth.

We all agree that what appears in a dream or as a result of a magical emanation does not refer to real, true phenomena, even if it might appear to be. While dreaming we believe that things are truly taking place, that there are real cars, houses, and so forth. Everything seems real, but in fact it is only a dream. Even in our everyday life, if something extraordinary happens to us we say, "It is like a dream," precisely to indicate that it does not seem real to us.

According to the Prasangikas, even the six perfections and buddhahood are like magic emanations or illusions. Nevertheless, although the six perfections are illusion-like, if practiced, they will allow us to attain buddhahood, which is also illusion-like. For this reason they state that, although phenomena do not truly exist, the realization of buddhahood is possible through the practice of the six perfections.

It is because of the existence of the six perfections, which depend on causes and conditions, that we can attain buddhahood, which also depends on causes and conditions. Even without investigating whether these causes are "true" or not, we can establish the functionality of the six perfections, because by actually practicing them we attain buddhahood. If, instead, we analyze them in order to understand their true mode of existence, we will then discover that they do not exist truly, or intrinsically.

For the Prasangikas, the conventional existence of phenomena can be ascertained without having to investigate whether they exist "truly" or not, whereas through analysis we cannot find the true existence of any phenomena. In fact, they say, "Even if phenomena do not exist on an ultimate level, they do exist conventionally if one does not analyze them, and it is therefore not a contradiction to practice the perfections such as generosity and so forth in order to attain enlightenment." [4]

Exponents of the other schools argue with the Prasangika-Madhyamikas because they believe that if phenomena do not exist truly then they do not exist at all. They object as follows: "If nothing exists truly, then nothing exists. The six perfections also do not exist, nor does the buddhahood attained through practicing them."

The Prasangikas reply, "The six perfections and buddhahood do not exist by their own nature, and yet they do exist conventionally. Therefore, through the practice of the six perfections, similar to illusions, we can attain the state, similar to an illusion, of buddhahood."

Even sublime phenomena such as buddhahood and emptiness do not exist by their own nature. Through the six perfections we attain supreme happiness, and this is the reason we should practice them. If we desire happiness we should practice the six perfections; if we do not wish to suffer we should eliminate the six main afflictions.

Studying the Dharma, we become acquainted with the biographies of great saints such as Milarepa, and learn how difficult his life was. He ate only nettles and wild plants, and remarkable anecdotes are told about him. Once, for example, when a thief went at night into his cave, Milarepa told him with a smile, "If even I cannot find anything here during the daytime, when there is light, how then can a thief find something at night, in the dark?"

Even though Milarepa had no material possessions, he experienced no suffering because he had abandoned the six mental afflictions, and he was happy because he had mastered the practice of the six perfections.

This story itself is enough to make us understand that the Dharma is the only method to attain true happiness, and that if we strive with right effort, we will gradually succeed in attaining realizations.

In the teachings it is said that we should remember the impermanence of life and of all produced phenomena. Because life is impermanent, sooner or later we have to leave this physical body, as well as all other objects. At the moment of death, the only thing we can take with us is the virtuous or nonvirtuous karma we have created. Contemplating the impermanence of life is very important, especially for those interested in the study and practice of the Dharma.

When someone we know dies, we should remember that we too, sooner or later, will have to leave this body behind and take on another life-form. We should reflect that we also will not be able to take with us anything or anyone—not our children, our wife or husband, our relatives, or the possessions we managed to accumulate during this lifetime. Someone dying leaves everything behind, and in the future will not be able to use any of the things he accumulated in his life, except the karma he has created. If during this life he generated positive karma, he will surely obtain wealth and prosperity in the future, and if he purified negative karma accumulated in this and also in previous lifetimes, it will be of help to him.

If one waters and works the soil in a sown field, shoots will surely grow; if, on the other hand, seeds have not been sown, no amount of work, water, and the rest will cause anything to grow. Likewise, if we have not created a particular karma, there is no possibility of experiencing its results later.

If we pray that the positive karma of a dying person might speedily ripen, that person will quickly experience the results.

We should use the deaths of other people to reflect on the fact that we too must die, and so remember how important it is to practice the Dharma, seeing that it is the only thing that will help us both during the time we have left to live, and at the time of death. It is unwise not to make any preparations for when death arrives, using our lives, our physical energy, and efforts to solve only less important, mundane problems.

For example, one of a nation's main concerns is protection from external enemies. To this end, understanding the importance of living in freedom and autonomy, the rulers of a country assign part of their budget to the defense sector, even though they do not forsee wars in the near future. If war were to break out, however, the preparations will have been useful.

In our lives we face many problems—some of them are short-lived and last only a month, a day, or an hour, while others are more difficult to solve and carry on even for years. Some are solved easily, while others require greater effort, and others still require enormous effort. If we simultaneously had to face the problem that occupies us for a day and the problem that occupies us for a year and were to use all our resources to solve the former, this would not show much intelligence.

In life we come face to face with various difficulties. In order to overcome material difficulties, one solution is to obtain what we need in appropriate ways. If this is not possible, the alternative solution is to try to be content and satisfied with what we already have. Someone interested in the Dharma should choose this second solution above all.

As human beings we have various needs to satisfy, and must therefore use some resources to obtain what is indispensable to us. Toward superfluous things we should develop the type of mindfulness that recognizes the fact that it is not possible to satisfy all desires, even with much striving, and that it is therefore more convenient to try to be satisfied with what we already possess. If we can reason in this way and feel content, we will succeed in obtaining what we desire. The person who does not opt for the second solution will try to acquire everything he desires but will be unable to do so on many occasions, and in this way will have a new problem that will increase his unhappiness.

In trying to solve our problems, we should differentiate between the momentary and the long term and devote more time and attention to the latter. Certain kinds of difficulties can be easily overcome, but with situations that are hard to confront we should instead be content and tolerant, for in this way we will succeed in finding the solution.

In order to solve many of our problems, we can remind ourselves of the first teaching given by the Buddha: all existing composite phenomena are impermanent, and therefore our bodies are too. The death of our bodies, however, does not mean the end of us, because we will take on another physical form dependent on the karma we have created. In order to obtain a body, a better environment, and better circumstances in the future, we should create their specific causes now, by accumulating good karma. Even this is not enough, however—in fact, the human condition that we possess and our environment are already good, and in spite of this we still face much suffering and many problems. It is therefore necessary to find a definite solution and eliminate the causes of all suffering, even of the suffering that arises in favorable circumstances. The solution is to meditate on the nature of phenomena, realizing emptiness through the wisdom that perceives it directly. This is necessary not only for personal liberation, but also for the attainment of buddhahood.

Studying the ninth chapter, we can learn how bodhisattvas meditate on the emptiness of all phenomena. The way to establish emptiness is the same on both the Hinayana and the Mahayana path; the only difference

is motivation. Hinayana practitioners meditate on the emptiness of phenomena in order to attain personal liberation, whereas Mahayana practitioners strive to meditate on emptiness with the support of bodhichitta,
the mind that wishes to attain buddhahood for the benefit of all beings.
The difference between the two vehicles is therefore solely in the aim,
whereas the object of meditation, emptiness, is the same.

QUESTION: If I die, does the world disappear?
ANSWER: This is a good question, and it introduces a new subject. When
we speak of a mind that designates phenomena, we refer to mind in general—it can be yours or mine. If it were a specific mind and this disap-
peared, then certainly the entire world would also disappear. For example,
if there is a plane flying in the sky, the mind of a particular person might
think that there is a plane, but this is not necessarily the only mind capable
of formulating this thought. The thought can also be generated by the
minds of other people seeing the airplane fly.

We can say that if there is the appropriate basis, we are able to label that
particular phenomenon with the word "airplane," but if such a basis does
not exist then it is not possible even to generate the mind that attributes
the name "airplane."

Lobsang Dorje's existence depends on the name we gave him; therefore Lobsang Dorje exists in dependence upon that name. If Lobsang
Dorje existed in a different way than this, then when we search for Lobsang Dorje among the components of the parts or in the person himself
through analytical enquiry, in order to see whether Lobsang Dorje exists
by his own nature without having to attribute a name to him, we should
be able to find him. But on that basis we will not find Lobsang Dorje,
because Lobsang Dorje's head is not Lobsang Dorje, his hands are not
him, and neither is his body. And if we exclude all the parts that are not
Lobsang Dorje, we would still not find him.

Therefore, since Lobsang Dorje is not in his parts, nor in their assemblage,
but also not separate from them, we can say that Lobsang Dorje exists only
because we have given a name to a person, the one we call Lobsang Dorje.

Let us suppose a postman has a letter for Lobsang Dorje and looks
for him to deliver it. Someone indicates Lobsang Dorje to him and the
postman gives him the letter. If he simply accepts the information and is

convinced that that person is Lobsang Dorje, he will be satisfied, but if he is not satisfied and tries to find out who Lobsang Dorje truly is, he would not find him. Therefore, for the postman the mere name attributed to that person is enough—it is correct—and he will find Lobsang Dorje. If he wanted to find a Lobsang Dorje different from the mere designation of a name on a valid basis through analysis, he would not find him.

With regard to our mother, the nominal designation we make based on her person is our mother. Her body cannot be our mother, nor can her mind, nor can any part of her psychophysical aggregates.

An object's existence does not depend only on its parts, but also on our projection and on the name we give it. As soon as it appears in our mind, we give it a name.

At times while dreaming, we have the opportunity to meet our mother, and at other times we may meet an enemy. On these occasions, attachment and hatred may arise, respectively. These disturbing emotions arise because everything that takes place in a dream appears to be true. If while dreaming we examine the image we have of our mother, an enemy, or someone else, we would see that they appear to us to be self-existent, without depending on the mind that perceives them. But as soon as we are awake we realize that it was all merely an appearance, a dream, and not something real.

Why do we use a dream as an example? Because to someone unable to perceive the emptiness of phenomena, anything will appear as if it exists intrinsically, by its own nature, exactly like in a dream during which, although objects do not really exist as they appear to, they are perceived by the mind as if they existed externally. Therefore, to someone who has not realized the emptiness of phenomena, things appear in a similar fashion as they do to the person who is dreaming.

All phenomena depend on our mental designation. Since they do not exist intrinsically, we say that they exist in dependence upon our designation. If they existed by their own nature, we would not be able to say that the existence of phenomena depends on our designation. We never need to say, "I wear my ears on my head," because they are naturally joined to our head, but we do say, "I wear earrings on my ears," because earrings are not naturally there.

If we call a house "Tashi Rabten," that would be its name only because we gave it this name, but as it was being built no one would have said that they were building Tashi Rabten. The name is only an indication of that particular house, and what we call it.

Anything, as soon as it is labeled, is given a name. Therefore the phenomena that exist here exist solely because we give them a designation. We give a designation, a label, to a house, a table, or a tape recorder. The name we use to designate objects makes them exist. A glass, for example, does not exist by its own nature—we have given the name "glass" to a specific thing, and so the existence of the "glass" begins.

At this point, the following doubt may arise: "Does the existence of a tape recorder then depend solely on the designation attributed to it by the mind?" No. There must also be an appropriate basis upon which to designate the name "tape recorder," otherwise it would not be possible to record!

Let us imagine that we designate a rope with the name "snake." This is only a designation, but the real snake is also a designation, because in both cases the mind gives the name. The real snake, on the one hand, possesses an appropriate basis upon which we can conceptually attribute the name "snake," and it is therefore authentic. On the other hand, a coiled rope, even if our minds wrongly give it the name "snake," will never be an actual snake, since it is not of an appropriate basis.

Now, the two snakes are both mental designations, since neither exists from the side of the object. However, the first designation is supported by a valid basis, and its existence cannot therefore be harmed or contradicted by any valid mind. In fact, conventionally, there cannot be a valid mind that would establish that a real snake is not a snake. In contrast, with regard to the rope that appears to us as a snake, there will never be a sound mind establishing it as a snake, because this designation would be contradicted by another mind—a valid mind that utilizes logical reasoning to establish that it is not a real snake.

We have said that it is difficult to comprehend emptiness, because it is difficult to realize that phenomena are not self-existent. Once we do comprehend this, we then find it difficult to establish what exists from the side of the object. In other words, even if we understand that phenomena do not exist the way they appear to us, it will be difficult to establish how they do exist, function, and affect us.

If we had a magician in front of us who changed a pen into a horse, to our eyes that emanation would appear as a real horse, and our mind, too, unlike the magician's, would recognize it as such. In reality, because it is only an act of magic, that horse does not exist. Therefore on that same basis, one can have the perception of a horse with a real existence, or have this perception accompanied by the ascertainment of the lack of such existence, or have the pure perception of a pen.

The magician will see the pen as a horse but will not think that it is a real horse. Whereas to us, not only will the pen appear as a horse, but we will also think that it is a real horse.

This example helps us to understand the difference between the way we perceive phenomena and the way phenomena are perceived by those who have realized emptiness directly. Beings who realize the emptiness of phenomena directly do not perceive them in the same way as they appear to ordinary beings.

It is difficult for me to explain emptiness, and it is also difficult for those who are listening to understand its meaning, but anyway, we must first of all strive to understand that phenomena do not exist truly, or by their own nature, in the way they appear to us. We should try to reflect on this point often. When, through logical reasoning, we are able to comprehend that the existence of phenomena depends on their component parts, we succeed in establishing the lack of existence depending on its components, and when we realize that the existence of phenomena depends on the mind's designation, we will also understand that there is no phenomenon that is not designated by it and by its own nature. A wheel, for example, does not come to exist only from the side of the object, but above all because of the designation made by the mind.

Through the following arguments it will be clearer to us that phenomena do not arise from the side of the object. If you offer wine to someone who likes it and drinks it regularly, he will show his appreciation and will say that it is good. On the other hand, if you offer the same wine to someone who does not like wine, he will say that it is not good and will not show appreciation. If the attributes of the wine depended intrinsically on the object, there could not be two different opinions of the wine. But such a thing is possible, because the statements that the wine is either good or bad are both designations of the mind.

The same argument can be applied to the example of strong coffee— although it might be considered good by someone who drinks it often and likes it, someone who is not used to drinking it will not like it. If the coffee was good intrinsically, there could not be two different opinions on the matter. This happens, in fact, because the goodness or badness of the coffee is only a designation of the mind. If it depended on the coffee itself, if it was good by its own nature, it would then be considered good by everyone.

This analysis also applies to a person who is considered "good" by a friend of his and "bad" by an enemy. The enemy will not be able to see anything positive in that person, whereas the friend will notice many good qualities, and everything the person does will seem good to him. If goodness and malevolence existed in the person himself, there could not be two different opinions held by two different people. The fact that the friend sees good qualities, whereas the enemy sees defects, is due to the labeling mind, not to the person himself.

Let us reflect on another example. If we ask, "Is Venice far or near?" it is only by comparing its distance with other places that we will be able to say whether it is far or near. If you are now in Villorba, Venice is near compared to the distance that separates you from Milan or Rome. If, however, you compare it with the distance separating Villorba from Treviso, then Venice is far. Therefore the fact that things are far or near depends on something else. Without a relationship of interdependence we cannot say far or near.

Furthermore, this clock on my desk is not in itself large or small. We can say that it is large or small only by comparing it to something else. If someone says that it is large, it is only because in his mind there is a picture of a smaller clock, whereas if someone else has a mental image of a larger clock, he will say that this one is small.

Anything that appears to our minds exists because we designate it, therefore its existence depends on our label on a valid base, and not on the object itself. The way of distinguishing phenomena by saying "this book," "this pen," or "this chair" arises only by the nominal designations of our minds.

Vaibhashikas, Sautrantikas, Chittamatrins, and even Svatantrika-Madhyamikas are not able to establish that all phenomena exist merely as nominal designations of the mind. Only Prasangika-Madhyamikas maintain that each phenomenon exists merely because it is labeled by the mind and does not exist objectively, from its own side.

Exponents of the Prasangika-Madhyamaka system are Nagarjuna, Aryadeva, Buddhapalita, Chandrakirti, and Shantideva. They support this system because they actually know the authentic nature of phenomena.

Exponents of the Svatantrika-Madhyamaka system are Bhavaviveka, Shantarakshita, and Haribhadra. They maintain that phenomena have an inherent nature, and although they have already remarkably perfected the view of the lesser schools with regard to the mode of the existence of phenomena, they have not yet been able to ascertain and acquire the perfect view.

Exponents of the Chittamatrin system are Dignaga and Dharmakirti. They too maintain the existence of phenomena by their own nature, although there are differences between their view and the Sautrantikas'.

If we are able to maintain that phenomena exist as mere nominal designations of the mind, we can call ourselves Prasangikas. Whereas if we succeed only in establishing that phenomena do not truly exist, we can call ourselves Madhyamikas in general. However, we must understand this to refer to our actual view, and not merely our intellectual understanding of the subject.

It is not easy to see phenomena as existing merely as mental designations, and I myself do not think that I possess this view, although I certainly have an intellectual understanding of it.

If we manage to understand that phenomena come to exist only because they are labeled by the mind, we will also easily comprehend that they cannot exist by their own nature, without depending on the mind that labels them. When we realize this, if someone asks us whether phenomena exist by their own nature or merely as mental designations, we will reply without any doubt that they exist as mental designations. Besides, knowing that an apple, as with all produced phenomena, also depends on its own causes, we will be able to maintain that an apple that is not caused by its own seed does not exist. Following these convictions, we will be able to state that we too share the Prasangika view.

To succeed in generating even a small, coarse understanding of how things exist through designation is an excellent thing, even if ours is a mere intellectual understanding. And since we are now hearing teachings on these subjects, we will gradually be able to realize the authentic mode of existence of phenomena. It is said that by generating even just one doubt about the intrinsic existence of phenomena, it is possible to shake off the cycle of conditioned existence, in the same way that an old dress is easily torn when we pull at it.

In all philosophical schools except the Prasangika-Madhyamaka, it is maintained that phenomena have some form of intrinsic existence from the side of the object. Prasangikas hold exactly the opposite view, saying that phenomena exist only by mental designation, and that there is no kind of intrinsic or natural existence whatsoever from the side of the object.

All phenomena in the universe exist only through a mind designating them, just as maintained by the Prasangikas. Hence they do not exist with a nature of their own, intrinsically, or truly. It is important to understand the meaning of the term "truly," which in this context means "from the side of the object."

Furthermore, all schools apart from the Prasangikas maintain that if phenomena did not exist by their own nature, they would not exist at all. On the other hand, Prasangikas maintain that, although phenomena are only mental designations, they are able to carry out a function. If we bear this in mind, it will be easier to understand the text, since the exposition continues in the form of a debate between the Prasangikas and the other schools.

Madhyamikas maintain the non-true existence of phenomena, whereas the lesser philosophical schools (Vaibhashika, Sautrantika, and Chittamatra) maintain their true existence. The exponents of these three schools maintain that if phenomena did not exist truly, they would not exist at all. Therefore there would be no attainment of enlightenment through the practice of the six perfections, and consequently there would be no reason for practicing the Dharma. They ask, "If phenomena such as form, and so on, do not exist truly, why then are they established by a direct perception?"

They believe that if form and other sensory objects do not exist truly, then they do not exist at all; whereas if they do exist, they must exist truly. According to them, this is demonstrated by the fact that we can directly perceive the five types of sensory objects—visible forms, sounds, smells, flavors, and tangible objects—and therefore they object, "Since form and so on are established as existent through the proof of our direct perception of them, is it not a contradiction to say that they are false?"

The Prasangikas reply, "Form and other objects do not exist by their own nature, and do not exist truly, but through our direct perception they appear to us, because conventionally they do exist. Conventional existence is not true existence."

Through the five senses we perceive the five objects in a conventional way, but not in an ultimate way. The ultimate nature of the five sense objects cannot be perceived through the five sense organs, because if this were the case, yogis would not need to perceive it through their samadhi. [5]

Supporters of other schools refute the Prasangika statement that on the one hand, phenomena do not exist by their own nature and are therefore false, and on the other hand, they exist conventionally, by designation. They do not understand how these two realities can coexist.

The Prasangikas reply, "It is just like in the case of the impure body, commonly considered to be pure. In reality this cognition is false." [6]

When we wash, our bodies become clean externally, but not internally. If we do not believe that our body is dirty, let us try to imagine opening it up and observing what it contains.

Even though in reality our bodies are dirty, conventionally we say that they are clean. Likewise, even though phenomena do not exist by their own nature, they appear as if they do. This mode of existence is false. Therefore the existence of phenomena by their own nature is false, as in the example of the magician who makes a pen or another object have the appearance of a horse. The audience and the magician himself see a horse, whereas there is really a pen; for this reason it is an illusion! However, the magician knows it is an illusion and that there is no horse but only a pen, while the audience believes there to be a real horse. The appearance of phenomena as intrinsically existent is caused by imprints left on our consciousnesses by grasping to true existence.

The exponents of other schools observe, "If phenomena do not exist by their own nature, then this is in contradiction with what the Buddha has said—that the nature of all composite phenomena is impermanence."

The Prasangikas reply, "There is no contradiction in this statement. The Buddha was very wise and skillful in showing the mode of existence of phenomena, and did so gradually, not by expounding all his teachings at once. His intent was to guide ordinary beings onto the right path. First he said that produced phenomena are impermanent, and he then went further. This is his method of guiding in an appropriate fashion. Even if the Buddha has shown that phenomena are impermanent and therefore momentary, this is only a method to lead ordinary beings toward the correct view of how all phenomena truly exist. However, with that statement he did not mean to say that the momentary existence of impermanent phenomena truly exists." [7]

A question is posed to the Prasangikas: "You maintain non-true existence; why then has Buddha Shakyamuni taught true existence?"

The reply comes: "Yes, he has taught the true existence of phenomena even though they are not truly existent, but this was done with the aim of guiding ordinary beings who are not capable of differentiating between non-true existence and nonexistence. If the Buddha had taught the non-true existence to such people, they would have understood that phenomena do not exist. The Buddha's teaching on the true existence of phenomena is a teaching that must be interpreted. Nagarjuna himself has pointed out that the teaching on the true existence of phenomena must be interpreted, whereas the teaching on the non-true existence of phenomena is a teaching with a definitive meaning."

Prasangikas maintain that "things," which is synonymous with composite or impermanent phenomena, are not truly impermanent, because if they were, they should be so in an ultimate way, and this is not so. "Truly impermanent" does not exist, because it is not one with "impermanent," nor is it different from "impermanent." Things are impermanent, but not impermanent by their own nature or intrinsically.

An impermanent tape recorder exists and has the characteristic of being momentary; but a truly impermanent tape recorder does not exist, since it cannot be truly one with "impermanent," nor truly different from "impermanent."

Let us consider the "momentary tape recorder" and the "tape recorder." These two, being existent, must necessarily be either the same or different. In this case we can say that they are different because their name is different. The truly momentary tape recorder, however, cannot be identified as the same thing, or one with, "momentary." Nor can it be considered to be different from "momentary."

Others have maintained the following. "Since the Buddha has said impermanent phenomena exist, it follows that 'impermanent' must be 'truly' impermanent." But the Prasangikas, although accepting the fact that composite phenomena are impermanent, do not accept that they are truly impermanent, impermanent by their own nature, or intrinsically impermanent.

If they were, they should be either the same thing or different, but "truly impermanent" is neither one nor the other with regard to "impermanent."

For example, the impermanence of a pillar is accepted, but its true impermanence, or ultimate impermanence, or impermanence by its own nature, is not; if it were, it would follow that that quality would be the same thing as "pillar" or different from "pillar."

If the true impermanence of the pillar were one with the pillar, impermanence could no longer be separate from the pillar, being truly impermanent. If it were different, there would be no relation between the pillar and true impermanence, as they would be truly different. In other words, "impermanence" and "pillar" exist as different things, but the "true impermanence" of the pillar, if it exists, should be either one with the pillar or different from it.

However, they are not one, because "impermanence" and "pillar" are two. That is, they are different in spite of being related. Also, they are not different, because if they were, there would be no relation between them. This is not the case, since impermanence is a characteristic of the phenomenon "pillar."

"Pillar" and "impermanence" exist conventionally as different phenomena, and "pillar" exists conventionally as a single phenomenon, being one with "pillar." Conventionally, "one" and "different" are possible, even if not ultimately. In fact, any existent phenomenon is necessarily either one or different. Therefore, if truly existent phenomena really existed, they should also be so. But in fact something truly existent can be neither one nor the other, because it does not exist.

For example, the "flowers of space," which in reality do not exist, are neither one with nor different from any other phenomenon. Likewise, the true or intrinsic existence of any phenomenon is neither one with nor different from the phenomenon itself, being nonexistent.

In order to clarify the matter further we can reflect on the following. The "I" is not separate from the five aggregates. Since the five aggregates are terminologically a name, the "I" ascribed onto them is another name. However, the nature of the five aggregates and of the "I" are the same, because we cannot separate them. We have given the name "I" to the group of five physical and mental aggregates. Hence between the "I" and the aggregates the difference is in the name, although the basis upon which these names were given is one and the same.

On a conventional level, the way in which phenomena appear does not correspond to the way in which they exist for any being who is not a buddha, although on an ultimate level they do. Therefore, since conventionally it is possible that the actual way a phenomenon exists is different from how it appears, the "I" and the five aggregates can exist as "one" and "different," because their existence can be differentiated. On an ultimate level, however, since the actual way in which they exist must correspond to what appears, the distinction between "one" and "different" is no longer possible.

If the "I" existed truly apart from the five aggregates, then it would exist by itself as different, separate, and with no link to the five aggregates. Consequently we could not say that the "I" is named on the basis of the group of the five aggregates.

In short, from the ultimate point of view it is not possible for the "I" to exist, but it is possible on a conventional level.

When we qualify any phenomenon as "truly existent," some problems arise because a phenomenon is not truly existent as one with or as different from its parts.

QUESTION: Why is it that if something is truly existent, it should exist in the way it appears?
ANSWER: When, for example, you say that someone is lying, this is because what he is saying is different from how things are. On the other hand, when you say that someone is telling the truth, this is because what he says is consistent with what is. We can use another example. Sometimes we see someone killed or a house burned down on television, and according to appearances it seems that someone has been killed or a house has been burned down. This is not so, because what appears on screen and the actual reality are two different things.

Also, "truth" and "truly existent" are two different things. We have "truth" when what appears to be and the real situation are not different. Whereas "truly existent" means that phenomena exist by their own nature, exactly as they appear to us, without being designated by mind. But in this case, even without a name attributed to them, they should nevertheless exist. It has been said before that phenomena exist because we give them a name. For example, this book exists because it has been labeled "book" by the mind, and therefore it depends on the mind that has labeled it so, whereas a truly existent phenomenon must not depend on anything. If phenomena were self-existent, without the need for a mind designating them, then if searched for, we should be able to find them. In actual fact, when we analyze, we do not find them.

Let us say I ask you what a "book" is. It is not the second page, or the back of the book, and so forth—it is none of these things, even though it does not exist apart from its components. Therefore we can say that the "book" has been designated by the mind, and for this nominal designation to take place there must be some valid reason. When all the right conditions are there, we can label "book." Without having a valid basis as reference, if I say "book" and indicate another object, this object could not be the book, because a correct basis for designation would be lacking. If there is an appropriate basis and a mind designating it as a book, then the book exists and we should be satisfied with this designation, because otherwise we will not find it.

QUESTION: Since there is no "I," who watches the mind?
ANSWER: We need to make a distinction. There is no "I" outside the five skandhas, but a conventional "I" does exist. In fact, I say, "I do, I speak, and so on." There is not an "I" emerging from the five skandhas, but there is an "I" labeled on the basis of the five skandhas. This conventional "I" is the one that watches the mind. Apart from this designated "I," there is no other "I" that exists from the side of the skandhas. The skandhas, of which the mind is one, are what is being designated, hence they are the object, not the subject that watches. A man who looks after sheep is called a shepherd, and likewise there is a name—"I"—for what watches the mind. On the basis of these skandhas we have the sense of "I." If the five skandhas were the "I," then the "I" would not be a name given on the basis of the five skandhas. The skandhas are there already, and on their basis we designate an "I." It is very difficult to have an accurate idea of the conventional "I," because the "I" does not exist above or apart from the skandhas—it is only a label given to the group. So, the tape recorder does not exist of its own nature, but there are parts that are assembled together, and to this group we give the name "tape recorder." The same happens with the conventional "I."

Going back to the text, at this point the Prasangikas, referring to the statement of the Buddha that explains that composite phenomena are impermanent and therefore momentary, explain, "Conventionally, we say that composite phenomena are momentary; but on an ultimate level they are not, because nothing exists truly."

The following objection is raised. "You say that ultimately impermanence cannot be seen, because transience of phenomena exists only conventionally. This also cannot be true. You accept conventional existence of phenomena because you maintain their nominal existence (because of the name attributed to them). Yet not even the conventional existence of phenomena as momentary or impermanent is possible, because the object in the morning is recognized as being the same object in the evening. If it were momentary, the object in the morning could no longer be the same as the object in the evening, and yet we generally say that it is. Therefore, conventionally, too, momentary phenomena are not possible."

Now, conventionally we say that a glass seen in the morning is the same as the glass seen in the evening. In reality, that perceived object is no longer the same. The glass of the first moment is not the same as the glass of the second moment, because at every instant it undergoes changes, but we generally maintain it is the same, because of having understood it incorrectly.

Not everything we conventionally designate to be existent actually exists. Things that exist in conventional reality cannot be contradicted by logic, whereas things that do not exist, even though we give them a name, are in contradiction with logic.

We say, for example, that our bodies are pure, but this is only a statement. In fact, the body is not pure, but impure.

So, not everything that is seen or conceived as being a certain way is so in reality. How can we make this distinction among things we see? If someone, supported by sound logical arguments, says that in reality a particular thing is just as it has been established by valid cognition, then we can consider it to be so, but what is not sustained by logic should be considered false. Someone might object, "Although we say that impermanent phenomena are momentary and therefore the glass seen in the morning is not the same as the glass seen in the evening, we think that the glass is the same, because it appears to us to be so." This way of thinking, however, is not correct, because the glass we perceive in the evening is not the same as the one we perceive in the morning—it undergoes transformation moment by moment, since it is impermanent. However, we believe it to be the same because of our attachment to the self of phenomena, which means the glass appears to us as if it were truly existent.

There are people who, through samadhi, directly perceive the subtle impermanence of phenomena. To them, the glass appears as momentary—that is, the glass of a particular moment is no longer perceived later as the same glass. Because we ordinary people grasp at the true existence of impermanent phenomena, we perceive them in the same way that we perceive the existence of the glass—as if, at any given moment, they will always be of the same substantial nature.

Hence there are two different ways to perceive impermanent phenomena: as momentary or as non-momentary (as if they constantly have the same substantial nature). The latter is ordinary people's perception and is caused by the ignorance that grasps at the self. Because of the view that grasps at true existence without the support of valid arguments, they cannot understand the true nature of phenomena. Whereas people who perceive the transience of phenomena directly through samadhi are supported by logic, and we can definitely say that their view is the perfect one.

Our bodies, made of blood, flesh, and bones, are not as attractive as they might appear. Yet we nevertheless consider them to be clean, beautiful, and desirable because of our grasping at them as such. Likewise, although produced phenomena are impermanent, we do not accept their transience and instead consider them to be identical at each moment.

When training in wisdom, it is important to analyze our habitual modes of thinking.

If we look at ourselves closely, we understand that we lack the mental qualities that we should have, and are richly endowed with negative attitudes that we should not have. Nevertheless we have a positive side, which is the ability to understand that we can gradually free ourselves from current mental afflictions and obtain all the qualities we lack. For this reason we are striving in this direction, and since this is a good quality we possess, we should be able to appreciate it and be happy because of it. Since it is possible to eliminate our afflictions, it is right to rejoice at this potential and at the qualities we already possess, whose nature is such that they can be augmented.

While studying the Dharma, we should generate interest in its aims by eagerly persevering in the practice and not being like a flower under the hot sun, weakened by lack of water. We must be active and start immediately to examine our storehouse of mental afflictions. In order to do so, we must comprehend and retain that the mind grasping at phenomena as if they were truly existent is a kind of ignorance.

Vaibhashikas, Sautrantikas, and Chittamatrins formulate the following objection to the Prasangikas: "If phenomena do not exist truly, maintaining the impermanence of phenomena on a conventional level is contradicted, since in that case forms and so forth could not be impermanent, even conventionally."

The Prasangikas reply, "Although phenomena do not truly exist, forms and so forth are, on a conventional level, established as impermanent by valid cognition." [8]

Phenomena do not exist independently, do not exist by their own nature or by their own characteristics, and do not exist only from the side of the object—that is, without depending on the mind that designates them. But the ignorance that grasps at true existence conceives the nature of phenomena in a wrong way. Such an erroneous concept is akin to finding a piece of brass and believing it to be gold. Likewise, our minds apprehend phenomena as if they were truly existent, as if they existed by their own nature and from the side of the object, and these are indeed wrong conceptions.

Understanding that the piece of brass is not gold is the right way of knowing it. In the same way, if we understand that phenomena do not truly exist, that they do not exist naturally and from the side of the object, but are instead mere designations of the mind, we can say that we have generated the correct view with regard to their existence.

Let us take another example. When a magician turns some wood or a stone into a horse, people who see it galloping do not realize that in reality it is not a horse. They perceive it to be a true horse, and this is a wrong conception with regard to that piece of wood. If, however, someone starts to think, "It is true, I see a horse galloping, but in reality that is only a piece of wood that the magician has turned into a horse," at that moment he will understand the reality of that piece of wood. That ignorant mind that previously grasped at the emanation as if it were a true horse no longer exists, because the mind has apprehended the object correctly. Therefore the wrong conception related to it cannot arise anymore. The two thoughts—the wrong one and the correct one—cannot coexist. When the mind understands correctly, the wrong conception disappears.

Those people who, because of magic, perceive the emanation as a real horse grasp at that idea, but the magician, although he sees the appearance of the horse, knows that it is only a creation, and does not grasp at the idea that it is a true horse.

All phenomena that appear to us exist in this same way. Their existence is not found on their own side, in the object, in the same way that we cannot find the horse created by the magician through a piece of wood.

The way that the things we perceive exist does not correspond to the way that they appear to us. We should therefore try to change our view and reflect on the fact that, although they appear to us to be truly existent, their authentic mode of existence does not correspond to this perception. At present we continually think that phenomena are concrete and that they exist from their own side, and not that this way of existing is only an appearance. Now we can start to change that view, trying to see them as akin to an illusion. We should not have a view of phenomena like that of spectators who watch the spell of the magician, but instead think like the magician who sees the horse, but knowing that it is not true, does not grasp at that appearance. While asleep, anything that appears to our minds seems real, and it is the same with all actions we perform in our dreams. As soon as we awake, however, we understand how none of this was real.

The Hinayana arhats, the bodhisattvas who have reached a certain level, and the buddhas see all phenomena as mere appearance. They are free from the mind that grasps at phenomena as if they existed concretely, and therefore they do not have attachment for them. We, on the other hand, do not have the strong conviction that phenomena do not exist as they appear, but believe them to exist concretely, from their own side, objectively, and by their own nature. Therefore we grasp at them and because of this generate attachment, hatred, and so forth. This conditioning is created because we are not satisfied to think that phenomena are only an appearance, but believe them to be something more.

Another objection of the three lesser schools is the following: "If phenomena were not truly existent, then the Buddha too would not exist, and therefore one could not accumulate merits through offerings made to him."

The Prasangikas reply, "Buddha does not exist 'truly,' but he does exist conventionally. Therefore it is conventionally possible to accumulate merits by making offerings to him."

The correct attitude toward the mode of appearance of phenomena is not easy to acquire, because for a long time we have been used to thinking in an erroneous way and have many imprints of wrong views in our mind. If we pour scented water into a wooden container and then empty it and even wash it, the container will retain that scent for a long time. The same happens with our mental imprints.

Since lesser schools than the Prasangika are not able to comprehend that phenomena do not exist "truly," by their own characteristics, when the Prasangikas state that phenomena do not exist by their own nature, the other schools think that these do not exist at all. This is why they object, "If phenomena are illusions, it follows that the Buddha too is only a magical appearance, and the offerings made to him are also illusory. Therefore by making these illusion-like offerings to an illusion-like Buddha, we cannot accumulate any merits." They maintain this because they think that if Buddha is a phenomenon that does not exist by his own nature, and the same is true for the offerings made to him, both the Buddha and the offerings do not exist at all.

They then carry on with their objections: "Since phenomena do not exist by their own nature, it follows that they do not exist, and if something does not exist and we speak of it, it is like speaking of an illusion or a spell. The offerings we make to the buddhas would then be illusion-like offerings made to illusory buddhas, and through them we would not be able to accumulate any merit."

The Prasangikas reply, "Just as you maintain that it is possible to make truly existent offerings to a truly existent buddha, and that through that it is possible to accumulate truly existent positive karma, with the same argument we maintain that we can accumulate merits by making illusion-like offerings to illusion-like buddhas." [9]

For Prasangikas, even if phenomena appear as real, they do not exist "truly," but are like an illusion.

The exponents of the three lesser schools now ask another question to the Prasangikas: "If ordinary beings are like illusions, how can they be reborn after death?"

The Prasangikas reply, "When all conditions are there, sentient beings are reborn, just as it occurs with magical emanations that manifest when all necessary conditions are assembled, whereas if those conditions are not there, they cannot be produced." [10]

A magician needs specific conditions in order to perform his magic: he will have to assume a certain posture and have certain objects at his disposal. He will be able to perform his magic only when all the necessary requirements are fulfilled. Likewise, when the main causes and the circumstantial conditions are present, sentient beings take on a new birth.

Anyway, when the Prasangikas maintain that phenomena are like an illusion, they use this analogy only in order to explain the conventional reality of phenomena; they do not mean to say that phenomena are actual illusions.

Hinayana arhats, arya bodhisattvas, and buddhas are no longer reborn through the power of negative actions and mental afflictions, whereas we take on conditioned rebirths because these two factors are present.

Exponents of lesser schools observe, "With regard to magic, we can understand that what you say is possible, because magic lasts for only a short time. But with regard to living beings we do not think this is so, because they appear for a long period of time, since they take on one rebirth after another. Besides, if beings were like an illusion, it would follow that one does not commit a negative action in killing another being, just like a magician does not create negativity when he makes the horse that he himself has created through magic disappear."

The Prasangikas reply, "Because an illusion-like sentient being has a mind, those who harm him generate negative karma and those who benefit him generate positive karma." [11]

If spectators observing a horse or a human being created by a magician kill him with a gun, this action will create negative karma, since the intention to kill—that mental factor that wants to kill a horse or a man, thinking that it is truly a horse or a man—has been generated. However, they would not have committed the action of actually killing (physical karma), because there is no horse or man but only the illusory appearance of such, which is devoid of a mind. In contrast, it is possible to create virtuous and nonvirtuous karma, both physical and verbal, in relation to sentient beings who are like an illusion and who possess an illusion-like mind.

How can people or animals appear through magic? This happens as a result of the power of mantras or other means used by the magician. However, they cannot produce a mind, but only the appearance or the semblance of human or other beings. For this reason no negative karma is created in relation to them.

Results arise only through a variety of cooperating circumstantial causes and conditions, and not from a single cause alone. [12–13]

What is essential to understand is that the Prasangikas maintain a difference between "not truly existent" and "nonexistent," whereas supporters of other schools are not able to make that distinction, and think that what does not exist truly does not exist at all—for them the two statements are the same.

Thinking that phenomena exist truly is like walking on the edge of a mountain path, with the risk of falling. Thinking that phenomena do not exist at all, not even conventionally, is like walking on the opposite edge, running a similar risk. Thinking that phenomena exist conventionally, but not truly, is the right and correct view, akin to walking in the middle of the path. The term *Madhyamaka* means "middle way."

"Conventional existence" of phenomena means that they exist because of the name attributed to them, whereas "untrue existence" means that phenomena do not exist by their own nature, intrinsically, without depending on something else.

QUESTION: Why can't one cause alone produce many results?
ANSWER: Can you give me an example of something that is produced by one cause alone? In reality even a single raindrop arises from several causes and conditions. Likewise, a single ear of corn is produced not just by one, but by many causes and conditions. Therefore no Buddhist believes that a single cause alone is able to produce many results. On the other hand, some non-Buddhist schools believe in something of this kind. For example, the Hindu school of the Samkhya believes in the existence of a primordial substance that alone can create all phenomena, and another school believes that Brahma is the sole cause of all phenomena, just like Christians believe in God.

QUESTION: If I want to hit someone who stands behind a shop window, I shoot, and the bullet breaks the glass and kills the man.

ANSWER: But even in order to bring this action to completion you need many conditions. You must have a gun and some bullets, there must be a man to shoot at, and that man must possess a mind. You need the intention to kill him, a shop window, and someone who has built it, and someone who has manufactured the gun.

QUESTION: But if there are many people observing the same phenomenon, this will bring about many different perceptions, according to the number of people watching it.

ANSWER: Certainly, but at this point it is necessary to clarify the difference between "sole cause" and "cause." For example, an apple tree certainly has a substantial cause. However, this is not the only cause involved in producing the tree; in fact, many other circumstances act together. If we speak of a sole cause, we mean a cause that is not accompanied by any other—a single cause. It is possible for a cause to generate many effects. For example, a hen can produce one hundred eggs, but the hen is not the "sole cause" of the eggs, because there are many other cooperative conditions. A tape recorder, too, needs many causes in order to work, and if only one single cause is present it cannot record. The statement that a sole cause can produce many results is presented by those who follow a doctrine supporting such a view, but in fact, according to Buddhist philosophy, this is not possible. Anyway, all this cannot be understood right away, speedily; one needs to reflect on it for a long time.

QUESTION: Is it possible to discover all the causes that have produced a particular phenomenon by analyzing it?

ANSWER: Yes, if we are able to think and analyze the matter correctly.

What do you think when it is said that phenomena are like an illusion? Are you able to understand that, in spite of being like an illusion, they nevertheless perform a function? Or is stating that phenomena are like an illusion equal for you to saying that they do not exist?

Carrying on our reflection, if we understand that phenomena are like an illusion, our attachment to them and any other negative mental attitude will disappear, in the same way that we will not feel attraction or anger toward a person who we know to be solely the illusory creation of a magician. Right now we continually create desire, hatred, and other disturbing emotions in relation to phenomena just because we are not able to understand that they are like an illusion. But when we are able to do that, all our mental afflictions will no longer have a basis upon which to rise, and will fall naturally. When our clinging to phenomena as truly existent weakens, it is possible to eradicate the wrong conception we hold toward them.

We should therefore analyze deeply what has been explained, and try to understand whether the arguments expounded here are well founded, or if instead our ordinary way of thinking is correct. Whenever we have time at our disposal, we can use it to reflect on these subjects.

Since we wish to eliminate all our mental obscurations, and given that engagement with the Dharma is the only way to do this, we must strive in this direction even if it takes a long time. If there were other means to effortlessly remove wrong conceptions and achieve the desired aim, then it would be right and appropriate to use them, but until now no other means have been found apart from this.

Practicing the Dharma means applying the method for the attainment of happiness and the elimination of unhappiness. We must therefore commit ourselves to studying it and actualizing it continuously, not only in this lifetime, but also in future lives, and the best form in which to do so is the human form.

In order to attain liberation, one needs to engage in the threefold superior training of morality, concentration, and wisdom. The superior training of morality refers to the ethical conduct a practitioner should observe, and includes rules to be followed by monks and laypeople.

The superior training of concentration consists of focusing one's mind on a particular object over the desired period of time, in order to attain calm and mental stability. At present, if we judge our mind objectively, we see that it is so unstable that it does not allow us to concentrate for even a few seconds. However, if we train, we will succeed in doing so for an increasing length of time. Concentration is obtained only through practice. Someone coming to the center for the first time will perhaps not be able to sit on a cushion because of pain in his legs, but by persevering, he will gradually succeed in sitting comfortably in that position for longer periods of time.

With regard to wisdom, there are many kinds of wisdom: knowing that produced phenomena are impermanent, knowing that they are devoid of self-existence, and so forth.

With regard to impermanence, we differentiate coarse impermanence from subtle impermanence. Understanding coarse impermanence means understanding that, for example, we no longer exist after death, or that when the candle has reached its end, the flame too is extinguished. Understanding subtle impermanence means understanding that moment by moment all composite phenomena undergo change, and that a phenomenon that exists at a given moment will no longer be the same the next moment, or understanding that the tape recorder of a given time is no longer the tape recorder of the previous moment.

Realizing the change of phenomena in the smallest time interval means knowing subtle impermanence. If we ask ourselves, "Are we now the same as this morning?" the answer is that right now we are not the same as we were a moment before, therefore we are also not the same as this morning, because at each moment we change. Also, we will not be the same tomorrow. Therefore if we do not practice in this moment, this moment will pass and will not return, and we will have wasted it. Whereas if we practice from now on, we will not have wasted this opportunity. The "I" of the first moment no longer exists in the second moment, and so, if we look closely, this "I" that we consider so precious is no longer there a moment later.

Impure phenomena cause suffering. For example, if we do not inquire thoroughly, we might believe that our bodies are a source of happiness; but if we look deeply, we understand that they are the cause of all our suffering.

Who is sending us to work? It is our bodies, although one might ask, "How can the body send us to work?" When we get up in the morning, we must wash, have breakfast, and get dressed. Since our bodies have numerous needs, we must go to work and earn money in order to satisfy those needs; that is why we say that our bodies force us to work.

Let us have a look at the money we earn through our work. Everybody thinks it is the source of happiness. But if we reflect deeply, we understand that it is also a cause of problems, because in order to earn it we must perform work we do not like and that we find tiresome. We could think, for example, of someone who has cows. Superficially, this might seem a favorable situation, because cows give milk that can be sold, thus providing a necessary means of livelihood. But their ownership also implies continuous work: you must give these animals hay and water, and the stable needs to be clean—all of this solely in order to have some milk.

Our bodies, caused by mental afflictions and karma, are included within the classification of impure phenomena, whereas the bodies of buddhas, of bodhisattvas who have attained the path of seeing, and of Hinayana arhats dwelling in nirvana, are not.

Just as someone who lives in jail and does not see his life as unpleasant will not aspire to freedom or attempt to find means of escape, so we, if unable to see this cyclic existence as something undesirable that creates great suffering for us, will not be able to generate the desire and the aspiration to be free from it, nor will we make any effort in that direction. Cyclic existence is not only outside ourselves, not only the universe in which we live, but it is also the body, since they are both of the same nature.

Why is it that we do not like being in prison? Because there is no freedom there, no possibility to choose, and no happiness. Likewise, with this body we also have no freedom or possibility to choose, and because of it we experience problems and suffering. Since our bodies are like prisons, we should therefore desire to be free from them.

Who are the jailers in the prison of our bodies? The chief jailer is ignorance; then there is hatred, attachment, and other mental afflictions. Who has been imprisoned in this body? Our "I." And while we are in this prison, what brings us some solace through pleasant experiences from time to time? Our positive karma.

But if this body is like a prison and causes us so much suffering, what should we do with it? At present, we can do nothing. Committing suicide is not a good solution, because we would only have to take on another body that was also the result of karma and mental afflictions, and experience the same problems again.

Some prisoners decide to escape and study a plan to kill the jailers and burn down the prison. Likewise, if we practice the threefold superior training, we are burning down the prison of our bodies, and thus we will be free from it.

The superior training of wisdom refers to the highest wisdom, the wisdom that perceives the empty nature of phenomena. We should therefore concentrate and meditate upon it in order to attain supreme enlightenment, but also just in order to be able to free ourselves from all the suffering in the cycle of conditioned existence, and to attain nirvana.

The prison of our bodies is controlled by the three root mental afflictions, but mainly by the ignorance that grasps at phenomena as existent from their own side. However, if we apply the direct antidote of the direct perception of emptiness to this wrong conception, it will be the definitive solution. Therefore to understand that phenomena do not exist by their own nature, or intrinsically, is imperative, and for this reason it is important to discuss and analyze this subject.

Resuming our commentary on the text, the Prasangikas at this point state that phenomena do not exist by their own nature, and the same applies to our minds, which are by nature pure and free of flaw. We have taken on this rebirth because of impure actions and mental afflictions, and as long as we do not block them, we will continue in the same way in our future lives. As machines are propelled by electricity, so our wheel of rebirths is activated by the ignorance that grasps at a truly existent "I." It is therefore necessary to eliminate this ignorance.

The actual nature of the mind is beyond any impurity, and has always been ours from beginningless time; in fact, the mental afflictions we possess do not have a permanent nature, but are only a momentary, transient obscuration of the mind.

Prasangikas state that it is the mind itself that turns in the wheel of cyclic existence, but that the mind's nature is emptiness. The exponents of the lesser schools raise their objection to this statement, saying, "You maintain that since the mind does not exist by its own nature, cyclic existence too does not exist by its own nature and, furthermore, that the nature of cyclic existence is the same as nirvana. If this is so, it then follows that the Buddha, in his state of nirvana, is nevertheless still in cyclic existence, and that therefore there is no use in practicing what the Buddha practiced—that is, the six perfections and so forth." [14]

They raise the above question because they are unable to distinguish between "nirvana" and "natural nirvana" (or emptiness nature), unlike the

Prasangikas, who answer, "We do not maintain that the Buddha exists in the wheel of conditioned rebirths, because he has gone beyond these forms of existence. We differentiate between nirvana and natural nirvana, saying that nirvana is that state of the cessation of suffering obtained through applying the direct antidote to the mental afflictions that obscure the mind, whereas natural nirvana is the very nature of the mind itself: its emptiness."

Nirvana is the state of mind in which all causes of suffering, and therefore suffering itself, have ceased, the state attained only after having completely purified the obscurations of all mental afflictions and having thus gone beyond cyclic existence. Natural nirvana, on the other hand, being the ultimate nature of the mind, or its emptiness, is a characteristic accompanying it all the time, and is not therefore a successive attainment. The meaning of "natural nirvana" is that the nature of the mind is empty of intrinsic existence.

No mental training is needed in order to realize natural nirvana, whereas in order to attain nirvana it is necessary to follow the path and, through it, achieve purity of mind by removing from it transient stains. As long as stains exist, ordinary sentient beings will continue to wander in samsara in the same way that a magical emanation will manifest if the appropriate conditions are present. The Buddha, having discontinued its causes, no longer wanders in samsara, whereas ordinary beings, not having eliminated them, continue to do so. Cyclic existence exists if its causes exist, and it ceases if its causes cease.

This argument is being brought forward because it allows us to establish the correct view with regard to the nature of phenomena: the emptiness of true existence, the direct antidote to the mind that grasps at the true existence of phenomena. In order to establish the right view we must first of all distinguish the correct way of thinking from the erroneous one.

When the Prasangikas state that phenomena do not exist truly, or by their own nature, the exponents of the lesser schools do not understand, and think that the former maintain that phenomena do not exist at all. The aim of this discussion is precisely to clarify this misunderstanding.

It is not easy to explain and understand the content of this chapter. It is necessary, in order to more easily access the meaning of the philosophical principles expounded here, to have a good foundation in this knowledge, which means having already listened to and studied the Dharma in its general aspects, and therefore knowing what is meant by conventional existence. Without these prerequisites, hearing particular terms such as "natural existence" might seem very strange, even bizarre.

Let us suppose we find a snake in our home: we will no doubt attempt to send it away, but if we do this unskillfully and without care, it will be very dangerous, for it could bite us. Likewise, if we lack a correct approach to the study of the emptiness of phenomena, it might harm us rather than benefit us. We could, for example, reach the conclusion that phenomena do not exist, and so believe that there is no such thing as creating positive or negative actions, which would be an erroneous conception. Therefore when we study emptiness, we must be careful. Saying that phenomena do not exist truly does not mean that mountains, houses, or people do not exist.

When we project a film onto a white screen, the screen is actually white, but we see all sorts of images upon it. However, if we direct a flashlight with a very powerful beam onto those images, they will disappear. The flashlight can be compared to the mind that examines true existence, seeking ultimate existence, and finds nothing. The mind that examines the conventional existence of phenomena apprehends things in the way the images appear on the screen when no light is projected onto them. Hence there are two types of mind: one is the mind that examines the ultimate existence of phenomena and does not see them; the other is the mind that examines their conventional existence and can see them.

The meditation on the two truths, ultimate and conventional, should be done alternately, because only buddhas can perceive the two levels of reality simultaneously. We should first meditate analytically on ultimate truth and understand the meaning of the emptiness of an object—for example, the emptiness of a vase; then we should meditate on its conventional truth, in order to understand how it exists conventionally.

We can see Lobsang Dorje without any analysis, but if we were to investigate who he authentically is, whether he is his hair or hands, we will not find any Lobsang Dorje there in the object, and only the idea or the concept we have of him will remain. Therefore, not being satisfied with the conventional Lobsang Dorje and going to look for Lobsang Dorje on an ultimate level, we will not find him. This is just like when, not being satisfied with the images we see on the screen, we direct a flashlight with a powerful beam toward them in order to see them better, but in so doing, the images vanish.

It is said that phenomena do not exist "truly" because without analyzing them we can perceive them, but once we analyze them we are no longer able to find them.

When we name a house or a flower, we do so with the mind that simply labels. When, however, unsatisfied with a mere designation, we seek further in order to understand what a particular phenomenon is, the mind that examines ultimately is present, and it does not find the object. The mind that perceives the conventional existence of phenomena is not the same moment of mind that perceives their emptiness (with the exception of the mind of a buddha).

In order to attain buddhahood it is necessary to realize bodhichitta and the wisdom that perceives emptiness; therefore, if we want to be free of this body, which is like a prison and gives us unhappiness and suffering, we should concentrate on both. Although the understanding of emptiness is of fundamental importance, our practice at present is to observe our actions, try to abandon the negative deeds that produce suffering, and practice the positive deeds that produce happiness.

When we walk to a remote place, we need to look not only far ahead but also close by, and pay attention, otherwise we risk falling. On the other hand, if we are certain that there are no hindrances between here and our destination, we can focus our gaze on our objective or even walk with our eyes closed. Likewise, while walking on the spiritual path, we should observe our actions and their effects.

The root of all mental afflictions is the erroneous conception that grasps at the true existence of phenomena. Were we to perceive a human as a nonhuman and a nonhuman as a human, ours would be a wrong conception toward a human being, but this could vanish if we changed our view: if we perceived a human as human and a nonhuman as a nonhuman. Likewise, if a person is able to see phenomena only as mere mental designations, the mind that grasps at true existence—that is, the mind that perceives them as existing from their own side—will disappear.

Refuting the Objections of the Chittamatrins
Concerning Ultimate Truths

The Chittamatrins maintain the true existence of *other-powered phenomena*—impermanent phenomena they consider to be under the influence of causes and conditions that are other, or different from, those phenomena in question—but state that these do not exist as substantial entities external to the mind. In other words, they believe that the objects we see are of the same substance as the mind perceiving them because they arise from the same imprint and that therefore they do not exist externally.

When we visualize the mandala of the deity, it is not something separate from the mind perceiving it, since it is a manifestation of the mind, an object visualized by the mind. Whatever the object might be, they say, it is always of the nature of the mind perceiving it. For example, if we dream of the body of our father, though he is not actually there at that moment, the mind perceives it as if it were present. So, that body seen in the dream is a phenomenon produced by that same dreaming mind.

Instead, Prasangikas say that phenomena do not exist by their own nature as they appear to, and this is precisely why they are like an illusion. Furthermore, since mind too is a phenomenon, it also lacks natural existence or existence by its own characteristics, and is similar to an illusion, just like all other phenomena. Then the Chittamatrins object to the Prasangikas: "Since according to you, phenomena do not exist by their own nature or are like an illusion, it follows that they do not exist at all and that also the mind that perceives phenomena as illusions does not exist. What then perceives phenomena as illusions?"

The Prasangikas reply by asking in turn, "Do phenomena exist the way the mind perceives them—that is, as they appear? If they exist in the way they appear to the mind, that means they exist externally, because the way in which they appear to the mind is that they exist externally. But this would be in contradiction with your own view."

The Chittamatrins must necessarily answer that even though phenomena appear as if they have external existence, actually they do not. For them, the appearance of phenomena as external objects is a deceptive appearance, and this leads them to state that phenomena are illusions.

However, this answer is also in contradiction with their view, because stating that phenomena are like illusions is for the Chittamatrins like stating that phenomena do not exist by their own nature, which according to their own system would mean that they do not exist at all.

In summary, the Prasangikas ask the Chittamatrins, "Do phenomena exist the way they appear?"

If the Chittamatrins' answer is no, the Prasangikas retort, "If phenomena do not exist the way they appear, then they do not exist by their own nature; and therefore, according to your previous objection (if phenomena do not exist by their own nature, they do not exist at all), it follows that they do not exist." If the Chittamatrins' answer is yes, then they are in contradiction with their own view (that phenomena do not exist externally), because phenomena appear to the mind to be externally existent. Therefore their thesis is proven wrong.

There are cases in which the exponents of a school, even though they do not accept at first a certain conclusion from another school, on the basis of their own premises, must welcome in the end what the others propose.

The Chittamatrins then try to state their view by saying, "According to us, phenomena are not entities external to the mind that perceives them, but are of its same nature." They maintain that phenomena partake of the same substantial nature of the mind; they also maintain that, although phenomena do not exist externally, they appear to exist that way, that therefore they are like an illusion, and that such illusion-like phenomena are perceived by a truly existent mind. The Chittamatrins do not say that phenomena are like an illusion, because for them the mind is not like an illusion.

The Prasangikas instead say that a "truly" existing mind cannot be accepted—they admit the external existence of phenomena, but maintain that the mind does not exist by its own nature. The Chittamatrins, on the other hand, do not accept the external existence of phenomena, and maintain that the mind does exist by its own nature. It is on the basis of these different views that the Chittamatrins and Prasangikas are in disagreement.

In this context, the Chittamatrins try to refute the Prasangikas' view with the following objection: "You maintain that phenomena are like an illusion because they are not truly existent, but in that case they would not exist by their own nature; therefore they would not exist. Who is it, then, that understands that phenomena are like an illusion?" [15]

The Prasangikas reply by applying the same logic used by the Chitta-matrins, and in turn formulate a question. "You maintain that only the objects' appearance is external to the mind, and this is the meaning you attribute to existing like an illusion; but we maintain that objects exist externally. Now, since you accept that the existence of phenomena is like an illusion, you must also accept that phenomena do not exist with a nature of their own; consequently the mind too cannot exist with a nature of its own, which for you means it does not exist at all. But if the mind does not exist, who maintains and perceives the appearance of phenomena as an illusion?" The very same question that had been formulated by the Chittamatrins, followers of the "mind-only" school, is now being asked by the Prasangikas!

The Chittamatrins answer, "Phenomena as they are perceived, as sub-stantial entities external to the mind, do not exist. They exist in another way—that is, they have the same substantial entity of the mind, since the aspect of forms appearing to the perceiving consciousness is itself mind. For this reason objects are suitable to be perceived by consciousness." [16]

The Prasangikas reply by asking a further question: "Since you main-tain the true existence of the mind and deny the existence of phenomena as substantial entities external to the mind, who is it that understands such true existence of the mind and that it is of a single substantial entity with the phenomena it apprehends? What proof do you have that the mind exists truly or intrinsically?"

The Prasangikas ask this question because they want to know how Chit-tamatrins can establish the existence of true mental consciousness. Since the Chittamatrins maintain that the mind exists truly, the Prasangikas ask them which mind is able to know this.

The Chittamatrins answer, "There are two types of mind: one perceives only sense objects and so forth, and the other perceives only the mind perceiving the objects, and it is called self-perceiving, or self-knowing, or self-cognizing."

What is this self-perceiving mind? To clarify, the Chittamatrins use the following example: when a visual consciousness that perceives the blue color of an object is generated, at the same time that there is perception, there is also another mind that apprehends that perceiving consciousness, and this is the self-perceiver.

When I spoke of this type of mind at the Lama Tzong Khapa Institute in Pomaia, asking at the end what people had understood, someone replied with the following analogy: "It is like a man who looks at the color blue from behind the lens of a camera. The camera can be compared to the consciousness that perceives the color blue, and the man behind the camera is like the self-perceiver, perceiving the consciousness that perceives the color blue."

The self-cognizer is in any case a type of mind accepted only by the Chittamatrins, and is not accepted by the Prasangikas, who say that the Buddha himself has stated that the self-cognizer does not exist. To this purpose the text proclaims, "It has been said by the protector of the world that the mind does not have the ability to behold itself." [17]

The Prasangikas then state that the self-cognizer should not perceive mind as external to itself, but rather should perceive it in a nondualistic way; otherwise it would not make sense to say that it is a self-perceiving mind. The Chittamatrins continue, "Normally when we perceive things, we do so in a dualistic way. But the self-cognizer apprehends the mind that perceives the objects in a nondualistic way, since mind itself is its own object."

But the Prasangikas answer back that this cannot be so. With the attribute "dualistic," a separation is implied between the perceived object and the mind perceiving it, whereas "nondualistic" refers to a modality according to which there is no perception of object and subject as separate. This meaning of nonduality is the same that is used when speaking of emptiness.

When we think, "I am going," there are not two things involved but one, whereas when we think, "I am eating an apple," there are two—the eater and the eaten. Therefore, the self-cognizer should not imply two separate entities, but should instead be one with its object. When we say, "I am unhappy," or "I am happy," we do not have the sense of two things, but of one, whereas when we say, "I do good to that person," two entities are involved—the other person and ourselves. In the case of the self-perceiver, defined as a mind that perceives itself, there should not be two different things involved, since the mind that perceives and the mind that is perceived are not different.

According to the Chittamatrins, there is no dualistic perception because this self-perceiver is not a deceptive mind. If it were such, it should per-

ceive things in a dualistic way. However, the Buddha has said that there
cannot be a mind that perceives itself the very same instant of knowing
another object, in the same way that there cannot be a blade of a sword that
can cut itself. Therefore, although the Chittamatrins believe in the existence of this type of a mind, this view is not shared by the Prasangikas—if
there were a mind capable of perceiving itself, it should also be possible for
the blade of a sword to cut itself! [18]

QUESTION: But isn't consciousness aware of itself?
ANSWER: There are various types of consciousness and mental factors.
Mindfulness is a kind of memory, and introspection or vigilance is a kind
of wisdom. Mindfulness is conscious not of itself, but of another object.

According to the hypothesis of self-perception, there is a mind that
perceives the color blue, and at the same time there is a mind that perceives that same mind that perceives the color blue. The reason the Chittamatrins maintain the existence of such a mind is because we have the
capacity to remember past experiences. In other words, they maintain
that when we perceive an object—for example, the color blue—at the
same time there is always a mind that beholds the perception of the color
blue. In India many pandits maintained the existence of such a mind,
whereas others maintained the opposite. For this reason it is difficult for
me to explain this subject, and difficult for the translator to translate it.

All living beings, whether human or nonhuman, desire happiness and do
not desire unhappiness. We suffer because of the wrong conception that
considers what is impure to be pure, what is the nature of suffering to be
happiness, what is impermanent to be permanent, and what is devoid of
a self to have a self.

In what way do we experience suffering on the basis of considering
what is impermanent to be permanent? By thinking, for example, that
our relationships with our friends, children, and relatives will last a very
long time. We are actually used to thinking of them as having a permanent
nature, and because of this wrong conception, we experience attachment.
However, since they are impermanent, sooner or later we will have to
separate ourselves from them, and at that moment, bewildered and upset,
we will think, "How is it possible that this is happening to me?"

This used to happen in Tibet too. Although there, because of a greater awareness of death, the monks seemed to experience less suffering. They did not have the great regret for the loss of their relatives that laypeople experienced. If we are conscious of impermanence and of the uncertainty of life's duration, we realize that death can catch us at any moment, and when this happens, it will not seem unusual.

Concerning the experiences of suffering we generate by considering what is impure to be pure, we can take as an example our own body and the bodies of others. We conceive of the body as pure, and therefore we are attached to it, but its nature is impure. If we realize this, we will no longer desire to possess our own body, nor the body of another, and being without such desire, we will not suffer even when we have to separate from it.

Every type of worldly happiness arising from our contaminated actions and from mental afflictions, though it might appear to us as pleasant, is instead the nature of suffering, because it can cause us unhappiness at any moment.

When we have some money, we feel safe and experience a kind of solace because of it; however, since the money will inevitably disappear, this being its nature, we will also find reason for worries.

When we go to the seaside and dive into the water, we first experience a pleasant sensation; but if we stay long enough in the water, this pleasure will turn into discomfort.

When we meet friends that we have not seen for a long time, we immediately experience great joy; but if we stay with them long, this joy will turn into its opposite.

The pleasure generated by contact with an object of an impure nature, whatever that may be, will nevertheless turn into suffering. Whereas the happiness of nirvana, since it is obtained after the liberation from the conditioning of mental afflictions, is a permanent happiness, because, no matter how long we experience it, unpleasant sensations will no longer arise.

Because we grasp at the concept of a truly existent "I," we discriminate between friends and enemies—we have attachment for the former and hatred and resentment for the latter. This sensation of non-equanimity causes us unhappiness, due precisely to our grasping at the "I," and cannot be eliminated by material means, but only through the holy Dharma.

When the desire to be free from the suffering of cyclic existence arises, it is called *definite emergence,* or renunciation.

As soon as we have spontaneously generated this feeling, we can say that we have boarded the train leading us to liberation, nirvana. If we then apply the same analytical process we have used to understand our own state of suffering to others, we will understand that all beings have the same desire that we do: wanting to be free from suffering and to attain happiness. Following this reflection, we will then generate the determination to achieve buddhahood so as to be able to help others to do so, and we will consequently develop the mind of awakening, or bodhichitta.

We know that all beings possess buddha nature and can therefore attain enlightenment. We also know that a buddha can show the way to eliminate suffering and can benefit all beings. Why then aren't we capable of engaging in the practices of the inner path? Because we do not reflect adequately on our own suffering.

It is important to have compassion for others, but in order to generate it we need to understand their suffering, and to succeed in this we should first of all realize that we ourselves are suffering.

The Hinayana arhats have eliminated the cause of cyclic existence and have attained the state beyond suffering, but they have not been able to enter the Mahayana path because they have not generated great compassion toward all beings.

In the *Abhisamayalamkara* it is said that by having great compassion one will not fall into the extreme of personal peace, by which oneself alone experiences the happiness of liberation. The realization of the authentic nature of phenomena will prevent us, on the other hand, from falling into the extreme of cyclic existence. Hence, we need the wisdom that realizes the nature of all phenomena in order to free ourselves from cyclic existence, and not only in order to attain buddhahood. To this aim we should know what this wisdom is, and it is for this reason that we are now studying the ninth chapter of the *Bodhicharyavatara.*

The Prasangika-Madhyamikas state that phenomena do not exist by their own nature, by their own characteristics, or intrinsically, and both Madhyamaka schools, the Svatantrika and Prasangika, maintain the non-true existence of all phenomena.

Unlike the Prasangikas, the Chittamatrins refer all objects of knowledge to three categories: *other-powered natures, thoroughly established natures,* and *thoroughly imputed natures.*

For the Chittamatrins, all composite phenomena are other-powered natures, dependent on the power of the causes that produce them.

Thoroughly established natures refers to the lack of external existence of phenomena, to an object's lack of existence by its own characteristics as a basis of nominal designation, and to the lack of self-sufficient and substantial existence of the self of the person. "Emptiness" in the Chittamatrin system refers precisely to these three forms of "lack."

Finally, they attribute some permanent phenomena (such as space) and imaginary phenomena to thoroughly imputed natures. For the Chittamatrins, only the third category is empty of true existence, whereas they maintain that the first two exist truly. This is also true for the mind, which is included.

Furthermore, they maintain the existence of the self-perceiver—that is, of a mind that perceives the mind that perceives the object. For them, the entity of this mind is no different from the substantial entity of the mind that perceives the objects. However, its aspect is different, because its object (the perceiving mind) is different from the object of the mind perceiving the objects. Their way of perceiving is therefore also different; in fact, the mind that perceives the objects is turned outward, whereas the self-perceiver is turned inward and has the function of allowing the memory of the mind that has perceived.

The Chittamatrins maintain that both the self-cognizer and the mental consciousness that perceives the objects are truly existent and also that they are of the same entity. These statements are in contradiction, however, because stating that they exist truly and that they are of the same entity does not allow one to simultaneously say that they have two different aspects. This is why the Prasangikas refute this view, using the argument of being "one with" or "different from."

If consciousness and the self-cognizer were truly existent as one entity, then they should be only "one," and this is in contradiction with saying that the self-cognizer is the perceiving subject and that the consciousness is the perceived object. If they were truly different, then there should not be any relation between the two types of consciousness, because in this case they should be two totally different phenomena and generating one should not depend upon the other.

On the other hand, if these two aspects of the mind existed truly, separately, it would follow, given that the self-cognizer does not know itself, that there should then be another self-cognizer that knows the first one, then another one that knows the second, and so on, ad infinitum, but this too is impossible. The Buddha himself said that the mind cannot perceive itself in the very same moment.

The Chittamatrins persist in their argument by saying, "Light is able to illuminate phenomena and also itself." But the Prasangikas reply, "Light can illuminate other phenomena but cannot illuminate itself. If it could, it also would follow that darkness could obscure, and if this were the case, we could not see it. Just as darkness cannot obscure itself, light also cannot illuminate itself. It follows that mind cannot know itself and that this self-perceiver cannot be accepted." [19]

The Chittamatrins try to further defend their position, supporting the existence of the self-cognizer by presenting the following example: "Let us consider two types of blue: the blue of transparent crystal, whose color depends on having been placed on a blue cloth, and the natural color blue of lapis lazuli, which does not depend on anything. The transparent crystal can appear to be blue if placed on a blue cloth, but a lapis lazuli does not need to depend on something else in order to appear blue, because its very nature is blue. Likewise, the visual consciousness, as well as other types of sensory consciousness, must necessarily be related to an object that is not consciousness, whereas the self-perceiver exists as consciousness without having to be related to anything but consciousness itself."

The Chittamatrins maintain that the self-perceiver does not arise in dependence on something else because it is one with the sense consciousness that perceives an object, and is generated simultaneously, whereas sense consciousness arises depending on its object. But the example that they present is not correct, because in fact lapis lazuli is not blue by its own nature but depends on causes and conditions to produce the color blue. [20]

The Chittamatrins then correct their previous statement, stating, "You say that light does not illuminate itself; however, it illuminates. Likewise, although you say that mind cannot know itself, without doubt it knows. How, then, can it be established that it knows?" If answering that, with regard to one mental continuum there is a mind that knows the mind that knows, it would follow that there should be an infinite number of these minds. If we were to answer that no mind knows the consciousness that knows, we could not maintain that the mind knows at all.

This debate originated with the Chittamatrin statement that mind or consciousness exists truly. In order to refute this, the Prasangikas ask, "On what basis can you state that the mind is truly existent?" The Chittamatrins reply by maintaining the existence of the self-cognizer, but have not been able to prove it. The Prasangikas, in order to refute this, present three analogies: the blade of a sword that cannot cut itself, the light of a lamp that cannot illuminate itself, and darkness that cannot obscure itself. It follows that the mind does not exist "truly," and that we cannot speak of a mind that knows "truly" or of any of its true characteristics. That would be as meaningless as speaking of the smile of a barren woman's daughter. [21–22]

This debate is about the mind's ultimate mode of existence and not about its conventional mode of existence.

A truly existing mind does not exist because there is no mind that can know it, just as there is no such thing as horns on a rabbit's head, for there is no valid mind that can perceive them. And we cannot discuss whether a truly existent mind is pure or not, just as we cannot discuss the attributes of a mule's offspring, since mules are sterile.

If the truly existent mind existed, the mind that perceives it should also exist. There is no fire in the ocean at night, for there is no valid mind that can perceive it.

We have mental afflictions because we possess the mind that grasps at the true existence of phenomena; we should therefore eliminate this mind through the wisdom that perceives the empty nature of phenomena. If we succeed in attaining this wisdom, which is the true antidote that eliminates the four wrong conceptions, we can also eliminate the suffering that arises from them.

The Chittamatrins maintain the existence of phenomena that are generated in dependence on something else and of phenomena that are generated independently of something that is other. For them, an other-powered nature is like the blue of transparent crystal that is lying on a blue cloth, whereas a thoroughly established nature is like the blue of lapis lazuli, which does not depend on anything else for its color. The self-cognizer of consciousness that experiences happiness or suffering is a thoroughly established nature, like the blue of lapis lazuli.

This view is refuted by the Prasangikas thus: "External phenomena, such as form and so on, exist in relation to something other (the consciousness that apprehends them), as in your example of the transparent crystal, which is blue if placed on a blue cloth. At the same time, consciousness also exists in dependence on many conditions, and so it is with the blue color of lapis lazuli."

The Chittamatrins carry on maintaining that the self-cognizing mind exists, and when the Prasangikas ask them, "What reason do you present that can support this?" they reply, "The self-cognizer exists because when the mind perceives the color blue, later you can have the memory of having perceived the color blue. Such memory is due to the self-perceiver, and if this did not exist there could be no memory of that perception."

The Prasangikas object, "In order to remember an experience—for example, the perception of the color blue—it is not necessary for another consciousness to apprehend the mind that had the direct perception of the color blue."

Let us suppose that someone gives us poisoned yogurt and that we drink it without knowing that it is poisoned, thinking that it is ordinary yogurt. After a while, when the effects of the poison start to manifest, we run to a doctor who will diagnose the poisoning. At this point we will start to wonder how this could have happened, and after careful reflection, we conclude that the yogurt we drank was poisoned. But while drinking it we did not know this—knowing this is only a result of the later events that we have understood. So, although the direct perception of the poison did not arise at the same time as the perception of the yogurt, we nevertheless realize what has happened.

The recognition of a past experience (such as having drunk poisoned yogurt) does not require a direct perception in order to be established, since, although we did not perceive the poison in the yogurt, we can later recall the fact that we drank it. This memory exists in spite of not being preceded by a direct perception of the object.

Therefore the Chittamatrins do not put forward a valid argument when they use the presence of the memory of an experience as the reason to support their presentation of the existence of the self-cognizer.

In the text the example of a bear is presented. During hibernation the bear is bitten by a mouse, but does not realize it until springtime. Once it wakes up and feels the poisonous effects, the bear understands what has happened. Although the bear does not perceive being bitten at the actual moment the event occurred, and although much time has elapsed since the event, he is able to establish the cause of his discomfort. The process through which a moment of consciousness is remembered is similar to the above, and does not depend on the existence of a simultaneous self-cognizer. [23]

The next reason the Chittamatrins give in order to maintain the existence of a self-cognizer is this: "If a person who has attained calm abiding and other conditions can perceive even faraway objects as a result of his clairvoyance, how much more so will he be able to perceive his own mind, which is much nearer."

The Prasangikas reply, "This is not necessarily true because, for example, by applying eye lotions blessed with the power of mantras, one can see objects buried underground, but it is not possible to see the eye lotion itself." [24]

The Chittamatrins say, "If the self-cognizer were not there, the other cognitions, such as seeing, hearing, and smelling, also could not exist." But the nonexistence of the self-cognizer does not imply the nonexistence of other-cognizers, and the Prasangikas reply, "We do not want to deny the mere existence of seeing, hearing, and so forth. What must be changed is the conception of them as truly existent, since it is cause for suffering. Seeing or hearing do not by themselves bring about suffering, nor do the perceived objects. The causes for all suffering in cyclic existence are grasping at true seeing, true hearing, and so forth. [25]

For the Chittamatrins, phenomena are "like illusions" because, even though to the perceiver they appear to be external to the mind, the phenomena and the mind perceiving them arise from the same imprint. On the other hand, they are also not the mind itself, although they both possess the same substantial nature. Still, according to the Chittamatrins phenomena exist truly, although they do not exist externally. But, as we have seen, for phenomena to exist truly they must exist in the way that they appear to—that is, as external to the mind.

The Prasangikas say, "If you state that phenomena exist truly, given that in order to exist in this way they should exist as they appear, you contradict your own statement that phenomena are not external to the mind, although they appear to be so. And if an object is external to the mind, how can it arise from the same imprint as the mind that perceives it? If you say phenomena are not different from the mind, then you must also refrain from maintaining that they exist truly."

The Prasangikas wish to clarify that it is a contradiction to state that phenomena are on the one hand truly existent and on the other are different from the perceiver itself, the mind. Phenomena, in order to exist truly, should exist as they appear. But the fact that they appear to be external contradicts the Chittamatrins' statement that they exist truly and that they have the same substantial nature as the mind.

The Chittamatrins believe that composite phenomena exist truly because they arise from causes and conditions. This argument is opposite to the Prasangikas', who state that produced phenomena are not truly existent because they arise from causes and conditions—but for the Chittamatrins this position is illogical.

The Prasangikas say, "If things were truly existent, they should exist in the way they appear—that is, as external to the mind—but you Chittamatrins do not accept this." They refute the Chittamatrins' view by pointing out the contradiction of maintaining that phenomena exist truly although they exist differently from the way they appear.

Furthermore, the Chittamatrins maintain that forms are neither mind, nor other, nor different from the mind. But this too is refuted by the Prasangikas, since if forms did not exist in either of the two modes, it follows that they could not exist at all—things must be either mind or other than the mind. [26]

The Prasangikas explain to the Chittamatrins that illusion-like phenomena, such as forms and so forth, even if they do not exist truly as they appear, are objects of knowledge. In the same way, mental consciousness is a cognizer even if it does not truly exist. In other words, the perceived object and the perceiving subject are both non-truly existent, although they exist on a conventional level.

They continue, "Even if you, Chittamatrins, were to succeed in ascertaining that external phenomena are not truly existing, but continued to state that the mind exists truly, this would be equally unacceptable;

because if perceived objects are not truly existent, the mind that perceives them also cannot be truly existent."

The Chittamatrins maintain that "conditioned existence" or samsara (the state in which subject and object appear as two separate entities) must have something real as its basis—that is, a nondual, truly existent consciousness—or else it would be a state like space, non-caused, permanent, in which phenomena could not appear as real. [27]

The Prasangikas reply, "If samsara had true existence as its basis, liberation would not be possible, nor would it be possible to die or to fall into the inferior realms. A truly existent phenomenon would be permanent, and so it could not be the cause of any phenomenon, it could not produce any effect, and it would be independent. A truly existent phenomenon could not produce fruit because doing so would depend on other factors, whereas if it is truly existent it must not depend on anything." [28]

For example, a truly existent fire cannot produce smoke.

According to the Chittamatrins, phenomena do not exist as substantial entities external to the mind. They are empty of external existence. Therefore they state that phenomena are like illusions, because although they are of the same substantial nature of the mind they appear to be external.

The Prasangikas state that phenomena are like illusions because they do not exist as they appear—that is, as truly existent—and that the mind is illusory because it perceives phenomena to be real although they do not exist "truly."

Then the Prasangikas observe, "The mind of ordinary beings is accompanied by dualistic perception; if it were free from dualistic perception, as you say, it would be similar to the mind of a buddha. In this case, what would be the point of practicing the path, since all sentient beings would already be enlightened? And what would be the advantage in accepting your view that considers the objects of cyclic existence are only mind?" [29]

QUESTION: The Chittamatrins maintain that if the self-cognizer did not exist, the sense cognitions would also not exist. Why?
ANSWER: It has been said that one can ascertain the perception of the color blue because this self-cognizing mind, through which one can establish the existence of the knowledge of other objects, exists. According to the Chittamatrins, if this self-cognizing or self-perceiving mind did not exist, one

could not maintain the existence of sense consciousness and consequently also could not maintain the existence of phenomena, since in order to establish the existence of a phenomenon there must be a valid mind, and in order to establish its existence and memory, they say, there must be a self-cognizer.

QUESTION: Why does a phenomenon need to be as it appears in order to be truly existent?

ANSWER: When we say that the face appearing in the mirror is not real, it is because there is not a face inside the mirror, but only a reflection. When we say that emanations by a magician are not real, it is because what we see is not really there. When we say that a person is lying, it is because what he says does not match reality. When we say that a thing is true, it is because it exists precisely in that mode. Therefore, if one says that a phenomenon is truly existent, it must be exactly as it appears.

QUESTION: Why must this be the proof that an object is not truly existent? It might be that the mind perceives it in an erroneous way but that it is nonetheless truly existent!

ANSWER: By "not truly existent" we do not mean that a glass is not a glass, nor do we mean that in spite of not being a glass it appears as such. The human beings we see are human beings. We are not saying that non-humans appear to us as humans.

What we mean is that we believe that any object we see exists by its own nature, as if self-existent, independent from the mind's designation, whereas in reality that object is not truly existent because it comes to exist in dependence on a name that is attributed to a valid basis. We perceive a person to exist in the five aggregates that are the compoments of a person, but in reality he or she does not exist in them. Objects appear to exist from their own side, but they do not exist in such a way. For this reason we say that phenomena do not truly exist.

QUESTION: Which part of the body is the mind?

ANSWER: Each of us can say, "I came from a certain place, I have a brother, a mother, I am happy, I am unhappy." Who is saying all this? It is something that remembers, and what remembers is the mind. Mind and body are two separate things.

QUESTION: What is the nature of detachment (renunciation): happiness or unhappiness?

ANSWER: Aversion to samsara has a connotation of happiness, because when a person realizes the nature of suffering of cyclic existence and that there is a possibility to be free from it, this makes him happy. The reason we meditate on death is that later we will have to be reborn, and it is therefore necessary to prepare favorable conditions for a fortunate future life. The Kadampa geshes used to say, "If we do not have negative karma, we have no reason to be afraid." A spiritual practitioner without negative karma should not be afraid of anything.

All problems arise from the fact that we conceive phenomena in the wrong way. If someone harms us, we feel that he has wronged an "I" that we picture as very solid and real, that can be pointed out. We think that the person who has caused the harm can also be found as a concrete one. But if through analysis we look for the person who harmed us, we will not find what we expected.

Let us take, for example, a person toward whom we feel attachment: he or she appears to exist in a concrete and solid way, but if we look closely we will not find a truly existent person inside or outside of her for whom we can say we feel attachment. If it were possible to find that truly existent person, she would exist.

On the other hand, if we analytically examine a person who has caused us harm, we will find that he is not his head, his hands, and so forth, and continuing our investigation, we will not succeed in finding that person. We will not find either the person we feel attached to or the person we feel aversion to, because that person, like all phenomena, does not exist truly.

In stating this we are not proposing that the object that conditions us does not exist at all, but only that it does not exist independently, from its own side. If we understand the interdependent nature of phenomena, the ignorance that grasps at their true existence disappears. The Prasangikas are those who correctly know the authentic nature of phenomena, whereas the Chittamatrins, not having understood it, state that phenomena exist truly.

At this point, we should consider the fact that since phenomena do not exist truly, the mind that perceives them also does not exist truly.

Establishing as the Path the Knowledge
That Conventional Truths Are Like Illusions

The Chittamatrins say, "You state that phenomena do not exist truly and are therefore like illusions, but to present this view as an antidote to mental afflictions is unacceptable, since when a magician creates the appearance of a woman through magic he may still desire her, even knowing that she is an illusion that he himself has created." [30]

To this objection the Prasangikas reply, "The magician can experience attachment to a woman he himself has created because he has not yet succeeded in eliminating the wrong conception of the true existence of the illusory woman. Since he has not realized the emptiness of all phenomena and has no familiarity with the illusory nature of what he himself has created, he still has the tendency to grasp at true existence. Consequently, he has not yet eliminated the natural predisposition to generate desire for pleasing objects. Therefore, even if he understands that the object appearing to him as a woman is in fact not a woman, he will grasp at the concept of true existence of that appearance."

Understanding that the illusory woman is not a real woman does not automatically imply the understanding of the non-true existence of the woman's appearance, and therefore of her existence as an illusion. This is why the magician can feel attachment. One can feel attachment for the reflection of an object in a mirror, because the non-true existence of that image has not yet been realized. The mere understanding that the image reflected in the mirror is not the true face is not enough to prevent one from experiencing attachment.

The magician can understand that the emanated woman is illusory, but if he does not realize that her appearance does not exist truly, his understanding of her illusiveness will be very coarse. It is necessary to acquire the understanding of subtle illusiveness, and this is possible only by realizing the non-true existence of phenomena. When we correctly realize the way that phenomena exist, we will no longer experience any attachment toward them. [31]

Knowing only intellectually that phenomena do not truly exist is not enough. After having understood that all phenomena are devoid of true existence, one needs to reflect and meditate single-pointedly and for a long time on the mental image of the lack of true existence. Only after having obtained the natural and spontaneous view that phenomena do not exist truly and having realized that emptiness itself is devoid of true existence will there be no possibility for the mental afflictions to arise. [32]

If we investigate true existence appropriately, we will understand that it does not exist. And when we realize it, the true existence of phenomena will disappear—that is, the object that must be negated will no longer be an object conceived by the mind.

What we must do in practice is try to understand the meaning of the true existence of phenomena and then try to negate it through analytical meditation; subsequently we need to perceive their non-true existence through concentration. During meditation we deny the true existence of phenomena and, by the end of the analysis, what remains before the mind is only their non-true existence, their emptiness—but then, understanding that emptiness itself is empty of true existence, the concept of the true existence of the emptiness of phenomena also dissolves. [33]

Someone could think, "Phenomena are devoid of intrinsic existence, but emptiness is real." Actually, the emptiness of phenomena does not exist truly or intrinsically either. This is what we mean when we speak of the "emptiness of emptiness." When the lack of true existence of things and non-things is understood, the mind that grasps their true existence is completely pacified. And at the moment when that mind perceives emptiness directly, the dual appearance that is typical of conventional existence disappears. When things (for example, the vase) and non-things (for example, its emptiness) are both understood to be non-truly existent, the mind's grasping at the true existence of things and non-things will be completely pacified.

For the yogi who possesses more than a mere intellectual understanding of emptiness, during meditative absorption on the ultimate nature of phenomena the appearance of true existence will disappear, and there will not be any kind of conventional appearance. In contrast, one who possesses only a conceptual realization of emptiness will know that phenomena do not exist truly but will not have eliminated the duality between conventional appearance and the non-true existence of phenomena.

Exponents of other Buddhist schools ask, "When a buddha concentrates on the authentic nature of phenomena, all kinds of conceptualizations disappear. How then can he act for the benefit of beings since, in order to do so, some kind of conceptual activity is needed? And given that conceptual activity is illusory and that a buddha no longer engages in any illusory activity, how can he help beings?" [34]

The Prasangikas reply, "When the Buddha was a bodhisattva, he prayed that he would be capable of benefiting all sentient beings, and therefore, his mere appearance is beneficial to them. However, for a buddha to appear and give teachings also depends on sentient beings' accumulation of merit."

As a cloud gives rain without need of conceptual activity, so the buddhas give teachings and benefit all beings. It is like the wish-fulfilling gem that, although devoid of conceptual motivation, through its mere existence fulfills a desire whenever someone expresses one. It is like the wish-granting tree found in the heavens that, although devoid of concepts of doing or non-doing, produces a particular thing for the simple reason that someone desires it."

The other schools still ask, "If the Buddha had this aspiration long before, how can its effect be produced at the moment of his enlightenment?" [35]

The Prasangikas reply, "This is possible. For example, a long time ago the Brahmin Sanku blessed Garuda's reliquary with the strength of his mantras, and to this day it still has the power to neutralize poison. Likewise, a bodhisattva, because of his prayers, aspirations, and dedications, is able to benefit beings once he has become a buddha, in spite of not having any conceptual motivation." [36–37]

The Vaibhashikas and the Sautrantikas then say, "If a buddha is not engaged in conceptual activity, how can praying and making offerings to him generate merit?" In other words, since a bodhisattva does not have a conceptual mind but only direct perception, and therefore lacks the conceptual thought that accepts or does not accept offerings, how can merit accrue from offerings addressed to him?

The Prasangikas reply, "It is said in the sutras that one accumulates merit in making offerings both to a relic of the Buddha and to a living buddha." [38]

The Vaibhashikas and the Sautrantikas reply, saying that a person cannot accumulate merits by making offerings that do not exist truly to a buddha who does not exist truly. The Prasangikas, however, refute this argument by observing that if it is possible to accumulate merits by making truly existent offerings to a truly existent buddha, likewise it is possible to accumulate merits by making non-truly existent offerings to an illusion-like buddha. [39]

Although the other schools debate with the Prasangikas in order to state their philosophical principles, only the Prasangikas possess the knowledge of the way in which phenomena exist, and what they state is correct. However, until we acquire more familiarity with this view, it will be difficult for us to understand all the implications of what the Prasangikas are saying.

The points that are stated by the Prasangikas and the points that are maintained by the other Buddhist schools have all been stated by the Buddha. He expounded different philosophical views according to the different capabilities of sentient beings, with the knowledge that every sentient being would not immediately understand the Prasangika view. Buddha gave teachings at different levels with the aim of guiding beings gradually toward the highest aim and view, not unlike a doctor who prescribes medicine to his patients in ever-increasing doses, with the purpose of curing them in the best way.

If we think that the Chittamatrins' view, for example, is more suitable for us, we may adopt it. For the Chittamatrins, external objects, deities, mandalas, and all other objects of visualization are of the same nature as the mind perceiving them.

Phenomena are said to be "dependent arising" because they arise in dependence on *causes and conditions,* they arise in dependence on *their own parts,* and they arise in dependence on *a mental designation.*

The characteristic of arising in dependence on causes and conditions refers only to impermanent phenomena, and all Buddhist schools accept this, maintaining that composite phenomena, are produced by causes and conditions.

Arising in dependence on parts refers to both permanent and impermanent phenomena.

Impermanent phenomena arise in dependence on their parts like the wheel depends on its spokes, its rim, and so forth. This is accepted by both the Madhyamikas and the Chittamatrins, but not by proponents of the lesser schools such as the Vaibhashikas, who do not accept the divisibility of the atom, which they consider to be devoid of parts. Actually, even the smallest material particles depend on their respective parts, and in fact the right side of each of them is different from the left.

According to the Madhyamikas, "arising in dependence on parts" also refers to permanent phenomena since permanent phenomena, such as space, for example, exist only if considered in relation to their parts. This is not accepted by the Chittamatrins, who do not speak of such dependent arising of non-composite phenomena.

Finally, arising in dependence on a mental designation is accepted only by the Prasangikas.

GESHE-LA'S QUESTION: "When the Prasangikas say that phenomena do not exist by their own nature, how do the Chittamatrins reply?"

STUDENT'S ANSWER: "Chittamatrins believe that if phenomena do not exist by their own nature, they do not exist at all, and that if this is the case, then neither positive nor negative actions, nor even the Buddha himself, exist."

GESHE-LA'S ANSWER: "Yes, for the Chittamatrins, composite phenomena, the 'external' phenomena and the mind, all have the same type of true existence because they arise from causes and conditions."

The supporters of both Madhyamaka schools maintain that phenomena do not exist truly. The Svatantrikas, however, state that phenomena have some sort of natural existence by way of their own characteristics, and this view is shared also by the Chittamatrins. The Prasangikas, however, maintain that phenomena do not exist intrinsically, truly, by their own characteristics, or by their own nature. All these terms have equal meaning for the Prasangikas, just as non-true existence, non-intrinsic existence, and so forth, are synonymous with emptiness and lack of self.

The Svatantrikas understand emptiness to be the non-true existence of phenomena. They accept that on an ultimate level phenomena do not exist truly, but they do not deny that phenomena exist conventionally by their own characteristics.

Both the Chittamatrins and the Svatantrikas believe that if phenomena did not have some sort of natural existence, if they did not exist by their own characteristics, they would not exist at all, and there could not be cause and effect, the four noble truths, and so forth. The Prasangikas maintain the opposite: "If phenomena exist truly and are not empty or devoid of natural existence, for precisely that reason there cannot be cause and effect, the four noble truths, and so forth."

It is difficult to understand all of this in minute detail, but at the very least we should try to understand the main reasons that one school asserts a certain mode of existence and establishes reality in a different way. We must also observe our own way of thinking, read texts, and discuss our ideas with others, and in this way deepen our understanding. It is difficult to understand all of this deeply, but at the beginning it is enough to have even just a superficial, coarse idea, and then gradually progress.

Until we acquire an understanding of emptiness we will not be able to eliminate the mental afflictions, and until we are able to block the disturbing mind, we will not be able to avoid experiencing suffering.

Mental afflictions cannot die or be destroyed by an air raid, but only by the wisdom that perceives the ultimate nature. No matter how many difficulties we might face, we should nevertheless try to achieve the understanding of the ultimate nature of phenomena, because buddhas and bodhisattvas have also realized emptiness through striving and perseverance, and not by sleeping.

QUESTION: Why do the Chittamatrins use the example of dreams in order to state that the mind exists truly and that objects do not exist externally? ANSWER: For them the mind exists truly because it arises from causes, and objects do not exist externally because they are like phenomena appearing in a dream. They appear to be external to us, but they are of the same substantial entity as the mind. While dreaming, are the objects that appear to you external or internal?

Just as the object of the dream is of the same substantial entity as the mind, so, for the Chittamatrins, what we see as an external object is of the same substantial entity as the mind. The fact that you can perceive objects is due to mental energy, to the power of the mind. In tantra too, when you visualize the mandala and the deities, these appear as external objects, but in fact they are only manifestations of your own mind.

When you watch a film projected onto a white cloth, even though it seems that there is something on the cloth, the image actually comes from the projector. If the projector stops, the images also vanish and no longer appear. To believe that the mind is like a projector, that there are no external phenomena but only mind, is the Chittamatrins' position, but in fact this is not the case: the Prasangikas accept external objects.

Establishing as the Path the Knowledge
That Ultimate Truths Are Emptinesses

Among the four Buddhist philosophical schools, the two Hinayana
schools maintain that in order to attain nirvana it is not necessary to realize the emptiness of phenomena; it is enough to realize the four noble
truths. These two schools do not accept the selflessness phenomena, only
the selflessness of persons.

Unlike the Vaibhashikas and Sautrantikas, the Madhyamikas state
that without comprehending the empty nature of the true existence of
phenomena, the final aim of Mahayana or Hinayana nirvana cannot be
attained. The Prasangikas maintain that this is written in the Mahayana
scriptures, in which it is stated that one who possesses the view of phenomena as being truly existent cannot understand or see the truth, or
realize awakening. Furthermore, in order to attain liberation, a follower
of the Hinayana path must study and realize emptiness as explained in the
scriptures on the perfection of wisdom. [40]

The Prasangikas have the oral transmission of this teaching: the Buddha
explained emptiness to Manjushri, Manjushri explained it to Nagarjuna,
and Nagarjuna to other masters. As for the path of bodhichitta, the Buddha
expounded this to Maitreya, Maitreya to Asanga, and so on. It is understandable that Hinayana followers would not recognize these Mahayana
teachings as credible, since the Buddha transmitted them only to those who
were able to understand them. The Hinayana followers, not having ever
heard these teachings, are not familiar with them and consequently deny
that he gave these teachings at all.

Furthermore, only in the Mahayana teachings do we find explanations
on the four *kayas,* or bodies of a buddha, of which there is no mention in
the Hinayana school. Consequently, the followers of these schools do not
know or understand these either. At first, those who follow the Hinayana
may be unable to accept all of these teachings; nevertheless, the Prasangikas quote the related lineages, so that Hinayana followers may ascertain
their validity later on.

The reason that the Prasangikas provide these references to the
Mahayana sutras is twofold. On the one hand, they address the Hinayana
followers—they present the view of emptiness as an authentic teaching

of the Buddha in order to give Hinayana followers a point of reference for the future. On the other hand, they address their Mahayana interlocutors, the Chittamatrins and Svatantrika-Madhyamikas, offering them immediate proof of validity, since these schools already have a certain familiarity with the aforementioned Mahayana lineages.

The Buddha taught according to the various capabilities and inclinations of beings, as a good doctor prescribes medicines according to the nature of the patients' illnesses and does not prescribe the same medicine for everyone, claiming that it is the best cure. If someone is capable of practicing the Mahayana teachings, those teachings are given to that person; if someone is able to practice the Hinayana teachings, these teachings are given instead, regardless of the fact that the Mahayana teachings expound a deeper path and view.

If the Hinayana path is more suited to someone practicing the spiritual path, it is good for that person to follow it, because he or she will benefit more from it. Those who do not know their abilities and go in search of the most renowned and highest teaching will find it difficult later on to understand and practice it, and will soon grow tired.

Tantra is a powerful path that can make the attainment of buddhahood possible within one lifetime, but before practicing it, it is necessary to generate renunciation for samsara, as well as bodhichitta and the understanding of emptiness, and be steadfast in these practices, which are the three principal aspects of the path. If a practitioner has the prerequisite of a mind thus trained, it will then be possible for that person to attain enlightenment even within a single lifetime.

At present, in countries such as Thailand, Sri Lanka, and Burma, the Mahayana teachings, and of course the tantric teachings also, are not accepted as authentic teachings of the Buddha. But in fact these teachings are a body of the Buddha's teachings that the Tibetans received from Indian masters through an uninterrupted lineage, and have preserved in purity to this day.

Many erroneously think that Buddhist tantra derives from or has been influenced by Hindu tantra, because they maintain that the Buddha did not expound the tantric path at all. This is completely false.

In order to refute erroneous conceptions, the Prasangikas ask the Vaibhashikas and Sautrantikas, "How can you establish that the teachings that you accept are teachings of the Buddha, and that the Mahayana teachings are not?" The Vaibhashikas and the Sautrantikas reply that their scriptures are trustworthy because they have been established as words of the Buddha by both Hinayana and Mahayana followers.

The Prasangikas object that the same people who dispute that the Mahayana sutras are the teachings of the Buddha accept the Hinayana sutras as his authentic words simply because they know them. [41]

When those people were born, they held no opinion with regard to the Hinayana sutras; only later, having received teachings on them from the masters, did they begin to understand them, find them relevant, and therefore consider them to be the words of the Buddha. Now, all these reasons that we apply to the Hinayana sutras we can also apply to the Mahayana sutras!

When we hear that all conditioned phenomena are impermanent and that impure phenomena, produced by karma and mental afflictions, are in the nature of suffering, we can reflect and easily realize that this is true and that these teachings are valid. Likewise, if we have the patience to listen to and reflect upon the Mahayana teachings as well, we can verify their validity and thereby establish that they have been expounded by the Buddha.

The Prasangikas continue, "If you say that the Hinayana sutras are the words of the Buddha because they are accepted as such by both of us, as well as by many others, then the Vedas and other non-Buddhist scriptures are also true, because they are accepted by many people." [42]

In fact, it is illogical to believe that something is true simply because it is accepted as such by many people.

Another reason the Hinayana followers maintain that the Mahayana sutras cannot be the words of the Buddha is that there are those who dispute them. But this too is illogical, since the Hinayana scriptures are themselves disputed by some Buddhists and non-Buddhists alike. There are some schools within the Hinayana tradition that dispute certain sutras, and furthermore there are some who even criticize the teachings of the Buddha and do not consider them perfect. According to that logic, one should not believe in any Buddhist sutra, since they are all disputed and refuted by someone else. [43]

Lesser schools maintain that their sutras alone are the word of the Buddha, arguing that these sutras mention the three higher trainings of morality, concentration, and wisdom. "But this must then hold true for our scriptures also," reply the Prasangikas, "and since they too contain the three higher trainings, you should accept them."

The Prasangikas state, "You say that after the Buddha entered the state beyond suffering, the arhat monks became the lineage holders of his teachings and are responsible for their propagation. Furthermore, you consider arhats to be the root for establishing the presence of Shakyamuni Buddha's teachings. But if, as you say, they have not comprehended that all phenomena are empty of true existence, if they still grasp at true existence, it would be truly difficult to say that they are *arhats,* or those who have freed themselves from cyclic existence." [44]

To this objection the Hinayana followers reply that in order to realize nirvana or liberation from cyclic existence, it is enough to meditate on the sixteen aspects of the four noble truths, such as impermanence and so forth, and that it is not necessary to realize emptiness as stated by the Prasangikas. They maintain that liberation is attained by realizing the selflessness of persons—that is, by realizing that persons are devoid of that self that appears on the basis of the five aggregates and is thought of as self-sufficient and substantially existing. [45]

The Prasangikas object, "By realizing the lack of self-sufficient existence of the self of the person, it is possible to neutralize and subdue only the coarse mental afflictions, but not to eliminate every affliction from its root. According to you, nirvana can be attained by simply neutralizing the mental afflictions that are manifest. This is not true, because these practitioners you call arhats will still grasp at the self of phenomena, even if they have eliminated grasping at a self-supporting self of the person, and on this basis they will generate karma, which will not allow them to free themselves from samsara. [46]

The Hinayana followers say that the arhats have realized the sixteen aspects of the four noble truths, and that they have therefore eliminated the mental afflictions, including greed, which is the main reason for rebirth in cyclic existence, and consequently are no longer forced to be reborn.

But these so-called arhats will still take on a new birth in samsara because the causal condition of having sensations associated with the perception of true existence is still present, and this will produce attachment. [47]

In other words, the Hinayana followers state that the basis on which to establish the teachings of the Buddha is what they call *arhats,* but they do

not understand what it means to be an arhat according to the Prasangikas'
philosophical view. According to the Prasangikas, the arhats have actually
eliminated all mental afflictions, and therefore have also eliminated the mind
that grasps at true existence, and have thus attained complete cessation.

According to the Abhidharma, two types of confusion, or ignorance,
are described: the ignorance that arises due to disturbing conceptions,
which is a mental affliction, and the ignorance that is not a mental affliction but instead an obstruction to knowledge. Hinayana followers accept
both, and for this reason the Prasangikas say to them, "You accept the two
types of confusion, but you should also accept the two types of attachment
or greed: the attachment that arises in dependence on grasping at the
self-sufficient, substantially existent self of persons, and the attachment
that arises in dependence on considering persons and phenomena to be
truly existent."

The point is that there are two definitions for two different categories
of mental afflictions—one is given in the texts common in the Hinayana
school, whereas the other is present only in Mahayana texts and refers to
the subtle mental afflictions that derive from grasping at true existence.

The attachment that arises in dependence on grasping at the self-
sufficient, substantially existent self of persons is coarse attachment, and is
mentioned in the Abhidharma. The attachment that arises in dependence
on grasping at the truly existent self of persons and phenomena is subtle
attachment, and is described only in the Mahayana texts.

Since the Hinayana followers do not know of the existence of subtle mental afflictions of this kind, they have no antidotes to eliminate
them. This point is explained in the *Madhyamakavatara* by Chandrakirti
through the following analogy. Let us suppose that a person is afraid of
snakes and thinks that there is a snake in his house. If someone tells him
that there are no snakes, since he has not seen any, his fear will disappear.
If, however, the person tells him instead that there are no elephants to be
found in that place, it will be no help whatsoever in dissipating his fear!

Likewise, the logic applied by the Hinayana followers is incapable of
destroying, and is not an antidote to, the conception of true existence,
because it is directed only at eliminating the conception of self-sufficient
existence. The statement that there is no self-sufficient existence of the self
(equal to saying that there is no elephant in the house) cannot be an antidote

to grasping at the true existence of the self (equal to the snake), and therefore does not allow for the realization of emptiness.

As it is said in the *Guru Puja,* we do not desire even the smallest suffering and we are never satisfied with the happiness we have. These attitudes are present both in our minds and in the minds of others. We can therefore pray that all beings may attain all the happiness they desire. Although we do not desire the smallest suffering, we suffer continuously; this suffering does not arise from nowhere but from specific causes, which in turn derive from mental afflictions, which themselves derive from the ignorance that grasps at the true existence of phenomena.

We can eliminate this ignorance by comprehending that the object of its grasping is erroneous. When we understand the correct mode of existence of phenomena and are able to differentiate what is authentic from what is not, we will then be able to eliminate the ignorance that grasps at an erroneous way of seeing things.

There is no way to eliminate the root of the mental afflictions without understanding the real nature of all phenomena.

Once we possess this wisdom, all mental afflictions will finally be eradicated and will not arise again in the future under any circumstances. If, on the other hand, we only subdue the manifest afflictions, they will arise again whenever favorable circumstances present themselves. So, in order to be free from samsara and thus put an end to all suffering, realizing the non-true existence of all phenomena is indispensable. [48]

Hinayana followers maintain that, in order to attain the state of an arhat, it is enough to meditate and realize the sixteen aspects of the four noble truths, and that once this is done, the practitioner experiences sensations of pure happiness.

The Prasangikas reply, "Since the Buddha himself has said that in order to be free from samsara and attain both the Hinayana nirvana and buddhahood it is necessary to realize the emptiness of true existence, how can you Hinayana followers maintain that there are arhats who have freed themselves by simply meditating on the lack of existence of a coarse self? Without having developed the wisdom that perceives the non-true existence of phenomena, those experiences of happiness are still impure, and will therefore generate attachment."

The Prasangikas are not saying that the Hinayana arhats have not abandoned mental afflictions. Their objection is raised because, according to the Hinayana practitioners, arhats do not need to realize the non-true existence of phenomena in order to attain nirvana. If this were the case, however, when they experienced a pleasurable sensation they would perceive it as truly existent, and, since this conception of true existence causes the grasping mind to arise and is the basis of all mental afflictions, the arhats would still have mental afflictions, whereas in fact they do not have them anymore.

In the end, the crucial question is, "How can we free ourselves from samsara?" The appropriate answer is, "Through the realization of the emptiness of the true existence of the self, and not only of its self-sufficient existence!"

It is therefore essential for us now to receive teachings on the correct mode of existence of the self, which must be differentiated into two categories—the *self of the person* and the *self of phenomena*.

When bodhisattvas realize emptiness, they acquire the state of aryas. Because they have developed great compassion for beings who are imprisoned in the suffering of cyclic existence, and since they are now free from any fear of the suffering of samsara and from any attachment to the happiness experienced within it, they dwell there for a long time, simply in order to benefit sentient beings. It is therefore very important to meditate on emptiness and understand its meaning. [52]

All criticism leveled at the view of the lack of intrinsic existence of phenomena is unacceptable, because it does not relate to the facts. On the contrary, without any doubt, meditation on emptiness is the antidote to the obscurations caused by the mental afflictions and to the obscurations to knowledge. [53]

Why then don't those who desire to attain buddhahood meditate on emptiness? [54]

Someone might reply that he does not want to because he is afraid. And in this case the Prasangikas reply, "One must not be afraid to meditate on emptiness, because the realization of emptiness pacifies suffering. [55] One could be afraid if any truly existent self was there, but since there is none, who is there to be frightening, and who to be afraid?" [56]

The Lack of True Existence of the Person's Self

GENERAL REFUTATION

The considerations that lead to the establishment of the non-true existence of the person's self are thus expounded in the stanzas of the root text.

> Teeth, hair, and nails are not the self; the self is not bones nor blood; it is neither mucus nor phlegm; nor is it lymph or pus. The self is not fat nor sweat; the lungs and liver also are not the self; neither are any of the other inner organs; nor is the self excrement or urine. Flesh and skin are not the self; warmth and energy winds are not the self; neither are bodily cavities the self; and at no instant are the six types of consciousness the self. [57–59]

This is because if one is searching for a truly existent self in the name that designates it or on its basis—the person it is attributed to—one does not find it. So, an intrinsically existing self does not exist, but the self does exist.

REFUTATION OF THE VIEWS PRESENTED BY SOME HINDU SCHOOLS WITH REGARD TO THE PERSON'S SELF

The school of the Samkhyas (the Enumerators) maintains that the self is consciousness, and that it is permanent. An objection is made that auditory consciousness that perceives sound, for example, cannot be permanent, because when its object—sound—ceases, its particular knower, or perceiving subject, must necessarily cease too.

The two non-Buddhist schools of the Vaisheshikas (Those Who Differentiate) and Naiyayika (Logicians) are considered together because, in spite of slight differences in some doctrinal principles, they share a similar philosophical view. They both maintain that the self is matter and that it is permanent. The Prasangikas' objection to this is that atoms are not the self because they do not possess the nature of mind. The Vaisheshikas and the Naiyayikas reply that the self is a very subtle energy that is able to experience when it comes in touch with a mind that is separate from it and can know objects.

The Prasangikas reply to the above statement by saying that a self knows only when encountering its specific referent. This means that before the self has come into contact with the object, it cannot know it, but it apprehends the object a moment later, when encountering it. Therefore, if the self of the first moment does not know the object, whereas the self of a moment later does, that self cannot be permanent, and is in fact impermanent. It is precisely because the self possesses a mind and is impermanent that it receives benefits and suffers changes.

The Vaisheshikas and the Naiyayikas continue to maintain that the self has no consciousness and that it is separate from the function of performing activities and producing effects. The Prasangikas reply that if their presentation of the self is true, then one could say that space is a self.

Their interlocutors then say that if the self were not permanent, the relation of cause and effect could not work. They state that the self must necessarily be permanent, because the self that accumulated the cause must be the same as the self experiencing the effect, and to this purpose they say, "Since as Buddhists you maintain that the self is impermanent, the self that accumulated the cause cannot be the same as the one experiencing its effect." [70]

To this objection the Prasangikas reply, "The self of a previous life accumulates karma, whereas the self of a later life experiences its effect. This is possible because the self of the past life and the self of the future life are two different states of the same continuum." They add, "One does not experience the effect when accumulating the cause, and does not accumulate its cause when experiencing its effect. We agree on this point, but what differentiates our view from yours is that you state that the self is permanent, whereas we say that the self is not truly existent, and that if it were permanent, it could neither perform the action nor experience its result, and therefore there is no basis for our debate." [71]

Also, those actions whose effect is experienced in the same lifetime cannot be established by stating that the accumulation of the cause and the ripening of the effect occur simultaneously, because even in this case karma must still be accumulated in a moment previous to the ripening of the effect. In any case, Buddhists state that the self is impermanent, although continuity exists between the person performing a deed and the person experiencing its effect. [72] Therefore, if we are looking for a permanent, truly existent self, either in its name or in the basis of its designation, we do not find it, in the same way that no essence is found in the trunk of a plantain tree. [73–74]

The state of buddhahood is characterized by perfect renunciation and by complete accumulation, a state in which all afflictions have been eliminated and all positive qualities have been accumulated. Given that we wish to attain this, we must embark on the path that leads us to it.

The best method to purify our minds is the wisdom that perceives the ultimate nature of all phenomena, their emptiness. Emptiness means that each phenomenon exists only as a designation made by a valid mind on a correct basis, and not objectively, from its own side.

It is difficult to comprehend the ultimate nature of phenomena; in fact, when we say that things do not exist truly or intrinsically, doubts or misunderstandings may arise, such as thinking that phenomena do not exist at all.

Since the Prasangika school states that phenomena do not exist truly, non-Buddhists ask, "If phenomena do not exist truly, then they do not exist at all, and therefore beings do not exist; what then is the object of compassion? And what is the point of generating it?"

The Prasangikas reply, "Although ultimately phenomena do not have intrinsic nature, and therefore do not exist truly, they do exist conventionally. Therefore sentient beings, objects of compassion, exist conventionally as a designation of the confused or ignorant mind." [75]

Non-Buddhists ask, "If sentient beings do not exist, who will attain buddhahood?"

Prasangikas reply, "If you try to argue about the existence of phenomena by saying that they do not exist, then we repeat that they do exist conventionally, because the conventional mind has logically designated sentient beings, and they are the objects of compassion, even though they are not truly existent."

We cannot reject the existence of the conventional mind in order to attain liberation from suffering. On the contrary, the conventional mind is compulsory to this process, because it performs the function of knowing what to accept and what to reject. Furthermore, in order to pacify the suffering of sentient beings completely, we cannot reject compassion. [76]

Even though it is possible that someone might not be able to overcome the obstacles to complete omniscience right away, they will nevertheless need to abandon grasping at the self. Pride and other disturbing emotions arise and grow because of our ignorance of the self, a mental affliction that must be abandoned.

Non-Buddhists object, "But there are no methods to reverse this confusion or ignorance!"

The Prasangikas reply, "There are indeed, since it can be eliminated. Its antidote is the wisdom developed through meditating on the lack of an intrinsic self." [77]

When this direct antidote is present, the erroneous conception vanishes; therefore the best thing to do is to familiarize ourselves with the meditation on the selflessness of persons and phenomena. The ultimate nature of phenomena is their non-true existence. Once we have acquired and realized this, the mind that grasps at true existence cannot arise again.

Up until now we have been reborn into conditioned existence because we have been unable to understand the authentic mode of the existence of phenomena. Shantideva, having meditated and attained realization of the lack of self of persons and phenomena, speaks about this in his text, and we too must strive to understand and meditate on the teachings we receive. We must study the texts that explain this subject and later on ask for further teachings, in order to improve our understanding even more.

Wisdom does not arise in our minds unaided, nor is it like dust that naturally accumulates in our homes—this is the reason we must strive as much as necessary to develop it.

Since the mind that grasps at true existence can be eliminated, all our mental afflictions can be abandoned and the causes of suffering can be thus eradicated. In time, by creating the appropriate causes, we can attain buddhahood.

Some non-Buddhist schools state that the self of the person is the mind, whereas the Buddhist schools state that this is not the case. Still others say that the self is a material substance, but this view too is negated by the Buddhists. The physical body and the mind are the bases on which we designate the self of persons, hence these bases cannot be the self. This self does not exist by its own nature, from the side of the basis itself, but is simply a nominal designation made on this basis.

If we see a striped rope at sunset we think it is a snake, but in fact there is no snake from the side of the object—we imagine it to be there and, because of this, generate fear. In the same way that we label "snake" on the basis of a folded rope, so we put the label "I" on the basis of body and mind. And in the same way that the snake does not exist objectively, so also the "I" does not exist objectively.

However, with regard to the designating mind there is a difference, because in the first case the mind is wrong, whereas in the second case it is valid. On the basis of the piece of rope, no snake exists, but on the basis of mind and body, a conventional "I" does exist. Since the designated "I" does exist, the person who lives in conditioned existence, practices the Dharma, and attains buddhahood exists also—whatever is done is done by the conventional "I."

If we are able to understand the lack of self of persons, it will be easier to understand the lack of self in phenomena as well.

The Lack of True Existence of the Self of Phenomena

As the *four noble truths* are found in both Mahayana and Hinayana texts, the same is true in the case of *thirty-seven branches in harmony with enlightenment*. These are as follows:

- the four close placements of mindfulness
- the four perfect abandonments
- the four legs of magical emanations
- the five powers (faith, enthusiasm, mindfulness, meditative stabilization, and wisdom)
- the five forces
- the seven branches of enlightenment
- the aryas' eight paths

In order to understand the lack of self of phenomena, we meditate on the four close placements of mindfulness. We will find the explanation of these four points by the Prasangikas later on in the text. The four are the close placement of mindfulness on the body, on feelings, on the mind, and on phenomena.

CLOSE PLACEMENT OF MINDFULNESS ON THE BODY

The feet and the calves are not the body; the thighs and the hips are not the body; the abdomen and the back are not the body; and neither are the chest or the arms. The ribs and the hands are not the body; the armpits and the shoulders are not the body; all inner organs are not the body; neither the head nor the neck are the body. Therefore, what truly existent body is there among these parts? [78–79]

If the body truly existed, since it has many parts, each individual part would be the body, and yet it is not possible for a part to be the whole. The doubt may then arise that the assemblage of limbs might be the body, but this is also not the body. The body is made up of the head, the trunk, the four limbs, and so forth. But if we look closely, the leg is not the body because it is only a limb, and so on. [80–81]

When we speak of one year, we are referring to the period of twelve months; therefore the first, second, or third month cannot be the year, because they are only parts of it. The parts of the year are twelve—the twelve months—but a month does not have twelve months as its parts, and therefore a month of the year is not the year. Since a month does not contain twelve months, it is not a year. A year is designated by the duration of twelve months.

As a part of the year cannot be the year itself, so a part of the body cannot be the body itself. When we look for the body among its various parts, we do not find it, but we also do not find a body separate from them. If we look for the body using analysis, not being satisfied with the fact that it exists conventionally as a mere designation of the mind, we will not find any body at all. This is why we say that the body does not exist truly or intrinsically, beyond a name given to its parts.

Some non-Buddhist schools say that there is a body beyond its parts, but the existence of this body is not possible, because if we take away its parts we do not find the body.

According to our philosophical system, the parts and the whole have the same nature. Some non-Buddhist schools say instead that the parts and the whole are of a different nature, and that the same applies to the body and the self. They consider the body to be impermanent, but the self permanent.

The Prasangikas ask the exponents of these schools, "Does the body exist as partially distributed among all of its parts, or is it entirely contained in each of its parts?" If their answer is that the body can be found equally distributed in each of its parts, then they are contradicting their own statement according to which the body is indivisible, without parts. If they say that a body can be found in each of its parts, then they will have to accept that there are as many bodies as there are parts. [82]

Therefore the body does not exist truly, but, because of the confusion with regard to its parts, a mind is generated that erroneously conceives of it as a truly existent body. The body, however, does not exist the way it is perceived by that mind. This is like when we see a pile of stones from afar and mistake them for a man because they are set up in a form similar to a man's. In the same way that a pile of stones resembles a man for as long as the causal conditions to mistake them for a man are assembled, so the hands and so forth appear as a truly existent body for as long as the causal conditions to mistake them for a body are present. [83–84]

However, we cannot say that there is a body distinct from its parts, as a bottle is distinct from the glass—the body cannot be distinct from its parts, even though it is not the parts.

And the parts of the body also do not exist truly, or intrinsically. Any phenomenon has its parts but is neither one with nor separate from them. This is why we say that phenomena do not exist truly. For example, we cannot say that the month and the year are the same. If they were, then when the month is finished, we should say that the year is over too. Since we designate the year on the basis of the months, if we take out a month, we can no longer have a year.

If it were possible to say that eleven months make a year, we could also say that ten months make a year, or eight, or seven, and so forth. The year cannot be separate from the months, nor the months from the year. We cannot find the truly existent year, because it is a mere designation based on the twelve months. Likewise, we call thirty days a month, and twenty-four hours a day—an hour is designated on the basis of sixty minutes, and a minute is designated on the basis of sixty seconds. In short, phenomena do not exist truly, precisely because they are mere nominal designations based on their parts.

If phenomena do not exist by their own nature, or truly, then how is it that they appear to have intrinsic existence? This is so because we have a confused mind that grasps at the existence of phenomena as if they were true. Our grasping at the true existence of the body arises because we have not understood the way in which it came to exist—that is, by the designation of a name to its parts. Without this mindfulness, we have the concept of a body existing intrinsically.

For example, when we see a scarecrow from afar in the middle of a field, we think it is a man because it has a head, two arms, and is wearing a shirt. A body is also designated on the basis of its parts, but we believe that on that basis it exists truly. When we see a body, because of the imprints in our minds that cause us to grasp at true existence, we project onto its image a kind of concrete existence, and therefore think that it actually exists in this way.

A buddha, although he perceives the body, does not see it as intrinsically existent, because he has eliminated the imprints of the mind that grasps at true existence. Arya bodhisattvas who have reached the eighth, ninth, and tenth bhumis, shravaka arhats, and pratyekabuddhas all perceive the appearance of true existence, but do not grasp at it. Arya bodhisattvas from the first to the seventh bhumi still have some grasping to true existence even though they nonetheless recognize it as only the mere appearance of this.

The body is designated as such in dependence on its parts; parts too are designated in dependence on their respective parts. The hand is a part of the body, and it exists in dependence on its own parts—fingers, joints, skin, and so forth. But if we are not satisfied with the fact that it exists as a designation and look more deeply, we will not find a hand. [85]

The hand is therefore a designation on the basis of the various parts that constitute it. Fingers are themselves a designation based on their various parts. For example, the phalanx is a designation based on its own parts, which in turn are designations of the subparts that constitute them and so forth down to the smallest atomic particles, which still depend on their eastern, western, northern, and southern parts. Even the smallest particles are devoid of intrinsic existence—everything is found to be as empty as space! [86]

Whoever is intelligent enough to understand the authentic mode of existence of phenomena, and of the body in particular, can no longer have attachment to what does not exist intrinsically, or by its own nature. This illusory body is like a body appearing in a dream, so how can one be attached to it?

In order to eliminate the coarse aspect of attachment to the body, one can meditate on its impurities, but in order to eliminate attachment completely, even subtle attachment, it is necessary to meditate on its emptiness.

Meditation on the lack of intrinsic existence of the body is what is known as the close placement of mindfulness on the body. At times we generate attachment to the body because we see it and consider it healthy, strong, and beautiful; to meditate on its impermanent nature, reflecting on the fact that its strength and beauty will not last long because it is subject to continuous change, is also known as the close placement of mindfulness on the body. *Close placement of mindfulness* means keeping our minds constantly tied to the chosen object.

Since a body endowed with intrinsic nature does not exist, we cannot differentiate between a truly existent female body and a truly existent male body. [87] And given that the body does not exist naturally or intrinsically, how can a person exist naturally or intrinsically? A naturally existing male person does not exist, nor does a naturally existing female person, and therefore no naturally existing person exists.

CLOSE PLACEMENT OF MINDFULNESS ON THE FEELINGS

Feelings are also not truly existent, because if they were, they would be permanent. A feeling of joy would last forever and the same would apply to an unpleasant feeling. In reality, feelings change and are not permanent, and this demonstrates their non-true existence, or lack of intrinsic existence.

If feelings were truly existent, each time we experienced a feeling of suffering or mental unhappiness, we would not be able to experience pleasant feelings anymore, and vice versa. The feeling of suffering does not exist intrinsically and neither does the feeling of happiness, because one can arise when the other ceases.

When we enjoy good food, we experience a feeling of pleasure in the taste, but if this feeling of pleasure were truly or intrinsically existent, each time we ate that very same food we would experience an identical feeling of pleasure. In reality this is not so, as in the case of a person whose father has just died and does not enjoy eating good food as he normally does.

If the feeling of pleasure existed naturally or intrinsically, it would exist forever, whereas as soon as a feeling of suffering arises, the feeling of pleasure ceases. [88]

On the other hand, it is also unacceptable to think that nevertheless some subtle feeling of pleasure is present. Some maintain that such a feeling of pleasure exists naturally or intrinsically, that it is there even when a feeling of pain arises—the pleasure is simply overshadowed in that moment and thus cannot be experienced. How is it possible to maintain such an argument? If we accept this, we should also accept a category of feeling that is not experienced, which is impossible. Therefore the Madhyamikas object, "If something is devoid of the defining characteristic of a feeling—namely, experience—how can it be a feeling?" [89]

The other schools reply, "They are feelings because an experience, however subtle, is there. For example, only coarse aspects of suffering are dispelled by a strong pleasure, and in this case a slight pain remains, whose nature is a weak feeling of pleasure, distinct from the coarse sensations of pleasure." [90]

The Madhyamikas object, "But this subtle experience cannot possibly be a form of suffering, because you now say it is a form of pleasure." [91]

If that person whose father has just died and who experiences a strong feeling of pain eats good food, at times his experience of suffering will be neutralized, and at other times it will not. If, for example, he has been offered *momos* (Tibetan dumplings), then these could somehow hinder his feeling of pain and engender a feeling of pleasure. Therefore, food may or may not act as an antidote to an experience of pain, and may or may not act as a condition for a pleasant experience. The same person can experience pleasure or no pleasure at all eating momos, according to the conditions. If momos produced an intrinsically existent delicious flavor, then pleasure should arise at any moment or in any circumstances in which one eats them. But when we are angry, for example, even exquisite food cannot give us pleasure.

The reason that the same food at times gives pleasure to some, while at other times or to someone else it does not, is that the "pleasant" characteristic associated with its flavor does not exist intrinsically. Another example is the fact that some people like black coffee while others do not.

Feeling too is therefore a designation made by the conceptual mind, and does not exist intrinsically. The mind that grasps at feelings as being intrinsically existent generates attachment, and for this reason we must meditate on the lack of intrinsic existence of feelings and acquire the yogis' understanding of the way in which all phenomena exist, supporting this with the nourishment of meditative absorption that arises from unifying calm abiding with superior view. [92]

We depend on food for the sustenance of our physical body and likewise, in order to develop the capabilities of a yogi, we depend on the meditation of *shamata* and *vipashyana*.

The ignorant mind that grasps at the true existence of feelings engenders desire and other mental afflictions, which in turn produce suffering. Therefore, in order to eliminate afflictions, we should meditate in this way and acquire the profound understanding of the non-intrinsic existence of feelings. This will serve as an antidote to conceiving of them as truly existent.

REFUTING THE TRUE EXISTENCE OF CONTACT

The perception of a blue object depends on three factors: the object, the consciousness perceiving it, and the organ of seeing. The substance of the blue object is in the object itself, whereas the perceiver of the blue object is found in our bodies. For the Chittamatrins there are no objective, substantial entities external to the experiencing mind, whereas the Prasangikas accept the external existence of objects.

Now, some could ask, "Does perception (for example, the perception of the color blue) depend on the contact between the object and the sense organ? Furthermore, is there space between the atoms of the object (visual forms) and the atoms of the seeing organ?" It is in reply to this question that the Madhyamikas present their reflections by which they specifically refute those who maintain the true existence of atomic particles devoid of parts.

If there is space, there is no possibility of contact between two phenomena; if there is no space, then they would be one. But if they were one, we could not speak of contact, because that implies the meeting of two phenomena. We could not say that two distinct atoms are one, because in fact they are two. If two atoms join, the volume increases; if two people are together, their total weight will be the sum of their individual weights. When two atoms come into contact, there is a change of weight and space, and we cannot ascertain whether one can completely melt into the other without any changes occurring. Since the two atoms are not completely absorbed but nevertheless meet, this means that a part of each of the two atoms is in contact, but not the other parts. For this reason we cannot state that atoms are devoid of parts and indivisible. [93–95]

Even the smallest atoms have particles, since they have eastern, western, northern, and southern sides. We are talking about particles of various dimensions—our sense organs can perceive the large ones, but not those that are infinitesimally small.

So far we have discussed the impossibility of an intrinsically existent contact between the atoms of sense organs and the atoms of objects. We have analyzed the body in an increasingly specific way, from its coarsest parts to its smallest atomic particles, but we have not succeeded in finding something truly existent in any of these parts.

Now we find stated the impossibility of establishing a contact, or relation by its own nature, between the mind and the external object. Since consciousness is devoid of atoms, form, or matter, it cannot come into true contact with what has no form. [96]

Furthermore, the same consciousnesses, if analyzed, cannot be found or established as truly and naturally existent.

The contact we are talking about is the same that is explained in the chain of the twelve links of dependent arising, and it is the link that generates feelings.

Since a true contact does not exist, how can true feeling exist? It is possible to produce a non-truly existent effect from a non-truly existent cause, but we cannot have a truly existent effect from a non-truly existent cause.

Doubt may arise again: If the contact is not truly existent, then its effects—feelings—are also non-truly existent and do not exist at all; why then should we strive to acquire pleasant feelings and avoid painful ones? But, once again, what is denied here is the intrinsic existence of both pleasure and pain. [97]

If the meeting of object, sense faculty, and consciousness does not exist truly, how can feeling truly exist? If the meeting between the above three elements does not exist intrinsically, neither do the feelings of happiness and suffering exist intrinsically, or naturally.

Meditating on this, we will no longer have attachment to feelings of happiness or revulsion for feelings of suffering, having understood that they are not intrinsically existent. Continuing to familiarize ourselves with this view, we will free ourselves from samsara. [98]

Mental consciousness is a mere knower that apprehends and experiences and does not enter into true, intrinsic contact with material objects.

Since all sense objects, forms, sounds, and so forth are devoid of true existence, even though they appear to possess it, their nature is like a dream or an illusion. Consequently, the mind that experiences them, that has feelings, is also devoid of true existence. If the subjective mind were truly existent, then feelings could never be experienced by the mind that is generated simultaneously with them and that is said to be the experiencer, because such a mind could not have any relation with its object. [99]

The aim of meditating on the non-true existence of feelings is to understand that object, feeling, and the consciousness that experiences feelings do not truly exist. In this way we eliminate the cause of conditioned existence. If we are able to understand the non-true existence of feelings, we will no longer generate attachment toward pleasant ones and, by not having attachment, we will no longer be tied to cyclic existence. At present we crave the experience of pleasant feelings because we grasp at their true existence, but instead we should strive to perceive everything we see and hear as a dream!

For every feeling, the consciousness that experiences that feeling simultaneously arises, and this consciousness is of a different nature than the sensation and is unable to perceive it truly. Therefore the next moment within the same continuum of consciousness can only remember that feeling, not perceive it. Furthermore, according to the same logical argument already used to refute the existence of the self-perceiver, the feeling cannot perceive or experience itself. [100]

Besides, if there were a truly existent consciousness separate from feelings, it could not experience them, inasmuch as they are different phenomena.

Since the feeling does not exist truly, the object related to the feeling also does not exist truly, nor does the person experiencing it. [101]

Among the five aggregates, feeling is the one conventionally said to determine an effect of experience in the person who is designated on its basis, but this is neither a truly positive effect, nor a truly negative one. We should therefore practice the close placement of consciousness on the feelings, apprehending them as non-truly existent.

If feelings were truly existent, we would experience them all the time, without change. Instead, precisely because they are not "true," we sometimes have feelings of pleasure, and other times feelings of suffering. Buddhas and arhats experience pleasurable feelings, but because they do not apprehend them as truly existent, they are not attached to them. Whereas we, whenever we experience pleasurable feelings, grasp at the concept of their true existence, and therefore generate the desire to repeat them because we do not understand their authentic nature, their emptiness. If we are not constantly aware of the non-true nature of feelings, we cannot eliminate attachment for pleasurable feelings or aversion for non-pleasurable feelings.

The subject discussed here is particularly difficult—both for me, who is explaining it, and for you, who are listening. We are nevertheless making an effort, and will succeed in the end in acquiring some understanding. In order to develop the wisdom that realizes the authentic mode of existence of phenomena, we cannot neglect study and reflection on their nature. This is the only way to attain liberation and buddhahood—these cannot be achieved by any other means, neither by airplane nor spaceship. Even just thinking that the text of the *Bodhicharyavatara* contains something useful to understand contributes to the elimination of our ignorance. And merely by listening to the teachings on the emptiness of the true existence of phenomena, even if we do not believe in this reality, can help us to dispel the ignorance that perceives the true existence of phenomena. Although we might not be able to study the great treatises that explain emptiness, nevertheless it can be useful simply to understand that objects do not exist from their own side.

Aryadeva has said that samsaric existence is like the tip of a needle—there is no possibility of happiness in such a condition. As long as we are not able to free ourselves from this physical form and this type of mind, which are both acquired through karma and mental afflictions, there is no chance of escaping suffering. The bodies we now have work as the basis for all types of suffering, and will also cause us suffering in the future, because in order to satisfy their needs and desires we accumulate much negative karma.

The texts explain that even if we are reborn as gods—with nothing but favorable conditions, with lives full of pleasures and bodies of light—at a certain point we will have to abandon that domain and be reborn into the lower realms. One of the disadvantages of cyclic existence is that, despite obtaining good social conditions, when that positive karma exhausts itself, we fall back into lowly conditions, and others will mistreat us. Although we may now enjoy wealth and jewels, at some point we will have to leave it all behind. What we have at present is borrowed, because sooner or later we have to return it. Although we might possess beauty, it will fade fast, just like a flower in autumn. Everything we find in samsaric existence is in the nature of suffering, and everything we regard as happiness or pleasure is in the nature of impermanence, and therefore cannot be depended upon.

Following this understanding, and given that our life is as ephemeral as lightning in the sky, we must try to attain liberation from conditioned existence. If this is what we desire, it is possible to accomplish it.

All impermanent phenomena exist in dependence on causes and conditions; no phenomenon exists independently. If we understand this, the mind that sees or conceives of phenomena as truly existent will be eliminated. With the realization of the emptiness of phenomena, conditioned existence is dissolved.

The Hinayana arhats, having attained the cessation of all suffering and therefore of conditioned existence, dwell in a state of individual bliss. But if someone is endowed with love and great compassion for all beings, he will not have any desire to attain liberation only for himself. One of the texts on mental training reads, "If all beings who have been our mother are now suffering, what is the point of seeking only one's own happiness?" So, desiring to be of benefit to others, we must reach the state that will allow us to help all beings equally, the state of buddhahood.

CLOSE PLACEMENT OF MINDFULNESS ON THE MIND

Mind, mental consciousness, and consciousness are synonyms. There are six main consciousnesses (visual, hearing, smelling, taste, tactile, and mental), six sense faculties or sense powers (of eye, ear, nose, tongue, body, and mind), and six objects (visual forms, sounds, smells, flavors, tangible objects, and objects of the mind).

Visual consciousness cannot be generated independently of the sense faculty of the eye and of its object, a visual form.

A truly or intrinsically existent consciousness does not exist, because we cannot find it either in the object, the sense faculty, or between them. Neither is there a truly existent consciousness inside or outside the body. [102]

There is no truly existent single aspect or function of mind. The mind, having emptiness as its ultimate nature, abides in the state of natural nirvana. [103]

If we look for the mind analytically, inside or outside the body, or within the visual faculty, and so on, we will not find it, because a truly existent mind does not exist. If mental consciousness existed intrinsically, or independently, we would be able to find it, but the fact that we are unable to do so is already proof that it does not exist in that fashion.

Realizing that the mind does not exist truly, attachment to a truly existent mind disappears. If we have a high opinion of someone, we cannot simultaneously hold a low one, and vice versa. Likewise, when we are able to realize the non-true existence of mental consciousness, the mind that grasps at true existence can no longer abide within us.

This natural characteristic of phenomena—and in particular, of the mind (i.e., its emptiness)—is the reason that liberation and buddhahood are attainable. It is this very non-true existence of the mind that we call the "lineage of the Buddha" or buddha nature, because it allows us to transform the ordinary mind, stained by temporary mental afflictions, into the omniscient mind of a buddha, in the same way that a prince, the son of a king, possesses the potential to become a king himself.

Mental consciousness is therefore not in the body, nor does it exist as intrinsically separate from the body. Even if we say that mind does not truly exist, we are not denying its existence. There is a mind, and this physical body acts because of its presence. And there is a good mind and a bad mind. It is one thing to say that there is no mind, and quite another to say that there is no truly existent mind. We say that mental consciousness exists, but not a truly existent mental consciousness.

The five sense consciousnesses are also established as devoid of intrinsic existence. If this were not so, we would encounter numerous contradictions. Actually, if a sense consciousness existed independently of any cause and condition, it would exist before, simultaneously with, and subsequently to its object. Now, if perceptions were there before its object, what object would it be conscious of, given that without a referent a sense consciousness cannot arise? However, if they were simultaneous, the consciousness could not arise from the object. [104]

For a perception or a particular experience to be present, the object of mental consciousness must exist before the mind that perceives it. This process is not unlike what occurs when we come to a Dharma center—first we see the building from the outside, then we come inside.

Perceiving consciousness arises from three factors—an object of perception, the sense faculty, and the immediately preceding moment of consciousness. Given that perceiving consciousness arises from these, we cannot say that it is independent and exists truly, because if it did, it would not depend on anything.

The Madhyamikas' statements deny the true existence of the mind but not its existence; the mind actually does exist and performs the function of knowing.

CLOSE PLACEMENT OF MINDFULNESS ON PHENOMENA

By means of the above reasoning we come to understand that all phenomena, being conditioned, do not arise independently or intrinsically, and therefore do not truly exist. [105]

The objection that the other schools now raise is that if all phenomena are not intrinsically generated, then the two truths (conventional and ultimate), as they are explained by the Prasangikas, do not correspond with reality. If conventional phenomena exist solely in dependence on a nominal designation by an erroneous mind (like the snake that is designated on the basis of an entangled rope), it should follow that the two truths and sentient beings are false and that their conventional existence is no longer possible. Therefore they ask, "How can the two truths exist? And how can beings attain nirvana and enlightenment?" [106]

The Prasangikas explain that there is no contradiction. Maintaining the conventional existence of phenomena means establishing their existence solely in dependence on the name attributed to them according to the conventions recognized by the world. According to the Prasangikas' system, existing conventionally does not mean that things are designated by an erroneous conception begetting a false type of existence. On the contrary, all conventional truths are designations made by a valid mind on a valid basis. The conventional existence of phenomena is not a mere creation of the ignorant mind—conventional phenomena, although not truly existent, nevertheless perform a function and produce effects. There is a deed, one who performs the deed, and a result, even though none of these three exist intrinsically. [107]

Also, subjective perception, perceived object, and nominal designation are all established in a mutually dependent way, none of them having any form of intrinsic existence.

The existence of a phenomenon is established in dependence on other phenomena. Visual consciousness is established on the basis of a form, the visual organ, and an instant of consciousness immediately preceding it. An object is established on the basis of the consciousness perceiving it—the knower and the known can only be established mutually. Hence all conventional phenomena can be established as existent by means of logical reasoning of dependent relation. For example, whether something is good or not depends on how it is considered or seen; therefore it exists relatively and is neither good nor not good in itself. [108]

When we understand that an object does not exist by its own nature, we can also understand how the mind, that which knows the object, does not exist intrinsically.

A further objection to the Prasangikas is raised by the other schools: "When the analytical mind reaches the conclusion that all phenomena are devoid of true existence, that analytical mind is not able to realize itself as being devoid of true existence. In this case, must there be another analytical mind that realizes that the previous analytical mind is not truly existent, or not? If there is not such a mind, then the initial analytical mind must be truly existent, which would invalidate your doctrinal system. If there is, then the subsequent analytical mind should in turn be analyzed by another mind, and hence the basic object of analysis would never be attained." [109]

The Prasangikas reply, "When the object of analysis has been perfectly analyzed and established to be empty, there will be no need to investigate the analytical mind in order to establish its non-true existence. When we are able to establish the non-true existence of a phenomenon, we are also able to understand the non-true existence of the mind that has ascertained it." [110]

It is difficult to understand the non-true existence of phenomena, and this is why many objections arise. If there were no answers, one could not demonstrate or establish non-true existence, but it can be explained, since there are answers to all the objections.

Given that the non-true existence of phenomena is a fact and not an erroneous concept, it cannot be denied, and it can be known and realized, thus eliminating the mind that grasps at true existence and achieving buddhahood as a result. It is therefore important to study emptiness, and even though we may not be able to realize it in the short term, we will eventually succeed by means of arguments that support this profound view. Even our mere leaning toward it helps us in our study and analysis, and becomes the foundation of a sound practice.

At present the concept of a truly existent "I" is due to our acquired familiarity with it. Inasmuch as we believe in, and grasp at, the concrete existence of an "I," we create a separation between ourselves and others, and nurture attachment toward ourselves and the things we possess, and aversion toward enemies and the things we do not like. Because of these mental afflictions, all the other disturbing emotions, which are the cause of conditioned existence, arise, and we must consequently experience suffering and all the related problems and discomforts.

We must therefore eliminate the cause of samsara, the ignorance that grasps at the truly existent "I." There is a prayer that says, "May I abandon this cycle of choiceless rebirths and put an end to all suffering." And a stanza from a lamrim text reads, "As a result of studying the texts, may we be able to practice the Dharma correctly, so as to be free from the prison of cyclic existence."

Refuting the True Existence of Subject and Object

According to the Madhyamaka school, phenomena do not exist truly or intrinsically. All other schools, Buddhist and non-Buddhist, though they may mean different things by it, maintain that both the object and the perceiving consciousness are truly existent, and as proof state that the true existence of the object is established on the basis of the true existence of the perceiving consciousness. They believe that the true existence of phenomena is demonstrated in this way, but, according to the Madhyamikas, this type of argument does not prove the true existence of objects. [III]

The other schools defend their view by saying that consciousness can be established as truly existent because it is conscious of the true existence of objects. The Madhyamikas reply that there is no valid perception that is able to prove the mind's true existence. Earlier in the text, the Chittamatrins proposed the existence of the self-cognizing mind as the best proof of the true existence of the mind, but this has already been refuted.

For the Madhyamikas there is no proof that can establish the mind's true existence, nor are there any valid reasons that demonstrate the true existence of objects of knowledge. They state that the existence of something can be explained only in relation to something else, whereas if a phenomenon existed truly, intrinsically, it would not need any support. Object and subject (consciousness) exist on the basis of mutual dependence. The existence of the object depends on the existence of the consciousness that apprehends it, and the existence of the cognizing consciousness depends on the object it apprehends. It follows that neither consciousness nor the object exist independently. [112]

All objects of knowledge exist only by means of relation or dependence. For example, we say that an object is short only in relation to a longer one; we consider a place to be distant because we relate it to a place that is nearer, and when we speak of an even more distant place, what we earlier defined as distant becomes close. Every phenomenon therefore exists in dependence on another. A man can be called a father only in relation to his son, and the son can be called thus only in relation to his father. As long as a man does not have a son, he will not be called a father. If a father were truly existent, he would have been a father since birth. If there is no father, there is also no son, and therefore father and son are interdependent and do not exist intrinsically.

Likewise, a mind exists only in dependence upon a perceived object, and an object exists only because there is a mind that perceives it. [113]

If something did indeed truly exist, it would have to exist independently from any other phenomenon.

Establishing Emptinesses from the Viewpoint of Causes

There are various arguments that refute the intrinsic existence of phenomena, and I will now try to expound them.

The first incorrect statement on the subject comes from the Charvakas (Nihilists). They maintain that all phenomena arise independently of causes. This is refuted by the argument that no composite phenomenon can arise without causes. The Charvakas maintain this philosophical view because their scriptures state that the beauty of a peacock's feathers, the sharpness of thorns, the softness of flowers' petals, and so forth do not have a cause that generated them, but exist by their own nature.

Such a statement is unacceptable, because through direct perception we can verify that effects are produced by causes. There is no harvest in summer without having sown seeds in the autumn, and the softness of flowers' petals, the roundness of peas, the sharpness of thorns are also produced by specific causes. [116]

The variety of effects is due to the variety of causes. The reason that composite phenomena have causes can be identified by the fact that they arise intermittently. Each time appropriate causes and conditions meet, a specific phenomenon is produced; when they do not meet, or are not sufficient, that particular phenomenon does not arise. [117]

Among the various non-Buddhist philosophical schools, such as the Hindu Naiyayika, Samkhya, and Charvaka schools, it is said that the latter hold the most harmful view because they do not accept rebirth and the relationship of cause and effect, and they maintain that phenomena arise without causes. If their view were correct, it would not be necessary to cultivate soil and plant seeds in the autumn, since a harvest would arise regardless, without effort. Furthermore, it would not be necessary to work in order to survive, nor would we feel hungry when we have not eaten, nor thirsty when we have not had anything to drink.

The purpose of acquainting ourselves with the views of other schools is that we too have confused ideas about phenomena in general, and about their true existence in particular. Therefore, it is crucial for us to try to understand others' beliefs and the arguments by which they can be refuted.

If we believe in the law of cause and effect and in past and future lives, it is not very important to us whether the Charvakas believe in these things. But if we ourselves hold beliefs similar to theirs, we must reflect on the questions and the relevant answers found in the texts and understand why a phenomenon, in order to manifest, must have its own causes, why it cannot arise without them, and so forth. We should understand in what way matter is produced by causes and conditions and generates effects, and apply the same principle to the mind, which is also an impermanent phenomenon, devoid of intrinsic existence.

Mental states are produced by causes, and so are our happiness and our suffering. If we do not believe in rebirths, we cannot make any preparation for future lives; and if we do not believe in the law of cause and effect, neither will we avoid accumulating negative karma, nor strive to create positive karma. Since cause and effect are a reality, the fact that we do not believe in them does not eliminate their existence. There is no result generated without a cause. If there were such a generation devoid of cause, according to the logic expounded in the text on valid cognition, the *Pramanavarttika,* this would be either present or absent at all times.

Other non-Buddhist schools, such as the Naiyayikas and the Vaisheshikas, state that phenomena have a cause, but that there is only one, the god Ishvara. The Naiyayikas believe that all existent things are created by the will of Ishvara, but this is refuted in that if all was produced by his desire, then there would be no need for us to do anything.

The Madhyamikas ask, "If you accept Ishvara as the cause of all beings and all phenomena, then please tell us, who or what exactly is Ishvara?" [118]

The Naiyayikas reply, "Ishvara is the five elements: earth, water, fire, air, and space, from which all phenomena arise."

The Madhyamikas then say, "It is true that these elements are the cause of the arising of the various composite or impermanent phenomena, but why give them the name 'Ishvara'? If Ishvara is a permanent god, without a cause, then your answer cannot be accepted. Elements are assemblages of atoms and are impermanent, since they change every moment. Besides, Ishvara cannot be permanent, because he has the desire to create, and possessing this desire indicates that his nature is impermanent. The five elements are devoid of mind and are not a deity. We ourselves use the elements and so, when walking on earth, we would be walking on Ishvara. Also, since elements can become impure, they cannot be considered pure, permanent, and divine." [119]

The Naiyayikas say that Ishvara is single, permanent, unmoving, and has the desire to create. But elements are manifold and cannot therefore be a separate thing; they are impermanent and cannot therefore be permanent. They are devoid of both conscious movement and the desire to create, and one cannot therefore say that they are Ishvara or that Ishvara is the elements. Nor can one say that he is empty space, which, not having movement and being permanent, does not have the capacity to create. If Ishvara were space, which is unmoving, he could not produce any effect. Furthermore, Ishvara cannot be a permanent self of persons, since this has already been refuted.

The Naiyayikas continue to argue, saying that it is not possible to speak of or imagine Ishvara himself, because he is an inconceivable creator.

So the Madhyamikas ask, "What is the need for believing in an inconceivable entity, about whom no understanding is possible?" [120]

They then ask their interlocutors what effects this creator Ishvara produces. The Naiyayikas answer that Ishvara produces the self, the atomic particles of the various elements, and the later continuity of himself. But all of these cannot be effects of Ishvara if, as they have stated, his nature is permanent. [121]

A permanent effect cannot be produced by a cause, nor can a permanent cause produce effects. "Permanent" refers to something that never changes, that has no kind of movement. Cause and effect are relevant only in relation to impermanent phenomena. There is no impermanent phenomenon that does not arise from its own cause, and indeed each impermanent phenomenon has a specific cause. Ishvara is said to be devoid of cause because he is permanent; but if he were a cause, he would still be different from the cause of water, earth, and so on, because he himself is neither water nor earth. In fact, he should not be different from the effects that he is said to produce!

Happiness too does not arise without a cause, nor can it arise from a cause of a different nature. Therefore, if we want to be happy, we must create positive karma. In the same way, there is no suffering without a cause, nor any suffering that arises from a cause different from its correspondent cause—that is, negative karma. For this reason, we are taught that we must purify and no longer accumulate negativity.

We are used to considering what is impermanent to be permanent, so I would now like to ask you, "Is the person who existed this morning here now? Is it the same person?" We are not permanent. A minute is divided into sixty seconds, and during each of them we undergo a change. When we move in order to reach a certain place, there is not a single instant in which we are still in the same spot.

The suffering we have experienced since time without beginning arises from specific causes: karma and mental afflictions. How then can we say that Ishvara is the cause that produces every phenomenon? And what is produced by Ishvara? [122]

Since both the happiness and the suffering we experience are produced by our karma, what does Ishvara produce? If he creates everything, then even the feeling we are experiencing now must have been produced by him; and since he has existed from time without beginning, then this feeling too must have existed from time without beginning, and the same would apply to the effect of our current feeling. Since Ishvara is considered permanent and a creator, then everything produced by him should exist simultaneously with him, since the beginning.

The Naiyayikas say that Ishvara is permanent, but that in order to produce something, he must come into contact with particular conditions. [123]

This can be disputed by the argument that if he is permanent, he should not be influenced nor depend on conditions, and that if he were, these conditions should be created by him. Since he would then produce causes and conditions, this means that he can create everything simultaneously. Why then does the creation of things depend on time, and why do cause and effect follow one another in different moments? We know that cause and effect cannot exist at the same time in the same way that father and son do not arise simultaneously—first there is father and then the son; the effect follows the cause.

If we still need causes and conditions to produce effects even if Ishvara exists, then what is the purpose of inventing him in addition?

The Naiyayikas maintain that Ishvara is permanent and therefore not subject to change. But from a permanent cause no effect can be produced! When a substantial cause encounters favorable conditions, and effects are produced from their concomitance (as in the example of a seed that produces a sprout when it joins the earth, warmth, and moisture), Ishvara cannot do anything to prevent this ripening, and is therefore without the power to produce results. [124]

Given that, even without Ishvara's will, we experience the suffering that ripens from the seeds of our karma, how can we say that he has power? In fact, he seems to be without any power, choice, or control.

If we say that phenomena arise because of Ishvara's desire, they would be produced by his desire and not by Ishvara himself. What is produced by Ishvara's desire depends on the desire. [125]

Fire is the cause and smoke is the effect; smoke exists only when there is fire. Therefore, if we see smoke, we can deduce that a fire was or is there. In this way we establish the relationship between fire and smoke.

All the effects we experience are due to our karma, not to Ishvara. If we have created the karma to be reborn as human beings, it will produce the ripening result of a human rebirth and, simultaneously, the view of human surroundings will arise. If we have created the cause for an unfortunate rebirth, such an existence will ripen. Ishvara does not produce these processes. If a farmer sows weeds he will reap weeds, and if he sows peas he will reap peas. Ishvara has nothing to do with the weeds and the peas, because they depend on their own particular seeds. If Ishvara were the cause of each phenomenon, it would be a non-correspondent cause.

With the above we have refuted the theory of Ishvara as the creator of everything.

A great kalpa is made up of eighty intermediate kalpas, subdivided into four periods. During the first twenty kalpas, or eons, the universe is empty. Following this period, there are twenty eons of formation, followed by twenty eons of stability and twenty eons of degeneration or destruction. The air element is formed during the first phase of the formation of the universe, followed by the water element, and then the earth element. The fire element is contained within each of them.

The formation of universes and worlds begins with the arising of higher levels of existence; hence the first beings born in the universe are born into these levels or realms. Rebirths into the lower heavens follow, and this continues in order down to the lowest level of the hell realms. The period of formation comes to an end when the first being takes rebirth in the Avici hell.

Causes can be individual or collective. The process that has just been described arises as a result of collective, or common, karmic causes, whereas the particular conditions of existence befitting each being depend on individual karma.

The Vaisheshikas state that the causes of each phenomenon are tiny particles of indivisible matter, devoid of parts and considered to be permanent. We have already refuted this assertion.

The Samkhyas, in contrast, assert that each phenomenon is derived from a primal substance, or a permanent general principle, which they believe is also the cause of all sentient beings. [126]

They maintain that such primal substance is a combination of three forces, or qualities, which they refer to in their system as purity, activity, and darkness. These can also be understood as the three types of feelings: pleasant, unpleasant, and neutral. If the three qualities are in a balanced state, they constitute the primal substance. If they are not balanced, they become its various manifestations—all phenomena. [127]

On the one hand, the Samkhyas assert that the primal substance is single; on the other, that it has three qualities. However, this is a contradiction, because it is not possible for something truly devoid of parts to simultaneously possess a threefold nature. [128]

Furthermore, matter, which is devoid of consciousness, cannot experience happiness and unhappiness, and so those qualities possessed by the primal substance cannot exist. Since a primal substance of this kind cannot exist, neither can its effects—all phenomena included in the twenty-five categories, such as sounds and other sense objects—which for the Samkhyas are of the same nature as their cause. [129]

If the primal substance were the cause of all phenomena, it would also be the cause of a garment, but since the primal substance does not exist, a garment also should not exist. Therefore the primal substance cannot be the cause of phenomena such as cloth, and these phenomena cannot be its effects (having to possess in that case the three qualities of happiness and so forth), nor can the primal substance be produced by these effects. [130]

Such a primal substance, which is described as permanent, does not exist, because there has never been a valid mind able to perceive it.

If happiness were permanent it would be continually experienced, even in unpleasant situations. Instead, at times we experience happiness and at other times unhappiness—this proves that happiness is not permanent. [131]

The Samkhyas object that this is not the case, asserting that when we are happy a coarse form of pleasure is present, and when we are suffering the pleasure still remains, but in a very subtle form.

To this objection the Madhyamikas reply that a permanent phenomenon could not change, becoming coarse one moment and subtle the next. If the feeling could change from coarse to subtle and vice versa, then it would not be permanent, but impermanent. [132]

Having already demonstrated that feelings are impermanent, the Prasangikas ask, "Considering the arguments stated above, why don't you accept that all other composite phenomena are also impermanent?" [133]

The Samkhyas object, "Although the various coarse and subtle states of happiness are impermanent, the nature of happiness itself must be permanent."

The Madhyamikas reply, "Since the coarse and subtle states of pleasure are not different from pleasure itself and are impermanent, then pleasure must also be impermanent." [134]

Are the coarse and subtle states of plesure one with pleasure, or are they different? If they are one with it, then when a coarse state ceases and becomes a subtler state, pleasure too must cease, and pleasure is therefore impermanent. If, on the other hand, they are of a different nature, this assertion is in contradiction with what has previously been stated by the Samkhyas—that coarse and subtle states of pleasure, although different from each other, are of the same nature as pleasure.

The Madhyamikas continue, "You state that the primal substance is a composite of the three qualities previously described, but since these are not permanent—since they are subject to change—then the primal substance too should change and therefore be impermanent, and not, as you say, permanent."

We all know from experience that states of pleasure and suffering are subject to change; and if the Samkhyas state that they are of the nature as the primal substance, this means that it too must change and cannot therefore be permanent. With regard to the statement that all phenomena are produced by this primal substance: since the existence of such a substance has been refuted, the existence of phenomena has also been refuted.

Phenomena do not arise without a cause, nor can they arise from non-corresponding causes, such as Ishvara. Everything that exists within cyclic existence has been produced by karma and by our own minds.

A prayer of aspiration says:

Through the strength of merit and wisdom
accumulated in the three periods by myself and all beings,
may we obtain the two bodies of a buddha
and benefit all beings by these.

The ultimate, highest purpose we can achieve is to obtain the two bodies of a buddha. These do not arise without a cause, but rather from two specific causes, which are the gathering of merit and wisdom. Therefore, if we aspire to buddhahood, we should complete these two forms of accumulation.

No phenomenon can arise without an appropriate cause and cooperative conditions, or from a single cause.

The Samkhyas accept something akin to the Ishvara of the Naiyayikas
and the Vaisheshikas, and call it the primal substance. In any case, whether
it is Ishvara or the primal substance, neither constitutes an appropriate or
corresponding cause, and it is therefore clear that phenomena cannot be
generated from them. The primal substance, which according to the Samkhyas is the appropriate cause of phenomena, cannot in fact be such, since
it is of a different nature than phenomena.

The Samkhyas also assert that effects are simultaneous with their
causes, and in response to this the Madhyamikas ask, "If you maintain
that effects are simultaneous with their causes, what is the meaning
of arising and manifesting? If a phenomenon is already present at the
moment of its cause, what need is there to say that phenomena arise and
then manifest?"

According to the Madhyamikas, each cause has a certain type of energy
or potentiality to generate its effect. For example, they say that a seed has
the potential to eventually produce a bud, but they do not say that the
bud is already present in the seed. If the seed is barren, it will not produce
a bud, despite having cooperative conditions.

The Samkhyas assert that the effect is already present in the cause, but
in a non-manifest way that our sense organs cannot perceive, and that it
becomes manifest the moment it arises.

The Madhyamikas reply, "If you say that the effect, in the moment
before its ripening, is already present in the cause in a non-manifest state,
and that it is manifest in the present, why don't you accept that it was produced at the same moment that it was made manifest? If you say that the
result is already present at the moment of its cause, then you should also
accept that excrement is already in food. Therefore, while eating food, we
would also be eating excrement, which is the result of food. Furthermore,
clothes are already present in wool and cotton, and we could then buy and
wear just wool and cotton, rather than clothes. However, since we cannot
find clothes in raw cotton and wool, we must accept that the effect is not
simultaneous with the cause." [135]

The Samkhyas observe, "Although food and excrement are of the same
nature, ordinary people, not being aware of this, do not eat the latter."

The Madhyamikas reply, "And your founder Kapila? Being omniscient, as you say, he should have by necessity known that excrement existed in food. Do you mean to say he ate it? [136]

"Besides, since you teach this view to others, why doesn't anyone understand and see that the effect already exists within the cause?"

The Samkhyas: "Ordinary beings' perceptions are not valid, hence they are unable to see the effect at the moment of the cause."

The Madhyamikas: "In that case it would follow that the visual perception of ordinary people with regard to a manifest phenomenon is also not valid, but false." [137]

In fact, conventionally, such perception is correct and not erroneous, with regard to its object. The Samkhyas nevertheless object, "Since according to you valid cognition is not truly existent, this must necessarily be false. Hence any object established by it would in the same way be false. In this case, the emptiness you speak about must also be false, since the valid mind that realizes it is false, and it follows that it would be pointless to meditate on emptiness." [138]

The Madhyamikas reply, "Even though the valid mind that realizes emptiness, and emptiness itself, are both non-truly existent and therefore illusory or false, in order to understand the meaning of the non-true existence of an object or phenomenon, one should first correctly identify true existence, which is the object to be negated. Without identifying the object to be negated, true existence, there cannot be perception of its nonexistence by a valid mind. It is necessary to know the fact of a woman's barrenness before saying that her children do not exist." [139]

In order to realize emptiness, we should first have a clear idea of what true or intrinsic existence means, and how true existence would be if it existed, because only after having established its characteristics can we understand that it does not exist. If we suppose that there is a thief in the crowd, we must first identify him if we want to arrest him.

When a mother dreams that her child is dead, she apprehends his non-existence. Such apprehending has the effect of eliminating the thought of the child's existence. Even though both concepts—her child's death and his existence—are in fact false because they occur in a dream, the former has, nevertheless, the ability to defeat the latter. [140]

Likewise, both the realization of emptiness and the thought that grasps at true existence are false, but the first has the ability to eliminate the second. And there is no contradiction in saying that the falsely existent realization of emptiness comprehends the falsely existent emptiness of phenomena.

When we have a valid cognition of conventional existence, that perception in itself is valid and correct. For example, we perceive a bottle, and it exists, but in addition the mind perceives a true existence, which, in fact, is not there. Hence we say that sense perception is illusory, or deceptive, but nevertheless valid. Emptiness itself is illusory because it appears to us to exist concretely and truly, when in fact it does not exist in this fashion.

There are two types of valid cognition: direct and inferential. The valid direct perception of emptiness is not illusory, but its valid inferential cognition, although valid, is illusory, because to this type of mind emptiness appears to be intrinsically existent.

The emptiness of each phenomenon is called *ultimate truth* because a direct perceiver apprehending it is devoid of any form of duality, and because its mode of appearance corresponds to its mode of existence.

In order to possess an accurate knowledge of the doctrinal principles of non-Buddhist philosophical schools, and in order to be able to understand correctly how their views are negated by the Buddhist schools, one should study Dharmakirti's *Pramanavarttika* and the *Drubta Chenmo (Great Treatise on Tenets)*, a text studied in depth at Drepung Gomang Monastery.

By means of the above analysis we have established that no impermanent phenomenon arises without a cause or from an inappropriate cause. In other words, each composite phenomenon is produced by a specific cause. Both happiness and unhappiness must therefore also have causes of a respectively similar nature—the first arising from positive causes, and the second from negative causes.

Effects do not truly exist either in single causes or in their assemblage, nor do phenomena exist separate from their own causes. [141] When a phenomenon ceases, it does not truly cease in order to go elsewhere. In short, both causes and effects arise dependently, and do not exist independently and intrinsically.

Since phenomena do not exist intrinsically or truly, but appear as if they do, they are said to be false, deceptive, and illusory. [142]

All Buddhist schools accept the principle of dependent arising between causes and effects.

Since there are many reasons demonstrating the non-true existence of phenomena, it is correct to think that phenomena do not exist truly. As the wisdom that understands emptiness can fight the ignorance that grasps at intrinsic existence, it necessarily has many valid supports. On the other hand, the ignorance that grasps at true existence has no logical support.

It is because of the obscuration caused by ignorance that forms, sounds, and so forth are perceived as truly existent. In spite of being thus perceived, such phenomena are not truly existent, in the same way that emanations produced by a magician are not. There is no difference between them—phenomena exist in dependence on causes and conditions in exactly the same way that the object emanated by the magician depends on its own causes and conditions. Phenomena appear to us to be truly existent, just as a horse emanated by a magician out of a piece of wood appears to be real. The horse that appears to us as a result of the spell is not a horse, and in the same way forms, sounds, and so forth, which appear to us as real, in reality are not so. We only perceive them as such because of our ignorance.

If composite phenomena intrinsically exist, then when they arise they should actually arrive from somewhere, and when they cease they should actually go elsewhere, but all impermanent phenomena, including the self of persons, come into existence solely as a result of causes and conditions. [143] As the bud arises from its cause, the seed, so karma arises from its cause, ignorance. If there is no cause, there is no effect—without ignorance, there is no karma, and without the seed, there is no bud. Hence there are no effects that exist by their own nature or intrinsically, because all arise dependently. Therefore the appearance of produced phenomena is like the reflection in a mirror. [144]

We are at present studying the Dharma, and once we have learned it, we will be able to practice it. It is also very important to have a good understanding of the way to practice it. When listening to teachings, you should not leave them unused, but analyze them with your intelligence and make them yours. At present we are not only endowed with human bodies but also with other precious conditions—intelligence, the time and interest needed for the practice of the Dharma, and the place to practice—and if we do not take advantage of these conditions, it is only because we are lazy.

The problems that come up daily in our lives are due to the fact that we give too much importance to ourselves and no importance to others. Since we all desire happiness, rather than thinking only of ourselves, we should extend this desire for happiness to others.

When we practice for all beings, the objects of our practice are boundless and the virtues we will accumulate are also boundless. An offering made to ten people is greater than one made to one person, and an offering made to all beings will be much greater than one made to a hundred beings. If we try to attain buddhahood for the benefit of all beings, the object of the creation of our merits is boundless, and the merits created will also be boundless.

In order to develop the altruistic motivation, we must consider its worth and realize its importance. At the same time, we should see a selfish attitude as negative and as something we would do well to eliminate, as it is disadvantageous to keep it within us.

People such as thieves, who care only about themselves and are not in the least concerned about the suffering they create for others by stealing their possessions, and assassins, who in order to satisfy their desires will even kill, exemplify the selfish attitude from which arises all the suffering of this and future lives. The *Guru Puja* says, "Because of this selfish attitude, we possess nothing that is worth giving to others; whereas it was because of the Buddha's altruistic attitude that he became a buddha."

Even though we are unable to perceive living buddhas, we can nevertheless see statues and paintings that represent them, and give them offerings and tributes. This is because the buddhas, possessing a mind dedicated to the benefit of others, have become objects worthy of respect and devotion, like the current Dalai Lama. This is due to his altruistic attitude.

The happiness we find in this life is the result of an altruistic attitude, as is the final state of enlightenment. A true practitioner gives more importance to the future, and a Mahayana follower gives more importance to others. Therefore, if we want to be Mahayana practitioners, we need to develop an altruistic attitude.

What we need to negate and eliminate is, on the one hand, the concept of a truly existent "I" and, on the other, our selfish attitude. These are the causes of all problems.

Establishing Emptiness from the Point of View of the Effects

A bud arises from its seed, hence it is not independent but dependent, and it does not exist truly, by its own nature. Also, dependent arising itself does not exist truly.

If phenomena truly existed, they would exist without depending on other factors, in which case what would be the purpose of causes? Something that exists intrinsically, or naturally, is not subject to the relationship of cause and effect. On the other hand, if an effect were not at all existent (a non-thing), what would be the need of relating it to a cause, given that it does not exist? [145]

Since neither true existence nor true nonexistence exist, it follows that there cannot be a truly existent arising; but we can reasonably accept that there is a relationship between cause and effect, which is also akin to an illusion.

Non-Buddhist schools raise the following objection: "Although a cause is not apt to generate a non-thing, it can transform the non-thing into a thing."

The Prasangikas answer, "Even by means of a billion causes, a non-thing cannot be transformed into anything else, because it is permanent."

Even if there were many causes, a non-phenomenon cannot become a phenomenon, and vice versa.

To see if it is possible for a non-thing to be transformed into a thing, one ought to observe whether by making that transformation, the non-thing leaves its state of non-thing or maintains it. If it becomes a thing without leaving the state of non-thing, then it is simultaneously a thing and a non-thing, which is impossible. On the other hand, if we were to say that a state of non-thing is transformed into a thing, having left behind its state of non-thing, this too would be impossible, because what is that non-thing that can separate itself from the state of non-thing and transform itself into a thing? [146]

It is impossible for "nothing" to become an object and for an object to become "nothing," just as it is impossible for a permanent state to become impermanent, and vice versa. In the state of nonexistence there cannot be room for existence; therefore how can a non-thing become a thing? [147]

Just as a child cannot give birth to another child, so it is impossible for nothingness to produce anything. "Nothing" and "thing" have different natures and thus cannot exist simultaneously, and the state of nothingness cannot cease. Only something that is a not a non-thing can become a thing. A non-thing cannot turn into a thing, and vice versa, a thing cannot become a non-thing and still remain a thing, because then there would be a combination of two natures, which is not acceptable. [148]

All living beings are devoid both of a truly existent birth and a truly existent cessation and are beyond truly existent nirvana and samsara. Since true existence does not exist from the beginning, it is said that it is pacified from the beginning; and since beings are devoid of true existence, it is said that they abide in natural nirvana and are therefore beyond true suffering. It is not necessary to attain this natural nirvana because it is already there and is the non-intrinsic existence of the mind. It follows that there is no such thing as a truly existent production, or a truly existent cessation. Since there is no intrinsically existent cessation, we can therefore establish that all sentient beings have never truly been born and have never truly come to cease. They have always been devoid of intrinsic existence, hence they have abided from the beginning in the state of natural nirvana. [149]

Sentient beings and all phenomena, even though they appear to, do not truly exist, and are like a dream. On a conventional level, impermanent phenomena exist and perform a function, but if we analyze them in some depth, their conventional existence also disappears.

It is like a large trunk of a banana tree: if we try to find an essential core within it by removing the various layers of bark, we will not find anything. Hence, within emptiness, there is no difference between those who have attained nirvana, the state of peace, and those who are still caught up within samsara, the state not beyond sorrow. Furthermore, nirvana and samsara are the same, with regard to the fact that they are both devoid of intrinsic existence. [150]

The Results of Having Generated Wisdom

Since all things are devoid of intrinsic existence, what is there to gain or to lose? How can there be intrinsically existent sentient beings who praise you, who give you offerings, who please you or harm you in a truly existent way? [151]

From where does the happiness of being benefited, or the suffering of being harmed, come? What is the use of being displeased with something unpleasant and pleased with something pleasant? If we look for ourselves from the ultimate point of view, we will find that the person and sentient beings do not exist intrinsically and that there is no form of natural existence. [152]

How then can there be intrinsically existent birth and death? How can there be intrinsically existent relatives or friends who benefit us in an intrinsically existent way? All these are devoid of intrinsic and natural existence. [153]

Since nothing exists intrinsically, there is nothing to gain or to lose truly, even if we have attachment or anger. Conventionally, there are those who pay us respect and those who abuse us, but in reality there is no concrete individual who respects or harms us.

Happiness is the object of our desire, and unhappiness is the object of our aversion, but neither exist truly. Likewise, there is nothing we can love or despise truly. By means of examination we see that we cannot find the object we feel attached to. Both the person who feels the attachment, the attachment itself, and the object of attachment do not truly exist.

Conventionally, death exists, but there is no truly existent death, nor a true future rebirth, nor truly existent friends benefiting us, nor enemies harming us, although they all exist conventionally.

Once we have really understood this, we should try to equalize the eight worldly dharmas. When we realize the profound meaning of emptiness, the eight worldly dharmas will no longer be divided into the four desirable objects and the four objects of aversion: we will no longer differentiate between happiness and unhappiness, praise and reproach, gain and loss, fame and disgrace. Once we have acquired the right understanding, we will no longer grasp at the thought that differentiates those who benefit us from those who harm us.

There are ten different meanings of the word *dharma*. This is the word used to name all phenomena (including the aforementioned eight worldly aptitudes), the Buddhist spiritual path, the overcoming of suffering (nirvana), the objects of mental consciousness, merits, the phenomena belonging to the duration of this life, the sacred texts, what will be generated, renunciation for the causes of suffering, and religious or doctrinal systems in general.

In order to be a good practitioner we should succeed in not being concerned about the eight worldly dharmas. If we try to practice the Dharma in order to be happy in this life, our practice will be impure.

Shantideva exhorts those who are engaged in understanding the meaning of emptiness to recognize that all phenomena are like space, or not truly existent. [154]

Before continuing the exposition on the subject we are discussing, Shantideva states that the Dharma is as vast as space and its explanation very difficult; he apologizes for not possessing the qualities and abilities required to explain it adequately. Nevertheless, he cannot refrain from expounding and commenting on it, since this is both useful and precious.

We too must appreciate and rejoice in it! In reality, in the *Bodhicharyavatara*, Shantideva has given the complete explanation of wisdom and bodhichitta, which lead to the attainment of buddhahood. In spite of having discussed these subjects extensively, he shows humility, which is a sign of his greatness.

Wisdom is like the sword that is able to cut at the roots of all suffering; and bodhichitta, concurrently used, is the path that leads to buddhahood. These subjects are therefore very important, and in spite of the difficulties, Shantideva has generated the necessary courage needed to expound them.

We too say at times that we had to accept an undertaking that was beyond our abilities, and apologize for having done so, and Shantideva expresses the same in a verse.

Despite our desire for happiness, we ourselves create the causes that lead us to unhappiness because of our wrong understanding. Because of our desire we feel attachment for our relatives and friends, and because of hatred we have aversion toward our enemies.

When we do not find the objects that we desire, we feel sad but still strive to obtain them, even at the cost of arguing and hurting one another, because we think that this is the right thing to do. Our desire to obtain something favorable has caused us to perform many negative deeds, and we live in a state of great difficulty. [155]

All beings who act in this way are objects of great compassion. In spite of being born many times as gods or humans, during these lifetimes we have always and solely sought temporal pleasure, and for this reason we were reborn into unfortunate realms, where our stay was longer than our time in the fortunate realms. [156]

The wisdom that realizes emptiness and the ignorance that grasps at true existence are in contradiction with one another. [157]

Even though we find ourselves within conditioned existence, we have come across this favorable opportunity to discuss the empty nature of phenomena, their non-true existence. We should use this incredible good fortune for as long as it is there in order to understand and familiarize ourselves with this view, the realization of which will allow us to be free from cyclic existence. Finding the opportunity to study and analyze the authentic nature of phenomena is almost impossible, but it has happened to us, and we should therefore strive to realize the emptiness of phenomena. Otherwise how are we going to be free from this ocean of misery?

Although we have now been reborn as human beings, the merits we have created are very limited, and the negative karma vast; we are therefore left with little hope. We have obtained this human life, by means of which we can accumulate many positive causes, but it is very brief, and its duration uncertain. [158]

Under the pretext of becoming healthy, we spend much time massaging ourselves, having baths, following special diets, curing ourselves with particular medical treatments; and in order to fend off hunger we are forced to work for our food, which we must buy and cook. Also, we must sleep in order to not feel tired. We can see therefore that there are many obstacles to practice. We are also subject to illnesses and various circumstances that harm us, and have friends with whom we spend much time in idle chatter—in other words, we spend our lives not being able to do many useful or purposeful things. [159]

It is also difficult to meet beings endowed with profound wisdom, and yet we have met them, and we are intelligent; we should use these favorable opportunities to investigate the nature of phenomena. We could also think that it is extremely difficult for us to practice because our minds are inclined to distraction, we are not used to being attentive, favorable conditions to the practice of the Dharma are very rare, and unfavorable conditions are numerous. [160]

However, we should not allow these thoughts to arise in our minds, because they could cause us harm, even though it is true that favorable conditions are extremely rare and unfavorable conditions very common.

There are four *maras* that can throw us into the suffering of samsara:

impure aggregates, mental afflictions, death, and one called *devaputra* (sons of gods), which refers to habitual attachment to sensory gratification.

We could think that because we have been reborn as humans it is easy to accumulate merits or attain liberation. In reality this is not so, because it is uncertain whether we will meet the right path, since mistaken paths are many and we could also be doubtful about which is the right one. [161]

It is also not certain that we are going to meet the perfect master. Besides, despite having the right inclination and favorable circumstances leading us toward the Dharma, as a result of our laziness we may think that we can postpone our practice until the future or our next fortunate rebirth, and in this way fail to utilize our current opportunity. Even thinking that we can practice in two or three years, or when better opportunities arise, is wrong and constitutes an obstacle, because the length of this life is uncertain and we do not know when death will come.

Now we have a human life and propitious circumstances, and we should take this opportunity by developing a firm determination based on the following three convictions: we must practice the Dharma, we must practice in this lifetime, and we must practice right now.

Practicing the Dharma does not mean offering one's labor and abilities to centers, communities, or groups of people without receiving any personal benefit. On the contrary, we certainly will receive benefit. Although this may not be measured in wealth and possessions, it will be measured in the accumulation of merits and spiritual energy.

Thinking that since it is hard to forsake erroneous conceptions, all the sentient beings in samsara will continue to experience the suffering of birth, illness, old age, and death without interruption, we will feel very sad. [162]

It is therefore necessary to endeavor to acquire the appropriate methods to free everyone from samsara. Recognizing that we are within samsaric existence, whose nature is suffering, we must seek the path that can lead us to liberation. It is right to be sad and have compassion for beings who, in spite of their suffering in conditioned existence, are unaware of it and in this way are not unlike children. [163]

Everything we consider to be happiness at present—such as eating, going to the mountains, or enjoying a day on the beach—is not really pleasure or happiness, for it is of the nature of suffering.

Some followers of non-Buddhist schools think that bathing in the Ganges River, jumping in fire, and performing other arduous ascetic practices constitute the path leading to liberation, and are therefore happy to endure them, and consider them pleasant. [164]

But in order to attain liberation we should develop the wisdom that realizes the authentic nature of phenomena, for this is the right path to reach that goal. Fasting, being in the water a long time, or entering fire are not adequate paths to liberation.

We have not attained nirvana, we are not yet arhats or aryas, and yet we live as though there were no aging or death. But even if we are calm, mistaking suffering for joy and failing to understand the real nature of samsara, at some point the "lord of death" will come and lead us into the lower realms, where we will have to endure great suffering. Why don't all beings tormented by suffering see that by acting as they do, they not only experience suffering now but also accumulate new causes for suffering that will ripen in the future? [165]

All of them are objects of great compassion. Sentient beings abide in cyclic existence, which is comparable to a burning fire. If someone is enveloped in flames, a good-hearted person will try to free him from that suffering, and we too must develop love and compassion by thinking like Shantideva:

"May the merits I have accumulated through the practice of the various perfections become clouds full of rain, able to extinguish the fire of suffering that devours beings." [166]

The last verses are in the form of a dedication of the merits accumulated by Shantideva, so that they may serve to alleviate the suffering of beings. Shantideva himself is in great haste to benefit them all—as when feeling extremely impatient awaiting for the arrival of a friend—and practices the six perfections together with the understanding of the non-true existence of all phenomena. For example, by practicing generosity he sees that the gift, the person receiving it, and he himself are not truly existent, and that by means of this wisdom that realizes emptiness one is able to attain enlightenment. And in fact this is how Shantideva concludes this chapter: "By having respectfully completed the gathering of merits without referring to a true existence, when will I be able to reveal emptiness to others, who are wretched through wrong views?" [167]

Any wealth we accumulate during our lives will have to be abandoned at the moment of death. Someone taking care of another, and finding a home for him and the food that he needs, will be considered a great benefactor, but in fact he has not done a great deal, since this benefit is limited in time and, in any case, that person will have to die. By developing the wisdom that realizes emptiness, on the other hand, it is possible to eliminate all mental afflictions and attain complete liberation from samsara.

By depending on the wisdom that understands the lack of self in persons and phenomena, it is possible at first to reduce the strength of the coarse mental afflictions by making them non-manifest. Later, by continuing to familiarize ourselves with this view, we will completely eliminate all disturbing emotions, even the most subtle, and their seeds. Having cut the root of suffering, we will attain liberation.

Hence this gift of the Dharma, and in particular the explanation of the wisdom that realizes emptiness, is of inestimable value. Only the Dharma can eliminate mental afflictions, which are our true enemy, and by means of practice we will attain the final result, non-abiding nirvana, a state that does not dwell within the two extremes of conditioned existence and personal liberation.

In order to cultivate great compassion, we should keep all sentient beings, who are tormented by suffering, as the referents of our meditation, and generate the mind that meditates on compassion in the aspect that wishes to see them free from suffering and from the causes of suffering.

Explaining the Title of the Ninth Chapter

The extensive title of the ninth chapter is "*Showing the Perfection of Wisdom.*" Through this chapter the expert pandits of the path of the Middle Way have established the non-true existence of all phenomena by means of valid logical argument and scriptural quotation.

The learned pandits of the Chittamatrin school argue that if things do not truly exist, they do not exist at all. To this purpose they establish and accept phenomena as truly existent. The Madhyamikas say that phenomena, although not truly existent, are not nonexistent. They are in fact able to establish the existence of phenomena precisely on the basis of their non-true existence.

Again, there is a difference between "non-true existence" and "nonexistence." A vase, for example, is not truly existent, but it is not nonexistent. Likewise, there is a difference between "existence" and "true existence." For example, the vase exists, but does not exist truly. For these reasons, according to the Madhyamaka school, all conventional phenomena, such as form and so forth, are seen as illusions. Saying that phenomena exist as illusions does not mean that they are unreal; the vase exists as an illusion, but at the same time is a real phenomenon. Why are conventional, composite phenomena, such as the vase, like an illusion? Because the vase appears to be truly existent, but abides or exists without true existence.

Through single-pointed meditation, which has the ultimate nature of phenomena as its referent, the practitioner realizes the truth—the lack of intrinsic existence of phenomena, or their emptiness. Later, arising from meditative equipoise and entering the post-meditative intervals, the practitioner acquires the state known as *subsequent attainment of truth.* From that moment on, we perceive phenomena as akin to illusions.

I conclude the ninth chapter here, having used the commentary by Gyeltsab Je Rinpoche in addition to texts of other great Tibetan masters of the past as my sources.

All the positive energy generated by our endeavor produces benefit, and therefore we now dedicate it by generating the aspiration and the wish that the accumulated merits may lead us to the complete realization of the meaning of the *Bodhicharyavatara* so that we can practice it correctly and, by following the path walked by all bodhisattvas, that we may attain perfect enlightenment.

·: IO :·

DEDICATION

THE TENTH CHAPTER describes the way in which bodhisattvas, the spiritual children of the buddhas, dedicate the merits of their actions for the benefit of all beings. In the opening verses the bodhisattva Shantideva dedicates the merits generated through having composed this text so that all beings in all directions may engage in the bodhisattva's conduct. [1]

May they be free from suffering and obtain an ocean of happiness and joy. For as long as they remain in cyclic existence, may their happiness never decline, due to the virtues of buddhas and bodhisattvas. May all the suffering of the lower realms vanish, and may all beings dwelling there experience supreme bliss. May these merits allow those experiencing intense cold to find warmth, and may those oppressed by heat be cooled. [2–5]

There are some lower realms in which the beings are forced to walk on razor-sharp leaves, wounding their legs and feet, and in the text the wish is expressed that those places be transformed into pleasant groves, as a result of the merits of buddhas and bodhisattvas. In the lower realms there is also a particular tree that looks beautiful but is in fact made of knives and swords, so that the being climbing it is wounded—the wish is expressed that this may transform into the wish-fulfilling tree. [6]

Although now the hell realms are places of suffering, may they become places of joy, with vast and fragrant lotus pools echoing with the calls of swans and wild ducks. [7]

May the heaps of burning coals produced by the flames of the hell realms be transformed into jewels, may the burning ground become a polished crystal floor, and may the mountains, which move closer and closer to crush those who inhabit the hell region, become celestial offering places. [8]

May the rain of blazing lava and weapons become a rain of flowers, and may the continuous battling with weapons among the beings dwelling there become a playful exchange of flowers. [9]

There are hell regions in which the beings are caught in fiery torrents of acid, and others where insects eat the flesh of those who live there; may these places be transformed into cool lakes as a result of the merits of having composed this text, and may those beings obtain celestial bodies and enjoy the company of divine consorts. [10]

The verses declare that, at a certain moment, the henchmen of the lord of death and the vultures move away, the sky suddenly clears, and more extraordinary events occur in the lower realms; the beings living there look up at the sky and see the form of Vajrapani, which gives them joy and consolation. Through the force generated by their joy, may they follow him. [11]

When the beings who suffer the pain of the hot lava of the hell realms see it extinguished by a rain of falling flowers mixed with scented water, may they experience sudden joy and an end to their torment, and, wondering whose work this was, may they realize that it is Padmapani's and develop great devotion. [12]

When the hell-realm dwellers admire a great radiant light and wonder whose work it is, they see the young Manjushri who dispels all fears and is respected also by the kings of the heaven realms, such as Shiva. [13]

Others see Manjushri and his retinue of bodhisattvas who offer him diamonds and jewels in enchanting palaces resounding with hymns sung by thousands of female deities; may those beings, upon seeing this sight, be free from suffering and full of joy. [14]

In the dedication verses we then pray that all beings may truly find solace in the cool and scented rain falling from the clouds created by Samantabhadra, one of the eight main bodhisattvas, together with Manjushri and Avalokiteshvara. May the merits of having composed this text allow everyone to eliminate their suffering and problems, to see those bodhisattvas, and, through the power of their blessings, enjoy all kinds of happiness that can be found in human and divine rebirths. [15]

Having accumulated these merits, may they be dedicated to the attainment of perfect enlightenment for the benefit of all beings, for the continuation and non-degeneration of the teachings of the Buddha, and for the long life of our masters.

The main fear in animals is of being devoured, and Shantideva dedicates his own merits to free them from that terror. [16]

Since the hungry ghosts suffer hunger and thirst, while the people of the northern continent do not have this concern, he also prays that the pretas be as happy as the humans, and that a stream of nectar may continuously flow from the hands of Avalokiteshvara, and its solace eliminate their suffering. [17]

May the blind see forms again, may the deaf find again the power of hearing, and may women give birth without pain. [18]

May all beings experience the joy of gods and goddesses as an illusion. May the naked find clothing, and the thirsty find delicious water. [19]

May the poor find wealth, and those weak with sorrow and pain find joy. May the forlorn find new hope, constant happiness, and safety. [20]

May the sick be free from their ills, and may even the mildest disease in the world never occur again. [21]

May the frightened cease to be afraid, and those bound be freed; may the weak or powerless find both strength and power, and may people think of benefiting one another. [22]

May travelers find happiness wherever they go, and may they effortlessly accomplish what they set out to do. [23]

May those who sail in ships and boats obtain whatever they wish for; and having safely returned to the shore, may they joyfully reunite with their beloved ones. [24]

May wanderers who have lost their way meet with fellow travelers, and may their journey be without any fatigue or fear of thieves and tigers. [25]

May the benevolent local deities protect children, the elderly, the insane, the unprotected, and those who find themselves in trackless, fearful wilderness. [26]

May all beings possess faith, intelligence, and the excellent conduct derived from observing the law of cause and effect. [27]

May they obtain treasuries extensive like space and always enjoy them, and, as a result of their mindfulness, may they avoid becoming the source of dispute or harm. [28]

May those who have little splendor come to be endowed with majesty, and may those whose aspect is ugly find magnificent and noble bodies. [29]

May beings with unfortunate life-forms obtain higher rebirths with more opportunities and energy for practice of the Dharma. May the lowly obtain grandeur and may the proud be humbled. [30]

May the merits accumulated here become the antidote to the sufferings of beings and to its cause. [31]

May these beings never be parted from the awakening mind, and may they always engage in the bodhisattvas' conduct by practicing the six paramitas; may they be guided and protected by the buddhas, and may they relinquish all evil actions. [32]

May all beings have long lives, live in contentment and joy, and never have to hear the word "death." [33]

May the gardens of wish-fulfilling trees abound in all directions with the sound of the Dharma proclaimed by buddhas and bodhisattvas. [34]

May the land everywhere be pure, devoid of rocks, smooth like the palm of a child's hand, and of the nature of lapis lazuli. [35]

May bodhisattvas dwell in every land, adorning them with their excellent manifestations, and may they give discourses and teachings surrounded by circles of disciples. [36]

May all creatures uninterruptedly hear the sound of the Dharma. May they always meet with buddhas and their spiritual sons, the bodhisattvas, and may these masters of the world be worshipped with endless clouds of offerings. [37–38]

May celestial beings bring timely rains, so that harvests may be bountiful. May kings rule in accordance with the Dharma and thus make the people of the world prosper. [39]

May all medicines be effective in healing all ills, and may the cure of repeating mantras also be successful. May dakinis, yakshas, and the others possess a mind endowed with compassion and love. [40]

May no living creature suffer, harm others, or fall ill; may no one be afraid or belittled, and their minds never become depressed. [41]

May the temples and monasteries where reading and recitation of texts is practiced flourish and remain, and may the Sangha members live in harmony and their purposes be accomplished. [42]

May monks and those desiring to practice find quiet and solitary places, and may their meditation be successful, having abandoned objects of distraction. [43]

In the old days in India there were fully ordained nuns. The text expresses the prayer that these bhikshunis be materially independent, abandon quarreling with each other, and be unharmed. Similarly, may all those who are ordained never let their morality weaken. [44]

May those with the misfortune of having allowed its decline repent and purify themselves; and as a result of having eradicated all evil, may they obtain the happiness that derives from a higher rebirth, and may their spiritual conduct not decline there. [45]

May the wise, richly endowed with knowledge, receive alms and honors, may they have a pure mind, and may their fame spread in all directions. [46]

May beings obtain a form superior to the gods. [47]

This is being said because gods, although enjoying great happiness, do not practice the spiritual path. We therefore need a higher rebirth in order to swiftly attain buddhahood.

May sentient beings again and again make offerings to the buddhas, and be joyful for their bliss. [48]

May the bodhisattvas see their desire of serving all beings be fulfilled, and may these beings receive everything the buddhas have intended for them. [49]

Similarly, may the pratyekabuddhas and the shravakas find happiness. [50]

Now Shantideva speaks in the first person: "And until I reach the level of the Joyous One, through the kindness of Manjushri may I be mindful throughout my lives and always obtain ordination." [51]

"Although sustained by simple, common food, may I enjoy a strong and healthy body, and in all my future lives may I not lack all other necessities and the ideal place for practicing the Dharma." [52]

"Whenever I have doubts about the practice, or wish to ask even the simplest question, may I obtain the vision of Manjushri himself and through his blessing understand every meaning and pacify all doubts." [53]

Manjushri developed the mind of enlightenment and then practiced the six transcendental perfections. "May my life be like his and may I in this way obtain final realization." [54]

All practice must be motivated by the desire to benefit beings; subsequently we strive in various types of meditation, such as analysis on refuge, as well as others, and end by dedicating all accumulated merits to the attainment of our initial aim. If our dedication is made in this way, not even hatred and other mental afflictions will be able to destroy it.

I will pause the commentary on the final verses at this point for auspiciousness and give some explanation about the *lamrim*—the progressive series of meditations on the path to enlightenment—followed by some general points about the qualities of bodhisattvas and a summary of Shantideva's text.

Tibetan Buddhism has four main traditions—Gelug, Kagyu, Sakya, and Nyingma—and all of them teach the lamrim in their own way.

Milarepa, the Kagyu saint, summarizes the lamrim in the following three points:

> If we do not contemplate the nature of the law of karma—that is, the way in which good and bad actions produce their respective results—the subtle power of the characteristic of ripening karma can bring about an unendurably painful rebirth. Hence, cultivate mindfulness with regard to actions and their effects!
>
> If we do not contemplate the harm of indulging in sense pleasures, and do not cease attachment to them completely, we will not be free from the prison of conditioned existence. Hence, cultivate the mind that perceives all as an illusion and apply the antidote against the origin of suffering!
>
> If we are not able to show kindness toward all living beings in each of the samsaric realms—that is, to those who have once been our own parents—we fall into the limitations of the lesser path. Hence, cultivate the universal mind of enlightenment, which looks at all beings with great love and concern!

As is stated here, we should meditate on such general, preliminary practices until we obtain stable conviction.

The Sakya school has a brief text called *Parting from the Four Attachments*. Among the four stanzas that constitute the text, the first states that a person who is attached to this life is not a spiritual practitioner, and that we must not concern ourselves with our current fame and wealth, but instead practice toward the attainment of better lives in the future, and that if a layperson were to do this, he or she would be a great Dharma practitioner.

The second stanza contains the exhortation to develop pure renunciation and to aspire to a higher level of existence. A person who is happy and comfortable in prison won't want to escape. Likewise, if we are attached to the transient happiness of conditioned rebirths, we will not strive to free ourselves from them.

The third stanza proclaims, "Worrying only about oneself prevents the attainment of the altruistic mind of bodhichitta." A bodhisattva seeks happiness and liberation for all beings, whereas we seek our own pleasure and are concerned solely about ourselves.

The fourth stanza says, "As long as we cling to the concept of intrinsic existence, we will never obtain the right vision of emptiness." This point has been explained in the ninth chapter of the *Bodhicharyavatara*.

All the teachings present in the lamrim are contained in essential form in the four stanzas of this Sakya text.

For the Gelug tradition, they are found in the text called the *Three Principal Aspects of the Path*. The three aspects of the path are renunciation, bodhichitta, and the correct view of emptiness. The first two of the four attachments the Sakya text refers to are included in renunciation.

In the Nyingma school these same concepts are expressed in four reversals: reversing the interest in this life, reversing the mind that seeks transient pleasures, reversing the mind that cherishes only oneself, and reversing the mind that grasps at an intrinsically existing self within phenomena.

The three preliminary Kagyu practices, the four separations from attachment of the Sakyapas, the three principal aspects of the path of the Gelugpas, and the Nyingma practice of four reversals are all consistent. They all point out the advantages of practicing and the disadvantages of not practicing, and stress the importance of trying not to be reborn into the lower realms. As a second stage, they exhort us to free ourselves from samsara through renunciation. Finally they tell us to abandon attachment to ourselves by benefiting others, together with developing supreme wisdom.

Above all else, we should strive to listen, reflect, meditate, and practice, which means that after having understood the benefit of the Dharma, we need to bring its content into our own life. In short, the essence of what we have discussed is that we must consider future lives more important than the current one, since they are more numerous, and we should therefore strive to practice the teachings and improve them. Once in a while it is also good for you to read other texts in order to deepen your understanding of what has been taught.

The pandit Asanga was able to directly perceive Maitreya as a result of his effort during many years of meditation, and he edited a text called the *Abhisamayalamkara,* which contains teachings he received from Maitreya. This text describes many of the qualities of buddhas and bodhisattvas and explains the various meanings of emptiness. This is the basis of the lamrim.

The first of the aforementioned qualities is that, while ordinary beings make a big display of, and exaggerate, their good qualities while hiding their shortcomings and errors, bodhisattvas act in exactly the opposite way.

The second quality of bodhisattvas is that they support the Dharma and teach beings according to their own experience and without an impure attitude, such as hiding personal shortcomings or emphasizing personal virtue and knowledge.

Bodhisattvas also possess the virtue of practicing the Dharma for the benefit of all beings, for their own and others' salvation. Bodhisattvas' minds are full of compassion for every creature, a compassion cultivated through the four unlimited meditations—on equanimity, love, compassion, and joy—and we should follow this example in order to obtain the same type of mind, richly endowed with all the aforementioned qualities.

Bodhisattvas are free from the slightest impulse of avarice with regard to the body, possessions, and merits, and strive to please their gurus with appropriate behavior of body, speech, and mind. They listen to and practice not only the Mahayana teachings but also the Hinayana, have a strong desire to be ordained, and somehow have an aversion to family life. They possess the aspiration to obtain the body of a buddha, and teach without setting limits on themselves—that is, without trying to hide or keep what they know for themselves but instead transmitting everything to others.

When we take the vows or commitments we try to keep them, and bodhisattvas speak and follow the truth just as if they had taken a vow. We can thus pray that we might one day possess the same qualities.

By obtaining the second ground of a bodhisattva, moral discipline (the first of the six perfections) is realized, and with it the firm determination to obtain not merely the level of a shravaka or a pratyekabuddha, but to follow the Mahayana path until the attainment of buddhahood.

In order to attain the state of enlightenment for the benefit of all beings, we need to generate the desire to work for them. To allow this thought to arise we should think of the kindness and benevolence that they have shown us, and have great patience according to the instruction of the *Bodhicharyavatara*. This means enduring all sorts of difficulties and suffering willingly, without reacting to the harm we receive and without being discouraged by the difficulties of the practice, such as those related to the realization of emptiness.

We also need enthusiastic interest in the spiritual path, love and compassion for all beings, and a sense of respect for our superiors. We should practice what we have learned from our masters, and have a positive and joyous attitude toward the practices of patience, enthusiastic effort, and meditation.

We should pray to be able to develop the qualities of bodhisattvas on the first and second grounds within ourselves, and be determined to practice all they practice. If we do this, it is truly praiseworthy, and by imitating higher beings, we in turn will set the example.

The *Bodhicharyavatara* was originally written in Sanskrit and subsequently translated into Tibetan. The first translation was by the Venerable Bhante Paltseg. This was followed by Rinchen Sangpo's translation, and it is good that we are now able to find translations in European languages.

To summarize the presentation of Shantideva's text, the first chapter of the *Bodhicharyavatara* discusses the development of bodhichitta, which is obtained by accumulating a great amount of merit, and the benefits derived from generating this mind. If we are completely enslaved by negativity, generating such a mind is very difficult. Therefore we must be purified of negative karma and mental afflictions, and this is the point that is discussed in the second chapter. At the same time the way to accumulate merits through the practice of the seven branches is explained.

Having purified negativity and accumulated merits, the practitioner is then ready to generate the mind of enlightenment and therefore takes the vows and practices the bodhisattva's conduct, as described in the third chapter. Having taken on these noble commitments, the practitioner then strives to honor them mindfully and conscientiously, as discussed in the fourth chapter.

The fifth chapter deals with discriminating alertness, the function of which is to verify whether one's conduct is appropriate to a bodhisattva or not; and like the fourth chapter, it addresses the first of the six perfections, morality. The sixth chapter discusses patience, the seventh chapter enthusiastic perseverance, the eighth concentration, the ninth wisdom, and the tenth and final chapter is the dedication.

In order to attain the final state of enlightenment, the omniscient state of a buddha, we must generate the altruistic mind of awakening, bodhichitta; and in order to advance on the path we must strive in the practice of the six transcendental perfections. Having succeeded in this, every mental affliction will be purified, all the perfect qualities of a buddha acquired, and at the same time it will be possible to work for the benefit of others. Our own objective is then realized, as is the objective of other beings', having obtained that state which is both of maximum personal benefit and of supreme benefit to others.

In other words, the final objective of practice is the attainment of the dharmakaya and the rupakaya; and in order to obtain these bodies of wisdom and form, we need to train in wisdom and method through listening, reflection, and meditation on the two truths, ultimate and relative.

Now we will return to the closing stanzas of the *Bodhicharyavatara.* It is said that beings will remain is samsara for a length of time as vast as space, and that the bodhisattva has the courage to remain there for this duration in order to guide and help them, and he therefore generates the altruistic mind and obtains the final state of buddhahood. [55]

When bodhisattvas reach the first and second level of the bodhisattva bhumis, they attain complete freedom from death and rebirth; they then choose a place to be reborn where they can be of the most help to beings who will benefit from their abilities. If, however, those bodhisattvas realize that their presence is not needed, since they have complete control over death and rebirth, they die, praying that all the suffering of samsara might ripen on them. Shantideva then wishes that, as a result of the power of the Sangha at the level of the arya bodhisattva, all beings might experience joy and happiness. [56]

In the text we find Shantideva praying, but actually all bodhisattvas do the same. The teaching of the Dharma is the sole medicine and antidote to the suffering of samsara, and the doctrine of the Buddha is the origin of every joy and happiness; for this reason may it be supported and honored and its practitioners helped and respected. [57]

These words also express the wish that spiritual communities might not endure financial difficulties and may be useful to those who turn to them, and that the Dharma may flourish and be preserved until the end of time.

Then Shantideva says, "Thanks to your power and inspiration, Guru Manjushri, I have been able to develop the enlightened mind and I have succeeded in composing this work. Therefore I prostrate to you respectfully and pay you homage. The possibility of contemplating the Dharma and developing my mind I owe to the kindness of my gurus; I therefore prostrate to you all, my masters." [58]

Finally we have the dedication's dedication, which refers to the dedication of the merits accumulated by composing the dedication, and these are always directed to the benefit of all beings, so that they may free themselves from samsara and obtain happiness. In this way the practice of generosity is further demonstrated.

The explanation of the root text is now complete, but according to tradition, once a commentary on a text is complete, one starts again from the beginning, and this is what I am going to do.

The title of the short poem I am going to comment upon is the *Bodhicharyavatara* in Sanskrit and *Chon Jug* in Tibetan, and it is studied and meditated upon by practitioners of the four Tibetan schools. The great bodhisattva Shantideva begins with verses of homage not only to buddhas and bodhisattvas, but also to all beings worthy of respect. After offerings and prostrations, he develops the determination to practice the six transcendental perfections.

Shantideva explains that his text will discuss the teachings of the Buddha and that therefore nothing new will be found that has not already been taught and discussed. He states that he is not well versed in the art of rhetoric and that he lacks the conviction to be of benefit to others, but writes so that the memory of the various practices he has worked on is not swept away by his mind; and so that, as a continuation of his experience, anyone who may possess the same good fortune might study this text, enjoy its benefits, and, by reading it and transmitting it, be able to understand its meaning. For example, we have now studied this text, and putting it into practice will depend on our diligence.

Since another tradition requires a teaching to be concluded with a positive, auspicious quote, I am going to finish with the following. Through reading and listening to teachings, we have accumulated a great quantity of merit, which we now dedicate to the benefit of all beings and so that the Dharma might be preserved for a long time. Now recite the last stanza in the text and meditate on the meaning of dedicating merits.

I prostrate to Manjughosha,
through whose kindness I generated virtuous mental states,
and I prostrate to my spiritual masters,
through whose kindness I then developed them.

GESHE YESHE TOBDEN'S DEDICATION

THE CONTENT OF the *Bodhicharyavatara* is as immense and profound as the ocean, and due to that immensity and profundity it is difficult to be able to completely grasp all of its subtle meanings. I have explained the text as one might draw a few drops of water from the ocean, but even in these few drops, mistakes may be found. Please forgive these flaws. I pray that in the future this book may be published in a form totally devoid of errors.

༄༅། །ཕན་བདེའི་འབྱུང་གནས་བསྟན་པ་དར་ཞིང་རྒྱས།

།བསྟན་འཛིན་སྐྱེས་བུ་ཐམས་ཅད་སྐུ་ཁམས་བཟང་།

།ལུས་ཅན་ཀུན་ལ་བདེ་སྐྱིད་འབྱུང་བའི་གནས།

སངས་རྒྱས་བསྟན་པ་རྟག་ཏུ་རྒྱས་གྱུར་ཅིག། །།

May the Dharma, source of benefit and happiness, grow and expand.
May all the holders of the Teachings enjoy excellent health.
May the Buddha's Doctrine, source of happiness and joy for all beings,
  grow endlessly.

Geshe Yeshe Tobden
Polava di Cividale del Friuli, Italy
September 11, 1997

APPENDIX

Key Points of the Ninth Chapter

SINCE THE MADHYAMIKA-PRASANGIKAS maintain that no phenomenon is endowed with true existence—meaning that nothing exists by its own nature, intrinsically, independently of its own causes, its own parts, or the labels applied to it—the Prasangikas' view opposes that of all other schools. The exegesis takes the form of a debate—shown implicitly in the root text and explicitly in the various commentaries—between the exponents of the lesser Buddhist and non-Buddhist philosophical schools (in italics) on the one hand and the Prasangikas (in roman) on the other.

1. Presentation of the general statement by the exponents of the three lesser Buddhist schools, by which they maintain that all or some phenomena have true existence.

The validity of their arguments is refuted by the Prasangikas. [stanzas 4–15]

a) *If all phenomena were like illusions and not truly existent, they would not exist at all, and therefore it would not be possible to attain enlightenment through the practice of the six perfections; furthermore the Buddha himself would be illusory, and no merit would be gained by worshipping him.*

Although phenomena do not exist by their own nature on an ultimate level, they exist conventionally; therefore, through the practice of the illusion-like six perfections, an illusion-like buddhahood can be gained, and by worshipping this buddha, illusion-like merits can be accumulated.

b) *The true existence of forms, sounds, and so forth is proven by the fact that everyone, both yogis and ordinary people, perceive them directly, and it is therefore wrong to maintain that they are false.*

The five types of sense objects exist conventionally, as ascertained by everyone through sense consciousness, but conventional existence is not true existence. On the other hand, the five senses cannot perceive the ultimate nature of forms, sounds, and so forth, which is realized only by yogis through the samadhi that unifies shamata and vipashyana.

c) *The Buddha said that composite phenomena have an impermanent nature, and it is therefore wrong to say that they do not exist by their own nature.*

Considering their apparent nature, the Buddha taught that composite phenomena are impermanent, and he said so in order to guide ordinary beings gradually toward the correct view of reality. However, he did not mean to say that the transient existence of composite phenomena exists truly or intrinsically.

d) *If sentient beings were like illusions, they could not be reborn after death; one would not accumulate merits by benefiting them nor accumulate negative karma by causing them harm.*

A sentient being is similar to an illusion but is not an actual illusion, and is furthermore endowed with a mind. Consequently, when all conditions are present, he takes on a new birth, and those who benefit him generate positive karma, whereas those who cause him harm generate negative karma.

e) *If, as you Prasangikas state, sentient beings were naturally dwelling in nirvana, in the state beyond suffering, and nevertheless wandering in cyclic existence, then the Buddha also would dwell within cyclic existence; therefore, there would be no reason to practice the life conduct of bodhisattvas.*

We must differentiate between nirvana and natural nirvana. The former is the state of the cessation of suffering, attained through applying the direct antidote to the mental afflictions that obscure the mind, whereas the latter is the ultimate nature of the mind, its emptiness, a characteristic that is always present.

It follows that each being possesses natural nirvana but not nirvana, the state beyond cyclic existence, and possesses this as long as he or she has not eliminated the causes for rebirth within cyclic existence. Since the Buddha has done that already, he definitely no longer dwells in samsara.

2. Expounding the specific view of the Chittamatrins with regard to the mode of existence of phenomena.
The validity of their arguments is refuted by the Prasangikas. [stanzas 15–29]

a) The Chittamatrins state that objects of perception, the other-powered natures, have true existence and are of the same nature as the mind perceiving them—that is, they do not exist externally. However, since they appear to us in this way, as external, they are like an illusion. For them the mind is also truly existent but is not like an illusion.

We Prasangikas maintain the external existence of objects of perception but state that they do not exist by their own nature, intrinsically, or truly. However, since they appear to us as if they exist intrinsically, they are like illusions, and deceptive in this regard.

Mind also does not exist truly, intrinsically, or by its own nature, and, like all other phenomena, is an illusion.

b) For the Chittamatrins, if phenomena do not exist truly, by their own nature, it would follow that they do not exist at all, and the same would apply to the mind that perceives them. In this case, they say, who is it then that understands that both phenomena and the mind are like illusions?

Since the Chittamatrins accept the fact that objects are like illusions, they should also accept that they do not exist by their own nature, and the same would then be the case for the mind, which for them would mean that the mind does not exist. In this case, who is it then that understands that the appearance of phenomena is like an illusion?

c) *The Chittamatrins maintain that there are two types of mind: one that perceives only sense objects, and the other, the self-cognizer, which perceives only the mind perceiving the objects, then ascertaining the true existence of this sense consciousness and, consequently, of its objects. Sense consciousness apprehends things dualistically, but the self-cognizer apprehends without duality, since the mind itself is its object.*

The existence of a self-cognizer cannot be accepted and it is not a proof, because a mind that can perceive itself does not exist, in the same way that a blade of a sword that cuts itself or a self-illumining light do not exist. Furthermore, in the case of a hypothetical self-cognizer, defined as a mind that perceives itself without duality, two different things (two minds) should not be involved and perceived as separate.

d) *If the self-cognizer did not exist, there could be no memory of the experience made by a consciousness when it has perceived its object.*

In order to remember or be aware of an experience in the past, it is not necessary for another consciousness that perceives the consciousness that had the direct experience to be present. Memory is present without depending on the existence of a self-cognizer. If a self-cognizer existed, it would need another mind in order to be ascertained, and so forth, ad infinitum.

e) *The self-cognizer exists because, as a result of particular realizations, through clairvoyance it is possible to perceive even remote or hidden objects, and even more so it is possible to perceive the mind, which is nearer.*

Applying eye lotions consecrated by the power of mantras, one can see objects buried underground but cannot see the eye lotion itself. Therefore the vicinity of an object does not give either certainty or proof of perception. And there is still no proof of a self-cognizer's existence.

f) By not accepting the self-cognizer, one also denies the other cognizers, such as the sense consciousnesses, with their functions of seeing, hearing, and so forth, because in this case there would not be a consciousness that would ascertain their existence.

It is not the mere existence of sense consciousness that is being denied, in fact they exist conventionally; and seeing or hearing, as well as the perceived objects, do not by themselves cause suffering. What must be denied is the concept of their true existence, which is the actual cause of suffering in cyclic existence.

g) The Chittamatrins maintain that phenomena are like illusions because they are not external to the mind, but that they are also not the mind itself, although they are one substantial nature.

If a phenomenon exists, it can be neither a thing nor something different from a thing. Therefore the statement according to which the objects of perceptions are neither mind nor other would lead to denying the possibility of their existence. But phenomena, which are like illusions, are objects of knowledge even though they do not truly exist; likewise, mental consciousness is a cognizer even though it does not truly exist. Therefore, we Prasangikas state that both objects of knowledge and consciousness exist conventionally.

h) Phenomena, though not existing externally, exist truly.

If phenomena were truly existent, phenomena should exist as they appear; therefore, the fact that they appear externally to the mind contradicts the statement that they exist truly but are of the same substantial nature of the mind that perceives them.

i) Composite phenomena exist truly because they arise from causes and conditions.

Composite phenomena do not truly exist precisely because they arise from causes and conditions.

j) Conditioned existence, the state in which subject and object appear as two separate entities, must have at the basis of its deceptive appearance something real—that is, a nondual, truly existent consciousness. Otherwise, it would be like space without cause—that is, a thoroughly imputed phenomenon, and not a state in which subject and object could appear as real.

If conditioned existence had true existence as its basis, one would not die, nor fall into the lower realms, nor attain liberation, because what is truly existent is permanent, independent, cannot be the cause of any phenomenon, and cannot produce any effect, since in order to do so it would depend on other factors.

Furthermore, the mind of ordinary beings perceives things in a dualistic way, whereas if it were endowed with the characteristic of nonduality (according to the theory of the self-cognizer) it would be like the mind of a buddha. In this case it would be pointless to practice the path, because all beings would already be enlightened, and there would be no gain in accepting the Chittamatrins' view, which considers "only mind" as the basis of cyclic existence.

3. Presentation of the various modes of reasoning of the exponents of lesser Buddhist schools, through which they try to prove that, in order to attain liberation from samsara, realization of the emptiness of true existence is not necessary.

The Prasangikas refute the validity of each argument brought forward, pointing out that this realization is instead necessary for anyone who wishes to achieve that objective. [stanzas 30–55]

a) The Prasangikas state that all phenomena are devoid of true existence and are therefore like illusions, and that such a view is the antidote to mental afflictions, which bind one to conditioned existence. But according to the

Chittamatrins, this is not acceptable; they state that if a magician produces the appearance of a woman through magic, he can still desire her though he knows that she is an illusion.

The magician can feel attachment for the woman he has manifested through magic because, not having yet realized the emptiness of all phenomena, he has the tendency to grasp at true existence, and consequently still has the predisposition to generate desire for pleasant objects. In other words, he grasps at the concept of the woman's true existence, in spite of knowing that she is a mere appearance.

If one trains in the understanding that all phenomena are devoid of true existence and subsequently in single-pointed meditation on the mental image of emptiness, when the natural and spontaneous view that phenomena do not truly exist is finally obtained, from that moment on there will be no possibility for mental afflictions to arise.

Furthermore, since the object to be denied, the true existence of phenomena, has been ascertained as being nonexistent, its emptiness is also recognized as being devoid of true existence. This is similar to the fact that, since the son of a barren woman does not exist, his death also does not exist.

A person who possesses only the intellectual understanding of emptiness has not yet eliminated the duality between the conventional appearance of phenomena and their ultimate nature. Whereas, for the yogi who has realized this, during his meditative absorption on the emptiness of phenomena, both the appearance of true existence and the conventional appearance of phenomena vanish.

b) The exponents of the other schools maintain that if this were the case, since a buddha is always dwelling on the ultimate nature of phenomena, all types of conceptualization would disappear for him, and consequently, he would not be able to act for the benefit of beings.

As a cloud lets the rain fall without any conceptual activity, likewise a buddha benefits all beings. This happens because of the strength of prayers made to this purpose when he was a bodhisattva, and because of the strength of merits accumulated by beings.

c) From this point forward the followers of the Hinayana schools refute the Prasangikas' view, and they begin by saying that if a buddha were devoid of true existence, no merits could be accumulated by worshipping him.

If some maintain that it is possible to accumulate merits by making truly existent offerings to a truly existent buddha, we Prasangikas instead say that it is possible to accumulate non-truly existent merits by making offerings to a non-truly existent, illusion-like buddha.

d) The followers of the Hinayana schools state that through the direct perception of the sixteen attributes of the four noble truths, liberation from conditioned existence is attained. Consequently, according to them, there would be no point in cultivating the view of emptiness propounded by the Prasangikas.

The view of emptiness of true existence, as explained in the Mahayana scriptures on the perfection of wisdom, is necessary. Those who grasp at the concept of the true existence of phenomena will not be able to attain the final aim, whether that of the Hinayana or the Mahayana nirvana.

e) The followers of the Hinayana refute the validity of the Mahayana scriptures, denying that they originate from actual words spoken by the Buddha, since they have never heard them. They maintain instead the validity of the Hinayana sutras, since they are accepted by the followers of both Buddhist traditions.

By applying the same logic, one can observe that those who deny that the Mahayana sutras are teachings given by the Buddha accept the Hinayana sutras only after having learned them. Furthermore, if something became believable and true only because it was accepted by many, then the Vedas and the other non-Buddhist scriptures would be so as well.

f) The Mahayana scriptures are not believable because there are those who refute them.

This is not a good reason either, because the Hinayana scriptures too are refuted by non-Buddhists, and some of them are also refuted by some Buddhists.

g) *The Hinayana scriptures are the authentic words of the Buddha because within them we find the teachings on the three superior trainings of morality, concentration, and wisdom.*

But these are also mostly present in the Mahayana scriptures, which must be recognized as words of the Buddha for the very same reason.

h) *If the Mahayana texts on the perfection of wisdom were true, the Hinayana arhats would have both understood and accepted them, but this is not the case. Instead, they have achieved liberation without having had to realize emptiness, but by meditating on the sixteen aspects of the four noble truths, and understanding the absence of a self-sufficient, substantially existent self of person.*

With such realization it is possible only to overcome coarse mental afflictions, but it is not possible to eliminate the subtle ones. The latter take place only by eradicating the mind that grasps at the true existence of the self of person and phenomena. If those whom the Hinayana followers call "arhats" had not comprehended that all phenomena are not truly existent, they would continue to grasp at the self of phenomena and on this basis they would continue to generate karma, which would not allow them to be free from conditioned existence. In fact, true arhats no longer possess mental afflictions, and are therefore free from samsara as a result of having necessarily realized the emptiness of true existence of the self, the effective antidote to the obscurations caused by the mental afflictions, as well as to the obscurations to omniscience.

The Hinayana followers cannot comprehend and accept this, since it is a very lofty subject that the Buddha made known only to those who were able to understand it correctly. The transmission of these and other Mahayana teachings therefore goes back, through a continuous lineage, to the Buddha himself, who explained emptiness

to Manjushri. Manjushri explained it to Nagarjuna, and this transmission continued down the line through the successive masters. As
for the path of bodhichitta, the Buddha expounded it to Maitreya,
Maitreya to Asanga, and so forth.

4. The exponents of other schools (non-Buddhist and lesser Buddhist)
ask what logical proofs the Prasangikas can provide in order to establish
the emptiness of true existence of the self.

The Prasangikas explain in detail the lack of true existence of the self
of person and then (through the four close placements of mindfulness)
the lack of true existence of the self of phenomena. [stanzas 56–110]

THE LACK OF TRUE EXISTENCE OF THE SELF OF PERSON

There is no truly existent self in a person, because if we look for it in its
basis (the psychophysical aggregates) or in the name by which it is labeled,
we do not find it.

However, a self does exist—that is, the self that depends on the designation made on a valid basis, on its own parts, and on its own causes (since
it is an impermanent phenomenon).

a) The non-Buddhist Samkhya school maintains that the self is the consciousness, and that it is permanent.

This is not acceptable, because, for example, the hearing consciousness perceiving sounds cannot be permanent, since when its object
is no longer present, the specific consciousness that apprehends it
must also cease.

b) The non-Buddhist schools of the Vaisheshikas and Naiyayikas maintain
that the self is a material phenomenon, devoid of parts, permanent, and
present in the individual.

Atoms cannot be the self, since they do not have the nature of the
mind.

c) The self is not conscious of objects, but is able to experience when it comes in touch with a mind, which is, however, separate from it.

This is illogical, because saying that such a self, which by its own nature is not conscious of objects, becomes aware of them as soon as the mind with which is in touch comes across them, contradicts the statement that this self is permanent (immutable).

d) If the self were not permanent, it would follow that the self of a person who has performed a particular deed could not be the same self that experiences the effect of that action.

The self from a previous life accumulates karma, whereas the self of a future life experiences its effect. This is possible because they are two different states of the same continuum. Also, the accumulation of causes that bring about the actions whose results are experienced in the same life always occur in a moment that precedes the ripening of the effect.

e) If beings were not truly existent, then they would not exist at all, and therefore there would be no objects of compassion, nor those who obtain results from having developed it.

Even though sentient beings, compassion, and its results do not exist ultimately, intrinsically, or truly, they do exist conventionally. In order to attain liberation from suffering we must not deny the conventional existence, but instead deny the ignorance that grasps at the concept of a truly existent self.

f) The non-Buddhists maintain that there are no methods for abandoning such ignorance.

On the contrary, there are such methods; therefore ignorance can be eliminated. The antidote is the wisdom developed through meditating on the lack of an intrinsic self.

THE LACK OF TRUE EXISTENCE OF THE SELF OF PHENOMENA

1. Close placement of mindfulness on the body

g) *Some non-Buddhist schools state that there is a body separate from its parts, and that its nature is different from its parts; the same should then apply to the body and the self. These schools in fact consider the body to be impermanent, but the self to be permanent.*

The body is made of the head, the trunk, and the four limbs, but if we look at it closely, none of these are the body itself, nor is it their assemblage. However, the body depends on these, and they share the same nature.

If the body truly existed, each individual part should be the body itself, but it is not possible for a part to be the whole.

A truly existent body cannot be found among its parts or separate from them; the body exists as a mere attribution of a name to these parts—that is, it is devoid of intrinsic existence.

The concept of concrete, true, intrinsic existence arises from a confused mind that perceives hands and other parts of the body as a truly existent body. This erroneous mind is like the mind that mistakes a pile of stones from afar for a person, when they are assembled into a person's shape.

Just like the entire body, each of its parts is in turn designated in dependence on its respective parts, and so on, down to the smallest atomic particles, which are also devoid of intrinsic existence.

By meditating on and realizing the emptiness of true existence of the body, one succeeds in eliminating attachment to it completely.

2. Close placement of mindfulness on feelings

Sensations do not truly exist. If they did, they should be permanent, whereas when a strong sensation of suffering arises, a preceding sensation of happiness ceases, and vice versa.

The "pleasant" or "unpleasant" characteristic of a sensation does not exist intrinsically. If it had true existence, the same object would be experienced by anyone and at any given moment in the same way, but this is not the case.

Sensations too are mere nominal designations made by a conceptual mind. Since the mind that grasps at them as if they were truly existent generates attachment and other mental afflictions, it is necessary to meditate on the lack of true existence of sensations, supporting this understanding with the meditative absorption generated by unifying shamata and vipashyana.

Contact, which is the cause of sensation, is also devoid of true existence.

h) Some schools maintain the true existence of atomic particles devoid of parts.

When a sense consciousness, the specific sense organ, and its object meet, we have contact, which produces sensation. This contact between the atoms of the various sense organs and the atoms of the corresponding objects cannot exist intrinsically, since its arising depends on their meeting. On the one hand, if there were space between the atoms of the perceived object of the sense organ, contact itself would not be possible. On the other hand, if there were not space, the two would be one, and equally we could not speak of contact, because in order to define it as such, there must be two phenomena involved.

Since when two atoms come into contact they are not completely absorbed, but they meet, this proves that a part of each is in contact, but not the others. For this reason we cannot say that atoms are devoid of parts and indivisible.

Also, contact established by its own nature between a sense consciousness and the external object is impossible, because consciousness is devoid of atoms, form, and matter, and cannot enter into true contact with what has form. Sense consciousnesses themselves, which are the subjects of perception, cannot be said to be truly existent, and neither can the perceived objects, since their nature is like a dream or an illusion.

Since true contact does not exist, true sensations too cannot exist. By meditating on this matter, one will no longer feel attachment for the sensations of happiness, or revulsion for the sensations of suffering.

3. Close placement of mindfulness on the mind

A truly existent consciousness does not exist, because one cannot find it either in its object, in the sensory faculty, or between the two. It does not dwell in our bodies either, or outside them.

Mind does not exist intrinsically, even in its smallest part; therefore the mind of every sentient being is, since time without beginning, of the nature of emptiness—that is, it dwells in natural nirvana.

Like mental consciousness, the other sense consciousnesses are devoid of intrinsic existence. If this were not so, each of them would exist before its object, simultaneously and successively. In fact, a perceiving consciousness arises in dependence on an object of perception, the faculty of the sense organ, and the immediately preceding moment of the mind; therefore, we cannot state that it is independent and that it exists truly.

4. Close placement of mindfulness on phenomena

Through the previous modes of reasoning, one will reach the understanding that all phenomena do not arise independently or intrinsically, and that therefore they do not truly exist.

i) The exponents of the other schools (now also including the Svatantrika-Madhyamaka) object that if phenomena existed only as mental designations from an erroneous mind, it would follow that the two truths and sentient beings are false, and that their conventional existence would also be false. Consequently, beings could not attain nirvana and enlightenment.

Existing conventionally does not mean that phenomena are designated by an erroneous mind conceiving a false existence; on the contrary, all conventional truths are designations of a valid mind made on a valid basis.

Although conventional phenomena do not truly exist, they have a function and produce effects. There is an action, one who performs it, and a result, although none of these exist intrinsically; the same is true for the subjective perception, the perceived object, and the nominal designation. When we understand that an object does not exist by any kind of own nature, we can understand as well how that which knows it, the mind, does not exist intrinsically.

j) The exponents of the other schools object that the analytical mind, which ascertains that all phenomena are devoid of true existence, cannot ascertain the same in relation to itself. Consequently, either there is another mind that realizes the non-true existence of the first analytical mind (and so on, ad infinitum, without ever being able to ascertain the object at the very foundation of the analysis), or this other mind is not there, and in that case the initial analytical mind must be truly existent, therefore invalidating the Prasangikas' theory of non-true existence.

When the object of analysis has been examined thoroughly and its non-existence has been established, there is no longer any need to investigate the mind that has made the analysis, because once the non-true existence of a phenomenon is understood, one is also able to understand that there is no truly existent analytical mind that might arise from it. This state of peace, in which neither intrinsically existing objects nor consciousnesses arise, is called nirvana, the state beyond suffering.

Note: *The presentation (in bold) of the four key points of the ninth chapter of the* Bodhicharyavatara *is the presentation of the Venerable Geshe Yeshe Tobden, whereas their elaboration was composed by Fiorella Rizzi.*

GLOSSARY

aggregates. See *skandha.*

Akashagarbha (Tibetan: *nam 'kha'i snying po*). Literally, "Essence of Space"; the name of a bodhisattva.

arhat (Tibetan: *dgra bcom pa*). Literally, "the enemy-destroyer"; one who has eliminated mental afflictions and attained liberation from cyclic existence. In the ninth chapter this term refers mainly to the Hinayana arhat.

arya (Tibetan: *'phags pa*). Literally, "superior being"; one who has attained direct perception of emptiness.

Avalokiteshvara (Tibetan: *'jig rten dbang phyug*). Literally, "World Sovereign"; the name of the bodhisattva of compassion.

bodhichitta (Tibetan: *byang chub sems*). The mind that aspires to attain the state of complete enlightenment of a buddha for the benefit of all sentient beings.

bodhisattva (Tibetan: *byang chub sems 'pa*). A being who, having developed the mind of enlightenment, dedicates his or her life to the achievement of buddhahood.

Brahma (Tibetan: *tshangs pa*). A worldly deity residing in the realm of form.

buddha (Tibetan: *sangs rgyas*). A being who has purified completely all mental afflictions (*sangs*) and who has realized everything that can be apprehended (*rgyas*).

calm abiding (Tibetan: *zhi gnas*; Sanskrit: *shamata*). State of concentration in which the mind abides univocally and effortlessly on the object of meditation.

chakravartin (Tibetan: *'khor lo bsgyur pa'i rgyal pa*). Literally, "universal monarch"; a worldly being of great power and wealth.

conqueror, or *victor* (Tibetan: *rgyal ba;* Sanskrit: *jina*). A epithet for a buddha, thus named because he has defeated the four demons.

cyclic existence (Tibetan: *'khor ba;* Sanskrit: *samsara*). The cycle of death and rebirth within the states of conditioned existence, characterized by suffering and produced by actions (karma) and mental afflictions.

dakini (Tibetan: *'kha 'gro ma*). Literally, "she who flies through space," where space must be understood here as perception of emptiness; a female being able to help the mind development of Tantra practitioners. Some are still tied to cyclic existence, others have completely freed themselves from it.

demon (Tibetan: *'dud;* Sanskrit: *mara*). One of the four types of malevolent forces: death, mental afflictions, psychophysical aggregates, and the celestial demon called *devaputra* (or "of the sons of gods").

desire realm (Tibetan: *'dod pa'i kham*). The realm that includes human existence. The two other realms are the form and formless realms.

Dharma (Tibetan: *chos*). Usually signifies religious doctrine—in particular, the doctrine of the Buddha. Can also refer generally to phenomena.

emptiness (Tibetan: *stong pa nyid;* Sanskrit: *shunyata*). The ultimate nature of all phenomena, their being devoid of intrinsic existence.

Hinayana (Tibetan: *theg dman*). The Small Vehicle, the spiritual path of shravakas and pratyekabuddhas, which terminates with the attainment of personal liberation from cyclic existence.

intrinsic existence. See *true existence.*

Ishvara (Tibetan: *dbang phyug*). A divine being who, according to some Hindu schools, is believed to be the creator of the world and of its dwellers.

karma (Tibetan: *las*). Action and its fruit. The law of cause and effect.

Karnapa. Name of a place in ancient India where ascetic competitions were held in order to establish who was able to endure the most intense suffering.

Kashyapa (Tibetan: *'od srungs*). An arhat disciple of Shakyamuni Buddha.

Kshitigarbha (Tibetan: *sa'i snying po*). Literally, "Essence of the Earth"; the name of a bodhisattva.

Mahayana (Tibetan: *theg chen*). The Great Vehicle, the spiritual path of the bodhisattva, whose ultimate aim is the attainment of buddhahood for the benefit of all sentient beings.

Maitreya (Tibetan: *byams pa mgon po*). The future Buddha, the next to manifest in the current cosmic era.

mandala (Tibetan: *dkyil 'khor*). Literally, "the center and the surrounding"; the universe and its content, purified in the archetypal representation of a celestial environment, at whose center is the manifestation of an enlightened being surrounded by his retinue.

Manjughosha, or *Manjushri* (Tibetan: *'jam dbyangs*). Literally, "Soft (mind) and Melodious (voice)"; the bodhisattva of wisdom.

mantra (Tibetan: *sngags*). Literally, "that which protects the mind"; sacred formula or prayer whose great power derives specifically from the energy of sound and symbols of the syllables composing it. In the context of the sutras, it protects the mind from afflictions; in that of tantra, it protects the mind from ordinary appearances.

Mayadevi (Tibetan: *lha mo sgyu 'phrul*). Mother of Shakyamuni Buddha.

merits (Tibetan: *bsod nams*; Sanskrit: *punya*). Positive energies and attitudes accumulated in the mind through virtuous actions of body, speech, and mind.

Mount Meru (Tibetan: *ri rab*). Literally, "supreme mount"; according to Buddhist mythology, the highest mountain, located at the center of the universe.

nirvana (Tibetan: *nya ngan las 'das pa*). The state of liberation from cyclic existence.

Padmapani (Tibetan: *phyag na pad mo*). Literally, "The Lotus Holder"; a manifestation of Avalokiteshvara.

pratyekabuddha (Tibetan: *rang sangs rgyas*). Literally, "solitary realizer"; a follower of one of the two Hinayana paths.

samadhi (Tibetan: *ting nge 'dzin*). The profound meditative absorption of a yogi.

Samantabhadra (Tibetan: *kun tu bzang po*). Literally, "Completely Good"; the name of a bodhisattva.

Sangha (Tibetan: *dge 'dun*). Literally, "he who aspires to virtue"; in particular, beings (*arya sangha*) who have realized emptiness and who support practitioners; in general, members of the Buddhist spiritual community.

shravaka (Tibetan: *nyan thos*). Literally, "hearer"; a follower of one of the two Hinayana paths.

skandha (Tibetan: *phung po*). Aggregate. There are five psychophysical aggregates, on the basis of which a person is labeled as such: body, sensations, discriminations, compositional factors, and consciousness.

sugata (Tibetan: *bde bar gshegs pa*). Literally, "one who has gone to the bliss"; a term for a buddha.

Sukhavati (Tibetan: *bde ba can*). The name of a Buddhist paradise, the pure land of Amitabha Buddha.

superior vision (Tibetan: *lhag mthong*; Sanskrit: *vipashyana*; Pali: *vipassana*). Profound vision and elevated analytical faculty of the mind, able to comprehend the subtle impermanence and the emptiness of all phenomena.

Supushpachandra (Tibetan: *me tog zla mdzes*). The name of a bodhisattva, whose actions are narrated in the *Samadhiraja Sutra*.

sutra (Tibetan: *mdo*). A discourse given by Shakyamuni Buddha.

tathagata (Tibetan: *sde bzhin gshegs pa*). Literally, "one who has thus gone"; a term for a buddha.

true existence (Tibetan: *bden par grup pa*; Sanskrit: *satya siddha*). The object that, being nonexistent, is negated in the analysis of emptiness.

Tushita (Tibetan: *dga 'ldan*). The pure land where the Buddha Maitreya resides.

vajra (Tibetan: *rdo rje*). Variously translated as "diamond" or "thunderbolt" and, as an adjective, "indestructible, invincible"; refers to what appertains to the pure essence of a being.

Vajradhvaja (Tibetan: *rdo rje rgyal mtshan*). The name of a bodhisattva mentioned in the *Avatamsaka Sutra*.

Vajrapani (Tibetan: *phyag na rdo rje*). Literally, "Holder of the Vajra"; the bodhisattva of power.

Vajrayana (Tibetan: *rdo rje theg pa*). Literally, "The Vehicle of the Vajra"; the teachings and practices of Buddhist tantra.

valid cognition (Tibetan: *tshad ma*; Sanskrit: *pramana*). An infallible mental state, able to correctly ascertain its object. It can be both conceptual and nonconceptual.

Vedas (Tibetan: *byed*). Ancient Indian hymns believed to be of divine origin.

Yama (Tibetan: *gshin rje*). The sovereign of death.

yogi / yogini (Tibetan: *rnal 'byor pa / rnal 'byor ma*). A practitioner (male / female) who has attained the unification of calm abiding and superior view.

ALSO AVAILABLE
FROM WISDOM PUBLICATIONS

PRACTICING WISDOM
The Perfection of Shantideva's Bodhisattva Way
His Holiness the Dalai Lama and Thupten Jinpa

A *Shambhala Sun* "Best Buddhist Writing" selection.

THE BEAUTIFUL WAY OF LIFE
A Meditation on Shantideva's Bodhisattva Path
René Feusi

"Ven. René Feusi's *The Beautiful Way of Life* is a beautifully written meditative guide to one of the greatest works of the Mahayana Buddhist tradition, and will be treasured by all those inspired by compassion and wisdom."
—Jonathan Landaw, author of *Prince Siddhartha*

SHANTIDEVA: HOW TO WAKE UP A HERO
Dominique Townsend and Tenzin Norbu

"In simple, compassionate language, this insightful book offers spiritual teachings, practical advice, and an entertaining story, all at once."
—*Foreword Reviews*

STEPS ON THE PATH TO ENLIGHTENMENT SERIES
Geshe Lhundub Sopa

An elegant five-volume comprehensive commentary on the *Lamrim Chenmo* by the renowned Buddhist scholar, Geshe Lhundub Sopa.

PRACTICING THE PATH
A Commentary on the "Lamrim Chenmo"
Yangsi Rinpoche, Tsering Tuladhar (Ven. Tsen-la), and Miranda Adams
(Namdrol)
Foreword by Geshe Lhundub Sopa
Preface by Lama Zopa Rinpoche

"Readable and to the point, it brings this great classical tradition 'into the very palms of our hands.'" —José Ignacio Cabezón, Dalai Lama Professor of Tibetan Buddhism and Cultural Studies, University of California–Santa Barbara

LIBERATION IN THE PALM OF YOUR HAND
A Concise Discourse on the Path to Enlightenment
Pabongka Rinpoche, Trijang Rinpoche, and Michael Richards

"The richest and most enjoyable volume from the lamrim tradition . . . published to date."—*Golden Drum*

THE WORLD OF TIBETAN BUDDHISM
An Overview of Its Philosophy and Practice
His Holiness the Dalai Lama
Foreword by Richard Gere

"A lucid and profound yet eminently readable introduction to this subject."
—*Library Journal*

THE COMPASSIONATE LIFE
His Holiness the Dalai Lama

"This sorely needed prescription for sanity and kindness in the world is unbelievably simple and unbelievably important, and therefore a practice worthy of our wholehearted commitment." —Jon Kabat-Zinn, author of *Wherever You Go, There You Are*

INTRODUCTION TO TANTRA
The Transformation of Desire
Lama Thubten Yeshe and Jonathan Landaw
Foreword by Philip Glass

"The best introductory work on Tibetan Buddhist tantra available today."
—Janet Gyatso, Harvard University

THE BLISS OF INNER FIRE
Heart Practice of the Six Yogas of Naropa
Lama Thubten Yeshe, Robina Courtin, and Ailsa Cameron
Foreword by Lama Zopa Rinpoche

"An impressive contribution to the growing body of Buddhist literature for an English-reading audience." —*The Midwest Book Review*

About Wisdom Publications

Wisdom Publications is the leading publisher of classic and contemporary Buddhist books and practical works on mindfulness. To learn more about us or to explore our other books, please visit our website at wisdompubs.org or contact us at the address below.

Wisdom Publications
199 Elm Street
Somerville, MA 02144 USA

We are a 501(c)(3) organization, and donations in support of our mission are tax deductible.

Wisdom Publications is affiliated with the Foundation for the Preservation of the Mahayana Tradition (FPMT).